ALSO BY JANE HEALY:

*Your Child's Growing Mind: A Guide to Learning and Brain
Development from Birth to Adolescence*

ENDANGERED MINDS

*Why Children
Don't Think—and What
We Can Do About It*

JANE M. HEALY, Ph.D.

A TOUCHSTONE BOOK
Published by Simon & Schuster

TOUCHSTONE
Rockefeller Center
1230 Avenue of the Americas
New York, New York 10020

7   9   10   8

Library of Congress Cataloging-in-Publication Data
Healy, Jane M.
Endangered minds : why our children don't think—
and what we can do about it / Jane M. Healy.
p.   cm.
Includes bibliographical references and index.
1. Learning, Psychology of.   2. Learning–Social aspects
3. Learning–Physiological aspects.   4. Neuropsychology.   I. Title.
BF318.H38   1990
155.4'1315–dc20   90-39897
CIP

ISBN: 0-671-67439-1
0-684-85620-4 (Pbk)

Dedicated to Mother Nature
and the gift—and responsibility—of neural plasticity

Contents

Introduction

It was a dreary, wet May afternoon ten years ago when I stumbled, bleary-eyed, into the post office to mail the final draft of *Endangered Minds*. I distinctly remember thinking, "Probably no one will ever read this, but at least I got it off my chest!"

As it happened, many others shared my concerns, and the book struck an immediate chord both in the United States and abroad. I started to receive notes from teachers that began, "So I'm not crazy! Kids really are getting harder to teach. . . ." and from parents along the lines of, "Thank you for giving us the courage to set some limits on TV in our house and spend better time with our kids." As a congenitally insecure author, I remain eternally grateful to all those who have taken the time to tell me that my ideas have helped. Just last month at a workshop, a participant passed me the following note, typical of many I have received that make all the effort worthwhile:

> Five years ago your book saved my career. I was just about to give up teaching, but you inspired me to re-think what I was doing in my classroom, stop blaming my students, and try some new approaches. My job is more fun than ever, and now I want to go back to graduate school to study the brain and learning.

What more could I ask for?

Now, given the opportunity to comment once more, I am heartened that the content of *Endangered Minds* has stood the test of time and further research, and that greater interest has been aroused about connections between neuroscience and education. I am dismayed, however, that we have not made more headway into curbing toxic electronic and educational environments for children.

I was pretty far out on a theoretical limb when I first presented the hypothesis that children's brains might be so significantly changed by contemporary culture as to be increasingly maladapted to our traditional notions of "school." In the intervening years, however, the concept of cortical plasticity—the process by which the brain shapes itself in response to various environmental stimuli—has become a staple of the mainstream press and has even sparked a White House conference.

Given this understanding, the following implication doesn't seem so far-fetched: Children surrounded by fast-paced visual stimuli (TV, videos, computer games) at the expense of face-to-face adult modeling, interactive language, reflective problem-solving, creative play, and sustained attention may be expected to arrive at school unprepared for academic learning—and to fall farther behind and become increasingly "unmotivated" as the years go by. The current educational scene attests to this misfit even more strongly than it did when this book was originally published. Just ask any teacher at any grade level. Moreover, when I warned about the "starving executive" in Chapter 9, little did I know that the fastest-growing category of learning/behavior disorder was soon to become something called "executive function disorder."

Neuroplasticity is now thought to include emotional/motivational as well as cognitive circuits. This would mean that a child's habits of motivation and attitudes toward learning don't all come with the package, but are physically formed in the brain by experience. Thus, if a child is discouraged, defeated, or emotionally abused by parents or teachers, she might develop physical "tracks" in the system or a negative pattern of neurochemical response that become increasingly resistant to change. When she enters a new learning situation, therefore, she brings a brain predisposed to apathy, negative response, and failure. Those of us who have worked with many such youngsters can readily accept this idea, but we also know that even the most "turned-off" kid has potential—it just takes a lot of time and hard work to reroute those maladaptive connections!

We see increasing confirmation of the reality of developmental stages (or "waves") and critical/sensitive periods in the brain's trajectory of growth. New stages of development may even occur into adulthood. And, hooray!—mental activity does indeed continue to improve the brain even into old age; serious mental decline is not inevitable for healthy adults, and those who keep their minds active may be better buffered from the effects of debilitating diseases (e.g., If you get Alzheimer's, you may not decline as rapidly.)

PERENNIAL QUESTIONS

I learn about the issues on people's minds during the question period at lectures and workshops. One of the big questions for parents and teachers continues to be this peculiar "epidemic" of attention problems, or ADHD. The diagnosis of attention deficit disorder is skyrocketing, and large numbers of children are given prescriptions for stimulant drugs. I have been in schools where teachers told me that up to 50 percent of the students in their classroom are on Ritalin! I know that people who say "I told you so" are pretty obnoxious, but I must point out that since I originally wrote this book, researchers have confirmed major involvement of the executive systems of the prefrontal cortex and its subcortical connections.

Although, believe it or not, we still await definitive research on media and the brain, I continue to believe this astonishing incidence of "illness" in kids results from several factors: heredity, pre- and postnatal brain "insults" from injury or toxic substances, frenetic and electronic mental environments that "upshift" a child's impulsiveness, lack of appropriate models and limits to teach children to control behavior, language erosion, and media that coach children in being thoughtless and disrespectful. We are asking a lot from our teachers to remediate the cultural debris of large classrooms of kids whose brains have been blasted into academic insensitivity since birth.

To this list, however, I must add school environments that place impossible attentional and academic demands (often in the name of "competency") on unprepared brains, and try to cram creative and lively children into boring mental boxes. Consider also some current idiocies such as limiting active play and recess to give kids more time to sit at their desks.

Thousands of pages have been written about effective approaches to treat attention problems. Among other imperatives is behavioral counseling to help parents, teachers, and the child structure the environment and learn strategies to manage the difficulty—either with or without drug treatment. But this approach requires adult time and patience that too many adults are unwilling to give. So we administer drugs and expect them to do the job. For many youngsters, stimulant drugs such as Ritalin, Cylert, or Dexedrine provide a gateway into new behaviors, but long-term treatment is still an iffy prospect. "Although children may calm down, concentrate better, and behave less disruptively while taking a stimulant, there is no solid evidence that their school work improves in the long run or that the adult outcome is affected," reported *The Harvard Mental Health Letter* in 1995. Certainly, adequate research on possible long-term side effects of these drugs should be undertaken immediately.

Another lingering question is whether deficits in a brain that has missed out on appropriate stimulation at any of its developmental stages can be made up. I wish I had a complete and satisfying answer to this question. My own experience suggests that, given the brain's long developmental trajectory, we should never give up on it. As it matures, learns, and develops new systems, and thus new types of learning potential, skills that were missed earlier may be taken up by different networks or accomplished in different ways (e.g., learning spelling through rule systems rather than visual memory). Moreover, if you can help the youngster (or adult!) develop more confidence, positive emotional response, and intrinsic motivation, you may see amazing results, since the brain's emotional centers are so intimately involved in priming circuits for learning.

On the other hand, certain types of deprivation or damage are hard to compensate for—consider the lasting effects of perinatal complications associated with cerebral palsy, for example. At more subtle levels, severe emotional deprivation or abuse during very early critical periods may permanently alter chemical receptors in the brain so that the individual may be predisposed to depression or violence. Lacking sufficient research, I say, "Go for it—try anything and everything, and have faith in the brain's powers of recovery." New interventions are constantly being developed for both physical and cognitive problems, but let's not forget that it's much easier—and less expensive—to do it right the first time around! (Please see Chapter 12 for a fuller discussion.)

Another issue dealt with in this book is bilingualism, which is still a hot topic. As stated here, bilingual or multilingual brains seem to end up with more neural turf and stronger language/cognitive skills than others if they develop the second language(s) in a natural and supportive environment—and if they do not have a language disability to begin with. Nevertheless, here is another area where we need far more good, *objective,* research. In the United States, at least, this field has been so fraught with political/economic influences (e.g., government funding for various types of programs), and many studies have been so poorly controlled, that it is hard to believe anything one reads. I believe we can state confidently that the phonology ("accent") of a language has a sensitive period in very early childhood, that the best way to learn a second language is generally in a bilingual, language-rich home, and that teaching should generally start at the oral rather than the written level; beyond that I do not see brain research yielding any firm prescriptions on this question.

The "reading wars" were just starting when *Endangered Minds* was first published, so I would like to take this opportunity to clarify my position on the issue of "phonics" vs. "whole language." (Practicalities of this question are detailed in my book *Your Child's Growing Mind.*) Let me just point out here that the unfortunate fiasco inaccurately labeled "whole" language ran into trouble because it neglected a major part of language: direct teaching of sound-symbol relationships ["phonics"] and spelling rules. Nonetheless, true whole language has a lot to teach us, not the least of which is that meaningful and involving content, with active questioning and writing by students, must be a part of the process. Reading is skill-based, but it also needs to be enjoyable, thought-provoking, and a pathway into imagination.

Parents are always anxious about when and how to teach a child to read. When a child is ready, interested, and has the requisite linguistic and cognitive skills to learn successfully, our approach should be flexible, including every technique available according to the individual's needs. Unfortunately, tests administered to elementary teachers now show up an alarming lack of familiarity with the rules of written language, "phonics," diagnosis of difficulties, or even how to go about systematically teaching a child to read. If we want to beef up children's reading abilities, teaching the teachers would seem a good place to start!

PROGRESS REPORT

Although awareness of the brain's role in learning has taken giant leaps forward and neuroscientist-educator dialogue has begun, caution is still advised in drawing overly specific implications of brain studies for classroom practice. Teachers sometimes ask me questions like, "What does brain research say about the eighth-grade social studies curriculum?" Certainly, some useful (and commonsense) principles can responsibly be drawn from the research—for example, the more engaged your students are in a topic, and the more modalities they use to process it, the better they will understand, remember, and apply it; or that not all eighth-graders have fully developed frontal lobes, so concrete, hands-on experiences will help them gain more abstract viewpoints. It is a mistake, however, to use our limited understanding of neuroscience to develop "formulas" for teaching or to support any sort of doctrinaire pedagogy.

Many parents now understand the necessity to limit TV viewing. Moreover, programs such as *Sesame Street* have made serious efforts to improve their formats and involve parents in active viewing (although much of the criticism in Chapter 11 still holds.) On the other hand, we witness alarming efforts to market video addiction and overstimulation at ever-younger ages, with so-called "educational" programs targeted at the infant-toddler set. Since these ages represent a particularly critical period when irrevocable foundations for emotional, social, personal, and language abilities are laid (or not), this commercialized assault on baby brains presages troubling long-term consequences.

Much of the time previously devoted to children's TV viewing is now occupied by computer use. I explore the positive and negative aspects in my book *Failure to Connect: How Computers Affect Our Children's Minds—and What We Can Do About It*. Suffice it to say here, as of this writing, there is plenty of bad along with the good. Parents and teachers should fully inform themselves before they expose their children's brains (particularly before age seven) to today's software or Internet use, and they should be on hand as an active part of their children's cyberlife.

LOOKING AHEAD

A number of interesting trends are emerging in the research. Most notably, the development of new methods of scanning the brain in action (e.g., PET scans, functional magnetic resonance imaging [fMRI]) presage better understanding of how to facilitate learning and why things sometimes go wrong. For example, studies have mapped the widely distributed brain areas involved in tasks of language reception, comprehension, and expression, as well as in reading. In the future, tests given early on may determine not only which children will be at risk for language or reading problems, but also what instructional method will be best for each child.

Such techniques complement basic research on neurochemicals (neurotransmitters, steroids, and peptides), which operate at the synaptic level to create our mental life—both cognitive and emotional. Brain scans can indicate how well neural systems are working; brain areas showing up as underactivated may indicate that the requisite neurochemicals are not available or properly utilized. For example, scientists have identified a so-called "biological signature" for attention deficit disorder. The implications of such findings are profound. It would be nice to be able to make a definitive diagnosis of this puzzling problem, but we must be wary of any arguments that "biology is destiny" and there is nothing to be done about it. The end point of such reductionist thinking might lead, for example, to testing all infants soon after birth and discarding or irrevocably labeling those who show up as potential troublemakers. After all, differences (or deficiencies) in brain function—even at the chemical level—can be learned as well as inherited, and there is every indication that positive environments and skilled teaching can influence even genetic deficits for the better.

The surge in research on brain chemistry, reflected in a proliferation of psychotropic drugs (e.g., mood enhancers for those suffering from depression, drugs for schizophrenia) will doubtless continue to be the biggest news in brain science in the near future and may answer some very important questions. How much of this neurochemical system is, in fact, "plastic"? Many people know that going out for some vigorous exercise can improve their mood, and even mustering up a smile may positively alter your neurotransmitters. On the other hand, if you grow up in an insecure or stress-inducing environment, your brain may always tend to be hyperreactive to frightening or stressful situations. What about the long-term effects on the neurotransmitter systems of youngsters repeatedly exposed to startling media and violent video games? What, too, are the neurochemical effects of long-term exposure to stressed-out or incompetent caregivers, or to nonhuman surrogates (TV, computers) which cannot respond in personal or emotionally supportive ways to young children? Interesting questions.

Increasing recognition of the close chemical links between brain, body, and emotions bodes some shaking-up of traditional educational practice. Exclusive emphasis on the cognitive brain must be reconsidered in light of the new information; the human organism is much more than a pure thinking machine. Even the immune system has reciprocal ties to the thinking brain. Certainly, trying to teach the head while ignoring the body and emotions may account for a great deal of school failure. But positive emotional climates are *not* those contrived situations in which students are constantly praised for whatever work they muster up the energy to do. Students need to be safe from physical danger and ridicule but challenged to master important content, listened to, and supported ("scaffolded") in achievement as a function of personal effort. If we could set up this sort of environment, many of our "educational problems" would probably vanish.

We will also see a reawakening of awareness about the close ties between brain development and the child's motor system, also slighted in our frenzy to make kids smarter. We may even prove that some regular downtime playing on a jungle gym or inventing social games contributes more to intelligence than grinding through yet one more page of rote arithmetic calculations! Likewise, as researchers begin to document the neurological contributions of music, visual arts, dance, pretend play, and other aesthetic or creative activities, those who recommend or allow the cutting of these "extras" in the curriculum will look even more foolish than they already do.

Finally, I would call attention to some redefinitions of intelligence that complement this more holistic view of the human brain. Straight academic learning is far from the only quality that makes for a successful person. Self-control, motivation, everyday problem-solving, self-awareness, reflection, and the intangible qualities of spirit may matter even more—and, according to today's teachers, are at least as endangered in our media-ized kids as are formal academic skills.

I have tried here to update some very complex arguments in a very few words. I recommend that you stay tuned to the research and remember that we still have a great deal to learn.

As to a short wish list for research, I would still like to see some cutting-edge studies of what our electronic baby sitters (TV, computer software) are actually doing to kids' brains. It would help with educational decision-making if we understood more about the developmental stages in the brain, with more specific markers of when it is most receptive to different types of experience. We could certainly use more specifics on critical/sensitive periods for the development of attention skills and motivation, or even for mental imagery and creativity. Many educators and parents wonder about the process of maturation as indexed by myelination and whether and how intellectual maturation can be enhanced. And what are the most effective long-term interventions when children have missed out on important experiences?

It will continue to be interesting to observe whether newer electronic environments will be developed to expand or contract the abilities of the brain. I continue to wonder how the human mind will evolve—and even whether it will end up as boss—in a world increasingly dependent on nonhuman cyber-entities. Doubtless progress toward a livable future will depend a great deal on the human values and interactions we offer our children today. In the long run, a society gets not only the leaders but also the young people it deserves. Given our children's native spunk, guided by the multitudes of parents and teachers who do care enough to spend the requisite time and energy, I think we still have a fighting chance.

Vail, Colorado
January 1999

Preface

Several people whom I respect very much advised me not to write this book. "You can't prove it—even if it's true," said the first neuropsychologist I called. "Why don't you write about something else?"

"Leave it alone. We've already had too much overpopularization of the brain. The public isn't ready to hear about these things," warned another.

"Don't give everyone more excuses to blame the kids," a thoughtful educator pleaded. "Teachers do too much of that already!"

I debated. Could I accurately explain to nonscientists that changing lifestyles may be altering children's brains in subtle but critical ways? Could I write a book that would tell the truth—without sounding like a crabby middle-aged academic? Should I go out on a limb with a thesis that available technology cannot test, much less prove?

On the verge of abandoning my idea, I scheduled more interviews, excerpts from which are included in the following chapters. These scientists had a totally different response. They got excited when I told them what I wanted to write about. Moreover, they convinced me that my ideas were not so farfetched after all. Some even told me to hurry up and get started. "These things need to be said—and the sooner, the better," one insisted.

They also goaded my own curiosity and provoked new questions. The process of tracking down the answers has been a rigorous one that has led me to offices, clinics, schools, and conference sessions in the United States, Canada, and Europe. Having produced some deeply troubling and eye-opening experiences, it has also yielded moments of refreshing optimism. I hope the reader will similarly be able to put the negatives into perspective and sense the promise as well as the obligation implied in the following chapters.

One of the most reassuring aspects of this search was the quality of the many people I met who are sincerely concerned about the intellectual development of children and teenagers. I would especially like to acknowledge my gratitude to a number of thoughtful scientists busy pursuing research on how the brain grows and learns but not too busy to answer phone calls, schedule interviews, explain complex ideas, and offer helpful suggestions on the manuscript. Their names are found, along with some gleanings of their wisdom, throughout these chapters. Scores of school administrators and teachers cared enough to write, phone, welcome me into their classrooms, and talk earnestly about their concerns, while at the same time communicating their dedication to students and to the art of good teaching. Above all, I am grateful to the students—my own and all the others—who keep me continually reassured that they really are worth the best efforts we can give them.

Of course, I must acknowledge that any work I do is the product of a joint effort: Angela Miller and Carole Lalli got this book off the ground, and the secretarial talents of Jane Piszczor have kept it aloft. I am particularly indebted to Bob Bender for stepping in at a critical moment with much-needed support and direction. My sincere thanks, as well, to the friends and colleagues who interrupted their own lives to read and offer thoughtful comments on the manuscript. Above all, my mother and the four wonderful men in my life have provided wise counsel and a necessary backboard for ideas to an oft-distracted writer. Special thanks to my husband, Tom, for using his "big picture" skills to keep me aware of what I am really trying to say.

Part One

———— ⚱ ————

CHANGING BRAINS

CHAPTER
1

"Kids' Brains Must Be Different..."

"Kids' brains must be different these days," I remarked half jokingly as I graded student essays in the faculty room late one afternoon.

"If I didn't think it was impossible, I would agree with you," chimed in a colleague who had experienced a particularly frustrating day with his English classes. "These kids are so sharp, but sometimes I think their minds are different from the ones I used to teach. I've had to change my teaching a lot recently, and I still wonder how much they're learning. But a human brain is a human brain. They don't change much from generation to generation—do they?"

"Changing brains?" mumbled a math teacher, putting on her coat. "Maybe that accounts for it."

Changing brains. The idea kept returning as I taught and watched students at different grade levels. I began to observe more carefully; these youngsters did seem different from those we used to teach—even though the average IQ score in our school had remained solidly comparable. Today's students looked and acted differently, of course, and they talked about different things, but I became increasingly convinced that the changes went deeper than that—to the very ways in which they were absorbing and processing information. Likable, fun to be with, intuitive, and often amazingly self-aware, they seemed, nonetheless, harder to teach, less attuned to verbal material, both spoken and written. Many admitted they didn't read very much—sometimes even the required homework. They struggled with (or avoided) writing assignments, while teachers anguished over the

13

results. When the teacher gave directions, many forgot them almost immediately; even several repetitions often didn't stick. They looked around, doodled, fidgeted.

Were kids always like this? I started to listen to the veteran teachers—not the bitter, burned-out ones who complain all the time about everything, but the ones who are still in the business because they love teaching and really enjoy being around young people. I visited schools. In every one, from exclusive suburbs to the inner city, I heard similar comments:

> Yes, every year I seem to "water down" the material even more. I request books for reluctant readers rather than the classics we used to use in these high school courses. I use library-research worksheets instead of term-paper assignments. I have to start from the beginning on conjugating verbs and diagramming sentences—and most of them still don't get it. Lectures can't exceed fifteen minutes. I use more audiovisuals.

> I used to be able to teach *Scarlet Letter* to my juniors; now that amount of reading is a real chore for them and they have more trouble following the plot.

> I feel like kids have one foot out the door on whatever they're doing— they're incredibly easily distracted. I think there may have been a shift in the last five years.

> Ten years ago I gave students materials and they were able to figure out the experiment. Now I have to walk·them through the activities step by step. I don't do as much science because of their frustration level.

> Yes, I've modified my teaching methods because of their lack of attention span and their impatience. I don't do much of the lecture-notetaking method. I'm using student workbooks, prepared worksheets and tests because they are readily available.

> I teach biology and I have them spend more time on paperwork just to get them to look at the material. They refuse to read the book, so I must keep trying techniques to get them to read it.

> I've been hoping someone would notice! I've been worried about this for some time. Kids' abilities are certainly different—I use with gifted

sixth graders a lot of what I did with average fifth graders in '65-'66. They complain of the workload.

It's scary! When I started teaching here [a "fast-track" private school] in 1965, I used *Evangeline* with the seventh grade. Imagine, *Evangeline!* And the kids loved it and understood it. Now there'd be *no way* . . . but I'm supposedly teaching the same kind of kids in the same grade!

Scary indeed! I became increasingly convinced that I was tapping into a major phenomenon with profound implications, not only for teaching and learning, but also for the future of our society. Scariest of all was the growing discrepancy between what children were apparently equipped to do and what teachers thought they should be capable of doing. Teachers of the youngest children, claiming they see more pronounced changes every year, warned that we haven't seen anything yet!

Changing brains? Could it be possible? As I went from school classrooms to professional meetings where neuroscientists were excitedly starting to discuss new research on the subtle power of environments to shape growing brains, I began to realize that it is indeed possible.

"Of course, experience—even different kinds of learning—changes children's brains," I was told again and again. If children's experiences change significantly, so will their brains. Part of the brain's physical structure comes from the way it is used.

"But," everyone always added, "there's no way to measure subtle neurological differences between past generations and this one. You can't prove such changes because the technology has not been available to measure them."

No "proof," but plenty of circumstantial evidence. I developed a questionnaire requesting anecdotal information on cognitive changes observed in students. I handed it out at national meetings and conferences to experienced teachers in schools where population demographics had remained relatively stable. Approximately three hundred teachers responded, and I was amazed by the unanimity of response. Yes, attention spans are noticeably shorter. Yes, reading, writing, and oral language skills seem to be declining—even in the "best" neighborhoods. Yes, no matter how "bright," students are less able to bend their minds around difficult problems in math, science, and other subjects. Yes, teachers feel frustrated and would like to do a better job. This was a long way from "proof," but I found it provocative—and troubling.

Meanwhile, newspaper headlines screamed daily about declining test scores. International assessments comparing math and science performance of thirteen-year-old students from twelve countries found U.S. students at "rock bottom," particularly in understanding of concepts and more complex interpretation of data. Analysts from the Carnegie Council on Adolescent Development suggested that test scores do not even reveal the total extent of the problem, as they are poor measures of the type of thinking abilities today's youth will need on the job. "Will our nation's young adolescents be able to function as the foundation for America's ability to compete in the global economy?" they wondered.[1]

News programs featured a report concluding that most American seventeen-year-olds were poorly prepared to handle jobs requiring technical skills and that only 7% could handle college-level science courses. A numbing national march toward mediocrity was predicted. A cover story in *Fortune* magazine compared the "crisis" in education to the attack on Pearl Harbor. "In a high-tech age where nations increasingly compete on brainpower, American schools are producing an army of illiterates," it proclaimed.[2] A survey found 68% of major business firms "encumbered" by the educational shortcomings of their employees; 36% were already offering remedial courses in reading, writing, and math, with another 28% acknowledging they were considering the possibility.

In a special issue focusing on problems in education, the *Wall Street Journal* documented the growing incompetency of high school graduates by surveying managers who have trouble finding even minimally competent workers to hire. "I'm almost taking anyone who breathes," said one bank manager whose new tellers can't add and subtract well enough to balance their own checkbooks. An advertising firm in Chicago admitted that only one applicant in ten meets the minimum literacy standard for mail-clerk jobs, and Motorola, Inc., provided statistics showing that 80% of all applicants screened nationally fail a test of seventh-grade English and fifth-grade math.[3] Clearly, opined the observers, schools are not doing their job.

Inadequate schools may well be a problem in a land where neither teachers nor the educational enterprise itself get a great deal of respect. Moreover, inferior graduates may well become inferior teachers. But is this the whole problem? Our knowledge about how to teach has actually improved during the last twenty years. I have been hanging around university education departments since the fifties; during that time professional training has been considerably up-graded. Thoughtful research on how children learn has paved the way for dissemination of better classroom methods and instructional materials as well as a much clearer understanding of students who have trouble learning in traditional ways. It hardly seems reasonable to believe that the majority of teachers have suddenly become so much worse. In any school I visit I find many good, dedicated professionals. They claim tried-and-true methods aren't working anymore. Why? Are children becoming less intelligent? Could changes in mental abilities reflect underlying changes in brain development as much as bad pedagogy?

What's Happening to the Test Scores?

In a highbrow private school in Manhattan, a college counselor laments, "Look at these verbal SAT scores! How am I ever going to get these kids into the colleges their parents want?" While this counselor has good reason for concern, he may be somewhat comforted by the fact that his students are certainly not unique.

Very few tests in the United States have stayed the same long enough to provide a long-range view of young people's abilities across the past few decades. Three organizations producing the most consistently standardized measurements have been the College Board, which publishes the Scholastic Aptitude Test (SAT) taken by students who intend to apply to college, the similar American College Testing program (ACT), and the National Assessment of Educational Progress, which tests academic achievement of school children at representative grade levels. As anyone who even scans the headlines knows, they have shown drastically declining scores, particularly in the areas of higher-level verbal and reasoning skills.

Although the SAT has been criticized for a number of failings, including various types of bias, it provides a consistent source of data over a period of years. Purportedly a test of ability rather than of what has been learned, the test is, in fact, highly dependent on background experiences such as vocabulary exposure, reading facility, and math courses taken. By the time students are in high school, it is difficult to separate out the various effects of school learning and native ability. Thus its scores reflect both basic intelligence and experience. Starting in 1964, average SAT verbal and math scores declined steadily until the mid-1980s, when they leveled off and then experienced a very slight rise. Subsequently, math scores have remained stable and verbal have begun another gradual decline. Overall, verbal declines have been considerably greater, 47 points by 1988 (from 475 to 428) as opposed to 22 for math (498 to 476).[4]

Losses of this magnitude have caused justifiable concern, and many reasons have been proposed for this apparent erosion of national brainpower. The fact that a less rarefied group of students, including more from less "privileged" educational backgrounds, now take the test has been shown to account for some, but not all, of the decline in average scores. Recently, in fact, scores of minorities are the only ones showing consistent improvement, with black students particularly making impressive gains. Moreover, the past few years have seen the growing popularity of courses that claim great success in coaching students in test-related subject matter and test-taking "tricks." These should have raised scores at least a little, particularly for the more privileged group who can afford the courses. Is it possible that without their influence, overall declines would be even greater?

For all students, steady increases in television viewing and less time spent reading are accepted as negative influences on verbal scores. The culpability of those factors, as we shall see in later chapters, goes far beyond what most people are willing to admit. Schools have also been blamed for giving less homework, lowering academic standards, and using less challenging materials. Of course, teachers complain they have been forced to these expedients because of skill deficits in the students they are attempting to teach. In short, no one really agrees on the reasons. Everyone agrees, however, that the situation is serious. Most alarming is the suggestion that the "top" layer of students, our potential pool of future leaders, is being seriously affected.

The "Best and the Brightest"

To investigate this possibility I contacted The Educational Testing Service, which publishes results of Graduate Record Examinations which are taken by a self-selected group of students who intend to pursue graduate study. I learned right away that it is hard to extract any firm evidence about scoring trends on these tests for several reasons, which I will explain shortly. Nevertheless, in digging through the data from the last fifteen years, I did find some interesting clues indicating that both interest and ability in primarily verbal fields of study appear to have declined rather startlingly.

The GREs include general measures of verbal, quantitative, and analytical ability as well as subject area tests in a number of disciplines such as history, English literature, psychology, math, etc. The subject tests are optional, as they are required for admission only to certain departments in certain schools. GRE scores must be cautiously interpreted in terms of general trends, since rising scores may indicate simply that brighter students, on the whole, are choosing to apply to graduate school, and vice versa. Moreover, the growing use of "prep" courses may also mask declining ability of GRE applicants.

Increasing numbers of students whose primary language is not English have unquestionably affected verbal scores on the general intelligence tests which all applicants are required to take. The percentage of total GRE test-takers who are not U.S. citizens has more than doubled since 1975 to about 16%. Since a large proportion of these students are math and science majors, math and analytic scores would be expected to rise, which they have. Between 1972 and 1987, average quantitative scores rose from 512 to 550; analytic scores have also increased. In the same period, however, verbal scores fell from 497 to 477.

This overall decline in verbal abilities may not be totally attributable to foreign-born applicants, since the same trend shows up on subject tests which are chosen only by students intending to study a particular field—in which they presumably consider themselves competent. Between 1972 and 1987, average scores of students choosing to take the English Literature test (who are overwhelmingly of English-speaking origin and have usually been English majors) declined from 545 to 526, while those on foreign language tests in French, German, and Spanish also tended downwards. The number of students taking tests in language or literary fields also declined precipitously; only one-half of the 1972 number took the English Literature test in 1985; the pool of French language test-takers declined to approximately one-fifth of its previous size. The same trends were evident in other fields heavily weighted toward verbal skills: History, Political Science, and Sociology scores fell off dramatically, as did the number of test-takers. In 1972, 1,354 students took the philosophy test; in 1984, only 252 signed up, and the test was subsequently discontinued.

These apparent declines in verbally oriented fields—even by native English-speaking literature majors—has troubled many observers who feel that a society needs good philosophers, statesmen, and writers as well as outstanding technological minds. In direct contrast, the same years have seen relatively large scoring gains in the fields of engineering, mathematics, psychology, and economics. For example, more students took the engineering test in 1987 than in 1972, and the average score rose from 593 to 623. The number of non-U.S. citizens in these technological fields who will decide to leave the United States after they obtain their advanced training is, of course, unknown.

Let me speculate for just a moment about what these changes might suggest. For reasons which I hope will become clear later in this book, sequential, verbal-analytic reasoning (such as that needed for fluent, accurate reading, writing, and oral language expression) depends on quite different uses of the brain than do skills depending more heavily on nonverbal, "simultaneous" mental processes (e.g., engineering, some aspects of higher mathematics). No clear statement, much less any conclusions, can be drawn from this spotty scenario, but one might be tempted to ponder whether, whatever the reason, we are seeing some sort of shift in abilities—or at least interest—among our future academic leaders.

. . . and Back in the Trenches

Of course, few of our students make it to graduate school. For the vast majority of American youngsters, declines in math and science achievement as well as in verbal skills are a source of national alarm. Recent scores on the National Assessment of Educational Progress (NAEP) have shown particular deficiencies in higher-order reasoning skills, including those necessary for advanced reading comprehension, math, and science. Although younger students, in the wake of a clamor for educational reform, seem to have improved test scores slightly, "most of the progress has occurred in the domain of lower-order skills." Math scores, according to the NAEP findings, are particularly dismal when students are required to sustain attention for problems requiring more than one step. For example, only 44% of high school graduates could compute the change that would be received from $3.00 for two items ordered from a lunch menu.[5]

The same deficiencies in sustained reasoning are found in other subjects. Thus, according to Albert Shanker, president of the American Federation of Teachers, only 20% of seventeen-year-olds could write an organized job-application letter, only 4% could make sense out of a sample bus schedule, and only 12% could arrange six common fractions in order of size. Dr. Shanker goes on to comment that only 20 to 25% of students currently in school can learn effectively from traditional methods of teaching.[6]

Particularly troublesome is the fact that, with the exception already noted of foreign-born math students, older and better students are falling behind similar students of previous decades.[7] Eroding abilities in the "best" students first started to show up in the NAEP results in the seventies. A similar trend showed up when a well-recognized test of basic skills for grade school students was revised in 1977. Scores of a nationally representative sample of 40,000 fourth and eighth graders were compared with those of their 1970 counterparts. "Average" fourth graders in 1977 were slightly worse in all areas than fourth graders of 1970, and "language usage" among the better students had dropped significantly. "Average" eighth graders of 1977 had fallen half a year behind those of 1970 both in language usage and mathematics concepts; the "fast" eighth graders had declined most of all. They scored significantly lower in all subjects, with a full-year drop in language usage ability.[8] As will be shown later, the effects of these universally noted trends have begun to show up even in highly selective colleges, as professors find they must water down both reading and writing assignments as well as expectations for analytic reasoning. Despite a serious effort on the part of elementary and high schools to beef up the curriculum, students of all ability levels show virtually no gains in higher-order skills.

Exhibit A in the current academic crisis is the state of reading abilities. Although declines in reading ability have already raised a loud outcry among educators and employers, most people are not aware either of the breadth of the problem or how the manipulation of test procedures are masking its real dimensions.

Exhibit A: The Crisis in Reading

Some of my seniors will graduate from *high school* reading on a lower level than the students who graduated from junior high school in 1970.
—English teacher, suburban school, Virginia

My students? Well, they don't read. The culture doesn't read. They don't use language above the colloquial expressions because the mainstream culture is dangerously indifferent to the importance of precise language. I don't have much hope of producing readers in the classroom until we can produce readers in the larger social context. I used to be able to use *Tale of Two Cities* in a good eighth-grade class; now, even with ninth graders I approach it warily. If they read it on their own, they miss the connections and so much of the meaning—particularly the subtle ideas. The syntax is just like a foreign language to them.

—English teacher, independent school, Ohio

Toward an Inarticulate and Aliterate Society?

The state of literacy in the United States today is declining so precipitously, while video and computer technologies are becoming so powerful, that the act of reading itself may well be on the way to obsolescence. The alarming incidence of illiteracy in the United States has been widely publicized, alerting the public to the fact that up to 23 million Americans in the work force lack the reading and writing skills necessary to compete in the job market.[9] No so readily recognized, or admitted, is a growing decline in skill and interest in reading among the functionally literate. Those who can read (or at least pronounce the words)—do not.

Approximately 90% of young people can read simple material. Yet the majority have difficulty understanding text above elementary school level, drawing inferences beyond simple facts, following an author's point or the sequence of an argument, or using facts to support an argument of their own.[10] As in other subjects, college-bound students have declined in both reading ability and interest, despite national and local initiatives toward improved instruction for them.[11] The NAEP's most recent report found that only 5% of high school graduates could satisfactorily master material traditionally used at the college level.

The situation may get considerably worse. Many of the upcoming generation of teachers dislike reading and avoid it whenever possible. One study conducted by two Kent State University education professors in a children's literature course found surprising changes in prospective teachers' attitudes. "Many students enter our courses with negative attitudes toward reading in general and, more specifically, toward the types of literature that make up the main content of our courses" (i.e., "good" books for children and adolescents). More than one-fourth of these potential teachers confessed to a "lifelong discomfort with print," and many acknowledged that they made it through English courses by relying on "Cliff Notes, book jackets, or cursory reading to supply them with just enough information to pass tests or to prepare book reports."[12] Others of us who are teaching teachers can unfortunately confirm that this observation is not an isolated one.

These young people, who will convey to the next generation not only the higher-level reading and reasoning skills they have so handily circumvented but also their own attitudes toward reading, are reflections of the society in which they live. Americans, on the whole, are not particularly entranced with the written word. Although sales of children's books to affluent parents, who want to give (perhaps literally) their child every educational advantage, are growing, no one is really sure who—if anyone—is actually reading the books. Despite incontrovertible evidence that children who read well come from homes where reading is a prominent part of life, most parents do not read themselves. Eighty percent of the books in this country are read by about 10% of the people.

The proportion of readers in the United States is continuing to become smaller with a steady and significant decline in the number of book readers under twenty-one, according to Dr. Bernice Cullinan of New York University. She reports on one large group of "typical" fifth graders queried about the average amount of time they spent reading outside of school:

50% read four minutes a day or less
30% read two minutes a day or less
10% read nothing

This same group of children watched an average of 130 minutes of TV per day. Yet, as Dr. Cullinan reminds us, children become good, insightful, analytic readers *only* by lots of practice with reading.

Our society is becoming increasingly *aliterate*, says Cullinan. "An aliterate is a person who knows how to read but who doesn't choose to read. These are people who glance at the headlines of a newspaper and grab the TV schedule. They do not read books for pleasure, nor do they read extensively for information. An aliterate is not much better off than an illiterate, a person who cannot read at all. Aliterates miss the great novels of the past and present. They also miss probing analyses written about political issues. Most aliterates watch television for their news, but the entire transcript of a television newscast would fill only two columns of the *New York Times*. Aliterates get only the surface level of the news."[13]

The serious audience for books in this country is getting steadily older and shows no signs of growing, confirms Jack Shoemaker, the editor in chief of North Point Press. "I think that a quick survey of some of the big independent booksellers will confirm my sense that there is no meaningful audience in their teenage years or people in their twenties. These [book] stores are largely supported by people in their late thirties to mid-fifties," he remarked recently.[14]

Similar although less dramatic trends are appearing in other countries as well. The Japanese publishing industry reports a steady decline in hardcover sales despite the fact that, comparatively speaking, the Japanese are voracious readers. Literary critics in that country complain that young people are not as interested in literature as previous generations.[15]

Despite similar murmurs from other countries, publishers in the United States have particular reason to be concerned that readers are an endangered species. Book sales in this country are twenty-fourth worldwide, and figures on newspaper sales show significant loss of readership; fifty-four daily papers have died since 1979, and papers sold per thousand residents are only half the number sold in Japan.[16] A proliferation of pictorial and technically oriented magazines (e.g., fitness, home design, motorcycles, computers) fill the newsstands.

The problem results not only from disinterest in reading but also from increasing numbers of students with poor reading skills. Curiously enough, many of these poor readers do not recognize they have a problem. A survey of 443 students entering a community college showed that although a horrifying 50% were reading *below ninth grade level*, only 80 acknowledged that they needed any help with reading! Even among the 221 who scored anywhere from third- to eighth-grade level, 178 believed they were doing just fine.[17] This all-too-typical statistic certainly hints at major inadequacies in the expectations of their previous schools. Even more, however, it may reflect on the value the students place on reading or their ability to take responsibility for and look inward at their own mental processes.

The Two-Minute Mind

Why don't—or can't—most young people read? One of the most common complaints among this generation is that books are "too hard" or "boring." Many have trouble with the mental organization and sustained effort demanded by reading. Coming to grips with verbal logic, wrestling one's mind into submission to an author's unfamiliar point of view, and struggling to make connections appear to be particularly taxing to today's young intellects.

Informal reports help explain the reality behind the statistics. Even some English majors now find sustained prose a drag. Kristin Eddy, a news aide at the *Washington Post* and a literature major at George Washington University, reported recently on a hands-up poll revealing that only half of her upper-level classmates had bothered to finish the assigned *All the King's Men*, a best-selling favorite of a previous student generation. Why? "Boring!" "Too hard to follow." Another classmate commented that Sarah Orne Jewett's beautifully written *The Country of the Pointed Firs* "went so slowly that it seemed like it was written by a retarded person."

To read well, minds must be trained to use language, to reflect, and to persist in solving problems. Students may learn to sound out the words, but unless they possess the internal sense of responsibility for extracting the meaning, they are engaging in a hollow and unsatisfying exercise. With major efforts, we have succeeded in teaching students in early grades to "read the words." Test scores jump off a cliff, however, when students must begin to plug the words into language meaning and grapple with the more advanced grammar, vocabulary, and the sustained intellectual demands of a real text.

Reading Abilities: Worse Than We Realize

Starting in the 1970s, reading test scores in American schools took such a dive that major initiatives were launched to improve instruction. Educators developed new materials based on research about how children learn to read, better training of teachers became a focus in many schools, and instruction in "phonics" (systematic sounding out of words) was stressed. A slight rise in reading test scores in the early grades resulted.

However, as Fred M. Hechinger points out, young students may be sounding out the words better, but they are actually understanding less.[18] Children cannot comprehend, remember, and apply what is read. The 1986 NAEP report found, as have other recent assessments, that students' related problems in reading and expressing ideas in writing stem mainly from difficulty with verbal reasoning.

"Reading instruction at all levels must be restructured to ensure that students learn to reason more effectively about what they have read," states the report, which showed such a drastic and "baffling" decline in reading performance of nine- and seventeen-year-olds that the report was delayed for five months while researchers refigured the statistics and reexamined the test items. They still could not explain the decline. NAEP officials had planned to publish a study showing trends in students' reading performance since 1971, but these plans were canceled because no one wanted to believe the results.[19]

Why We Shouldn't Trust the Tests

This fiasco only illustrates what educational psychologists already realize; strange goings-on sometimes occur in the name of "testing." Test results, in fact, can be quite misleading estimates of just how well, or how poorly, children can read. Perhaps the NAEP results really were accurate. They probably appeared so surprising because other current reading tests—believe it or not—actually make students' abilities look considerably better than they really are! Here are several reasons why most test scores should be taken with a large grain of salt:

1. What Is Reading?

How do you define "reading"? I have described in my first book an unusual group of children called hyperlexics, who teach themselves to read as early as age two and continue to read obsessively from any written material they can get their hands on. One five-year-old hyperlexic boy whom I tested brought the *New York Times* to my office and proceeded to read it aloud with flawless élan. Not surprisingly, he also scored at the level of an average high school senior on a commonly used reading test that measured how well he could sound out and pronounce words he had never even seen before! With scores like this, the child must be a gifted reader, right? Wrong. Unfortunately, he could not understand the meaning of even a first-grade story. Like others afflicted by this strange syndrome, he could "word-call," but he comprehended little.

The ability to "bark at print" is not reading, but many people, including well-meaning parents, think it is. Tests which show that young children's scores are rising may simply be focusing on the "lower level" skills of word reading while neglecting the real heart of the matter: How well do they understand what they have read? Can they reason—and talk, and write—about it?

2. How Do We Test It?

When testing children on reading skills, it is relatively easy to check out "phonics" and other word-reading abilities. It takes much longer to find out how well students have understood a passage. Because it is time-consuming to sit down with each child and do a thorough job, most standardized tests used today are given to large groups of children and scored by machines. They are poor vehicles for assessing comprehension because the student is not required to formulate (say or write) anything, merely to fill in "bubbles," to check off one of a given set of answers. Such multiple-choice tests receive a lot of well-justified criticism because they tend to concentrate on "lower-order" literal questions. Sometimes you don't even have to read the passage to get the right answer:

What color was John's wagon?
green
black
red

"It's testing for the TV generation—superficial and passive," commented Linda Darling-Hammond, director of education for the RAND Corporation. "We don't ask if students can synthesize information, solve problems, or think independently. We measure what they can recognize. But this is very different from what actually goes on in our information society. No one goes to work and finds a checklist on their desk."[20]

Even poor readers may manage to answer "little red wagon" questions, but they start to flounder when the language, the texts, and the questions grow up. One effective way to probe a reader's understanding is to ask him to "tell what happened," give a summary or a paraphrase. Many students today have particular difficulty with such questioning, perhaps because they have never been required to synthesize or talk about texts in this way; they've been too busy filling in the bubbles.

3. "Dumbed-Down" Tests

Most people are unaware that there has been a major "dumbing-down" of reading tests since the 1960s. It is a shocking fact, considering their poor scores, that our children are taking tests drastically more simple than those of only two decades ago. The evidence suggests that test-makers are making children look better than they really are by manipulating the level of difficulty of both the reading and the types of questions asked.

When discussing tests, I often think back to the mid-seventies, when I was principal of a primary school and we switched to the brand-new, updated form of a nationally normed achievement test. Every child's scores magically rose because the new test was so much easier than the previous one. By simply using the new form, we could raise scores significantly without even teaching anything! Educators went around at professional conferences that year telling each other, "If you want your school to look really good, switch to the new form of Brand X achievement test."

What a wonderful discovery! If scores continue to decline—why, just keep changing the tests.

Reading abilities of contemporary children cannot easily be compared with those from past decades because most of the tests have been changed every eight or ten years. In 1978, one college professor in Minnesota gave students in his classes the same reading test that had been used in 1928. Their scores were more like those of the high school students of fifty years earlier.[21] Such comparisons are not terribly valid for a number of reasons, including differences in standard vocabulary and usage from one generation to another, yet there is every indication that reading abilities have undergone even more accelerated declines since he did this research in 1978. At the same time, we have seen increasingly frequent revisions of the major tests. Do these more frequent changes reflect a greater need for a fix-up?

In 1987, Dr. James Cannell blew the whistle on test-changers. In an incendiary report he charged that the degree of difficulty in the reading comprehension section of the widely used California Achievement Test for second and third graders was a full grade level below that of the 1977 version of the same test. The equally popular Stanford Achievement Test, said this report, "showed a profound drop in expository reading difficulty between 1972 and 1982." Despite noisy protests from the testing establishment, the essential truth of Cannell's findings was subsequently confirmed by a federally sponsored analysis.[22]

Are the test-makers really at fault? "Norms," by definition, vary according to the abilities of the group of children used to develop the scoring system for any given test; if overall abilities decline, so do the standards of the test. If sixth graders in the 1980s are poorer readers than sixth graders were in the 1960s, the 1980s test has to be easier in order to get a "normal distribution" of scores, with many children receiving average scores and only a few out on the extreme high or low ends.

Moreover, because administrators tend to shun tests that make their children look stupid (and themselves incompetent), publishers are naturally pressured to produce tests to make kids look good. They appear to have done exactly what Cannell claimed. When I compared the 1964, 1972, and 1982 forms of a typical, widely used reading test, I was shocked to observe the differences. Each successive edition was so much easier than the previous one that it was hard to believe they were actually given to children of the same grade level! As just one example, Figure 1 shows comparable items (the last page) from the 1964 and 1982 forms of the test for fourth graders. You don't need a master's degree in reading to notice the increasing simplification of content, vocabulary level, sentence length, etc. This test, incidentally, is advertised as "the standard by which all other achievement tests will be measured."[23]

The most scary of all is a new "Advanced" form, designed for *ninth graders* and published in 1988 (Figure 2), which calls on such complex skills as reading a menu in a fast-food restaurant. This entire test is demonstrably easier than what fourth graders were expected to read in 1964.

Is the publisher's advertisement of this last instrument as "Testing Today's Curriculum" an unconscious irony? Personally, I find it incredible that this is called a "reading" test, yet it is one of the major instruments by which "competency" is evaluated.

4. Teachers and Administrators Can Cheat, Too

When the pressure is on for better test scores, administrators may report falsely inflated results to make their schools or districts look better. Cannell's study found, in fact, that all fifty states were above the national average,[24] although no one knows quite how this apparent miracle occurred. Teachers, too, are susceptible to pressure. When one's evaluation—and maybe one's job—is on the line, even a responsible teacher may slide into a seductive practice called "teaching the test." When the same test is used for more than one year and teachers become familiar with the questions, they tend, perhaps even unconsciously, to focus instruction on the items ("Remember this word—you just might see it again . . .") that will make their students shine statistically.

There are other clever little ways to manipulate test scores. One group of elementary teachers from Michigan told me they always give

A

Grade Four Reading Test, 1964

Test 2: Paragraph Meaning

Although we cannot always see the difference with the naked eye, stars are of different colors, and astronomers with 49 to aid them can see this. Since heat produces light, one thing that the different 50 of the stars tell us is the 51 of each star.

49	1 telescopes	3 eyes		1 2 3 4
	2 colors	4 charts	49	○ ○ ○ ○
50	5 colors	7 astronomers		5 6 7 8
	6 lights	8 telescopes	50	○ ○ ○ ○
51	1 distance	3 temperature		1 2 3 4
	2 size	4 weight	51	○ ○ ○ ○

The flowers of trees differ widely in their size and prominence, so that, while we all know the flower of the cherry tree, we may never have noticed that the oak has a flower. Yet, if we could trace back the history of every acorn, we should soon find that the oak does have a 52 . The size and appearance of what we call a flower usually depend on the part we call the petals, but these are not necessary parts of a flower at all; and there are many flowers which have no 53 . All 54 have flowers of some sort. They may be large or small, but they exist.

52	5 flower	7 seed		5 6 7 8
	6 trunk	8 root	52	○ ○ ○ ○
53	1 color	3 stems		1 2 3 4
	2 petals	4 size	53	○ ○ ○ ○
54	5 plants	7 parts		5 6 7 8
	6 petals	8 trees	54	○ ○ ○ ○

FIGURE 1. Comparison of Reading Achievement Tests, Grade Four: 1964 and 1982. (**A**, Stanford Achievement Test: 6th edition. Copyright © 1964 by Harcourt Brace Jovanovich, Inc. Reproduced by permission. All rights reserved. **B**, Stanford Achievement Test: Copyright © 1982 by Harcourt Brace Jovanovich, Inc.)

Grade Four Reading Test, 1964 *(cont.)*

Van Gogh was intensely conscious of life and creation, and the forces that govern Nature. Since he could not express what he felt by ordinary methods, he resorted to a strange manner of __55__ , drawing his pictures in masses of waving lines. It seemed to him that things so full of life as the sky, and the sun, and the earth could only be expressed by __56__ that seemed to be always moving and were as nearly __57__ as a line on a canvas can be.

55 1 living   3 feeling   1 2 3 4   55 ○○○○
2 painting   4 writing

56 5 words   7 lines   5 6 7 8   56 ○○○○
2 musical notes   8 ideas

57 1 alive   3 straight   1 2 3 4   57 ○○○○
2 precise   4 strange

Water is sometimes referred to as H_2O which is the chemical formula for water. This is the __58__ way of saying that every molecule of __59__ contains two atoms of hydrogen (H_2) and one __60__ of oxygen (O).

58 5 complex   7 chemist's   5 6 7 8   58 ○○○○
6 mathematician's   8 only

59 1 air   3 water   1 2 3 4   59 ○○○○
2 salt   4 chemical

60 5 drop   7 gram   5 6 7 8   60 ○○○○
6 molecule   8 atom

B

Reading Comprehension

I am awakened by the sound of thunder. Quietly, I sit up in bed. I am all alone in the trailer. The air holds mysterious sounds. "Are you safe, Jeremy?" I ask myself. I see a shadow in the window! The sight of it scares me. I slip beneath my blanket. The room is dark, except for the glow from the candle. I hear footsteps outside. Could they belong to some strange creature? I have never been this frightened before. Then I hear a tap on the door. "Who is it?" I whisper softly. What a comfort to hear Uncle Mike's voice!

50 What did Jeremy see in the window?
  f   a flame
  g   a shadow
  h   a tree
  j   an animal

51 This story takes place in a—
  a   barn   c   tent
  b   trailer   d   cabin

52 The footsteps belonged to Jeremy's—
  f   friend   h   uncle
  g   brother   j   cousin

53 Jeremy was awakened by—
  a   a knock on the door
  b   footsteps
  c   thunder
  d   a bright light

54 How did Jeremy feel at the end of the story?
  f   confident   h   sad
  g   tired   j   relieved

55 The author creates a mood of—
  a   warmth   c   peace
  b   sadness   d   excitement

FIGURE 1 (*continued*)

Grade Four Reading Test, 1982 *(cont.)*

School doors open
At summer's end,
In the lonely building
The children attend.

Faces happy, faces glad—
With faded jeans and wind-blown hair
Legs climbing.
Stair by stair.

Teacher waiting at her desk—
Room smells musty,
Walls are bare,
Books all dusty.

Goodbye, white sand;
Goodbye, pool.
Hello, Miss Rosen!
Hello, school!

56 The books need to be—

    f brushed off   **h** put away

    g repaired   **j** covered

57 Where is Miss Rosen?

    a in the schoolyard

    b in her classroom

    c in the hallway

    d on the stairway

58 In this poem, what do the children's faces tell us?

    f how hungry they are

    g how happy they are

    h how old they are

    j how well behaved they are

59 In this poem, the children are saying goodbye to—

    a their teacher   **c** summer vacation

    b their friends   **d** winter

60 The children's hair probably looks—

    f wet   **h** dusty

    g faded   **j** tangled

Grade Nine Reading Test, 1988

Treat Yourself

EVEN IF MONSTERS ARE ATTACKING THE CITY...

PIZZA PLUS

	SMALL	MEDIUM	LARGE
Stego-pizza Sausage, bacon, mushrooms, onions, beef, black olives, green olives, green peppers, pepperoni	4.50	6.00	7.50
Tyranno-pizza Sausage, mushrooms, onions, beef, bacon, black olives, anchovies, baby shrimp	5.00	6.50	8.00
Dino-cheese pizza	2.75	3.00	3.25
Dino-cheese & 1 topping	3.25	3.75	4.25
Dino-cheese & 2 toppings	3.50	4.10	4.70
Dino-cheese & 3 toppings	3.75	4.45	5.15
Each extra topping	.25	.35	.45

Extra Toppings: Bacon, sausage, pepperoni, Italian sausage, anchovies, shrimp, beef, green peppers, green olives, black olives, cheese, jalapeños, onions, clams, chicken, pistachios.

BRONTO-SPECIALS

Served all day Sat. & Sun.
Mon.-Fri. after 4 P.M.

The Bronto-Vore—Fresh spinach, onions, mushrooms, mozzarella with our own spicy sauce on a chewy crust and sprinkled with spices and more cheese.

The Tyranno-Vore—Generous portions of piping hot pepperoni, savory sausage, and mushrooms, layered with hot melted cheese. Or choose any three of your favorite ingredients and create your own TYRANNO-VORE.

sm. $6.85   med. $10.15   lg. $12.95

BEVERAGES:
32-oz. Soft Drinks.............................79¢

PASTA, SANDWICHES, & SALAD ALSO AVAILABLE
Special orders may take longer. Sales tax not included. Free delivery with minimum order. Limited delivery areas.

19972 Paleozoic Drive
555-1997

FIGURE 2. "Advanced" Reading Achievement Test, Grade Nine: 1988. (Stanford Achievement Test: Copyright © 1988 by Harcourt Brace Jovanovich, Inc.)

Grade Nine Reading Test, 1988 *(cont.)*

1   Before sales tax is included, a small Dino-cheese pizza with sausage, green peppers, and onions will cost—

   A $3.50
   B $3.75
   C $4.00
   D $4.45

2   Which dish contains spinach?

   F Tyranno-Vore
   G Stego-pizza
   H Bronto-Vore
   J Dino-cheese pizza

3   How much will the coupon *save* Bob if he orders a medium Stego-pizza and a 32-ounce root beer?

   A $0.79
   B $4.50
   C $6.00
   D $6.79

4   All of these can be ordered on a Dino-cheese pizza *except*—

   F clams
   G bacon
   H pistachios
   J mushrooms

5   This advertisement was *not* designed to be—

   A published in a newspaper
   B handed out at Pizza Plus
   C broadcast on television
   D distributed in people's mailboxes

6   You *cannot* get a Bronto-Special for—

   F dinner on Saturday
   G lunch on Friday
   H dinner on Friday
   J lunch on Sunday

the pretest (in September) late in the afternoon and tell the children they can go out on the playground as soon as they finish. For the "posttest" (by which the "gains" from their teaching are judged at the end of the year), they give the students orange juice and a healthful snack first thing in the morning; then when blood (and brain) sugar are at peak level, they hand out the test and encourage the class to take their time and stay in their seats to check answers if they finish early.

Why We Shouldn't Trust the Textbooks

"Johnny is only in third grade, but he's already in a fourth-grade reader!" carols a delighted mother. Unfortunately, she should not assume this accomplishment proves Johnny to be other than a mediocre reader, since many textbooks have also undergone "dumbing down." For some time, textbook publishers have been under pressure to make texts more "readable," unfortunately defined as having shorter sentences, less complex vocabulary, and more pictures. Elementary school textbooks ("basal readers") have increasingly contained short, unnatural sentences and awkward prose that can hardly be expected to endear to students the cadences of good language and literature.

Quality has also been jeopardized by superficial standards of reading "competency." According to a 1988 report of The Council for Basic Education, "Editors are increasingly organizing elementary reading series around the content and timing of standardized tests." The result? "A thin stream of staccato prose winding through an excessive number of pictures, boxes, and charts."[25]

High school textbooks (in science, history, etc.) have been pruned in response to complaints by teachers that students cannot understand books with traditional levels of complexity. Given the caliber of prose "infecting" current history texts, laments history buff Jack Valenti, they "would all fail the essential test: Was it read, enjoyed and remembered?"[26]

In a scathing critique published in *Education Week*, Arthur Woodward of the University of Rochester took textbook publishers to task for the new stress on visuals that drastically weakens texts. In many cases, he wrote, "instructional exposition takes second place to the design characteristics, which generally resemble those of a coffee-table picture book." He blames the high proportion of pages devoted to illustrations, often quite unrelated to the material at hand, for "the difficulty publishers face in handling given topics with sufficient substance."[27]

Even college-level texts have suffered by becoming more "homogenized," less academic, longer, easier, and more superficially glossy, claims Dr. Diana Paul of the University of Massachusetts and Harvard. These changes came about, at least in part, because "increasing numbers of college students were reading at a level that made it difficult for them to cope with traditional college textbooks," she explains.[28]

Overall, the state of reading points up fundamental changes, not only in skill levels, but also in the way today's students approach thinking and learning. Is it possible that reading is, indeed, an unnecessary relic of a passing culture? Could new habits possibly be more adaptive for today's kids or for society? While these are notions we will consider in the final chapter of this book, most educators see trends away from literacy as overridingly negative. Not only do they put students into direct conflict with the stated goals and methods of education, but they also render them less able to compete in the practical world of work in an information-processing society where verbal and problem-solving skills are in high demand.

Moreover, the expanded mental and human perspectives gained from reading may be a particular imperative for a generation destined to live—and provide leadership—in a technological culture. Do we want policymakers who are untroubled by the weighty realities of history because they have never read—or reflected—about them? Or business leaders who never heard of the likes of Babbitt? Or voters who have never peeked around the corner of their own thinking?

But Kids Should Seem Smarter!

Logically, one might expect that major changes in a generation of brains would show up on IQ tests. Do today's kids also get lower scores on them? No! Students today—at least the young ones—actually appear to score better than the children of previous generations.

To try and make some sense out of this apparent contradiction, I looked up the handful of studies that have surveyed trends in IQ scores over generations. I also compared scores on verbal sections of the tests (which require, for example, vocabulary knowledge, listening, verbal expression and reasoning skills) with the nonverbal sections (which contain items such as visual puzzles, mazes, imitating block constructions, etc.). Predictably, no easy answers were forth-coming, but studies over the last few decades did suggest that verbal abilities have recently begun to decline relative to nonverbal ones. This pattern, which has surprised researchers, is beginning to be seen in several European countries, but the United States is definitely leading the way. Whether these changes are attributable to some inherent weakness in the tests themselves or whether they represent an important trend has not yet been agreed upon.[29-31]

In fact, most researchers themselves have decided that looking only at people's "IQs" is not a very good way to compare mental abilities of successive generations. First of all, no one is really sure exactly what different types of tests actually measure—which may not be "intelligence" at all. Moreover, the "experts" have yet to agree about what "intelligence" really is.

According to total scores (verbal plus nonverbal) on the Wechsler Scales, probably the most commonly used IQ tests in the United States and several other countries, children appear to get smarter all the time. In fact, unlike reading tests, each new version of the test has been made slightly harder because scores have tended to rise across generations. People in this part of the testing business have come to expect that each generation will do better, on average, on the same types of items than did their parents. Yet, not surprisingly, this may only reflect the fact that more people have spent more years in school. No matter how hard test-makers try, it is almost impossible to test "intelligence" without including factors that are improved by atten-dance at school—not the least of which is test sophistication. More-over, as more parents attend school longer, more children are brought up by people who think and talk "in the culture of the tests"; so they may test "smarter" even if they are intrinsically no brighter. More-over, as more people go to school longer, their scores continue to rise even into their twenties, so that recent revisions of the test have actually seen adults getting proportionately "smarter" faster than adolescents.[32]

In addition, improvements in the average levels of nutrition and prenatal care naturally tend to raise the average scores of any pop-ulation. Since the 1930s, when tests for mental ability became widely used, average scores in the United States have increased substantially, with slight declines only for children born in the De-pression and the postwar baby boom. The latter drop is doubtless linked to another statistical fact: increasing family size produces lower average IQ test scores. Conversely, when people have had smaller families, IQ scores have normally risen, presumably because parents of fewer children have traditionally spent more time with each child.[33]

As standards of living have increased in countries around the world, so have IQ scores, and scores in the United States are now leveling off compared to those in other countries. Dr. James R. Flynn of the University of Otago in Dunedin, New Zealand, recently collated all available information on IQ trends over time. His study, the largest to date, took data from fourteen developed nations; overall, they showed "massive IQ gains."

Viewing these results in light of reality, however, Dr. Flynn became skeptical. Are people today that much smarter than the average man on the street in previous eras? "A generation with a massive IQ gain should radically outperform its predecessors. . . . [If these changes are real] the Netherlands alone has over 300,000 people who qualify as potential geniuses. The result should be a cultural renaissance too great to be overlooked," he wryly observed.

Yet, Flynn pointed out, a major survey in Europe "contained not a single reference to a dramatic increase in genius or mathematical and scientific discovery during the present generation; no one has remarked on the superiority of contemporary schoolchildren. . . . As for inventions, the number of patents granted has actually diminished."

Moreover, comparisons between IQ scores and results on other tests are puzzling, to say the least. As American IQs have continued a moderate rise, scores on the Scholastic Aptitude Test (SAT), have taken their major nosedive. Dr. Flynn comments, "Thanks to gains on [IQ] tests, it seemed that those entering American high schools were getting more and more intelligent, and yet they were leaving high school with worse and worse academic skills. Unless nonintellectual traits, such as motivation, study habits, and self-discipline were deteriorating at an incredible rate, how could more intelligent students be getting so much less education?"[34]

Flynn himself concludes that IQ tests really do not measure intelligence at all, but rather a specialized type of problem-solving that may not transfer very well outside of the test situation. Environmental factors only tangentially related to real intelligence may actually be responsible for the scoring gains, he suggests. Whatever the tests measure, however, the United States is leveling off faster on both verbal and nonverbal scales than other nations. "Evidence is pouring in from all over the technologically developed world that the U.S. gains are below average, and the new evidence sets aside any doubts about measurement error," he states.[35]

Let us return for a moment to Dr. Flynn's offhand speculation about the deterioration of "nonintellectual traits," which may deserve more emphasis than he gave it. In later chapters we will explore their underestimated importance as well as their endangered state. It should also become apparent that the parts of the brain storing information and producing high IQ test scores are essentially separate systems from those enabling people to organize, plan, follow through, express themselves accurately, and use the facts they have absorbed. These latter areas, probably an even more important source of "intelligence," are the ones the tests don't tap—and the ones most in jeopardy for children growing up in today's culture.

As we shall see in the next chapter, the power of children's brains can indeed be increased by good nutrition, adult companionship, and the stimulation of active play, toys, books, and games. Television provides many bits of knowledge that enable youngsters to look good on IQ tests, especially during early years. Computer use may also spuriously make young children look "smarter," although some ways of using computers may actually be detrimental to overall reasoning ability. These foundations are only the beginning, however. If no one shows youngsters how to use their brains for thinking, the apparent advantages will soon be lost.

CHANGING LIFESTYLES AND ACADEMICS

While society blames educators for academic declines, educators on every level complain that society is sending them children who are ill-prepared to learn. Almost everyone accepts the fact that "disadvantaged" youngsters need special educational attention; few realize that changes in contemporary lifestyles are affecting even "advantaged" children.

Voices From the Trenches

Dr. Shirley O'Rourke, a thoughtful analyst of the current scene and an energetic public school kindergarten teacher in a "typical" small Midwestern town, has children in her class from all socioeconomic groups. I asked her if she had observed any significant recent trends in the learning abilities of her students.

"You bet," she responded instantly. "They're neat kids. At this age they can make fantastic progress, but we have to work harder at it these days. And it's not always my children from the higher socioeconomic sections of town that do the best," she added quickly. "This is my sixteenth year, and I have found, over about the past seven or eight or so, the children from every neighborhood come with fewer social skills, less language ability, less ability to listen, less motor ability. I have my theories, of course—the TV, parents being so busy.

"Their social skills, the ability to interact appropriately, they're very rough, too. When I started teaching, children's first reactions would be through conversation; now, before they even find out if anyone accidentally bumped them, it's bam, slug it out—girls and boys both.

"Their listening is really worse. I always say 'excuse me' when I want them to listen to me; now I find myself having to explain what 'excuse me' means, that it's my turn to talk and their turn to listen. Kids used to know that conversation means taking turns; I don't think they know that now. Everyone wants to talk at the same time.

"Years ago, the children had experiences, their parents took them places, they talked to them instead of at them, they read to them. In sports, the parents would be outside, having fun casually. But today, the experiences are changed, what some adults seem to be calling 'experiences' is to go buy a workbook.

"I can't blame it on the fact that parents are working, because I've seen parents who are both working and doing an excellent job with their children in terms of experiences; I don't know if it is because others are too busy and don't realize how important experiences are. Without experiences, there are no concepts; without concepts, there's no attention span because they don't know what people are talking about."

Dr. O'Rourke remains hopeful, however, about possibilities for filling many of the gaps.

"I have some children from the saddest backgrounds and I will not believe anyone who tells me that a child needs to have all this special help when all they really need is to be actively involved, allowed to talk, allowed to relate to each other, and to use literature to develop that missing language."[36]

In a later chapter we will take a look at some teaching approaches that confirm Dr. O'Rourke's optimism. Clearly, new ideas and energy are needed at every level. In one well-known independent school, another master teacher, veteran of fifteen years in the same third-grade classroom, commented:

"Their attention span has gone way down. It's very short and they tune out all the time. Sometimes they tune out right at the beginning of a lesson or a discussion. One surprising thing—many of them tune out their peers as well as me! I associate it with TV, but that can't be entirely it because some who are watching the more worthwhile programs are very sophisticated in their knowledge.

"I really hate to generalize because some of them are so good, but *many* kids have trouble integrating what they learn. It seems that their personal experiences are so skimpy that they have trouble separating from the bang-bang stuff they see on TV. But you know, there are exceptions. I had one kid last year whose IQ was much lower than the rest of my class, but he really did well. His parents were so good—they read with him a lot, good worthwhile stuff, and they talked and discussed with him. We did one unit on Eskimos, and that father went with him to the library and they picked out two books and came home and they read them to him, and then they discussed them. Now this kid was so literal that if you said something about a 'bird's-eye view' he would go around looking for the bird, but when we talked about Eskimos in class, he really contributed some great insights.

"Then there are many others with much higher IQs whose performance is so poor—of course you never know how much of that might be a learning disability, but sometimes I think the environments they come out of can make those problems worse through a virtual neglect of enrichment. You might say they're making the worst of what they have rather than the best."[37]

Dr. Arthur Costa, president of the Association for Supervision and Curriculum Development, told me in an interview that he, too, believes there have been widespread changes in students that necessitate some serious educational rethinking.

"Not all kids, of course, but one thing so many are worse at is that they think episodically, they don't draw on past knowledge. Another is the lack of perseverance—they give up ('I don't want to do this, I don't want to do thinking; thinking is hard work'); another is their impulsivity: they take the first thing that comes to mind, they make immediate judgments, snap, snap. They seem unable to listen to ideas and carry them forth and interact with each other; they're so busy with their own point of view that they can't get into anyone else's thinking. They've also got a sort of lack of awesomeness, curiosity ('Who cares? It's boring, this is dumb!'). I don't want to say all kids; what I am saying is that many kids come to school and they lack motivation, restraint of impulsivity, they're disorganized, they're out of tune with phenomena. Yet these thought processes will be so essential in the future.[38]

Ohio Teacher of the Year Rosemary Gulick, interviewed in her first-grade classroom in a middle-class suburb, thinks poor learning habits become increasingly resistant to change. "Children today are definitely harder to teach. They expect learning to be 'fun,' and they can't wait for anything. Everything is instant. My biggest concern is that they can't think through problems. By the time I get them at age six it's almost too late!"

A visit to Ms. Gulick's classroom soon demonstrated that she hasn't used this as an excuse to give up. "I have to train them to talk, listen, pay attention—even show them how to work their way through problems; it takes time, but it's worth it!"[39]

Who's Minding the Children's Brains?

In the following chapters we will take a closer look at many interlocking factors of the scenario these educators are describing. New developments in the lives of today's children have the potential to put their brains at risk. The most obvious is increased physical danger from toxic environments, but intellectual hazards are also inherent in some of our society's favorite leisure-time activities, inappropriate educational methods applied to shape up lagging skills, and changing attitudes of adults toward the needs of children. All may be jeopardizing young minds in more subtle but equally significant ways.

Everyone wants our children to be smarter, but is anyone willing to take the responsibility? By 1995 more than three-quarters of all school-age children and two-thirds of preschoolers will have mothers in the labor force. Yet the quality of surrogate care is too often inadequate. It is estimated that 15% of primary-age and 45% of upper-elementary-age children come home to a house without a parent or other adult. As women return to work, community agencies that have traditionally depended on volunteer support are no longer available to extend social networks, sports programs, scouting, and other activities to children who lack enrichment at home. For preschoolers, fewer women are available to take care of other people's children, and makeshift caregiving abounds. Not many fathers have working conditions flexible enough to fill these gaps, and good day care is expensive and hard to come by.

"Because society does not yet wholeheartedly support working mothers, we have done little as a nation to provide optimal substitute care for small children. It is frightening to leave a small child in less than optimal care, and yet 50% of parents do not have adequate daycare available to them," emphasizes Dr. T. Barry Brazelton.[40]

Dr. Susan Luddington-Hoe, an authority on infant development in

California, is particularly concerned about the effects of inadequate environments on early brain development. She says that erosion of the quality of interpersonal interactions for youngsters may have long-range effects.

"It's really ironic, just as we're becoming so enlightened as to the importance of the brain's interactions during the first year of its development, we're having fewer interactions! Mothers are looking for other resources to baby-sit their babies, and as mothers pull away from babies, babies are not getting the challenge they need. You visit some infant care centers, and it is so sad; I went to visit one two doors down from me and they have eight to twenty babies there, all under the age of one. I walked in and there was absolutely nothing—I mean it, no pictures, no toys, nothing. The babies were just sitting there on blankets on this carpeted floor—this is a licensed, recommended infancy center in California. There were three care-givers: two were Spanish-speaking and one was Iranian; none of them spoke English, but all the babies were English-speaking. Children in settings like this are not getting the optimal brain growth, they're not getting the activity that establishes the cognitive pathways or keeps them moving."[41]

Professionals' concerns do not end with the early years. Continuing changes in language development, personal habits, and problem-solving abilities can be a function of alteration in adult-child interactions even into adolescence.

Dr. Dee Coulter, a Colorado teacher and lecturer on brain development and learning, is concerned about a seeming epidemic of attention and learning problems in older children. She comments, "TV is an easy scapegoat for everything bad that's happening. But I don't know if it's the TV per se, or if it's an indicator that the family has a fairly sparse repertoire of options—and I'm not just talking about kids in the ghetto. Maybe TV is the only way lots of kids can settle themselves down because no one is there to show them how to work with paint supplies, modeling clay, musical instruments; they have no other nurturance, no one to read them stories, no nature to walk out in, no pets to take care of. We are looking at the absence of all these things in so many children's lives. TV becomes a side effect."[42]

LOOKING AHEAD

The purpose of this book is not to criticize either parents or teachers. Both groups feel helpless in the face of contemporary pressures, and most do their best. They are fighting an uphill battle, however. Many parents realize only too well that old formulas for family structure and child rearing don't always apply. And while most educators—many of whom are parents themselves—would like to help, too many do not understand what is needed. Only when both groups become aware of what is really happening to children today can we all stop blaming each other and start working on solutions.

It makes no sense to blame the kids, although this is an expedient too often seized upon by frustrated adults. Of course, adults of every era lament the fecklessness of the upcoming generation. Cultural change is inevitable, and as the young rise to meet new sets of challenges, generational rifts in priorities naturally occur. In the long run, of course, things usually work themselves out (although a cynic might remark that many oft-quoted comments about the unworthiness of youth have been followed by the decline of the civilization in question). It is important to note, however, that within the vehicle of gradual change, parents and teachers have customarily remained at the wheel even while they complained about the noise in the backseat. From this position of control they continued to guide the mental habits of the young in the directions they deemed appropriate.

Currently, technological and social change have seized the accelerator, propelling us into an uncertain world—of video, computers, the "global village." In this vigorously bubbling "information age," many adults feel they have little control and perhaps even less knowledge than their children. Unlike their own parents, they may be reluctant to assert themselves against their offspring. The young, who appear to command the new machines—as well as the mores of the bedroom and the shopping mall—are sometimes viewed as having more wisdom than they really do. Parents, themselves overwhelmed, abdicate to the peer and popular culture much of the shaping of their children's mental habits.

We have failed to recognize, however, that if a society expects its young to master academic skills and intellectual content, adults must help prepare children's minds accordingly. The purpose of this book is to call attention to the brain's needs, the neural imperatives of childhood and adolescence. Many are currently being violated. What we do with, for, and to our children's growing minds will shape not only their brains but also the intellectual "standards" that represent our cultural future.

The primary thesis of this book is that we are rearing a generation of "different brains" and that many students' faltering academic skills—at every socioeconomic level—reflect subtle but significant changes in their physical foundations for learning. These fundamental shifts put children in direct conflict with traditional academic standards and the methods by which they are usually conveyed. Particularly at risk are abilities for language-related learning (e.g., reading, writing, analytic reasoning, oral expression), sustained attention, and problem solving. The following chapters will attempt to demonstrate how and why these changes are occurring, what should be done about them, and finally, what they may mean in terms of the future. How, specifically, can parents and teachers help children acquire the skills that will be needed in a new technological age?

Neural Plasticity: Nature's Double-Edged Sword

The large auditorium is hushed as the lights dim and a statistical chart appears on the screen. I reflect momentarily that I have never heard a large group of educators this quiet.

"Now, I'll show you the effects of different environments on our animals' brains." Dr. Marian Diamond wields her laser pointer triumphantly. "We've been working at this for more than thirty years, so I hope you'll forgive me if I skip just a little." The audience chuckles appreciatively and subsides into rapt attention as Dr. Diamond continues. "Here's a summary of the data comparing brain size and weight of rats reared in the standard cages, those who lived in the 'impoverished' environments, and here"—she pauses dramatically— "are the results with the animals who lived in the enrichment cages. Notice how, with increasing amounts of environmental enrichment, we see brains that are larger and heavier, with increased dendritic branching. That means those nerve cells can communicate better with each other. With the enriched environments we also get more support cells because the nerve cells are getting bigger. Not only that, but the junction between the cells—the synapse—also increases its dimensions. These are highly significant effects of differential experience. It certainly shows how dynamic the nervous system is and how responsive it is to its internal and external surroundings."

This international audience has gathered to hear many speakers describe new concepts for education, but Dr. Diamond is clearly the star attraction. A professor of neuroanatomy at the University of California, Berkeley, she has pioneered studies that have opened scientists' eyes—and minds—about the power of environmental factors in physically altering the dimensions of growing brains. In experiments described in her book *Enriching Heredity* [1] and elaborated on in the next chapter, rats in an "enriched" environment, actively interested and challenged by frequent new learning experiences, develop larger and heavier brains and also show increased ability to run mazes, the best available test of a rat's intelligence. Moreover, in a series of recent experiments, she has demonstrated for the first time that the effects of personal involvement in new learning appear to be so powerful that rats of any age can develop new brain connections if they intensely pursue new challenges. "Yes," she concludes, with a flourish, "if we work hard enough at it we can even change the very old brain."

She is immediately besieged with questions. Aren't there some basic learning abilities the environment can't change? What about heredity? "Heredity plays a highly important role in the form of these different [behavioral] repertoires," she acknowledges, "but we now have clear evidence that the environment can play a role in shaping brain structure and, in turn, learning behavior. It is the area of the brain that is stimulated that grows."[2]

The auditorium resonates with an undercurrent of response. An elementary school principal seated next to me whispers, "If this applies to human brains, too, think of the implications for teachers—and for parents!"

I am eager to talk with Dr. Diamond, and an hour later, when she has finally been released by a swarm of questioners, I have my chance. This world-renowned scientist turns out to be an approachable and thoughtful person—and it soon becomes evident that she takes her own theories to heart. Our conversation takes place as we stride vigorously through a nearby woods, impelled by the enthusiasm with which she approaches new ideas as well as new physical challenges. She has just returned from her first kayaking trip and is about to embark on a six-week teaching assignment in Africa.

Although Dr. Diamond is obviously convinced that stimulation is good for human as well as for rat brains, I am curious about how confidently we can apply her animal research to children. I explain my questions about the effects of contemporary culture on children's brains. Do neuroanatomists believe that the brains of children, like those of the rats, can be changed by their environments?

"To those of us in the field, there is absolutely no doubt that culture changes brains, and there's no doubt in my mind that children's brains are changing," she replies. "Whatever they're learning, as those nerve cells are getting input, they are sending out dendritic branches. As long as stimuli come in to a certain area, you get more branching; if you lose the stimuli, they stop branching. It is the pattern of the branching that differentiates among us. The cortex is changing all the time—I call it 'the dance of the neurons.' This is true in the brains of cats, dogs, rats, monkeys, or man."[3]

Many similar experiments have convinced other scientists of the changeability—they call it *plasticity*—of brains. Although it is obviously impossible to conduct similar studies on humans, researchers agree both on the validity of principles derived from animal experiments and on the fact that human brains are probably the most plastic of all. Another expert in the field, Dr. Victor H. Denenberg, recently commented, "One would expect even more powerful and more subtle effects with the human, whose brain is vastly more complicated than that of the rat, and who lives in a much more complex social and environmental milieu."[4]

With the reality of brain plasticity well-accepted in scientific circles, it was still a new idea for many of the educators attending Dr. Diamond's presentation.

"I guess it seems obvious, but I somehow never really believed that what I did in the classroom would physically influence the size or shape of my students' brains!" commented one teacher. "It does put being a teacher—or a parent, for that matter—in a whole new light."

Indeed it does. In order to interpret any research responsibly, however, it is necessary to understand it. Although scientists themselves do not claim to have any final answers, this chapter will summarize what is currently known about environments as sculptors of growing minds both before and after birth. Let us start by entangling ourselves briefly in a very old, but fundamental, controversy.

THE ADAPTABLE BRAIN

"Just as the twig is bent, the tree's inclined." Common sense suggests that growing organisms are highly adaptable to external influences, but what seemed so apparent to Alexander Pope has caused psychologists to argue bitterly for years. How much is mental ability shaped by environments and how much is in the hands of heredity? After all, the tree still develops bark, leaves, and a functioning root system no matter how the twig gets bent. Psychologists have tried to resolve this issue with studies comparing identical and fraternal twins. Currently, heredity and environment are each assigned roughly 50 (or 40, or 60)% of the credit. As parents of wiggly little children can understand, however, their physical behavior resists numerical formulas— and so does their mental behavior: learning. So-called "nature-nuture" interactions are complex. For example, in a case to be considered in a later chapter, a learning disability that runs in families may result from changes in the child's brain before birth. Cells in the fetal brain get rearranged by chemicals produced because of an inherited response of the mother's own autoimmune system (don't worry, scientists are confused, too)—which the child may also inherit. Would you say this disability is caused by heredity or by the prenatal environment?

In another controversial example, children from lower socioeconomic groups tend to score below average on standard IQ tests. Is this because poor environments depress their intelligence, or because they never learned good test-taking skills, or because, as some believe, families with nonstandard intellectual endowment might get trapped in lower socioeconomic groups? In another chapter, when we consider the results of efforts to alter such children's intelligence, we will see how difficult it is to sort out these factors.

Brain research is now giving these old issues an interesting new dimension by changing the focus from heredity *versus* environment to heredity *plus* environment. Until recently, so little has been known about the "brain" that most theorists sidestepped it when trying to explain intelligence (and they produced some mindless theories as a result). Now we acknowledge that the basic genetic architecture for our brains lies at the heart of all learning and even much of our emotional behavior. When these inherited patterns interact with the child's environment, plasticity guarantees an unlimited number of interesting variations. The final pattern is determined by the way each individual uses that unique brain.

Behavior Changes Brains and Brains Change Behavior

"Do you really mean that the way children use their brains causes *physical* changes in them?" Since I began the research for this book, I have heard this question from almost everyone to whom I have talked—everyone, that is, except the neuroscientists. Their response is quite different, more along the lines of, "So, what else is new?" These scientists already understand that experience—what children do every day, the ways in which they think and respond to the world, what they learn, and the stimuli to which they decide to pay attention—shapes their brains. Not only does it change the ways in which the brain is used (*functional change*), but it also causes physical alterations (*structural change*) in neural wiring systems.

"Would I be safe in saying that if you change what a child does with his or her brain, you're physically going to change that brain?" I asked Dr. Kenneth A. Klivington of the Salk Institute in San Diego, California.

"That's absolutely correct," he replied. "*Structure and function are inseparable*. We know that environments shape brains; all sorts of experiments have demonstrated that it happens. There are some studies currently being done that show profound differences in the structure of the brain depending on what is taken in by the senses."

We will return later to these and other studies, but before we get too far into the details, we should undertake a look at the way the brain develops before and after birth, focusing on this whole concept of its changeability. A good starting point is the brain's most basic structure—the cells and their connections—for therein lies the secret of *neural plasticity*.

Networking Neurons

All brains consist of two types of cells: nerve cells, called *neurons*, and *glial cells*. The neurons, numbering in the billions, arrive in the world ready and waiting to connect themselves together in flexible networks to fire messages within and between parts of the brain. No new cerebral cortical neurons will be added after birth, but since each of these nerve cells is capable of communicating with thousands of other neurons, the potential for neural networking is virtually incomprehensible. Surrounding glial cells provide the catering service for the nervous system, supporting and nourishing the neurons as they go about their delicate task of creating, firing, and maintaining the connections for thinking.

If you hold your hand out in front of you with fingers extended, you can get a rough idea of the shape of the average neuron. Your palm represents the *cell body*, with its central nucleus, and your outreaching fingers are *dendrites*. These microscopic projections extend in treelike formations to act as intake systems, picking up messages from other neurons and relaying them to the cell body. After reaching your palm, a message would travel down your arm, which represents the *axon*, or output system. When it reaches the end of the axon, it must jump across a small gap called a *synapse* before being picked up by dendrites from a neighboring neuron. This primordial intellectual leap is facilitated by chemicals called neurotransmitters or neuromodulators. It is repeated untold billions of times as this vast array of potential goes about the business of daily mental activity. The strength and efficiency of synaptic connections determine the speed and power with which your brain functions. The most important news about synapses is that they are formed, strengthened, and maintained by interaction with experience.

New Experiences: New Connections

Dr. Richard M. Lerner, professor of child and adolescent development at Pennsylvania State University, and author of *On the Nature of Human Plasticity*[5] points out that you can't have a developing, changing, responsive organism without its brain being able to be altered structurally by environmental encounters. Structural change, in this case, does not mean growing new neurons, but rather creating new structures, like road systems, between the ones that are already there. As the structures of dendrites and synapses change in response to experience, the new pathways formed allow different functions to follow them so the child becomes able to master new skills. The brain's flexibility is also increased, since new pathways provide alternate routes to the same destination. During our discussion, Dr. Lerner used the analogy of a road system in a developing town. At first, there may be only one road through town; as alternate routes form, a driver has more choices of how to get to a destination. The structural changes are comparable to building a new road, and the functional ones to deciding which of several roads to take to reach a goal. The systems are mutually interactive, since the roads are constructed as a response to demands for certain types of functions.

I asked Dr. Lerner about the possibility that children's brains today might be constructing slightly different road systems from those, say, twenty years ago. If they are being attracted to different types of stimuli, both structure and function could be altered, he acknowledged. Yes, taking a large group of children and exposing them to certain experiences might modify them in a particular direction. Of course, any conclusions of this sort would require a good deal of evidence, this conservative scientist hastened to add.[6]

Scientists hesitate to make definitive statements on this point because they have not had the technology available to get the evidence for large groups of "normal" children. Even with new computerized techniques of brain imaging, it is still difficult to pin down subtle changes at the level of the neuron. Moreover, most research dollars have gone to the pressing issue of serious disability, so most available evidence comes from youngsters whose brains have been injured through illness or accident. They provide dramatic evidence for plasticity. Frequently children master skills even when the neurons thought to be important are missing or damaged. For example, very young children with severe injury in the brain's language areas can develop remarkably good abilities to talk, understand language, read, and write. These brains have been able to develop new structural connections to bypass injured areas and also to reorganize functionally by using alternate, undamaged areas. With a cast of understudies, the final performance is usually somewhat impaired, but young brains are astonishingly flexible.

What about older ones? While new tricks are indeed harder for old synapses, studies of stroke victims prove that with sufficient effort the human brain may be remolded to some extent at any age. The latest research confirms this principle for healthy brains as well. In fact, as I write this book and you read it, our brains are not even the same from moment to moment. The very acts of writing and reading are doubtless changing, very subtly, the way some cells connect together. I find this idea thought-provoking, and I can even become somewhat confounded thinking that while I am thinking this thought-provoking thought, my brain is probably being changed by it!

It is much more difficult, however, to reorganize a brain than it is to organize it in the first place. "Organization inhibits reorganization," say the scientists.[7] Carving out neuronal tracks for certain types of learning is best accomplished when the synapses for that particular skill are most malleable, before they "firm up" around certain types of responses.

Hard Wiring and Open Circuits

Animal brains have an easy time of it. They carry out many of the basic routines of keeping alive, fed, and safe, reproducing and caring for the young, with preprogrammed neural systems that do the work without asking questions. While these more primitive brains are clearly capable of learning, more of their cells are committed to *hardwired* networks genetically programmed to function with a minimum of flexibility.

Human brains depend on these hard-wired systems, too, but we also have larger areas of *uncommitted* tissue that can mold itself around the demands of a particular environment. A human brain is thus well adapted for life in a complex society. Our species has a better chance for survival with mental equipment flexibly engineered for the challenges of an ever-changing world. Thus, human brains and the culture they generate are intertwined. As the culture acts to modify our brains, they, in turn, act to modify the culture.[8]

Researchers have debated heatedly about which learning abilities are hard-wired and which are more open to experience. One of the foremost authorities on early brain development, Dr. William T. Greenough[9, 10] of the University of Illinois, has recently found a new way of looking at this problem. According to his explanation, some systems, which he calls *experience expectant*, are specifically designed to be easily activated by the type of environmental information that a member of a species may ordinarily be expected to encounter. Most human infants, for example, have sufficient visual, auditory, and tactile experiences to activate circuits for seeing, hearing, and touching. These brain cells require proper experience at the proper time, but even a brief period of normal input causes connections to be formed.

Some aspects of more complex skills like language also seem to be built into this "experience expectant" system; the brain "expects" to be stimulated by a set of sounds and some basic grammatical rules (e.g., little children soon pick up the idea that verbs come before objects—"want cookie"), so these abilities are learned readily by children who have even minimal language experiences in early years. Experience-expectant neurons can be foiled, however. Later in this chapter we will consider what happens to children deprived of even basic sensory experiences.

The open circuitry that accounts for many human learning abilities, however, develops from connections that Greenough calls *experience dependent*. These systems are unique to each individual's experience and account for the fact that we all have quite different brains! For example, learning about one's physical environment, mastering a particular vocabulary, or trying to pass algebra means the brain must receive enough usable stimulation to carve out its own unique systems of connections between cells.

Since so many children these days seem to lack higher-level language development, I decided Greenough's research might offer a clue. I asked him whether all language should develop almost automatically from a minimum of environmental exposure (experience expectant), or whether higher-level language abilities might depend more on special amounts and types of input into the system (experience dependent).

"My opinion is that language development is heavily experience dependent," he replied, "and therefore would have a great deal to do with the way a child is reared. Hypothetically, children who grew up receiving a great deal of their input from television, for example, might be different from children who grew up getting input from an individual speaker."

"If they get different types of language input, could the language areas of children's brains be subtly different from those of twenty years ago?" I asked.

"I think you can make a case for it, although our work can only indirectly say anything about that. What we know is that the brain very selectively can be shown to respond to its particular experiences; if an animal, for example, learns a motor task, you see very selective changes in the brain regions that govern that task; so that there is no question that these changes are highly specific to the events that produce them. It's certainly quite conceivable that a major difference in the way in which kids grew up would lead to a major difference in brain organization for information processing. There's remarkably little evidence available, however," he added.

"Is it possible that the pace of our contemporary life, when many children are constantly being stimulated from outside so that they have little time to sit, think, reflect, and talk to themselves inside their own heads—could that make a physical difference in their brains?" I ventured.

"I think it's a reasonable hypothesis," Dr. Greenough responded thoughtfully.

In a later chapter we will examine research that sheds considerable light on some of the subtle language deficiencies shown by many of the current generation. For now, let us resume our survey of how the brain learns to think—and what happens if it doesn't. While I personally believe that most of the worrisome changes now occurring in children's brains are caused by intellectual environments, some drugs and chemicals to which children are now exposed before birth may also be contributing to the increased incidence of learning difficulties.

THE DOUBLE-EDGED SWORD

The very flexibility of systems that rely on experience for their shaping, or even for their survival, makes plasticity a double-edged sword. On one side is the optimistic news that brains are designed to make the most out of the situations in which they find themselves. At any age we take an active role in shaping our own brains according to what we choose to notice and respond to. On the other hand, however, lie several serious issues. What happens if significant numbers of cells are damaged during the process of development so they can't respond efficiently? What if the "right" stimulation is not available? Is it possible to focus too heavily on one set of stimuli and neglect others? In order to address these complex questions, we must first get an overview of the prenatal process that sets the neurons into place. Then we will move on to consider sources of flaws in the system.

Building the Fetal Brain: Neurons Compete to Survive

Most people are unaware that nature overendows us with brain cells, yet this apparent wastefulness is our assurance of adaptable mental equipment. In the nine months before birth, the fetal brain grows rapidly from a small cluster of cells into an organ that contains too many neurons. By the fourth week of gestation it has started to differentiate into separate areas. Neurons and glial cells are produced at a rapid rate and then, to the continuing amazement of neuroanatomists, manage somehow to "migrate" to the areas for which they were designed.

The first cells out form areas for more basic functions such as physical drives, reflex movements, and balance. Somewhat later come relay stations for sensory stimuli and some technical equipment to help with memory and emotion. These abilities are mainly "hardwired" into systems underlying the neocortex, whose convoluted surface covers the rest of the brain like an elaborate layer of gray frosting. Hardly a superficial addition, however, the cortex is the control panel for processing information at three levels:

1. receiving sensory stimuli
2. organizing them into meaningful patterns so that we can make sense out of the world
3. associating patterns to develop abstract types of learning and thinking

These later-developing "association areas," so critically important for planning, reasoning, and using language to express ideas, are the most *plastic of all;* their development depends on the way the child uses his or her brain at different stages of development.

Surprisingly enough, all these abilities emerge as a result of a violent competition by which the brain literally "prunes" out and disposes of its excess neurons. Because there is a limited number of available connection sites, the mortality rate for neurons is staggering. Even before birth up to 40–60% die off because they can't find a permanent home. During gestation, each cell migrating to the cortex tries to find a prearranged spot in one of six layers. They don't all arrive, however. The first cells out arrange themselves in the first, or inner, layer, and the later arrivals quite literally must climb between and beyond them, stacking themselves up until eventually all six layers have formed. The final layers hold the potential for the highest-order, latest-developing mental abilities, but these cells have the hardest job finding their proper station in life.

"So, you can see right away that we can all be considered brain damaged in one respect," wryly observes Dr. Jane Holmes Bernstein.[11] But some of us get labeled, and some don't. As we talk, I notice that one wall of her office in Boston Children's Hospital is covered with drawings made by some of the children that she sees every day. As a clinical neuropsychologist working with children called learning disabled, she attempts to understand behavior—primarily learning behavior—in terms of brain structure and function. She is convinced that brain shapes behavior, but also that experience in the world shapes the brain as it develops, through a process that she terms "competition for connections." This mechanism is initiated before birth by nature's clever overproduction of neurons.

"Cell death appears to be a natural consequence of the competition for connections: those cells that don't connect are lost. Ideally, this process will result in a very efficient structure, but it can go wrong, too. Sometimes damage before birth to an early-maturing part may lead to abnormal patterns of connections; if early-arriving cells pre-empt the connections that should belong to later arrivals, the later ones have nowhere to go and sort of fall off the cliff. It's important to realize that early development after birth may seem normal—after all, some basic connections have been made; later on, however, it's likely to be a different story. Higher-order thinking skills that should develop with maturation have no foundation!"[12]

What happens, then, to the potential learning ability of this brain? Why would nature set up such a risky system for developing mental connections?

"It seems to me that this sort of competitive connectivity model is the basis for a great deal of our uniqueness as individuals. The playing out of these patterns is presumably what allows brains to be generally competent at the same skills but different in the individual case," reflects Dr. Bernstein.

Not everyone agrees with Dr. Bernstein's terminology. "I hate the term 'brain damaged'!" Marian Diamond argues. "We each have different kinds of brains; the connections are different, giving us different kinds of abilities. Give the young people the benefit of the doubt . . . we have different brains to develop and this is a positive connotation, not a negative one!"[13]

Whatever words may be most effective in getting people to realize that not all children learn in the same way, it is clear that environments play an important role in these differences. Later, we will return to some of Dr. Bernstein's opinions about how neural patterns are being "played out" for today's children. Now, however, we should finish our look at prenatal life by considering some of the specific factors that may alter these patterns of connectivity—for better or worse. They fall generally into two categories: those that come in from outside, and those that are produced in the environment of the womb itself.

The Vulnerable Fetal Brain: "Birth Defects of the Mind"

The brain is always most plastic at times when it is growing fastest. The fetal brain is especially vulnerable, not only because of its increased metabolic rate, but also because of an underdeveloped ability to detoxify harmful substances. Not so many years ago, obstetricians earnestly assured their patients that the placenta was an effective screen for toxic materials, but they were wrong, as the thalidomide tragedies eventually demonstrated. We are now acutely aware that many toxins are able to cross the placenta. Because of its rapidly proliferating concentration of cells, the fetal brain is a natural target, and the systems growing fastest at the time of exposure are on the front line.[14]

Even toxic material that doesn't cross the placenta, such as residue from cigarette smoking, may accumulate in the placenta and disrupt the baby's nutritional intake. Many prospective fathers are unaware that they, too, can harm their unborn children. If they have been exposed to toxic substances, their contaminated seminal fluid may expose the fetus during intercourse or cause birth defects if toxins have damaged the genetic structure of the sperm.[15]

Because of the finely timed schedule of cell proliferation and migration, different effects may come from exposure at different times.

Some are more obvious than others. Damage during the first few days of pregnancy usually results in spontaneous abortion, of which the mother is probably unaware. From one to eight weeks of gestation, when cells start to move toward their target destinations, fetal death or major abnormalities usually result. After eight weeks, when neurons begin to settle into place, toxic exposure may result in subtle rearrangements of their placement or with their potential ability to communicate. These seemingly minor structural and functional abnormalities have aroused growing concern from a group of scientists in the new field of *behavioral teratology:* the study of the effects of toxic substances on the developing brain. These researchers are convinced of the potential of *teratogens*, or toxins, to cause subtle but pervasive difficulty with learning and behavior—the type of problems that, even years later, earn some children the label of "learning disabled."[16]

"Yes, it's a serious problem. There are clear links between substances commonly found in the environment and later development of learning and behavior difficulties," says Dr. Brenda Eskenazi of the departments of Maternal and Child Health and Epidemiology at the University of California at Berkeley. "You might call these 'birth defects of the mind.' The effects on the brain are so subtle they don't show up on routine screening measures, and it may be years before the problem gets identified."[17]

Most such problems are of three major types: motor clumsiness and/or perceptual difficulties; problems with attention; or disabilities in specific types of school learning such as reading or math. As Dr. Bernstein pointed out, while it is sometimes hard to understand how prenatal exposure can show up only years later in school, early damage to higher-order systems may not become apparent until those particular systems are called on, as, for example, in reading comprehension or math reasoning. Since exposure to toxins after birth may also invite subtle forms of damage, causality is hard to pin down.

Hazardous Substances for the Fetal Brain

What are the hazardous substances? Although many potential candidates have been identified, conclusive results from well-controlled testing are few and far between. Here is a summary of the current field:

Lead: Clearly implicated in mental retardation, lead exposure both before and after birth has been shown to lower IQ even in potentially gifted children as well as causing problems with attention and academic learning. Yet the source of the problem may go unrecognized. Dr. Herbert L. Needleman of the University of Pittsburgh School of Medicine is convinced that many children who have real learning and behavior difficulties in the classroom look "fine" when examined in a doctor's office. He estimates that as many as 650,000 American children may be affected. Authorities all over the world are beginning to share this concern.[18]

Other metals: Methyl mercury, arsenic, aluminum, and cadmium have all been implicated, particularly when combined with exposure to other toxins or with lead.

PCBs, PBBs, solvents, pesticides, and some chemical fertilizers: All contain ingredients that may affect the central nervous system. The presence of these substances in many work environments has resulted in new precautions and some regulations concerning exposure for people of childbearing age.

Recreational drugs: Alcohol may cause serious abnormalities in both mental and physical development or may exacerbate the effects of other toxins. The level of susceptibility appears to vary widely among individuals, and it is not known how to determine what amount, if any, is safe for any one person. Narcotics known to be toxic to the developing brain are heroin, methadone, and codeine. Most research on marijuana is out-of-date and poorly controlled; new studies suggest extreme caution by both potential mothers and fathers.[19] Likewise, many authorities warn that growing cocaine use by pregnant women will soon flood the schools with children who have attention, learning, and social problems. In all, drugs taken during pregnancy are producing a substantial subpopulation of children who begin life with significant neurological impairment. At this writing, it is estimated that at least one out of every nine babies born in the United States is affected.[20] And these children are not even included in our already declining test scores!

Prescription drugs: Prospective parents are advised to discuss potential childbearing with a well-informed physician who can advise them on current information regarding any medication they may be taking.

Over-the-counter drugs: Experts advise completely avoiding these during pregnancy.

When I began to investigate this topic for an article I was asked to write recently,[21] I found myself horrified by what I read and heard from experts in the field. Everywhere I looked, I could see (or breathe, or ingest) substances that were under investigation. How did my husband and I ever manage, I wondered, to have three healthy, well-functioning children? I procrastinated about writing the article, partially because I was worried about frightening expectant parents, yet I became increasingly convinced that this information should be promulgated. Finally, I placed another call to Dr. Eskenazi, who had mentioned the fact that she was expecting her first child. I asked her how she reconciled her own pregnancy with her extensive knowledge about hazards to her child's developing brain.

"You have to use common sense," she replied. "Even knowing everything I do, I don't get hysterical. I just maintain sensible precautions. I read labels and avoid situations where I might be exposed to toxins. I would certainly advise women to clean up their environments and their lifestyles before becoming pregnant, and then just be careful and relax as much as possible."[22]

This is good advice, but to what extent does our society help women "use common sense" or even inform them clearly about the issues involved? Where is the research that will clarify the dimensions of this worldwide problem? At every teacher workshop I attend these days, I am asked, "Do you think that drugs or medications taken by parents may be related to the rash of attention problems we are now seeing in schools?" Although I am convinced there are a number of other forces playing into children's attention problems, I am obliged to respond, "Yes, according to the research, it is certainly a factor."

One group of teachers in California, alarmed by newspaper reports about neurotoxic effects of crop spraying, wanted to know what connection it might have to an increasing number of diagnosed learning disabilities in their district. They are not the only ones wishing for better answers to questions like these. In recent testimony before a Senate subcommittee, Audrey McMahon of the Association for Children with Learning Disabilities appealed for increased research on this global problem, the threat of which, she points out, does not end when the child is born. The brains of young children remain highly susceptible. Contaminants come from a multiplicity of sources, such as air pollution, automobile exhaust, foods that have been sprayed with pesticides, clothing worn by adults in a contaminated workplace, and even breast milk that has absorbed toxins stored in the mother's body fat. During the course of my interviews, a doctor in Germany told me that he and other physicians are advising women who live near the Rhine River, which has been heavily contaminated with pesticides and industrial residues, not to nurse their babies for more than a few weeks.[23]

The Stressed-Out Fetus

Toxins are not the only influences by which the fetal brain can be altered. A mother's illness and accident pose obvious risks. Recently we have also become aware of the importance of her nutritional and emotional status. It is encouraging to learn that these two variables are themselves doubled-edged swords that give parents some control over the general course of their baby's prenatal life. A sensible, bal-anced diet containing reasonable amounts of protein during preg-nancy is a powerful protective factor against other risks. On the other hand, fetal brains are affected by malnutrition, and poorly nourished women also tend to give birth to children of low birthweight, who are statistically more at risk for learning problems.[24]

In today's fast-paced society, the subject of maternal stress is an issue that warrants better research. Animal studies have shown that stress during pregnancy can upset chemical transmission systems in the brain of the fetus,[25] possibly because hormone secretions associ-ated with stress cross the placenta. One recent rat study from Israel demonstrated that "random" stress during pregnancy (i.e., the preg-nant animal was exposed to loud noise or flashing lights on an unpre-dictable schedule) not only caused increased fearfulness and exaggerated stress response in the offspring, but also produced chem-ical brain changes resulting in permanent alterations in the relative size and shape of the two halves of the offsprings' brains.[26] (Is this an animal analogue for "different learning styles"?)

Published reports by several authorities have suggested that sus-tained stress during the first months of pregnancy may be a factor in the development of hyperactivity in children, but the professional litera-ture does not offer any definitive guidelines. Expectant mothers are well advised to avoid prolonged, excessive stress if they possibly can—although available definitions of what constitutes stress, or what "ex-cessive" means for any individual woman, are frustratingly vague.[27]

The Flexible Mind: Overcoming Prenatal Damage

Before we move on to consider the way brains develop after birth, let me digress for a note of reassurance. The idea that brains can get changed around like this is a bit less frightening if we consider the point that everyone is "brain different" in some respect. Many chil-dren emerge apparently unscathed from difficult pre- and postnatal environments, while others end up "learning disabled."

There are doubtless several reasons for these different outcomes.

First, environments continue to modify the brain long after birth, so their effects can actively counteract prenatal problems. Moreover, some children just seem to be genetically more resilient than others. Good prenatal nutritional and emotional environments provide additional insurance. Finally, because of the young brain's great structural and functional plasticity, it can arrange itself around some types of learning in a wide variety of ways, depending not only on innate predispositions but also on the way the material is presented.

Most school learning calls on many sets of connections, not just a single location in the brain, so some types of prenatal "damage" may be circumvented by later learning experiences. For example, youngsters learning to read by either sounding out words ("b-a-t") or by guessing at them from their general shape ("STOP") are using different systems of neurons in each case. Later, when they move on to rapid reading and comprehension of more complex material, they will connect up with higher-level systems. Thus, skilled reading is said to be "subserved" by a number of different combinations of brain cells in different locations. Some are obviously more critical than others (the ones that put the sounds together with the letters, for example), but it is possible to circumnavigate areas of weakness. Even without big "holes" in our brains, most of us have had to learn to compensate for certain sets of connections that don't hook up quite as easily as others! If you contemplate the potential arrangement and rearrangement of several billions (or hundreds of billions) of nerve cells, you get a notion of the infinite number of ways in which a system can get arranged.

If some kinds of damage happen early enough, this flexibility, teamed with a drive to succeed and the help of a supportive environment, can generate seemingly miraculous results. One of the most remarkable stories I have recently heard was from Dr. Isabelle Rapin of the Albert Einstein College of Medicine in New York. One of her patients was a girl who had been born with, quite literally, a "hole" in her brain—a large defect in the right rear quadrant of her cortex. Looking at an early brain (CT) scan of this child, which showed several distortions in addition to the large "empty" area, I had trouble believing she could ever have approached normal functioning. Yet, although she had some enduring visual problems, slow motor development, and trouble doing math, her verbal IQ registered in the superior range by the time she was nine years old.[28] When Dr. Rapin told me about this case, the girl was a student doing well at a well-known Ivy League university.

Some very specific types of damage or deprivation may noticeably affect basic "hard-wired" abilities, such as sensory discriminations (e.g., seeing visual features like vertical or horizontal lines; hearing certain kinds of sounds) because they are "localized" to very specific cells in the brain. Areas controlling attention and some related "executive functions" that will become important in later life (and in later chapters of this book) may also be vulnerable to early damage or deprivation. Many higher-level skills, however, can be approached in several different ways and thus may develop through more variable routes.

In his important book, *Frames of Mind*, Dr. Howard Gardner has suggested that separate types of intelligence call on many different brain areas.[29] A person may be highly gifted and have a wonderful memory in linguistic (language) intelligence, for example, but be unexceptional at music or interpersonal relationships. We can't draw a neat circle around any of these clusters in the brain, yet the various abilities within each seem somehow to work together. Specific skills within each cluster are developed at different stages of brain growth during childhood and adolescence.

Because the organization of the brain is so heavily influenced by the way it is used after birth, the home and school environment can do a lot to help potentially learning-disabled children learn more successfully. For example, as I have described in my previous book, a child's exposure to good language, a positively structured environment, and methods of instruction appropriate for his or her style of learning may determine whether learning problems materialize.[30] Moreover, the potential of teaching techniques to reorganize young brains is a hot new topic in the education world. We will see in a later chapter how one researcher claims to be changing brain function of reading-disabled schoolchildren with different teaching methods.

While the exact effect of brain-endangering substances remains undetermined, most of the academically injurious changes observed in today's children are probably much more a function of mental environments after birth. Fortunately, parents and teachers can actively do something about these influences. But they need to proceed wisely.

Engineering the Fetal Brain

Some people are in a real hurry to get started teaching their children. An increasingly popular attempt to "stimulate" brains artificially while they are in the womb is worrying many professionals.

"A lot of crazy, bizarre things are happening in the United States," reports Dr. Susan Luddington-Hoe, professor of maternal and child health at UCLA and author of *How to Have a Smarter Baby*.[31] "There are now over fourteen programs for *prenatal* learning! Pregnant women are wearing belts with stereo headsets to try and stimulate their infant's brain. Some people are even holding a card with, say, an *a* on it to Mom's belly and shining a flashlight through it while they say 'a, a, a' so the kid will supposedly be born knowing the alphabet. Let me tell you, I don't condone any of this stuff."

During a normal pregnancy, the fetus receives a great deal of stimulation from the mother's and its own movement, from the sound of her voice and heartbeat, and even from the taste and smell of the amniotic fluid. Although scientists—and mothers—confirm that a fetus can respond to some external events, notably sounds, organized "learning" by fetal brains has a rather tenuous base in research.

Studies have demonstrated that infant animals acquire preferences for tastes and odors *in utero*.[32] One researcher claims that human infants, while still in the womb, learn to prefer their mothers' voices and can even be "taught" to favor certain familiar stories that the expectant mother has frequently read out loud.[33] Dr. Luddington-Hoe's research has suggested that a fetus can differentiate its parents' voices immediately after birth.

Reports such as these have provoked a rash of commercial materials with which parents may attempt to create designer brains in their infants. There is even a "Prenatal University" for those who can't wait to get started paying college tuition.

"For heaven's sake," exclaims Dr. Luddington-Hoe, "nature has created the perfect environment; why should we mess around with it?"

Most responsible researchers agree that we do not yet know enough to do anything that risks distorting the natural processes of mental growth. Trying to "engineer" children's learning at any age can have disastrous emotional and neurological consequences.

The evolutionary history of our species has given us a neural architecture preprogrammed with a driving need to arrange itself adaptively. If a fetal brain is cared for and protected in following its own developmental timetable, it will emerge at the end of nine months ready to take on the challenge of molding itself around the demands of an awaiting—and constantly changing—world. We will now begin to examine this process.

Malleable Minds: Environment Shapes Intelligence

At birth, the average newborn brain weighs a mere 330 grams, one-forth of adult weight. By the time the child is two years old, its weight will triple, and by age seven its 1,250 grams will represent 90% of adult weight. Meanwhile, however, it is losing neurons as the internal competition intensifies and cell groups consolidate into more efficient systems. How does this growth occur? To this question both animal and human research have provided some useful and provocative answers.

THE YOUNG PLASTIC BRAIN

As both animal and human brains grow, three things happen that account for their increased size and efficiency. First, *dendrites* sprout many new branches and grow heavier as they reach out to receive messages and develop synaptic connections. Second, supporting *glial cells* increase in number. Both of these developments appear to respond directly to the types of stimulation sent in by the environment.

In addition, the *axons*, or output parts of neurons, gradually develop a coating of a waxy substance called *myelin*, which insulates the wiring and facilitates rapid and clear transmission. At birth, only the most primitive systems, such as those needed for sucking, have been coated with myelin, or *myelinated.* Myelin continues to develop slowly all during childhood and adolescence in a gradual progression from lower- to higher-level systems. Its growth corresponds to the ability to use increasingly higher-level mental abilities. The process of myelination in human brains is not completed at least until most of us are in our twenties and may continue even longer. While animal studies have shown that total myelin may reflect levels of stimulation, scientists believe its order of development is mainly predetermined by a genetic program.

While the system, overall, is remarkably responsive to stimulation from the environment, the schedule of myelination appears to put some boundaries around "appropriate" forms of learning at any given age. Before we go on to consider the exciting implications of the fact that environments can make brains grow, we should stop for a moment to discuss some potential hazards in trying too hard to "make" intelligence or learning happen. Some of the skill deficits of today's schoolchildren, in fact, may have resulted from academic demands that were wrong—either in content or in mode of presentation—for their level of development.

Forced Learning and Functional Mix-Ups

The same mentality that attempts to engineer stimulation for baby brains also tries to push learning into schoolchildren much like stuffing sausages. For example, some parents now wonder if their schools are any good if they don't start formal reading instruction, complete with worksheets, in preschool. Likewise, many schools have reading lists or advanced math courses for older children that look impressive but, being out of the reach of most of the students, convince them that reading or math are difficult and boring activities. I call this the "cosmetic curriculum" because it sounds impressive, but the learning is often, unfortunately, only skin deep.

Before brain regions are myelinated, they do not operate efficiently. For this reason, trying to "make" children master academic skills for which they do not have the requisite maturation may result in mixed-up patterns of learning. As we have seen, the essence of functional plasticity is that any kind of learning—reading, math, spelling, handwriting, etc.—may be accomplished by any of several systems. Naturally, we want children to plug each piece of learning into the best system for that particular job. If the right one isn't yet available or working smoothly, however, forcing may create a functional organization in which less adaptive, "lower" systems are trained to do the work.

As an example, I think of the many children we see in second and third grade who grip their pencil in the most peculiar ways; some crumple their fingers around it in weird arrangements that make letter formation difficult and cause their hands to tire quickly; some use the base of their fingers instead of the tips to guide the pencil so that the process of handwriting resembles a fencing match more than a fine motor activity; some clutch it in their fists like a weapon. Any teacher will tell you that trying to correct "habits" like these is an uphill—and usually unsuccessful—battle. The reason would seem to be that a strong network of synaptic connections has already formed around these maladaptive patterns, making them automatic and difficult to change because they are now built into the system. How much better if we had taken the time to teach it correctly the first time around!

Neuromotor development moves only gradually from "gross motor," large, global movements, to the smaller muscles farther away from the core of the body (in this case, from the palm out to the ends of the fingers). It is certainly easy to speculate that these children were given pencils and encouraged to write—without sufficient help on proper pencil-holding technique—before the appropriate motor areas were "ready." Thus they practiced and made this learning automatic in the brain areas that were most available at the time—to their lasting discomfort.

Can such changes in motor patterns really cause brain changes? In several provocative studies, monkeys whose fingers had been amputated showed altered brain structure as they learned to use different manual patterns. More subtle but equally striking changes occurred simply from having monkeys tap repeatedly with one finger; the related brain areas developed heavier sets of connections.[1]

This sort of study is clearly impossible to conduct on humans, and though we have come a long way, we are far from fully understanding which cell combinations mediate most higher-level learning. The way a child learns to hold a pencil will doubtless assume less and less importance in the age of computer word processors (see Chapter 15), but the same principles of neural readiness may apply to higher-level skills, since they are the most experience-dependent of all. As an example, let's take the kind of reasoning needed for *understanding* (not just memorizing one's way through) higher-level math. Perhaps some readers of this book shared a common experience when they took algebra: many of us functioned adequately until we reached Chicago, where two planes insisted on passing each other every day in class. When it wasn't planes, it was trains or people digging wells or other situations that did not seem in any way related to graphs and equations of X, Y, and Z. Personally, I found that the more I struggled, the more confused I became, until soon I was learning more confusion than algebra. Moreover, I began to believe I was pretty dumb. Was I developing what Herman Epstein calls "negative neural networks" (resistant circuitry) toward this worthy subject?[2]

Having fled from math courses at the first available opportunity, I have since talked to other adults who confided that, after a similar experience, they also avoided math until forced years later to take a required course in graduate school. At this point, their grownup brains discovered they actually liked this sort of reasoning, although they were still confused by the planes that meet over Chicago! I often wonder how many children decide they are "dumb" about certain subjects, when the truth is that someone simply laid on the learning too soon in a form other than the one they needed to receive it in at the time. Thus they were cheated of the chance to learn it in an appropriately challenging and satisfying way.

In this personal example, it is very possible that the necessary neural equipment for algebra—taught in this particular manner—may not yet have been automatically available in my early-adolescent brain. The areas to receive the last dose of myelin are the association areas responsible for manipulating highly abstract concepts—such as symbols (X, Y, Z; graphs) that stand for other symbols (numerical relationships) that stand for real things (planes, trains, wells). Such learning is highly experience-dependent, and thus there are many potential neural routes by which it can be performed. Trying to drill higher-level learning into immature brains may force them to *perform* with lower-level systems and thus impair the skill in question. Since every child's developmental schedule may be different for every type of learning (e.g., some get better at math faster than at English and vice versa), this concept of plasticity makes teaching a challenging task indeed.

I would contend that much of today's school failure results from academic expectations for which students' brains were not prepared—but which were bulldozed into them anyway. Deficits in everything from grammar to geography may be caused by teaching that bypasses the kind of instruction that could help children conceptually come to grips with the subject at hand.

The brain grows best when it is challenged, so high standards for children's learning are important. Nevertheless, curriculum needs to be considered in terms of *brain-appropriate* challenge. Reorganizing synapses is much more difficult than having the patience to help them get arranged properly the first time around!

Teachers and parents can prime children's brains for complex learning, but no one knows yet (if they ever will) how to "make" maturation happen. We don't, so far, know how to make myelin grow in human brains, although impoverished environments and inadequate intake of protein may stunt its development. The relatively fixed order of myelinization in different brain areas may provide a real biological basis for "readiness" for certain types of learning.[3] Even if we wanted one, there is no prescription for maturing brains—much to some parents' dismay.

Not long ago, a father of a teenage son blurted out a question in the middle of a lecture I was giving to a parents' group in an affluent suburb. "My son is fourteen now and he's been accused of being an 'immature late bloomer' by his teachers ever since kindergarten," he lamented. "Is there anyplace where I can buy myelin?" The audience laughed, and so did I. Many of us have done battle in that particular trench, but maturation is not so easily purchased. What is presented to the growing brain may indeed enrich it in many important respects, but the good intentions of adults who try too hard to manipulate the process can easily backfire.

Looking Inside the "Enriched Brain": What Works?

How, then, do we stimulate growing brains appropriately? And what can cause them to change for the better? In seeking an answer to these big questions, we can start once more in the rat laboratories, where, as visitors, we would observe colonies of rats living in very different types of cages. Although all get the same rations of food and water, some rats enjoy "enriched" environments while others live either in standard laboratory or "impoverished" conditions for mental growth. The "enriched" animals have larger cages and more playmates, but most important, they are also surrounded by toys such as wheels and balls, which they are busily investigating, pushing, rolling, and climbing through. These two variables—companionship and active involvement with toys—differentiate between "enriched" and "impoverished" conditions. According to Dr. Diamond, these environmental variations can change the size of the cortex by as much as 11%.

Other researchers have theorized that the areas maturing fastest at the time of stimulation are the ones in which the most growth is found. Thus, in a complex human brain, the same type of stimulation might affect different skills, depending on the brain's stage of development.

What happens to cells in the "enriched" brains? Dr. Mark Rosenzweig and Dr. Michael Renner, who started their work in Dr. Diamond's laboratory, describe several effects, "including changes in gross weight of the brain, weight and thickness of the cerebral cortex, microscopic changes in cell density and relative proportions of different cell types, and changes in the structure of individual neurons."[4]

Curiously enough, Rosenzweig has found that rats in the impoverished condition (IC) actually gain more in body weight than their counterparts in enriched condition (EC). Yet their brains are inferior in many respects, two of which are particularly significant. First, as Marian Diamond has shown, there are many more glial support cells in the enriched brains, and second, the neurons themselves have more dendrite spines and thus, presumably, more synapses.[5]

In another lab, Dr. William Greenough, also considering differences between groups of enriched and deprived rats, found differences in synapses as great as 20–25% in one area of the cortex. This finding, he says, "led us to consider what similar extremes might result if all neurons in the human brain were equally plastic. The difference of about 2,000 synapses per neuron in the rat would translate into many trillions of synapses on the 100–200 billion neurons of the human brain!"[6] Although, as we shall shortly see, the mere existence of many synapses does not necessarily mean "smarter," this potential for change is indeed impressive.

The critical question is, of course, do these changes in brains have effects on learning? Yes, indeed, say Rosenzweig and Renner, particularly on higher-level skills. "In problem-solving tasks," they report, "the more complex the task, the greater the likelihood that EC-IC differences will be found. In these tests, the primary sites of environmentally induced anatomical plasticity are in those regions of the brain associated with the more complex (and presumably higher-level) cognitive functions, [particularly] higher-level problem-solving skills." Moreover, even when not being tested, the behavior of the enriched rats is more active and organized when they are exploring new situations. They appear to be picking up more and different information during exploration as a result of their lively curiosity.

As a teacher, I invariably think of some of my students when I read studies like these. We must always be cautious, however, in applying such research to human learning. First, while facts about nervous system development can be extrapolated from one set of neurons and glia to another, it is quite another matter to start drawing parallels between animal and human behavior in complex learning situations. Second, while these environments clearly differed from each other, none of them approximated a rat's natural habitat. It is rare to find a human situation as "impoverished" as the IC cages, although in a later chapter I will describe the effects on a human child of one that might be considered comparable. Even the "enriched" environments are less stimulating than those in nature where rats are constantly exposed to the real challenges of living in a free environment, finding food, defending themselves, and moving about when and where they wish. Animals growing up "in the wild" in the Berkeley hills outside Dr. Diamond's laboratory tend to have larger and heavier cortexes than do those raised in the cages.

The basic principles of plasticity have been shown to be constant across such species as mice, gerbils, ground squirrels, dogs, cats, and primates (e.g., monkeys, Japanese macaques). What can we learn from animal research about how to stimulate children appropriately? Many studies support the notion that brains—and the organisms attached to them—tend to gravitate to the types of stimulation that they need at different stages of development. If we encourage children to make choices from a selected variety of available challenges, both environmental and intellectual, we are no doubt following the wisest course.

Whose Brain Is Growing Today?

Another lesson from animal research is the importance of active involvement and interest on the part of the animal. For example, Dr. Diamond and others have found that to keep the enriched rats' brains growing, they must frequently change their toys to keep them curious and interested. In another experiment, simply having rats climb over a pile of toys to get their food caused visual areas of the cortex to increase 7%.[7]

Greenough agrees. "It appears that active interaction with the environment is necessary for the animal to extract very much appropriate information. Merely making visual experience of a complex environment available to animals unable to interact with it has little behavioral effect." In support of the latter point, animals have been placed in small cages inside the enrichment cage so they can watch their brothers and sisters play, although they cannot themselves get at the toys. The brains of the spectators end up not much different from those of animals in impoverished cages.

As well-intentioned parents and teachers, we all sometimes end up taking charge of learning and trying to "stuff" in rather than arranging things so that the youngster's curiosity impels the process. Since I began reading this research, I often ask myself when I am struggling to "make" a student learn something, Whose brain is growing today?

It always helps to consider: Who is interested? Who is curious? Who is asking the questions? Children need stimulation and intellectual challenges, but they must be actively involved in their learning, not responding passively while another brain—their teacher's or parent's—laboriously develops new synapses in their behalf!

Any activity which engages a student's interest and imagination, which sparks the desire to seek out an answer, or ponder a question, or create a response, can be good potential brain food. Particularly in an age when we need "enriched" minds to grapple with increasingly complex problems, we should not encourage, or even condone, large doses of passive observing or absorbing for growing brains. Yet it is happening—not only in front of the TV, but in too many day-care centers, schools, after-school activities, and even in homes. How much does this learner passivity contribute to lagging academic skills? A great deal!

In the only human "enrichment" study she has done, Dr. Diamond compared sections from the brain of Albert Einstein with similar sections from average males. She found cellular enhancement of the same types that she had seen in her enriched rats.[8] In one particular area that makes higher-level associations between sensory systems, there were actually twice as many glial cells! She speculates that this unusual profusion could have resulted not only from inherited potential, but also from unusually active use of those particular cell groups.

CRITICAL PERIODS FOR LEARNING

What happens if the "right" stimulation is not available when the brain is ready for it? Are there certain times when the brain is more open to certain kinds of experience? When, if ever, is it too late to learn specific skills? Some of the most eye-opening research on neural plasticity shows that there are "critical," "sensitive," or "optimal" periods for some types of mental development. But if the right stimulus isn't available . . . too bad.

"In development it is now well known that there are certain times when an organism is ready to deal with certain stimuli," states Dr. Jane Holmes Bernstein. "And when those stimuli do not appear at the critical time, then it is likely that the brain structures that would have mediated them will not function and will die."[9]

Both animal and human data support this real-life phenomenon of *use it or lose it*. In order to understand its implications, we should first delve more deeply into the way by which the brain naturally hones itself into an efficient processing system.

Synaptic Pruning: What Gets Shaved and What Gets Saved?

Since an infant enters the world with more neurons than will ever be needed, the brain starts life in quite a disorganized state. Baby neurons that have survived the prenatal marathon to reach synaptic sites are already competing to reach out to other neurons by growing new dendrite spines. It will take many years—perhaps even a lifetime—for each brain's complement of synapses to form and become strengthened by repeated use. Particularly during the early years, the ones that get used are the ones that will be strengthened and survive. A major task during the years of childhood is to prune this mass of potential into networks of connections that are useful and automatic for the mental skills that this particular child is being encouraged to develop.

You might envision the newborn brain as a large mass of clay that has been formed in a rough template of a final product. On it, the environment acts as a sculptor. The types of stimulation that enter the brain determine to a great extent which material remains and which is shaved off and swept away from the studio floor. During sensitive periods, certain areas in the mass are temporarily warmed and softened, thus becoming more amenable to the environmental sculptor's knife.

This process proceeds quite automatically for the most part. Since the child can't possibly process all the available stimuli, he or she selects what is most interesting or personally relevant, thus building connections in the related brain systems. Adults' main task is to make a variety of stimulation available, at the same time considering carefully the choices their children are encouraged to make. Brains of youngsters who spend lots of time in front of a TV set, for example, may be expected to develop differently from those who pursue the physical, interpersonal, and cognitive challenges of active play. Children with plenty of time to "waste" can be encouraged to seek out activities that are appropriate for an individual brain's stage of development. Youngsters who are hurried from one activity to another may get lots of sensory input but be shortchanged on the time-consuming process of forming association networks to understand and organize experience meaningfully.

The pruning of many synapses is necessary to keep the child's mind from resembling a "booming, buzzing, confusion." Neuroanatomist Dr. Arnold Scheibel once described the immature brain as somewhat like a large tree crowded with many little birds, all singing weakly at the same time so that no individual song can clearly be heard. As the brain matures, gradually eliminating some connections and retaining others, the tree contains fewer but larger birds with strong, clear songs, well separated so that each can distinctly be heard.[10]

Although it seems logical to believe that the more neurons the better, this is not the case. The importance of pruning is demonstrated by studies that show some mentally retarded children have fewer synaptic connections than normal, while others have too many.

Researchers speculate that the retardation may be associated with the inefficiency of these overcrowded brains, although they unfortunately do not as yet know what to do about it.

Evidence for Critical Periods: Animal Research

The ground rules for plasticity often blur the line between efficiency and impairment. Evidence from both animals and humans shows that sometimes the brain's pruning mechanisms are carried too far.

What would the world be like if you could see everything—except vertical lines? You would probably have a lot of trouble getting through doorways, and it would be difficult to avoid bumping into trees and telephone poles. This experience happened to some kittens who were kept in an unusual environment during a short period when particular groups of cells called "vertical feature detectors" in the visual cortex were "ripe." During this time, the kittens never saw vertical lines. Despite a full dose of visual stimulation and otherwise normal vision later on, they never learned to see them. Later examination of their brains showed that the neurons designed to do this job simply failed to develop because they received no stimulation during the critical period of their development. Many different experiments have been conducted with kittens wearing specially designed goggles or blindfolds. The upshot of all of them is that the selective restriction of certain types of stimulation can structurally alter the animals' brains.[11] Naturally, function is also affected. I find two facts particularly interesting:

—Not only does severe visual deprivation result in changed neurons in the visual cortex, but it can also cause the auditory (hearing) cortex to develop more fully than would otherwise be expected.

—Structural changes occurring during critical periods result in behavioral changes later on when their "changed brains" cause the animals to pay attention and respond differently to different aspects of the environment.[12]

Other animal studies, even including such species as birds, crickets, and goldfish, have demonstrated many types of sensitive periods.

Sexual behavior of monkeys is later impaired if they are isolated during periods of normal sexual play during childhood. If mother cats do not bring live prey into the nest during a specific time frame, their kittens never develop the ability to become proficient hunters. In each of these cases, certain parts of the nervous system did not develop normally, and stimulation before or after the critical period does not have the same effect.

One interesting experiment illustrates the fact that animals will "work" for their stimulation when the critical period strikes. Kittens were reared in a dark room that contained a lever they could push to view a lighted scene especially designed to stimulate certain sets of visual "feature detectors." Before the onset of a critical period for this type of vision at about eight weeks of age, they occasionally depressed the lever but showed little interest in it, although their eyes had already opened. Suddenly, between eight and nine weeks, the relevant cells became "ripe" and action at the lever increased "dramatically."[13] We can assume the number of dendrites and synapses on those particular cells in their brains grew apace.

"Sensitive" Periods for Human Brains

Human brains have much bigger windows of opportunity because they take much longer to develop than do those of animals, so the terms "sensitive" or "optimal" periods are usually used. Studies to date have identified sensitive periods for two general types of abilities: basic sensory skills and higher-level ones, specifically some aspects of language.

Priming the Foundation Systems

Even when a child's ears and eyes are completely intact, visual and auditory processing may be impaired if cells in the parts of the brain that receive signals from these organs fail to fire during a particular time of development. A well-publicized example is the problem called lazy eye, or amblyopia. In this disorder, a young child fails to develop binocularity, the ability to use both eyes together efficiently, because one eye tends to wander, letting the other do all the work. Because the brain cells designed to receive the visual signals from the lazy eye do not get their proper dose of stimulation, they eventually stop firing. Doctors have learned that this condition must be treated before age five, if it is to be corrected, because the sensitive period for this particular ability may end at that time. The treatment, logically, consists of intermittently patching the good eye to force all cells in the system to do their work, develop their synapses, and survive. The same principle explains why cataracts on the eyes of infants must be removed before six months of age to avoid permanent visual impairment.

Still at a basic sensory level, the ability to discriminate fine differences between sounds of a language apparently must develop during early years, as well. An eighth grader I met recently simply could not "hear" the differences between some of the short vowel sounds and thus had trouble saying and writing them accurately. Her classmates thought that her substitutions, such as "osculator" for "escalator," were "cute," but her teachers were not similarly amused by her spelling mistakes. Sure enough, I discovered she, like many students with both spelling and reading problems, had suffered from early ear infections that resulted in sporadic hearing loss during preschool years. Because of this link with later learning problems, experts now recommend that parents watch children carefully for blocked hearing and get prompt medical attention for such problems before cells in the auditory cortex are permanently impaired by lack of exercise.[14]

Circuits for the sounds of different languages must apparently be stimulated during a critical period, as well. Dr. Jennifer Buchwald of the UCLA School of Medicine is interested in the way "the acoustic— that is, linguistic—environment during development is responsible for developmental differences in the brain." She is studying such differences in native Japanese and American speakers by measuring a special type of electrical wave, called P300, in their brains.[14]

Her research explains why adults who learn to speak a foreign language with different sound patterns than their own rarely acquire a flawless accent. Their vocal apparatus is not the reason; their brains are. While they may think they hear or mimic the sounds accurately, they really have lost the ability to perceive sound patterns that were not present in the environments during childhood. The distinctive accents of European, Middle Eastern, or Oriental speakers of English, which often reveal their particular national origins, provide living verification of the power of early environments to create lasting differences in some types of human abilities.

Does this justify teaching Japanese to infants—another current fad among the child-engineering group? At a recent conference Dr. Nico Spinelli responded with an interesting observation. "I think growing up bilingually wastes real estate in the brain. A better plan, in my opinion, would be for children to learn to pronounce perfectly fifty or so words of, say, German, French, Japanese, and Spanish. Later on, one or more of these languages could be learned more easily and with no accent, because the brain would have been primed for it."[15] Before parents rush for their foreign language dictionaries, however, I would like to reiterate the fact that any learning that has to be "pushed" into a child may end up doing more harm than good—for many reasons. Moreover, there is also evidence that the wrong kinds of foreign language input may tangle up the wires of some children for their native tongue. Caution is advised!

It seems logical that hard-wired sensory skills might have sensitive periods of development. But what about the type of association area brainwork that requires the integration of many different—and sometimes widely separated—neural systems? A few studies have been conducted which suggest that to develop active, intelligent responses to the world, a child needs specific types of interaction with caretakers at different times in development. For example, separate studies have shown that in normal children, direct kinesthetic (muscular) stimulation (e.g., parent moves child's arms or legs) is maximally effective during the first six months; maternal prompting ("Look at the bunny," "See the red fire engine") is more effective at some times than at others; and maternal gesturing has been positively related to comprehension in nineteen-month-olds but not in older children.[16] In the next chapter we will look at other ways in which "higher-order" skills such as language and attention may be affected by experience during specific times of development.

"NEURAL DARWINISM" IN THE COMPETITIVE BRAIN

Probably the most intriguing idea emerging from all this research is that brains are shaped and maintained by internal competition. The creative drama of neurons' endless battle, first for survival and later for connective power, is still not familiar to most people outside the research laboratories. Even many of those within the labs have trouble grasping implications of a major new theory proposed by Nobel Prize winner Dr. Gerald Edelman of Rockefeller University. His book, *Neural Darwinism*, outlines in complete detail what might be considered the ultimate argument for the environment's power in shaping the brain.[17]

In his theory and with "Darwin III," a computer that can replicate some aspects of human brain function in surprisingly lifelike ways, Edelman applies the laws of natural selection to the neurons in the human brain—and finds that they work. He first acknowledges, as we have already seen, that there are overall patterns of brain structure that are modified by genetic and prenatal history; in addition, he proposes a group of "secondary repertoires," formed only by stimuli to which a particular brain responds during its lifetime. In this constantly changing system, groups of neurons are locked in constant competition with each other to "capture" other cells for their group. The groups that get the most action grow stronger synapses, add to their networks, and survive; they are "selected" because they are more likely to be used in future behavior.

> As long as significant activation is achieved, the group can continue to consolidate its "hold" on cells. But other groups are constantly competing for the same cells, and any weakening of connections because of decreased activation puts the group at risk either of losing a few cells or, in the extreme case, of being divided and conquered.[18]

Ultimately, through a process that he describes as "reentrant signaling," the cell groups link themselves together in a coordinated system that can talk to itself. These systems communicate back and forth, spurring on their own development as they respond to internal and external stimuli. Thus our brains evolve, individually and collectively, according to what is useful and adaptive for the particular environments in which we find ourselves.

Committing Growing Neurons . . . to What?

Dr. Jane Holmes Bernstein is intrigued by Edelman's ideas. "It seems," she says, "the stimuli coming in are actually competing to have this brain take notice of them. When you're dealing with this idea of competition within the system, if those stimuli are not there at the right time, then the cells don't fire. The next set of stimuli coming in, competing madly for cortical connections, are likely to preempt what should have been a relationship in the cells."

But surely this doesn't mean that we're just helpless victims of whatever stimuli come along, does it?

Not at all, believes Dr. Bernstein. "It's not simply a matter of the stimuli being there; you have to do something with them." She describes a famous experiment in which identical-twin kittens were put in a large circular container painted with black and white vertical stripes—their only visual stimulation during a critical period of visual development. One kitten rode in a small basket that was attached to one end of a revolving balance beam. The other kitten was in a second basket attached to the opposite end of the beam; his legs, however, protruded from the basket. As he walked around, the beam revolved and his brother got a free ride. Both, of course, had the same visual stimulation of the vertical stripes. Later, it was discovered that visual receptor cells in their brains had developed differently, even though each had experienced the exact same scenery. The kitten who merely rode along was functionally blind for vertical lines!

"Only the kitten who had his feet on the floor, knowing where he was, aware of his position on the floor relative to the lines, developed those connections!" emphasizes Dr. Bernstein. "Experience shapes brains, but you need to interact with the experience."

Physical play is one of the main ways in which children interact with experience, points out Dr. Bernstein. "The most characteristic thing about the human is that we go looking for problems to solve—or in other words, playing. In fact, we usually worry about significant emotional issues in youngsters who are unable to look for problems to solve."

Before I left Dr. Bernstein's office I decided to get practical. If the brain responds physically to such environmental differences as whether a kitten walks or rides, what effects might today's environments—where many children spend more time watching a screen than with their feet on the ground—be having on mental abilities? What skills could they be gaining—and which ones might they be losing?

"Well," she replied, "there's nothing wrong with TV or computers per se. However, it may be an issue whether the kids are active or passive when working with the machines. *Sesame Street,* for example, has brought a great deal of information to children who might not otherwise have got it, but this may have been obtained at a price. I hear many teachers complain that children in kindergarten and first grade don't know how to *listen actively!* They're used to fast-paced segments of information that are constantly changing. They should be doing something with what they're getting.

"The *Sesame Street* population is actually at the greatest risk for not understanding that language is communication, a back-and-forth interaction between people. They aren't personally involved in using language to think and solve problems with. Children who have been talked to and had stories read to them are at a real advantage. They've learned how to listen and pay attention—and had fun doing it. These basic abilities are critical if a youngster is to benefit from education in the classroom!"

How about video games?

"In one very popular game, for example, children must learn to attend to increasingly complex clues. They're systematically encouraged to scan a visual array. But why not put a kid in a real-life problem-solving situation? This isn't being encouraged. We're not giving them the full range of opportunities and it's certainly possible that with such a degree of practice on one skill, the brain might commit too many cells and there would be fewer available for other things.

"Teachers worry about the amount of time children, even very young ones, spend these days encased in stereo headphones, listening to music instead of talking, reading or carrying on a conversation. What do you think that might be doing to their brains?" I asked Dr. Bernstein.

"I hate to think." She rolled her eyes.

"It seems as if we teachers have our work cut out for us," I ventured. "How much can schools change brains?"

Dr. Bernstein did not hesitate. "A great deal!" she replied emphatically.

In a Nutshell: Developing Brains

Genes set the outlines of mental ability, but the way children use their brains determines how their intelligence is expressed. The experiences with which a child chooses to interact determine each brain's synaptic structure as well as the way it functions for different types of learning. If children change the way they use their brains, their synapses are rearranged accordingly. The more they are used in a certain pattern of response, the less flexible they appear to become.

Nature provides a schedule for neural maturation, and increasingly complex modes of thinking emerge from an internal competition for connections at each new phase of mental growth. If a child is glued to an activity for several hours a day, connections for that specific activity will be built up, but something else is going to be diminished. Moreover, if certain kinds of skills remain unused during their appearance on the brain's developmental stage, neural foundations may wither away in the wings of potentiality.

Severe deprivation can have dramatic effects on the young, malleable mind. Less extreme variations in experience have less predictable consequences. The value of excessive stimulation to enhance development is unproven and risky. External pressure designed to produce learning or intelligence violates the fundamental rule: *A healthy brain stimulates itself by active interaction with what it finds challenging and interesting in its environment.* The environments that we provide for children, the stimuli with which we encourage them to interact, and the ways in which we demonstrate for them the uses of a human mind—these are the means at our command for shaping both their brains and our cultural future.

Part Two

———————— ✦ ————————

LANGUAGE, FUZZY THINKING, AND THE LANGUISHING LEFT HEMISPHERE

Who's Teaching the Children to Talk?

Language is not only a means of generalization; it is at the same time the source of thought. When the child masters language he gains the potentiality to organize anew his perception, his memory; he masters more complex forms of reflection of objects in the external world; he gains the capacity to draw conclusions from his observations, to make deductions, the potentiality of thinking.

—ALEXANDER LURIA[1]

Language is not the garment but the incarnation of our thoughts.

—WILLIAM WORDSWORTH

Language is our most powerful tool for organizing experience and, indeed, for constituting our social realities.

—JEROME BRUNER[2]

Sitting facing the television, muttering half thoughts or reactions into black space—this is the primary linguistic training ground for most of my students. It does not in any way adequately serve the goal of developing and strengthening verbal communication because there is no meaningful interaction. I have before me in my classroom a generation of youngsters whose world encourages linguistic passivity. I must build an awareness of the de-

mands of clear verbal communication on the most rudimentary interpersonal levels.

—A. JANE HAMILTON,[3]
MIDDLE SCHOOL TEACHER, HILLSBORO, NH

Language shapes culture, language shapes thinking—and language shapes brains. The verbal bath in which a society soaks its children arranges their synapses and their intellects; it helps them learn to reason, reflect, and respond to the world. The brain is ravenous for language stimulation in early childhood but becomes increasingly resistant to change when the zero hour of puberty arrives. Severe deprivation of language during early years guarantees lasting neural changes that noticeably affect speech and understanding. More subtle forms of language deprivation do not show up in such dramatic ways, but may ultimately affect abilities to think abstractly, plan ahead and defer gratification, control attention, and perform higher-order analysis and problem-solving—the very skills so much at issue in American schools today.

The brains of today's children are being structured in language patterns antagonistic to the values and goals of formal education. The culprit, which is now invading all levels of the socioeconomic spectrum, is diminished and degraded exposure to the forms of good, meaningful language that enable us to converse with others, with the written word, and with our own minds. The results are inevitable: declining literacy, falling test scores, faltering or circuitous oral expression, ineptitude with the written word that extends from elementary schools into the incoming ranks of professionals. Corporations run writing courses for budding executives, universities remediate basic skills, secondary schools lower standards, and elementary schools add more "learning disability" classes. Meanwhile bureaucrats and educational planners ignore the kernel problem and tout curriculum and methods devised for a previous generation. Bigger doses of "chalk and talk" are the weapons of choice against flagging attention, declines in reading comprehension, and superficial reasoning across the academic spectrum. But old methods are not working because young brains have not been shaped around language as a quintessential tool for analytic thinking.

If we want growing brains to build the foundations for traditional modes of academic excellence, we must confront the habits of our culture that are changing the quality and the quantity of our children's conversation—both interpersonal and with the written word.

Children immersed in what some linguists aptly term "primitive" language should not be criticized for failing to acquire linguistic sophistication.

Much of the blame inevitably falls on television, which is actually only one symptom of the problem. No one has defined long-term effects of stereo headphones versus conversation, of computer games or drills versus active social play, of videotapes versus books. How can children bombarded from birth by noise, frenetic schedules, and the helter-skelter caretaking of a fast-paced adult world learn to analyze, reflect, ponder? How can they use quiet inner conversations to build personal realities, sharpen and extend their visual reasoning? These qualities are embedded in brains by the experiences a society chooses for its children. What are we choosing for ours?

LANGUAGE, CULTURE, BRAIN: ARTIFACT AND ARCHITECT

According to many anthropologists, society, language, brain, and the human intellect have been shinnying together up the evolutionary pole since prehistoric times. Language, in fact, has been both artifact and architect of our human intellectual habits. The development of speech probably was inevitable because the human brain and vocal apparatus are uniquely suited for it. After the first words emerged, perhaps as a guttural expedient for some primitive man who wanted to summon a comrade when he was clutching a handful of tools, people discovered that talk could be useful. As they developed various uses for language, say some authorities, human evolution could have been pushed along by several notches. In turn, as language was used, the underlying brain structures may have been nudged into increased size and specialization.

The invention of writing also changed thinking. Many scholars believe the precision required to get thought into words on paper refined mental capabilities, logical thought, and the ability of a culture to reason about its complexities.[4] Neil Postman, author of *Amusing Ourselves to Death*, argues that the substitution of immediate, pictorial material for the written word may be destroying our societal ability to reason intelligently. "In a culture dominated by print," he points out, "public discourse tends to be characterized by a coherent, orderly arrangement of facts and ideas." It is no accident that the Age of Reason coincided with the development of print. Now, however, the content of much public discourse has become "dangerous nonsense." The Gettysburg address would probably have been largely incomprehensible to an 1985 audience, he suggests, even if the President could have constructed such long, complex sentences![5]

This "dangerous nonsense" is the introduction for large numbers of our young into the intellectual habits and values of adult society. It is also, for many, their primary linguistic model. From it, children get a window on adults' reasoning. "Language tells what a people thinks about itself and its destiny," maintains columnist Georgie Anne Geyer, but "television's abominable grammar has tarnished the beauty of the English language."[6]

Who Is Teaching Language to the Children?

Even if the linguistic quality of television were upgraded, however, the one-way nature of media talk makes it a poor teacher. Good language, like the synapses that make it possible, is gained only from interactive engagement: children need to talk as well as to hear. They need to play with words and reason with them. They need to practice talking about problems to learn to plan and organize their behavior. They need to respond to new words and stories to build a broad personal base of *semantic* meaning. They need personal adult guides to provide good examples of grammar—not primarily so they will sound "intelligent," but because word order, or *syntax*, is the means by which they will learn to analyze ideas and reason about abstract relationships. They need to hear and speak the tiny units of language—such as *ed, ing, ment*—that convey fine-grained differences between what happened yesterday and what will happen tomorrow, between actions and things, between the shades of meaning that give clarity to mental operations.

Good conversation is a *rara avis* in homes today. We know that most children do not read, but as we shall see, they also get little conversational training at schools. Moreover, school experiences may come too late or be of the wrong type. Traditional sources of language exposure have ceded much of their neural real estate to television and the peer culture.

Normal human brains will construct the essentials of a language even without much input: categories of word meaning, sounds, basic grammar. Deaf children invent basic symbols and the grammar of a primitive sign language even when they are not taught to sign. The brain dictates that some language will be learned; the form of the language then determines, to some degree, the form of the brain. If the deaf continue to use a visual language, their brains become significantly different from those of hearing children.

For children in more normal language environments, a minimum of exposure during the specific time period when the brain is "sensitive" for each type of development guarantees the unfolding of basic "experience expectant" systems. Refinements of language, such as more complex grammar, vocabulary, and social usage, however, don't arrive so easily; they depend on the quality and quantity of interactions in both preschool and elementary years. The most complex neural systems, which pull together abstract language and visual reasoning, develop only if challenging encounters with reading, writing, and verbal reasoning continue during the teenage years. Failure to stimulate these systems, which enable many of mankind's greatest achievements, threatens not only personal but cultural futures.

FAMILIES, SCHOOLS, AND GROWING BRAINS: THE IDEAL CONFRONTS THE REALITY

Language at Home Helps Children Create "Possible Worlds"

The person who teaches your child to talk also teaches a way of thinking. The ideas, values, and priorities of a culture are borne along on the stream of language that flows between generations.

Teaching children to speak not only helps them organize words in a sentence but also to organize their minds, advises Dr. Jerome Bruner. Bruner feels the type of symbol systems we teach children to use open "possible worlds" for them. The way we talk about the world and think about it in the "coin of that thought," he maintains, imposes a point of view and even creates a social reality. Nations differ in large part because of symbol systems. "Just as the little Frenchman becomes a consumer and user of French modes of thinking and doing, so the little American comes to reflect the ways in which knowledge is gained and reflected on in America."

Verbal interactions in the home are where it all starts. In a simple example, if your child is angry because a friend made off with a favorite toy, the words you use and those you teach the child to use will set lasting patterns of action and attitude:

"Go kick that little monster in the butt! We don't let people get away with things like that!" (Society is violent, and you must be prepared to defend physically against any who transgress on your territory. Don't stop to talk or reason; just act.)

"Let me call John's mother and settle this problem." (The world can be managed by persons in authority. Words are used for solving problems, but it is best to wait for someone else who knows more than you to do the work.)

"Let's go to John's house and you can tell him why you're upset. Hitting isn't going to do any good." (People are expected to take the responsibility for solving their own problems. Verbal negotiation is the accepted means.)

"Please be quiet; this program's almost over . . ." (Television problems are more important than real-life ones. Words don't seem to do much good, better try another way to get attention.)

Not all children have parents or caregivers who show them how to use words effectively, but these habits strongly influence the child's "possible worlds" when he gets to school. Dr. Gordon Wells, of the Ontario Institute for Studies in Education, has studied variations in the types of language training children get at home. "Everything that happens in a child's daily life is a potential subject for the sort of talk that facilitates attention, interpretation, and evaluation, but parents differ in the use they make of these opportunities," he observes. "In some homes, events are very much taken for granted, each one receiving the same sort of passing comment, whereas in other homes there is a much greater selectivity, some events being discussed in considerable detail and connections made with the wider context in which they occur."[7]

Social as well as thinking skills develop from children's language experiences, believes Dr. Bambi Schieffelin of the Department of Anthropology at New York University. "I think language is the thing that creates one's whole world view," she emphasizes. "I take a strong position that it's the structure of language that is important—you can use language to create worlds as well as teach how to think."[8,9]

The Importance of Talk

Dr. Schieffelin, like many others, is concerned that children are not receiving large enough daily doses of talk either at home or at school. With increasing numbers of young children spending time in day-care or school settings, we must pay special attention to their need to talk to adults and to each other, she insists. "I just believe that kids talking and having language experiences of all kinds, in any kind of medium, is just *critical*. Kids *have* to talk, they should

be encouraged constantly to talk, and older people need to participate with them, guide them, help them develop and expand their
abilities."

Many parents today try hard to provide elaborate "stimulating"
environments for their children, but not even designer toys substitute for good-quality conversation. Looking specifically at the behavior of the mothers in one typical study, researchers found that
"frequent, responsive mother-child language interaction" was the
most critical factor in raising mental ability, rather than "overall level
of maternal stimulation," i.e., how well the mother physically cared
for the child.[10]

A child's early experiences with language have powerful long-term
effects on school achievement. Studies of homes of children with
Down's syndrome show that parent-child interaction with language
can improve the future school abilities even of children viewed as
"retarded." By providing parents with training in language-rich "play
lessons" beginning when each child was thirty months old, researchers in one study found that ensuing gains in the youngsters' reading
comprehension lasted for at least ten years.[11]

Dr. Catherine Snow of Harvard University is conducting a large
study to find out which characteristics of family life are particularly
related to language development and—by extension—to school success. Some language skills, she finds, are much more valuable than
others in academic terms. For example, children who can come up
with good original definitions for words (as in "What does 'donkey'
mean?") tend to do well on standardized achievement tests. But
ability to mimic the behavior of a talk-show host interviewing an
adult for four minutes showed no relationship to success on the
tests.

The quality of the conversation adults have with children is extremely important, says Dr. Snow. In those precious times together
at the dinner table, for example, parents who take the time to discuss
topics thoughtfully, who talk about events and ideas, are helping their
children become much better thinkers than those who focus more on
the food or the situation at hand. Telling stories over and over, ex-
panding on characters, events, and ideas, also helps children learn to
think carefully and give good explanations.

The Importance of Words Without Pictures

Any activity that helps children use their brains to separate from the
"here and now," to get away from pictures and use words to manip-

ulate ideas in their own minds, also helps them with the development
of abstract thinking (e.g., "Let's guess what we will see when we go
to the park this afternoon." "I wonder what your coach's decision will
mean for next year's team."). Many experts believe this kind of "dis-
embedded thought" is encouraged by reflective conversations about
stories that have been read. Families with the time and patience to
talk thoughtfully with their children about the stories they read give
them a big advantage in school. Such activities are a difficult chore
when parents are rushed or tired, however. Who has the energy after
a day full of hassles?

Nevertheless, if parents expect their children to be good students,
they had better be prepared to make an effort. If they are too tired to
talk, they can at least read aloud from books that engage children's
interest and attention. In a large study in Great Britain following
children from preschool into elementary school, Dr. Wells and his
colleagues found that the most powerful predictor of their school
achievement was the amount of time spent listening to interesting
stories. Wells believes that such experiences teach children first about
the way stories (and later, other things they read) are structured, as
well as the types of language that may be expected in a variety of
types of written text. Even more important, however, is understanding words alone as *the main source of meaning*. Because the words do
not come with pictures attached, the child must come to grips with
"the symbolic potential of language"—its power to represent experience independent of the context of the here and now.

Experiences with pictures attached, even when they involve looking at picture books and learning new words, are not as valuable, says
Wells, because the child needs to learn "sooner, rather than later" to
go beyond just naming things that can be seen. He concludes:

> For this, the experience of stories is probably the ideal prepara-
> tion. . . . Gradually, they will lead them to reflect on their experience
> and, in so doing, to discover the power that language has, through its
> symbolic potential, to create and explore alternative possible worlds
> with their own inner coherence and logic. *Stories may thus lead to the
> imaginative, hypothetical stance that is required in a wide range of
> intellectual activities and for problem-solving of all kinds* . . . [empha-
> sis added].[12]

What is actually happening in today's homes? Teachers of young
children are worried that children aren't being read to enough at
home today. They say many of their charges now come to school

unfamiliar with the narrative staples of our literature: folk and fairy tales, "classic" children's stories, even nursery rhymes. Deficits are showing up especially among middle and upper-middle class children from "the type of families" where these stories were, until quite recently, standard fare. The librarian in one suburban school told me, "It's amazing to me that they come to kindergarten and first grade having no experience with nursery rhymes. It used to be they were all familiar with them and many could recite along with you; now hardly any are familiar. Is there such a thing as 'cultural illiteracy' for five-year-olds?"

Why are nursery rhymes so important? Not only do they get children "hooked" on listening to language, but they also teach valuable skills. "It's the patterns, the rhythms," she explains, "the way language is put together so pleasantly. Patterns are the most important for early reading—and even for math. Putting letters together in patterns, learning that everything in the world goes together in patterns—that's so important for the little ones."

"I have to start from scratch with most of these kids," said a kindergarten teacher in another school. "I'm supposed to teach rhyming words in the reading readiness program, but half these kids don't know what a rhyme is. And a lot seem to be missing that internal sense of rhythm."

Reading specialists tell us children's ability to discriminate and create rhyming words, as well as their sense of rhythm, are closely related to early reading ability. A child who has absorbed over and over—through the *ears*, not the eyes—such common word parts as "fun, sun, run" or "fiddle, diddle, middle" as well as the melody of their language is statistically destined to have an easier time learning to read.

Language Coaches

Ideally, children have one-on-one language coaches built into their lives from birth, when interactions between parent and infant lay the groundwork for nonverbal communication skills. Some parents mistakenly believe the first year is not important for language stimulation, yet during these months basic synapses of the language system are constructed by such "simple" means as nontalking games (pat-a-cake, peekaboo) between infant and caretaker. Turn-taking, even without words, is an important first lesson. During early months the brain also takes in its lasting repertoire of sounds for speaking and listening to the nuances of its native language.

Parents seem to have built-in knowledge of how to act as "language coach" while the child's abilities develop. Studies show that mothers instinctively shape and expand their child's language, tailoring their own responses precisely to each child's developmental need. They seem to know just how to pull the youngster's language up a notch by using forms in their own speech that are just one degree above the child's current level. Simply exposing children to adult language does not automatically make the learning "take," because youngsters can't repeat speech patterns that are much more complicated than those they are already using (another reason, incidentally, why most TV— even *Sesame Street*—is a flop as a language model).[13]

A burning current question asks whether other adults can also do this job. The few studies available suggest that fathers, too, may be quite skilled at tailoring language to a child.[14] Other adults and even older children can also be effective, but only if they have the skill to move on to more complex vocabulary and grammar when children are ready. When parents hire caretakers with different language patterns from their own, they should not be surprised if their child's development is affected.

Overall, being a parent may confer a special advantage. One recent study compared children's interactions with parents and with other well-intentioned adults who were not parents. Parents did a much better job of guiding the children's language, even if the children weren't their own.[15] Perhaps the secret is to be in close enough touch with a growing mind to become sensitized to what is happening inside it.

Development of brain systems beyond the most fundamental layers of language depend on the availability of the right kind of stimulation at the proper time. Anyone who has ever watched a small child pester an adult to get a certain kind of answer, realizes that children will try to elicit the right kind of conversation if adults are interested and available. This ideal scenario is increasingly missing, however, even in homes where parents expect to see their child on top of the academic heap. At this writing, the majority of babies born in the United States are placed in full-time day care within a year, commonly within two or three months, so their mothers can return to work.[16] American preschoolers spend a great deal of time watching television—missing both personal interaction and language content tailored to each child's developmental schedule. We don't know how many children are being encouraged to *be quiet* by overburdened caretakers, by parents who are pressed for time, or by hired baby-sitters who have poor mastery of English and would rather watch the soaps.

Are schools taking over the job? A resounding NO is, unfortunately, the answer. In many day-care centers and classrooms, teachers have too many children to see to and may even lack the interest or the skills to participate with them. Neglect of verbal interaction during the apex of the brain's sensitive period for language acquisition is a serious issue, but many so-called "reliable" programs overlook the priority of interactive talk. In one typical study, researchers observed the everyday interactions of children and their teachers in two well-regarded child care centers in the United States. They found:

> The children spent most of their time in teacher-directed large-group activities, and . . . most of their language behavior was receptive, such as listening to and following teachers' directions. Although teachers provided adequate oral language models, they were not active listeners, did not encourage curiosity about language, and did not spontaneously expand on children's vocabulary or concepts.[17]

In other settings the situation is even worse. Basic concerns for physical needs and safety predominate; even teacher talk is minimized. In some centers children watch video for substantial portions of the day.

For older children, too, schools neglect specific measures to make up for gaps in language development before it's too late. "We have to teach them the three R's and all the other stuff that gets neglected at home—from sex education to how to climb trees. Don't tell me we also have to teach them how to talk!" complained one school administrator.

"As a society, are we neglecting our children's language development?" I asked Dr. Schieffelin, who has compared language development in many cultures with that in the United States.

"That's what it looks like," she replied. "But I don't want to blame caretakers. Many mothers have to work. The problem is that there has to be some institutional support; someone has to help out, and that's not happening."

Dr. Schieffelin believes that we should rearrange our societal priorities to get children interacting with language. She says schools and day-care centers should encourage children to talk with peers as well as with adults. But classes are often too big. How, she asks, can teachers be expected to encourage language interaction when they must control overly large groups of children in classrooms—by keeping them quiet?

"We need to look at this ideology of silence; why is it that silence is seen as being in control and talk is seen as being out of control? Children can't be passive learners! I really think they need a lot of opportunity to experiment, talk to each other in ways that are not necessarily appropriate to adults—word play, sound play, role play—but teachers have so many kids in the room they can't tolerate the noise level."[18]

Passive "listening" does not build either language or effective listening skills. Our children today spend a great deal of time "listening" (to the TV, to the teacher), but they need to listen *better*, not just listen *more*. Real listening is an active mental process that serves understanding and memory. Classrooms where children are passively "listening" to teachers who do most of the talking are a dangerous anachronism. Studies of elementary and secondary school classrooms, where up to 80% of conversation is "teacher talk," even in primary grades, support Dr. Schieffelin's concern. When I visited a number of schools to record samples of children using language in the classrooms, I had trouble finding anything but isolated phrases or short answers to teachers' questions. Much of the "talk" was a one-way street, as the teacher presented material, gave directions, or asked factual questions requiring only brief answers. Only in rare classrooms were children encouraged to formulate complete sentences, expand on answers, or use more complex grammar. Even more rarely were children encouraged to talk to each other, ask each other questions—or even, in fact, to ask questions at all!

Children with insufficient language skills have difficulty requesting information or analyzing problems because they can't formulate appropriate questions. They register overall confusion ("I don't understand"), but lack the verbal tools to analyze the problem; they often remain silent because they can't get their curiosity into words. Their learning suffers accordingly, particularly in subjects such as math and science, where asking the right question is often as important as getting the right answer. In order to analyze problems and evaluate alternatives, children need active practice asking and attempting to answer their own questions. Too much "teacher talk" gets in the way of such higher-level reasoning because it prevents children from doing their own thinking! Observing in British primary schools, linguist Gordon Wells was struck by

> the very high proportion of teacher utterances that are questions, and of these what a very small proportion are questions to which the teachers do not already know the answer. Even when the form of the question seems to invite a variety of answers, there is often only one that is really acceptable to the teacher, and it is not uncommon to see children gazing at the teacher's face in an effort to guess what is in her mind, down to the precise word.[19]

In another era, when children's out-of-school environments provided richer language experiences, schools could, and did, assume that most children would arrive in the elementary or junior high school classroom with verbal skills adequate for their educational purposes. Now, a growing number of educational journals advise teachers not to assume skills of listening, verbal expression, verbal inquiry, and analysis. Children who come from homes where English is not the primary language particularly need special attention, special teaching techniques, and special sensitivity, but all students need an interactive language environment. Reality, however, trails good advice by at least ten years, and many, if not most, classrooms have too many children and insufficient support. Moreover, many also have such rigid "objectives" that even well-intentioned teachers may be forced to push pedagogy at the expense of curiosity.

As a society, we are inviting intellectual mediocrity if we neglect the quality of the language experience of our young. Linguistic passivity for large numbers of children of any age is a recipe for limitation, not only in their individual development but in the cut of our cultural fabric of thought.

What's Happening to Kids' Language?

Teachers today are variably puzzled, concerned, discouraged, and outraged by declines in native-English-speaking students' ability to use language coherently and analytically. Many are not aware that this problem also accounts for "fuzzy thinking." As I visit classrooms, I see ample reason for concern.

"Well, It's Like . . . You Know . . ."

In a suburban classroom eight fifth graders sit around a table reading silently from a textbook. Their teacher holds a manual from which he will read questions about the story. As the children finish reading, they look up expectantly.

"Who can tell me what Rebecca's problem was and how she tried to solve it?" asks the teacher. Hands shoot up. "Okay, Hank, give it a try."

"Well, it was like her friend Sam was uh—you know—uh—like there, er, trapped—uh—under a tree, you know, one that fell down, and Rebecca tried to use a thing—you know—a branch to, like, er . . ." Arms waving, Hank pantomimes a prying motion.

"Pry?" suggests the teacher.

"Yeah, to like pry the tree off him."

"Good, Hank. Susan, will you explain how well Rebecca's plan worked?"

"I'm not really sure," ventures Susan. "I sort of lost it after Rebecca yelled. Like who were those other people that came? I couldn't figure out whether this was before or after she ran into town."

Later, in the faculty room, the teacher appeals for help. "How can I teach these kids to express themselves better? They talk a lot but they have such trouble expressing their ideas clearly. I think it affects what they understand. We used to be able to use harder books in fifth grade, but now even when they can 'read' all the words, they can't seem to put it together. And you should *see* their writing!" He rolls his eyes. "Yet in so many ways these kids are really smart. Do you think I should be teaching them differently?"

Recently I observed a class of ninth graders in a private school discussing the book *Animal Farm.* The students were lively and interested, they clearly had some important ideas they wanted to express, and many did a wonderful job of it. But it was sometimes painful to hear others try. One snippet of dialogue that I jotted down occurred as a girl tried to describe the behavior of a tyrant:

"You know how he's like . . . ," she began. Then, abandoning that line of thought, she started again, "When he tried to . . . you know"—gesturing vigorously—"he did it."

As the conversation progressed, the teacher tried to get the students to compare themes in the book with issues in their own society. She posed the question of what people should do if someone starts acting like a tyrant.

"Oh, yeah," cried one student. "That was on *Magnum* last night."

"Couldn't you tell them . . . ," volunteered another, "I forget what it's called—couldn't you just tell them that they should get out?"

I do not wish to imply that these excerpts characterize all class discussions or that many, many students do not think clearly and express themselves well. Obviously, we cannot expect perfection from ten- and fourteen-year-olds. My concerns, and those expressed by many veteran teachers who have written and spoken to me, are more centered on the suspicion that more and more students are unable to use language—oral or written—with the types of precision that might reasonably be expected at any given age or supposed "ability level." This development goes hand in hand with an overwhelming barrage of reports about declining listening skills.

What the Teachers Say

Students have always needed help understanding and expressing themselves—otherwise they wouldn't be students. And some teachers have always complained. Nevertheless, an increasing number of teachers feel that declining verbal skills are partially responsible for their not being able to achieve the kind of standards in class discussions, reading, and writing that they once took for granted—with the same type of students. They repeatedly express a core of concerns:

- declining listening skills: inability to maintain attention, to understand, and remember material presented orally
- decreased ability to get facts and ideas into coherent, orderly form in speaking and writing
- tendency to communicate with gestures along with, or instead of, words
- declining vocabulary knowledge above fourth-grade level
- proliferation of "fillers" instead of substantive words ("You know, like, the thing, well, like the thing he did for his, you know, project . . .")
- difficulty hearing differences between sounds in words and getting them in order; this shows up in difficulty pronouncing and reading "long" words and in spelling
- faltering comprehension of more difficult reading material
- trouble understanding longer sentences, embedded clauses, more advanced grammatical structures in upper grades
- difficulty switching from colloquial language to written form

Not surprisingly, different concerns surface at different grade levels. Preschoolers are reported to have more trouble sitting still and listening to stories or short discussion than did children of previous decades, but they are often seen as having larger vocabularies ("Especially for clinical terms concerned with sex, reproduction, and disease," wryly commented one teacher) and a broader store of general information. Many little children appear to be "advanced" because they have adopted a veneer of sophistication from television.

In primary grades, most language demands can be handled by the brain's basic systems, which usually develop with any amount of normal input. Thus, although attention problems are always mentioned, language problems may not be specifically identified until about fourth grade, when the higher-level aspects—those that depend more

on enriched experience—are called on. At this point, the neural leg-
acy of contemporary culture creates an increasing mismatch between
students' language abilities and schools' expectations. Problems with
language understanding and usage become increasingly evident as
children move into grades that have traditionally demanded higher-
level thinking and organizational skills, comprehension of harder
books, and increased amounts of writing. Reading test scores start to
plummet.

As students move into middle school, teachers express greater concern about listening skills, vocabulary knowledge, reading comprehension, and the ability to use language to express ideas effectively.
Unless students read a lot on their own, their vocabulary growth
slows down somewhere near the fourth-grade level—approximately
the level of media language. Many schools try to remedy the deficit
by making kids memorize vocabulary lists, but students rapidly forget
words they rarely read, hear, or use in normal conversation. With
harder reading selections, comprehension problems also arise as children find the unfamiliar forests of more complicated texts (e.g., essays, poetry, literature with involved plots, plays) very bewildering
places indeed.

In high school, language difficulties continue to show up in subtle
problems with: planning, sequencing, and organizing ideas; classifying; grasping the fine distinctions between concepts; reasoning about
cause and effect (if A, then B; because X, then Y); understanding
relationships of ideas in their reading; reasoning in math and science;
expressing ideas accurately and directly; reflecting internally on their
own thinking, and even managing their own behavior.

Several university professors have recently told me they cannot
believe the difficulties students nowadays have with analytic thinking. For example, a well-known psychology teacher at a major university in Florida said, "It's a source of amazement to me how many
students can't link ideas together; they can't follow one idea logically
with another. I have older adult students and younger undergradu-
ates in my classes, and it's the younger ones I'm having more trouble
with. I really think it's because they have such poor verbal skills. If
you don't have a good grasp of the language, you have no tools to
think with. You haven't formed the appropriate categories verbally to
combine ideas. Language changes the way your brain sets up the
categories it works with. For these students the whole thought process just isn't there; the linkages between ideas that language provides are missing."

Wide variations in abilities to use language as a tool for thinking are a natural part of the human condition. There will always be students—even bright and talented ones—whose brains do not bend easily around analytic and logical uses of language. Children differ genetically in their aptitude for language learning, and it is clearly absurd to expect equal facility from everyone with any particular set of mental tools. The concern I hear expressed over and over is not that a few students are faltering, but that *many* are. These observations show a startlingly similar pattern at every level of the socioeconomic scale, with some of the most dramatic changes in children's language abilities reported by teachers at the country's most selective private schools.

Voices From Abroad

Is the problem unique to the United States? Apparently not, although it appears to be much worse here. One infant school teacher from Coventry, England, said, "We thought it wouldn't happen in England, but it is happening here, too. Children's language skills are suffering along with their ability to stop and think. The speed of life, what they're getting from T.V.—that lovely, typically British thing of standing and staring, reflecting, is being eroded."

"It's beginning—something we were trying to avoid for many a year," lamented a Dublin Montessori consultant. "Children are not speaking properly because they're not hearing words pronounced slowly. T.V. is too fast. Spelling is declining because they don't hear the sounds. If you hear two teenagers speaking, they can understand each other but we can't understand them. It's like a pidgin English—a shortened version of the real words. Teachers have to slow down far more than they ever did before. We're dealing with a different type of child. Children who are institutionalized from day one don't have the same rich language environment as those at home with only one or two adults."

Said a college professor from London, "It's very scary. I see it in the students at the college—they don't seem to be able to translate their thoughts from head to paper. We didn't used to see this, and it seems to be getting worse."

Educators in France have similar issues on their minds. The principal of a middle school (*college*) in southwestern France, said of his students, "Their capacities for listening have declined. Proper language use is poorly known; they don't understand the nuances of language. They write and spell very badly, and their grammar—it's horrible! They have smaller vocabularies and they chatter instead of reflecting before they talk. It takes them five or six sentences to say what they mean. One finds it even in the best students, deficits in attention and expression. I tell the teachers, we have to accept these children where they are; with all the distractions—music, television— society has changed."

As we concluded our interview, my French host remarked, "I have a daughter who is considered a good student now, but twenty years ago—she would not have been so good."

The Legacy of "McLanguage"

Observers tend to blame the schools for lack of training in the fine points of language and grammar. London columnist Brian Dunning, in a recent article entitled "Doesn't Anybody Here Talk English Any More?" decried a new generation in Britain "which runs a finger under words of more than one syllable," and students who, when shown a noun or a verb, will "blink like rabbits confronted with Wittgenstein."[20]

Unfortunately, when children come to school with a deficient base for higher-order language and reasoning skills, schools cannot simply "cure" the problem by waving a magic grammar or spelling book! One nationally noted learning specialist has some strong feelings about the real causes of the current problem.

"I call the trend in kids' talk today 'McLanguage,' " declares Priscilla Vail, author of *Clear and Lively Writing*[21] and *Smart Kids with School Problems*.[22] "It's verbal fast food made up of inflection, gesture, and condensation." Vail's consultations on bright children's learning problems in both public and private schools have convinced her that societal changes are overwhelming the schools with students who need remedial language training. Most learning disabilities are related to underlying language problems, yet increasing numbers of youngsters are permitted to be "linguistically malnourished," she says. The most basic problem is *they don't learn to listen analytically*.

"For one thing," Vail explains, "children can't spell because they are unaccustomed to separating out sounds and putting them in order—their listening experience has ill-prepared them to listen for fine differences in sounds or in meaning."

Good spelling, of course, also comes from seeing words in print (i.e., lots of reading). Research shows that a major factor contributing to both poor reading and poor spelling, however, is not lack of visual skill, but rather poor critical listening abilities. One typical study that compared good and poor readers showed that differences in a skill called "phonological awareness" was highly related to reading ability in both elementary school children and adults. "Phonological awareness" is the ability not only to hear the sounds in words but also to analyze their order. For example, the child is asked to: "Say 'smile' without the *s*"; move different-colored blocks to show the order of sounds in words (e.g., b-a-t, t-a-b); listen to a word and tell whether it is long like "bicycle" or short like "bike." Good readers (and good spellers, as well) are strikingly better at this type of listening than are poor readers, even when both groups have similar IQ scores.[23] Because these skills are accomplished in a special part of the *left hemisphere* of most people's brains, some researchers speculate that this complex of skills is related to inherited differences in brain structure, but studies have clearly shown that early exposure and practice also have a great deal to do with the way these areas develop. Today's children are exposed to lots of sound, but that is exactly what concerns Vail. "I am particularly worried about the kids who conform to the listening patterns of pop music," she says. "Their brains are being trained to listen uncritically to lyrics that are limited to repetitive syllables or short phrases that hardly sound like English. The beat overrides the melody, and there is no beginning, no middle, and no end. That is a poor training ground for understanding language!"

Interestingly enough, the parts of the brain that respond to this sort of musical immersion are in the *right hemisphere*, opposite from the areas that make people good at "phonological awareness." When we see young children encase their minds in stereo headphones, we should wonder what synapses are being strengthened—and at what cost?

Vail agrees, too, that children fail to develop skills they will need in school because conversation is suffering in homes. A veteran working mother of four, now a grandmother, she sympathizes with weary adults, but at the same time she worries about their children. "When you're tired, the last thing you want to do is have a long conversation with someone who's not on your level," she sighs. "Many children today, even in the 'best' homes, never hear rich, elaborated sentences. And when parents do talk with their kids, they do it with short sentences and a lot of gestures. These parents may have good language skills, but this is a culture of immediate gratification. We want instant information through eyes as well as ears, but academic learning requires the thoughtful mediation of language and the *delay of working through print*. We're giving kids competing messages when we raise them without any models of slow, thoughtful language and then expect them to listen to the teacher and understand what they read."

Whatever Happened to Storytelling?

Many children today are also missing out on a rich "oral tradition," in English or another language, that can enhance written language or stand by itself in a culture where writing is not generally used to communicate ideas. Although writing—and the kind of talking and thinking that go along with it—promotes the development of school-like ways of reasoning, the arts of storytelling, oral history, and conversation have their own special niche in developing reflective thought, memory, and attention. We will see in later chapters what an absence of good listening experiences may be doing, not only to attention spans, but to reading comprehension for today's students. For now, let us move on to explore some of the specific ways in which different forms of language usage may affect the modes of thinking—and the brains—that children take to school with them.

Sagging Syntax, Sloppy Semantics, and Fuzzy Thinking

If your language did not include the words *red, pink,* and *coral,* would your mind work the same way as it does now when you look at a geranium? How accurately can you compare democracy, communism, and socialism without using words? Without language, how would you go about planning and communicating the details of a party three months in advance?

No one denies that the way people use language is braided together tightly with the way they think. But exactly how much language actually shapes thought, and vice versa, is an old argument.

LANGUAGE AND THOUGHT

Do Different Languages Make People Think Differently?

One unresolved issue concerns whether speaking different types of languages makes people not only think differently about the world but also perceive things differently.[1,2] Some researchers have suggested, for example, that speakers of a language that includes in its vocabulary only a few color names (corresponding, perhaps, to shades of light and dark rather than hue) would perceive only the color values for which they had words. It is hard to grapple with the notion that in their minds geraniums might look quite different. According to this idea, Arctic Inuits who have several hundred words for different types of snow could be expected to reason more precisely about snow than members of cultures with fewer terms—and possibly, fewer shades of meaning.

Precision of semantic meaning can apply to verbs, adjectives, and adverbs as well as nouns (e.g., What is the difference between *hurl* and *toss*, or between *exquisite* and *beautiful*?). Language users who have these types of distinctions available may have mental access to more analytic forms of thinking than those whose lexicon is restricted to more general words (e.g., *throw*, or *pretty*).

The main danger of this position is setting up some types of language—and the accompanying thought—as arbitrarily "better" than others. Many linguists now view "good" reasoning as that which works best for the needs of the culture in which it takes place, and the best linguistic training as that which readies children's brains for the specific types of thinking valued and needed in their society. A child in a society primarily involved in food gathering, hunting, or navigation, for example, might never be required to write an analytic essay or research paper; one raised in a culture of artisans, where aesthetic beauty is of primary value, might not be encouraged to reason algebraically and therefore would not need the "language" of algebraic equations.[3,4]

In our Western culture, where we claim to value abstract, analytic reasoning, children are expected to be prepared to think accordingly. These higher-level abilities are not automatically built into the brain. They come only from specific kinds of language and educational experience that prod synapses into patterns we deem "more intelligent."

Many scientists have speculated about how language specifically affects intelligence. Alexander Luria, a renowned neuropsychologist who was fascinated by the workings of growing brains, insisted that language physically builds the brain's higher-reasoning centers. He claimed that, without language, humans would not have developed abstract, categorical thinking:[5]

> Language, in the course of social history, became the decisive instrument which helped humans transcend the boundaries of sensory experience, assign symbols, and formulate certain generalizations and categories. When the child names something, pronouncing, for example, "that is a steam engine," he begins to *understand* that in the movement of the machine named, steam plays a role and that it moves other objects. In mastering words and using them the child *analyses and synthesizes* the phenomena of the external world, using not only

his personal experience but the experience of mankind. He *classifies* objects, he begins to *perceive them differently* and with this to *remember them differently* [italics added].[6]

David Premack of the Department of Psychology at the University of Pennsylvania, wondering if language could change the reasoning skills of animals, taught a form of language to chimpanzees to see if it would improve their scores on IQ-type tests that were oriented toward verbal meaning. Although chimpanzees cannot speak, Premack taught them to communicate by arranging plastic chips standing for words into simple grammatical statements (e.g., "Give Suzie banana."). He then retested their ability to reason in certain ways and also tested human children on the same types of tasks. We should all be happy to learn that even educated apes are not about to take over the world, since Premack clearly showed that human children, even before they learn language, think more incisively than chimps do. Nevertheless, these experiments showed with equal clarity that language symbols did change the chimps' abilities to reason. Simply teaching them words for the concepts "same" and "different" enabled them for the first time to see this distinction among categories of objects and thus pass more of the tests.[7]

Language is, of course, not the sole route to thought. Chimps—and people—can reason nonverbally, and a lively human mental life also uses visual imagery and nonverbal symbols to interpret and remember experience. Painters, sculptors, and architects do not rely heavily on language to develop their artistic ideas. Likewise, highly abstract mathematical reasoning may ultimately call on systems in the brain other than, or in addition to, those used for language processing, even though the learner must master the basic language of adding, subtracting, multiplying, and dividing.

Despite the obvious importance of nonverbal forms of intelligence, there is as yet no substitute for language, used in tandem with visual reasoning, to hone precision of expression and analysis. In the schools to which we consign youngsters for so many hours of their lives, written language is the coin of the realm. Allowing children to enter with shallow linguistic resources puts them in intellectual jeopardy and creates dangerous tensions within education.

Syntax: The Grammar of Relationships

The grammar of language is one of the main ways by which people reason about relationships. When I speak of grammar, or "syntax," I am not talking about the rules we learned in school, but rather about the ones we figured out for ourselves, starting before age two. Putting the verb before the object ("Get cookie") and adding s for more than one are simple examples.

This ability to induce rules, for which the human brain is noted, is probably the reason basic syntactic abilities are said to be "experience expectant"; we aren't born with noun and verb rules clinging to synapses but rather with an innate ability to figure out categories and apply principles that let us generalize about the regularities in any domain of experience.[8] If a young child becomes frightened by a dog, for example, he may start to categorize all dogs as mean until he broadens his rule system to include friendly as well as unfriendly ones. When he notices that adding s makes more than one, he will apply this rule to all words ("mouses") until he broadens that system. The basic drive to make this kind of sense out of the world has doubtless helped keep our species alive.

Learning such rules takes many individual experiences before the general principle is finally internalized. Thus, children who are not frequently exposed to "literate language" may never internalize understanding of this kind of discourse, either its vocabulary or its grammatical rules. Children who do not have the sound of more complex language "in their gut" have particular problems understanding the subtle distinctions in meaning that are carried by abstract "little words" (or, if, would, might, did), and word endings ("I think" vs. "I am thinking"). The order of words in a sentence also conveys many important conceptual relationships that become increasingly important for clear thinking, reading, and writing after primary grades.[9]

Her father fed her dog the biscuits vs.

Her father fed her the dog biscuits.

Students not attuned to processing fine distinctions in the sequence of words get all mixed up by sentences like this, whether they hear or read them. Another frequent stumbling block is the grammar of *time sequence* and *cause and effect*:

Before John ate dinner, he played ball.

Because the last train had left, he stayed all night.

Still other confusing but common constructions are *embedded information*:

The bill vetoed by the President . . .

and *passive voice*:

. . . was not the one that had been recommended by our committee.

Understanding *tense* markers (when did the veto take place: before or after the recommendation?) also requires syntactic ability.

"These fine points of language take the person beyond the threshold of the visual world," says Priscilla Vail. "Without language, we're limited to our visual horizon; language allows children to move beyond that hidden machinery of cause and effect. If parents want their kids to do well in school or get into a good college, they have to start with language. A rich vocabulary is the foundation, but the ability to describe, compare, and categorize with language is what leads to our ability to think in analogy—that's the highest level, and it's also what is tested on the SATs!"

How the Brain Handles Grammar

In terms of what is happening to children's brains, it is important to understand that the orderly, grammatic, *syntactic* details of a language, its sounds, and probably the fine-grained distinctions in word meaning, are handled by the left hemisphere of the cortex in most right-handed people. More general understanding of word meaning, gesture, and interpretation of visual communication (e.g., facial expressions) is mainly directed for most of us by the less analytic right hemisphere.[10] In the sentence "The dog was chased by the cat," for example, right hemisphere semantic systems probably connect the words (e.g., *cat*, *dog*, and *chase*) with mental pictures and/or networks of previous associations. In order to understand the details of what happened (Who did the chasing? Is the time now, yesterday, or tomorrow?), we must use the left hemisphere. When I hear students' conversation these days, I often wonder if both sides are getting sufficient exercise!

Even verbal fluency, per se, does not signify full development of left-hemisphere language systems. Sometimes seemingly precocious vocabulary development and pseudosophistication fool adults who believe that a child who chatters a lot must have good language development. Not true! Some of the hardest learning problems to treat are those of kids who talk on and on but have trouble getting to the point. They have a large set of general associations, but they have big trouble synthesizing them and getting the details in order. Their words ride around their thoughts like Indians circling a wagon train, but they never get around to the attack. Many times, because these students also have trouble talking to themselves about what they're thinking, they don't even know what their point—or their question—is! "You know . . ." substitutes for verbal—and mental—precision; it is up to the listener to fill in the blanks. This problem is clinically classified as a form of "language disability," but it seems to be increasingly evident among "normal" students in today's "McLanguage" environments.

Since it has long been recognized that problems with verbal precision can result from deficits in the left hemisphere, language therapists speculate among themselves about how much the overwhelming visual presence of television and video may be exacerbating the problem by neglecting left-hemisphere language areas. In the next chapter and in our discussion of television, we will look more critically at this possibility.

Slipping syntax leads to fuzzy thought. Difficulties using grammatical language to identify relationships between ideas may account for many of the problems in logical thinking, science, and math that are becoming so evident in our high schools. Many problems with thinking go unrecognized until students must formulate ideas clearly enough to put them down on paper. In observing classrooms, I have commonly seen students "get by" in class discussions with short, superficial answers or a lot of gestures and verbal circling of the topic ("You know"—and the teacher does, so the kid is off the hook). The teacher is usually unaware that the class is responding at a conversational, not an analytic, level. When he assigns an in-class writing assignment, however, their cover is blown.

"These kids can't think!" wails the teacher.

Writing: The Last Straw

Writing is the road test for language as a vehicle of thought. An alarming number of students coming off our linguistic assembly lines are failing it. "Very few of our students can write well," states Archie E. Lapointe, executive director of the National Assessment of Educational Progress. "Most students, majority and minority alike, are unable to write adequately except in response to the simplest of tasks."[11]

Well-reasoned and well-organized writing proceeds from a mind trained to use words analytically. No matter how good, how creative, or how worthy a student's ideas, their effectiveness is constrained by the language in which they are wrapped.

Teachers are more discouraged by the quality of students' writing than by anything else except their ability to listen well. Why is writing so much more difficult than other language tasks? First of all, it demands a firm base of oral language skill. Students who have not learned to line up words effectively when they speak are not going to be able to do so on paper. Secondly, good written language is quite different from colloquial "talk written down." Awareness of its sound comes only from extensive listening to and/or reading quality prose and poetry. Moreover, expressing an idea on paper demands that the writer remove language from the here and now; gestures and "you know" 's just don't work!

Writing allows us to give our ideas a life of their own apart from the immediacy of speech, but this more abstract approach requires use of more complex syntax to link ideas together. Otherwise we get what I call "Dick and Jane" prose ("See Spot. See Spot run."). The most difficult aspect of writing clearly, however, is that it demands the ability to organize thought.

A teacher who was trying to help her second graders learn to write fluently came to me for advice about an otherwise good student who was having terrible trouble producing even a simple story. Her handwriting was good, she could copy anything quite easily, and when answering questions raised by the teacher she used age-appropriate language. When she tried to write anything original, however, she and the paper remained equally blank.

We decided that the teacher would offer to act as "secretary" and ask the little girl simply to *tell* her a story. Here is a sample from the child's first narrative:

And then she was . . . Dan . . . she was . . . Danny was probably wondering what Tanya was thinking.
'Cause he was wondering like . . . Tanya was, um, smiling . . . she was probably thinking and . . .
Danny was thinking what . . . was wondering what Tanya was thinking.

No wonder this child can't get ideas down on paper! She has not yet learned to arrange them in her mind.

When students in second grade show such difficulties, we expect to work with them to correct the problem. Now, however, university professors are starting to complain that they must also teach writing and thinking skills they used to take for granted. A Harvard professor recently began sending thank-you letters to the high schools of his students who can write clearly and intelligently.

"As I note the increasing roughness in student prose, I find myself heartened by rare examples such as the one presented by Miss X," he wrote in one. Later, in a telephone interview, he explained, "I think there's a definite decline in the quality of student writing. There's something fuzzy there; it's actually an imprecision of language reaching into a fuzziness of thought. They're beginning to lose the concept of words like *better*, so they think of *good* and *best*, or *tall* instead of *tallest.* What is interesting to me is how frequently I cannot get my students to write down what they mean. I spend a lot of time with them on their writing—far more than I think I should have to at a college like this. They simply can't do many of the things that were fundamental fifteen years ago when I started here."

The Grammar of Mathematics

Most people, even math teachers, are not aware that problems with language can cause difficulties in mathematical reasoning. The verbal tools that clarify relationships in reading and writing do the same job in math, and studies of children with exceptional mathematical talents often reveal similarly high verbal skills.[12] On the flip side, even bright hearing-impaired children are likely to have problems with math beyond computation, possibly because they have not had experience with the necessarily precise, sequential uses of language.

Some words important in beginning math are those that tell about the direction in which the numbers and the thinking go: (e.g., *before, after, into, above, under, away, over*); causation (e.g., *if:then, because*); or actions (e.g., *add, multiply*). The terms *borrowing from, dividing into,* or *multiplying by* are only a few examples that often confuse children who have trouble attaching the sequence of the language meaning to the numerals on the page. Advanced math courses such as algebra demand special skills in logical, sequential reasoning that often come wrapped in a form of syntax.

"Paying attention to words can help students cope with numbers," declares Joan Countryman, a nationally known math teacher who is working on a book called *Writing to Learn Mathematics*. She has found that having students write about problems helps them with the kind of logical thinking they need to come up with good solutions. Improving their language skills is her first step in improving mathematical reasoning.

Other teachers have hit upon this idea out of desperation. One algebra teacher from Tennessee, who described today's crop of students as "terrible problem solvers," commented, "I think the lack of understanding of English is the problem. I have to go through each problem step by step, underline the subject, the verb; we look for the verb that shows what equals what, then we take the prepositional phrases and analyze them. If we have a problem with a statement like 'It took John two hours longer to go the same distance,' they have to understand the language before they can get a picture in their mind about what is happening. Until then, there is no way they can really understand what kind of an equation is needed."

In her book *Twice as Less*, Eleanor Wilson Orr describes her own awakening to the ways in which use of prepositions, conjunctions, and relative pronouns can affect students' concepts of quantitative relationships. Working with students who spoke nonstandard English, she became convinced that their "reasoning problems" were, in actuality, reflections of differences in use of the language.

> In a chemistry class a student stated that . . . the volume of a gas would be *half more than* it was. When I asked her if she meant that the volume would get larger, she said, "No, smaller." When I then explained that *half more than* would mean larger, indicating the increase with my hands, she said she meant *twice* and with her hands indicated a decrease. When I then said, "But twice means larger," . . . she said, "I guess I mean *half less than*. It always confuses me."

By initiating math and science courses that start with words as a basis for understanding, Ms. Orr is helping students improve their learning by using the "power of language as an instrument with which one can reason beyond the observable."[13]

Differences in the way children are taught to talk about numbers may even account for some of the gaps between achievement of Japanese and American children, according to two California researchers. In a new and provocative study they demonstrated that language differences make it easier for Japanese children to understand "place value," a cornerstone of math competency and one of the things teachers have a lot of trouble getting most American children to understand. The reason for the difference, they say, may be that, unlike English, many Asian languages have spoken words for numbers that systematically describe their written relationship to ten. For example, in Japanese, *11, 12,* and *20* are spoken as "ten-one," "ten-two," and "two-ten(s)," much less confusing for a child than the terms *eleven, twelve,* and *twenty,* which do not easily translate into any linear numerical equivalent. Many American youngsters mix up such numbers as *seventeen* and *seventy;* Japanese children can understand them more easily because *17* is spoken as "ten-seven" and *70* as "seven-ten(s)."

In a study of forty-eight high-achieving first-grade students in both countries, these researchers showed dramatic differences in their ability to represent numbers according to place value, giving the Japanese a real leg up on more complex computation and reasoning.

Whereas American teachers labor mightily teaching place value for addition and subtraction in second grade, Japanese students at the same level master it handily and move on to multiplication. While one variable clearly cannot account for all differences, additional research on the way language shapes mathematical thinking may show other important variations.[14]

Why Aren't Children Learning Grammar?

The solution to all these problems seems to be simple. The schools should teach grammar. When schools attempt to teach "grammar" as they currently define it, however, they try to paste labels (e.g., "adverb," "clause") and rules ("adverbs modify verbs, adjectives, and other adverbs") on a system that needs to be embedded in the brain in a fundamentally different way. Without the foundations, beating "grammar" rules into brains is difficult; sometimes it seems impossible.

Evidently, little grammar is learned from watching television. Children may gain some vocabulary knowledge, but no one has shown that they pick up syntactic forms. Studies of preschoolers who watched *Sesame Street* showed that they learned to recognize more words than children who had not viewed the program (the tests merely asked them to point to pictures representing words, not to say anything), but no syntactic gains were noted. In another study, experimenters showed Dutch children TV programs in German in an effort to get them to learn German. They did not.

Several interesting studies have shown that TV was an equally poor language coach for normally hearing children raised by deaf parents. In one example, two normally hearing brothers were cared for at home only by their deaf mother until soon after the eldest was enrolled in nursery school. When the children were first tested at ages five and two, their only language experience had come from television and, for the elder child, brief exposure at school. His language, particularly his grammar, was peculiar and his younger brother had no language at all. Fortunately, both children were still within the sensitive period for language development, so their progress was rapid once they began to interact with other speakers. The investigators commenting on this case point out that, beyond the most basic level, *grammatical speech (and its understanding) seem to be the aspects of language acquisition most vulnerable to deprivation* and also that *children must use language in an interactional setting to* discover and learn the rules. "All these interactional aspects of communication are missing when language is heard from an indirect source. Even an indirect source that used simpler language than that used in adult speech (for example, television programs for children) would provide a poor context for language acquisition," they state.[15]

Studies of normally speaking mothers and their children confirm the importance of direct personal experience for learning these refinements of language. Although youngsters pick up basic vocabulary words and meaning quite well despite the speech style of their mothers, they miss out on higher-level grammatical abilities if their mothers fail to use them. It may not matter very much what language is being spoken, as long as the brain learns to process *some* well-developed system of grammar.

Some interesting recent studies of deaf persons who learned American Sign Language (ASL), which has a complete set of grammatical rules comparable to those of spoken English, have also proven that there are special slots in the developmental schedule for mastery of more complex syntax and for the little words and endings that carry subtle meanings (e.g., the differences between saying "A teacher is in the room." and "The teacher is in the room."). Dr. Elissa Newport tested deaf adults who had first been exposed to ASL at different ages: at birth, between four and six years, or after age eleven. She became a believer in sensitive periods for the development of syntax when she discovered significant differences in the subjects' proficiency depending on the time of their first exposure to ASL—even though these people had all come from similar school and environmental backgrounds and were between fifty and seventy years old at the time of the study. After age eleven, it appeared, their brains had lost the ability to master more complex forms of syntax. They made the same types of errors that show up increasingly in the writing of today's schoolchildren.[16]

Clearly, to be well prepared for reading, writing, listening, and speaking, *children need to interact with increasingly advanced language during the years of childhood.* But consider briefly the current situation:

- Busy schedules or uninterested caretakers militate against oral reading and thoughtful dinner-table conversation. Much of the "talk" that does take place, even in concerned families, may center around the mechanics of the moment (e.g., "Get your hat and mittens." "When does your shift at Burger King end tonight?" "Finish your homework or no TV.").
- The quality of language models in the media is highly variable.

Even if the child chooses programs with more complex language, it may be of little use without an adult around to encourage verbal response.

· Most elementary-level children read textbooks that contain a thin, watered-down syntactic gruel.

· Time and motivation for reading are increasingly usurped by television and other nonliterary demands such as extra-curricular activities, computer practice, or drill-type homework.

Is it reasonable to expect that an English teacher can patch up all the holes—and still do a thorough job of teaching literature, expository writing, spelling, public speaking, poetry writing, reading comprehension, etc.? When kids arrive in middle and high school, we assume they should be able to ask good questions and write a grammatically coherent essay—but most of them cannot. We also expect them to understand the books that have always been staples of the curriculum—but whose syntax sounds to them like a foreign language!

Tom could not get away from it. Every reference to the murder sent a shudder to his heart, for his troubled conscience and fears almost persuaded him that these remarks were put forth in his hearing as "feelers"; he did not see how he could be suspected of knowing anything about the murder, but still he could not be comfortable in the midst of this gossip.

—*Tom Sawyer*

Unless such literature is *carefully taught* by a skilled teacher who knows how to make the text come alive and who is able to make the huge time commitment to help students with unfamiliar vocabulary, grammar, and voice, I can tell you what many kids do—they simply don't read it. Instead, they continue to practice—and to embed in their brains—language that some linguists refer to quite descriptively as "primitive." Herein lies one of the major sources of tension between students and the curriculum.

"RESTRICTED CODES" AND THE LOSS OF THE ANALYTIC ATTITUDE

Linguists argue over whether calling a language "primitive" is either fair or accurate, but most agree that languages differ in complexity. Consider this sentence which most adult English speakers can easily understand:

The woman who lives next door brought the flowers that are on the table.

Some languages, however, can't get all these thoughts into one sentence because they lack devices to subordinate information. Speakers of such a language are limited to simpler propositions:

> *A woman brought the flowers.*
> *They are on the table.*
> *She lives next door.*[17]

As another example, compare this description of a cause-effect relationship:

The meeting was not productive. The chairman was frustrated. The chairman appointed a new committee.

with this one:

Because the meeting had been unproductive, the frustrated chairman appointed a new committee.

In the first example, the absence of complex syntax forces us to infer why the chairman changed the committee and also obscures the time sequence of the events. Forms of language that contain these more complex grammatical devices are called *elaborated codes*. Those conveying ideas without such complex grammatical structures are called *restricted codes* and are the ones viewed as more "primitive." They are most useful when one speaker can see another's gestures and already knows the details of the message. "The expressions used by many peoples standing at a primitive level can be understood only if the concrete situation is known and if their gestures are observed," says Luria.[18] The simple, visual content of many television programs lends itself particularly well to this type of talk.

According to Dr. Paul Kay of the Department of Anthropology at UCLA, elaborated codes can be distinguished by their longer sentences and more varied and explicit vocabulary. They have more expressions for logical connections (e.g., *thus, therefore, moreover, because, if, since, nevertheless*). Restricted codes, on the other hand, are much more immediate, requiring the listener to fill in the gaps that the speaker has not made explicit (e.g., placing one's own interpretation on devices such as "You know").

Both types of speech obviously have their uses in everyday life. If you had to deliver a lecture at a neighboring university, you would be well advised to stick to elaborated codes, but if you used them when making love to your spouse, they might not be too appropriate. The trick is to be able to "code-switch" and use the best kind of syntax for the situation at hand.

Elaborated and restricted codes also differ in the use of two types of words: content words and function words. *Content words* are our descriptive palette of verbs, nouns, and adjectives referring to specific things, actions, or attributes (e.g., *house, beautiful, running*). They are also called "open class" because we keep adding and subtracting new words to these categories all the time. Our new gastronomic lexicon (e.g., *quiche, sushi, pesto*) or some discarded relics (e.g., *buggy whip*) are examples of changing open-class words. Such words are used in both types of codes and are primarily handled by the right hemisphere.

On the other hand, *function words* are used in more elaborated codes. They are harder to understand because they don't stand for real things. These "little" words, word endings and prefixes, conjunctions, prepositions, auxiliary verbs, etc. (e.g., *if, but, so, did, might, un-, -ment*) develop much later in a child's speech. Also called "closed class," their usage changes only slowly over time. Function words require use of the more analytic left hemisphere.

Use of these different types of words enables different degrees of complexity in language. Sentences containing mainly content words

> *Children like to run.*
> *Children like prizes.*

are the type termed "restricted," or "primitive." Adding some function words enables expression of more complexity.

Some of the children in this group might like to run if we offered a prize.

Brain circuits for getting beyond restricted codes and using language analytically ("If you have already spent your allowance on a videotape, you may not be able to go to the movies tomorrow") do not develop automatically. One linguist who recorded mothers' conversations with their preschoolers and then measured the children's language development found that unless mothers used function words themselves, their children did not pick them up.[19]

Languages are always in the process of change. Traditionally, open-class nouns and verbs have been the ones that have changed most rapidly. Among the young, however, it appears that the closed-class and syntactic markers are fast becoming obsolete. These differences may represent the source of many of the declines observed, not only in academic achievement, but also in traditional, formal reasoning.

Who Is "Primitive"?

The words *primitive language* are loaded ones because they imply some sort of cultural judgment. Researchers who tried several years ago to apply this concept to groups of children got into trouble because they unfairly concluded that lower-class children are socialized to use only primitive, unelaborated, forms of language and are therefore incapable of learning elaborated speech and irrevocably doomed to school failure. Subsequent research has drastically modified this overgeneralization. It is true that families with less educational background are more likely to use language that is not "schoollike," and that children from homes of "lower socioeconomic status" (which is predicated on both educational and occupational levels) may have less experience than others with the types of language found in books (although this situation may be changing, as we will see in a later chapter). Few would argue with the reality that the ability to use "elaborated codes" confers a real advantage in our culture both in school and in many occupations, but assuming that all members of "lower classes" lack this tool and that all "upper classes" have it is clearly ridiculous.

Dr. Paul Kay, who is regarded as an expert in the evolution and cultural development of language, believes that issues of class and language are important but should not be overgeneralized. First of all, a more complex society has traditionally impelled all its members toward more abstract speech. In a simple "face-to-face" local community, he explains, everyone shares common experiences and can get by with simple words, short sentences, and a lot of gestures. As people become more separated, they need to develop ways of communicating about problems that are much more abstract and emotionally neutral. The more specialized we become, particularly when we begin to reason in specialized technical fields, the more we need elaborated codes. Having to put new concepts in writing, Kay believes, provides a special impetus to keep us from reaching an intellectual "dead end."

In any society, he says, some people need elaborated codes more than others. "When a society develops writing and differentiates into social classes, literate persons will usually have more occasion to speak explicitly and will tend to develop a speech style more attuned to explicit, technical, context-independent messages." *But speech that sounds elaborate does not necessarily signify higher class or intellectual quality.*

A businessman recently handed me a letter that he says typifies much language usage in today's business world. It begins: "Reference is made to the above automobile which was purchased at your dealership on November 30, 1988." For two closely typed pages, the author attempts to sound important while he "explains" a simple problem of replacing a fuel pump. Eventually we reach his concluding statement: "I request your explanation in writing that all of the pumps are this way or, however you phrased it, as you again refused replacing this pump saying it was replaced once already." This man seems to believe he knows what he is thinking, but his overelaborate language suggests only confusion.

Look out, warns Kay, for the difference between "speech that is 'better' only in the silly snobbish sense and speech that is in some real sense more effective, which communicates the speaker's message more explicitly and economically." "Bureaucratese," for example, is a "misguided attempt to achieve a high-sounding style" based on someone's confusion about what educated speech really sounds like!

Columnist Russell Baker recently engaged in a bit of elaboration himself when he lambasted some political language: "whiny, oily, sneaky, deceptive words posing as the soul of uptown refinement and civilized polysyllabic politeness." Baker thinks that the public should rise up and protest the meaningless and deadening "cotton wool" that constitutes American political discourse.[20] But how will the upcoming generation know the difference? When teachers tell me that their students seem more inclined to mouth gobbledygook than effective and economical language, I am not terribly surprised. They are, after all, saturated with models of pretension masquerading as precision.

Code-Switching: From "Teenage" to English

To think and express themselves clearly, reason and write well, and understand what middle and high schools expect them to read, children need to learn the codes of formal education. Yet, the communication style of many adolescents, even when they are trying to cope with academic language, is often in the "primitive" category. And because they seem to be less able to "code-switch," they are even more at odds with the adult world than teens of previous eras.

It is nothing new for teenagers to talk differently in English class than when hanging out in the cafeteria. The itchy autonomy of adolescence requires its own lexicon. Yet, in order to adapt to school demands, students must be able to change languages when they cross the border.

Until recently, children growing up could hardly avoid exposure to elaborated codes. In the media, most characters at least tried to talk like grown-ups, and families sat together and discussed what they saw on the news. Time was spent in talking on other occasions, as well. "Kids used to have to be able to code-switch to talk to their grandparents," commented one linguist. "But the grandparents aren't around the house anymore, and if the parents are home, they seem more willing to switch to the kids' form of talk than to try and force the issue."

Now, for a quantity of hours that exceeds that spent in school, even preadolescents are isolated in their own culture. TV and video talk (if they do at all) either in the teens' own language or in the increasingly agrammatical obfuscations of Madison Avenue. With a few notable exceptions, programs rely heavily on picture, gesture, music, and color to get much of the message across. Who needs "talk" containing long clauses, subordinated ideas, and connectives such as "meanwhile," "however," "nevertheless"? Emotionally charged words, not syntax, carry the news. Careful listening becomes irrelevant. Reasoning defers to the surge of immediacy; language use focuses on the literal, the here and now.

Even "literary" models for teenagers are beginning to emphasize the rift with adult culture and its language. In a recent interview, the twenty-five-year-old editor of a new magazine for teenage girls attempted to describe her mission: "Other magazines have, like, a stereotypical or idealized vision of teenagers," she said. "Maybe what parents or teachers would like. Not really what teenagers are about, you know."[21]

School is a foreign country! "It's like, well, you know" does not fly on essay exams. Untrained neural circuits rebel as lectures get longer. Increasingly, students tune out when the teacher talks, avoid literature whenever possible, work silently at their desks or with computer programs, and wait for lunchtime when they can have a "conversation" that makes sense to them.

Should it be any surprise that when they get to the syntax of Mark

Twain, the analytic reasoning of math and science textbooks, or the abstract organization needed to write clearly about something not personal or present, they are lost? Their brains have been molded around language, culture, and thought that are alien, even antagonistic, to those of the school.

Language Changes Brains

"For heaven's sakes, don't say that kids are becoming more right-brained!" pleaded a well-known neuropsychologist when I initially discussed this book with her. "There's been so much garbage published about the hemispheres."

She is right. Although research about the two sides of the cerebral cortex sheds considerable light on different ways in which people learn, it has frequently been oversimplified—mainly by the notion that people are either "right-brained" or "left-brained." Yes, the two halves of the brain have different modes of responding to experience. Yes, individual people have different ways of using them. Yes, many of our emotional, intellectual, and social differences are related to their intricate balance. But only major surgery can make anyone "right-" or "left-brained."

HALF-BRAINED? WHOLE-BRAINED?[1]

When parents come to me to explain that their child isn't getting along well in her (left-brained) school because she is so right-brained, I hasten to remind them that, like all of us, their child has one fully functioning brain with a right and a left half—unless, of course, she has a large scar in her scalp.

On the other hand, particular aspects of a child's environment may alter the relative power of these two sides—and the abilities that go along with them. Learning a language appears to cause some of the most significant changes. The issue of which language and/or dialect is learned is probably much less important than the extent to which refinements of syntax and meaning are mastered. The brain seems to change most dramatically in response to the first language acquired; second-language learning may well be handled by somewhat different areas. So far, neuropsychological research on second-language learning has not come up with any clear-cut explanations.

It appears, once a child has one type of grammatical speech under her belt (actually, under her scalp), the brain is primed to master others more easily at any time during the life span.[2] For this reason, teachers of foreign languages should look warily at children with inadequate mastery of their mother tongues and/or dialects, whatever they may be. How much of students' declining attention to foreign-language study can be attributed to brains that have never been primed by an internal feeling for grammatical relationships is anyone's guess. It goes without saying that parents hiring non-native-speaking caregivers should evaluate their overall linguistic proficiency along with other qualities.

In order to understand how language learning affects the hemispheres and to speculate about what may be happening to the brains of today's youngsters, it is necessary to review the functions of the two sides of the cortex.

The Well-Balanced Mind

So-called right- or left-brained thinking actually fluctuates on a continuum between these two extremes:

Linear, Analytic, Sequential (Left)

vs.

Holistic, Global, Simultaneous (Right)

The left hemisphere works by splitting up, analyzing, and arranging things in an orderly sequence. Because sounds, words, and the grammar of sentences require this type of arrangement, the left hemisphere is specialized in most people, probably from before birth, for speech and several other aspects of language processing.[3] In contrast, the right hemisphere is used to give us the "big picture" or *gestalt* of a situation. It cannot deal with sequences and fine details (e.g., grammar, word endings, order of sounds, fine motor movements required for writing) or fine-grained listening, but its holistic, visual abilities make it well adapted for many artistic pursuits. This does not mean that English teachers are "left brained" or that artists are "right brained." It may, however, mean that their brains find certain modes of processing more comfortable, so they tend to approach certain types of information with a preferred "style" for learning—more holistic or more analytical. Nor does it mean that language, per se, is *located* within the left hemisphere and artistic ability in the right.

All thinking, even language processing, calls upon both hemispheres at the same time. The trick, in a well-functioning brain, is to mix and match the abilities of the two hemispheres so that the most adaptive processing "style" is brought to bear on any learning situation. Since the hemispheres carry on continual and rapid communication over the bridge of fibers (*corpus callosum*) that connects them, their ability to interact is probably the ultimate key to higher-level reasoning of all kinds. In general, researchers currently believe:

Right Hemisphere

- responds to *novelty*
- works with wholes, not parts
- is visual, not auditory
- is associated with intuition and the ability to "size up" social situations
- in music, picks up the melody and disregards the lyrics or the sequential details of notation patterns
- is specialized for understanding the relative position of objects in space and mentally turning around three-dimensional figures (remember those items on IQ tests that showed you a funny-looking shape and then asked, "Which one of these, if upside down, would be the same as the first?"). Many video games probably call heavily on these abilities.
- in language processing, is well adapted for:
  —understanding general meaning and some aspects of word meaning (e.g., content words)
  —getting the "gist" of the speaker's intent
  —picking up the contours and melodic pattern of spoken language (prosody)
  —gesturing and "body language"
  —thinking metaphorically

Left Hemisphere

- deals with *"automatic codes"* (quick recall of specific words and letters, accurate spelling, math tables)

- analyzes and arranges details in order, e.g., time concepts, cause-and-effect relationships (first X, then Y), and the sequential patterns of small motor movements (e.g., tying shoes, forming letters with a pencil)
- is auditory rather than visual
- in music, it mediates the notation and lyrics rather than the melodic patterns
- in language processing, it mediates:
  —fine distinctions between sounds (phonology)
  —the order of sounds in words
  —the order of words and their relationships (syntax)
  —some types of word meaning (e.g., function words)
  —other aspects of language comprehension

As both hemispheres work in tandem, they constantly toss the mental ball back and forth as they deal with different aspects of a problem. Some educators have suggested children today are more "right brained" because they rely too heavily on abilities commonly associated with the right hemisphere to handle academic "balls" that should be fielded by the left. It is true that traditional school-oriented tasks such as reading, spelling, computing accurately, writing logically, and reasoning analytically depend heavily on left-hemisphere systems, but they cannot be accomplished without the help of the right. The critical question, therefore, is really not if children are "right brained," but if their environments are equipping them to use both hemispheres interactively.

"STYLES" AND STRATEGIES FOR LEARNING

Most of us have our own "style" for approaching certain types of problems, depending on the way we mobilize the different systems of the two hemispheres. These strategies may or may not be appropriate for the task at hand. For example, some people are inclined to focus on details and accuracy; this approach works well in accounting. It is not adaptive for creating a picture, designing a building, or repairing an engine, activities that are done best by visualizing the configuration of how the details fit together.

The way children deploy these different "styles" influences their success in school. Good spellers can visualize the whole shape of the word and also remember the sound of the details in order. Many poor spellers try to visualize the general outline of words rather than sequencing the details accurately, and the result is often something that looks more like abstract art than orthography. Poor readers deficient in left-hemisphere analytic/sequential processing skills may also rely too heavily on "wholes." They guess at words by their general configuration and don't analyze the order of the sounds or syllables. Language-disabled children who depend on gestures and short phrases, who have difficulty coming up with the word they want ("The um . . . you know . . . thing"), are also believed to have deficiencies in left-hemisphere language areas.

Why do different people use different strategies? Neuropsychologists believe that these different "styles" for learning come both from inherited differences in the brain and from the way a child's experiences train it to work. During development, neurons in both hemispheres must compete for synaptic sites, so the type of input growing brains receive is undoubtedly important for its final hemispheric balance. Learning that builds both analytic and holistic abilities is doubtless good for the brain, but many schools, unfortunately, focus heavily on stuffing in fragments of knowledge at the expense of more general comprehension, e.g.:

- phonics drills without meaningful reading
- repetitive pages of math "facts" lacking word problems or any connection to real objects
- memorization of lists of isolated facts, dates, names, etc.

Yet contemporary life seems to focus on more holistic and visual skills, often at the expense of language and analysis, e.g.:

- video games with lots of novelty and movement
- fast-changing scenes on TV
- music in which lyrics are secondary to the "feel" of the music
- gestural, telegraphic speech

Not only are these two types of training directly in conflict, but we must also ask if we are providing our children sufficient experience with more interactive uses of these different approaches to information. Are we showing them how to link facts and analysis to understanding by giving them interesting problems to solve inside their own heads? Are we encouraging them to make pictures in their minds as they read or listen, and allowing them plenty of time and attention for discussing what they are doing, feeling, or seeing on TV? Are today's environments encouraging the most useful hemispheric development for our society's future needs?

There is virtually no research on normal children to determine how much environments can alter hemispheric balance. Studies of several extreme cases suggest that it can be shifted rather dramatically by early experience. They also show that higher-level language systems of the left hemisphere are particularly vulnerable; with more evidence, we may discover that more complex functioning in both hemispheres and the important connections between them are also experience sensitive.

HEMISPHERES, LANGUAGE, AND PLASTICITY: UNUSUAL CASES

Altered Brains

The growing cortex is so plastic and so intent on being "whole brained" that it tries to reorganize itself even in the face of highly abnormal challenges. One such situation involves drastic surgery in infancy. It is hard to believe that several competent adults, leading normal lives today, are missing one entire half of the cortex because, as infants, they underwent a rare operation in which one hemisphere was removed because of serious disease. Naturally, physicians feared that their patients would have drastic learning problems, but to everyone's astonishment they grew up with what appeared to be quite normal learning skills. Children without a right hemisphere learned to solve visual problems; children without a left hemisphere mastered language, reading, and spelling. Extensive testing has shown that in each case the remaining hemisphere managed to take over many of the functions of the missing one. For a while it appeared as if the brain were almost totally plastic for learning abilities—as long as the injury occurred early enough, preferably in infancy, and as long as the injury was sufficiently large to impel the brain to reorganize radically.

Later studies have modified this unqualified optimism. In three individuals who have been studied most extensively, all of whom were operated on before the age of five months, it appears that total IQs are not quite as high as would otherwise be expected. Moreover, sensitive tests of language development show that the right hemisphere can compensate for injury to the left only up to a point—because it simply cannot manage complex syntax. For example, the adults missing their left hemispheres could not use and understand constructions such as passive voice, and they had difficulty judging whether complex sentences were grammatical, partially because of difficulty with function words, one of the left hemisphere's specialties.[4]

"Wild" Children

Three cases of so-called wild children, who grew up without normal human interaction, also show evidence that the ability to use and understand certain aspects of grammar develops fully only if specific parts of the brain are stimulated at the right time. In one famous case, a little girl named Genie was kept in a closet by her psychotic father until she was found at age thirteen, after the critical period for language acquisition had passed. Genie had heard almost no language, understood only a few individual words, and did not speak. Although she showed considerable right-hemisphere development, her left hemisphere seemed to be almost "dead" for some of its usual functions. Genie learned quickly, particularly skills associated with the right hemisphere (e.g., puzzles, mazes, and other signs of nonverbal intelligence). Her brain was also still adaptable enough to master some language, although this kind of learning was much more difficult for her. She developed a vocabulary of content words, but the refinements of speech, function words, and standard grammar continued to elude her. Even after eight years of extensive language therapy her sentences remained "largely agrammatic," according to her devoted therapist, Dr. Susan Curtiss. For example:

> "I like hear music ice cream truck."
> "Like kick tire Curtiss car."
> "Genie have Mama have baby grow up."

Because the neural connections for more advanced syntax were not stimulated before puberty, they appeared to have withered permanently.

In another bizarre case, which occurred in the 1880s, a boy named Kaspar was isolated in a small room from about age three until age sixteen. Although Kaspar only lived for five years after he was found, he showed every evidence of being extremely bright, making striking progress in drawing, reasoning, memory, and even gaining some competence in mathematics. He mastered enough vocabulary in German (his native language) to converse about philosophical issues, but had difficulties with syntax. Function words (e.g., conjunctions, pronouns) were a continuing problem.

A third case, also described by Dr. Curtiss, involves a thirty-year-old hearing-impaired woman named Chelsea, who is now trying to learn language for the first time. Like Genie and Kaspar, Chelsea is having a particularly hard time understanding and speaking grammatically.[5]

It is clearly impossible to compare children in such strange situations to children in more normal settings. Yet this evidence strongly suggests that the acquisition of function words and of syntax—particularly higher-level forms—depends on input to the left hemisphere during a certain time in development. Although the brain can probably master new vocabulary at almost any time of life, full development of language is, as Dr. Curtiss says, a "special talent" that we should not take for granted, even in normal children. How much stimulation is needed to keep these circuits alive? No one knows.

Plastic Hemispheres: Evidence From the Hearing Impaired

The severe deprivation of oral language input that is inevitable for hearing-impaired children drastically changes the way their hemispheres mature. The left hemisphere arrives in the world specialized to receive and respond to oral language, but the brains of hearing-impaired children who grow up without this kind of stimulation readapt themselves both structurally and functionally until their hemispheres are quite different from those of children with normal hearing.[6] Moreover, the importance of different types of input at different ages is once again shown by the fact that children who are deaf from birth use their brains quite differently than do those who lose their hearing later on.[7]

Dr. Helen Neville of the Salk Institute in San Diego is one of the foremost researchers studying brain responses of both deaf and hearing children. In several studies she has demonstrated that the auditory areas of deaf brains show characteristic changes.[8] More surprising to the scientists, these children's visual systems are altered as well. "If you're deaf from birth, with no auditory input at all, then the visual system seems to expand and take over regions of the brain that would normally process auditory information. This is another indication of the extreme plasticity in the human brain, and this occurs in a limited time period, probably the first four years," she reports.

Dr. Neville believes her research will eventually have important implications for normal children. "At the moment we can say with certainty that early language and sensory experience can dramatically alter brain development and that different inputs have the ability to make these changes only at certain times in development," she told me. "It will be really important to document precisely what these times are for specific types of input."[9]

For all children, development of language skills is tied up with social, emotional, and motivational factors, scientists emphasize. They theorize that brain responsiveness and variability during critical periods may be related to such aspects of home environment as adult models of language and hours spent watching TV.

Is Eleven Years Old Too Late?

This research also suggests real limits to our window of opportunity for helping children develop good language usage and understanding. There is, of course, a great deal of discussion among researchers about the exact parameters of sensitive periods for language development. It is obviously difficult to conduct such studies with children from "normal" environments. Recently, Dr. Roderick Simonds and Dr. Arnold Scheibel completed a study of the motor-speech area in seventeen normal brains of children aged three months to six years. They acknowledge that their limited number of subjects provide only tentative evidence but are convinced they have found evidence for a "critical window" in language development. Patterns of dendrite branching in these brains appear to have an age-related order of development which is responsive to environmental enrichment. Later-branching systems appear to be most susceptible to environmental input.[10]

Dr. Scheibel is personally convinced that interaction with adults, including language stimulation, is one of the growing brain's most important assets. "Without being melodramatic," he told me, "I think it would be very important to tell parents they are participating with the physical development of their youngsters' brains to the exact degree that they interact with them, communicate with them. Language interaction is actually building tissue in their brains—so it's also helping build youngsters' futures."[11]

It has been recognized for years that normal children who sustain brain injury, especially before age two, have a good chance of recovering most aspects of language functioning, but rehabilitation becomes much more difficult after adolescence.[12] There are probably many different sensitive periods in language development, which calls on functions of many different brain regions that mature at different times. The same experiences, before, during, or after the sensitive period, may have different effects.

Little experimental data relates to the type of degraded language exposure in a natural environment that today's children may be experiencing. Since one of my favorite jobs is teaching writing to young adolescents, I personally refuse to believe that all hope is lost when we enter the gates of puberty. It does, indeed, take a great deal of time and practice to implant "because" or "although" clauses in unfamiliar neural territory, but it can be done. Often, however, I wish that the syntactic scaffolding were a bit sturdier so that I could spend my precious instructional time in ways other than repairing participles and mending tenses.

I take considerably less pleasure in trying to teach remedial grammar to mainstream university juniors who will be language-arts teachers within two years. Evaluating the written and oral expression of some teachers currently working in the schools can be depressing, too. Who will be available to teach good oral and written expression to the next generation? Could we be witnessing the beginning of a major change in the way the human brain processes information?

LANGUISHING LEFT HEMISPHERES?

Perceptive professionals report that children in classrooms seem to be thinking and learning in increasingly more nonsequential and visual ways. Are shifting environments creating shifts in hemispheric habits? Since research offers interesting clues but no conclusions, we can only speculate on the basis of what is known:

1. Most researchers agree that the hemispheres are specialized differently at birth. What develops is the ability to recruit the most efficient and appropriate strategies for solving the problems the environment sets.
2. High-level thinking in any domain requires using the most appropriate hemispheric strategies and shifting flexibly between strategies when needed.
3. Inability to achieve coordination between hemispheres may jeopardize academic success.
4. The development of each hemisphere as well as their balance of power and their ability to communicate effectively with each other are affected by the growing child's experiences at certain times during development.
5. Higher-level language skills, particularly syntax, use of function words, and the ability to use language analytically, can be ac-

complished only by the left hemisphere and depend on specific types of input during development. These skills are integral to the elaborated codes used in traditional academic learning.

6. Language that always comes with pictures attached will produce different brain organization than that which must be processed only through the ears.

7. The experiences of children today may be predisposing them to deficits both in effective coordination between hemispheres and in higher-level linguistic and organizational skills of the left hemisphere. They may particularly lack practice in the use of left-hemisphere systems of auditory analysis and in the skills of logical, sequential reasoning.

8. The language of a culture inevitably changes, but current change is accelerated by widespread media communication. The trend toward use of less elaborated codes appears to be creating a severe mismatch between students and their schools. How successfully these skills can be taught to brains that may have passed a "sensitive period" for syntactic development is unknown, but it is presumed to take longer than if input is received during more appropriate times in development.

Even the foremost researchers in the field, such as Dr. Sandra Witelson of the Department of Psychiatry at McMaster University, admit they can only speculate about what is actually happening to growing brains. "From my review of the literature, I don't think one can completely change what the left hemisphere is predisposed to do—that is, language," Dr. Witelson told me in a telephone interview. "On the other hand, what teachers could be seeing is that children come in with some undeveloped cognitive skills because those cognitive skills, or similar ones, were not introduced or reinforced. It's possible that when a child is given a certain kind of task, he may choose to do it in an analytic or in a holistic, configurational way. They can read in a configurational way, or try to write on the basis of a visual image if they don't have the phonetic code. Then the child could experience difficulty because he's doing things in a different way, not the way the teacher may expect, and possibly not the best way to deal with English."[13]

In summary, it seems clear that a brain's organization, its proficiency with language use and understanding, and its very patterns of thinking may be physically changed to a significant degree by early language environments. By the time we have research to clarify exactly what may be happening to today's children, they will have grown up and become teachers and parents of the next generation. Will they be equipped with brains influenced more by sound and sense or by nonsense?

As we move into our next focus of concern—how children learn or don't learn to pay attention—we will see other reasons for the importance of efficient interaction between the hemispheres. It will also become apparent that the left-right distinction represents only part of the story. Other, less popularized dimensions of growing brains are equally critical to learning—and may be equally at risk.

Part Three

ATTENTION, LIFESTYLES, AND LEARNING DISABILITIES

Learning Disabilities: Neural Wiring Goes to School

"How can I teach these kids? They *can't* pay attention!" An insistent whine of complaint rises and gathers like a sinister haze over classrooms from preschool through college. Rather than serving as a warning, however, it has become a smoke screen for teachers and parents who belabor the young for failing to learn, and for politicians and professors who take potshots at the schools. While the adult community sanctimoniously bewails erosion of academic rigor and achievement, however, it perpetuates the practices that are shortening children's attention spans and rendering their brains unfit to engage in sustained verbal inquiry. Meanwhile, the schools, inundated with students who can't listen, remember, follow sequences of directions, read anything they consider "boring," or solve even elementary problems, have resorted to classifying increasing numbers of students as educationally sick.

"Learning disabilities," both formally diagnosed and unofficially suspected, are now blamed for a large proportion of learning casualties, from "underachievers" to school dropouts. The vast majority involve problems with skills of listening, language, and/or attention. Yet even "normal" students show increasing difficulty keeping their brains focused long enough to learn in traditional ways. Is something wrong with the kids? With their teachers? Or with the "fit" between the brains they bring to school and our expectations for them?

Attention, learning abilities, and learning disabilities are predicated on motivational and cognitive development in the brains of the learners. Each baby brain comes into the world uniquely fitted out for various forms of academic pursuit, but its pedagogical prognosis is largely determined by the ongoing mental traffic that trains it how to think and learn. For children, *habits of the mind soon become structures of the brain*—and they absorb their habits, either directly or indirectly—from the adult culture that surrounds them. For many, the habits of the mind that they take with them to school predispose them for trouble.

To understand the growing number of educational casualties today, we must face some often unrecognized realities about the brain-culture partnership. Particularly troublesome are some new factors that fuel the anomalous category of "learning disability," for which children are treated with educational prescriptions, and its frequent companion, "attention deficit disorder," for which many receive brain-altering drugs. Here are some questions that we need to address in these three chapters:

1. What is the real meaning of the term "learning disability" and why are there now so many in our schools?
2. Do children inherit learning problems—or are they caused by the environments in which they grow up?
3. What is an "attention deficit"? Why do increasing numbers of children seem to have them?
4. Should children receive drugs because they can't pay attention in school?
5. What are the physical foundations of attention and how can they be damaged by toxic and noisy environments or sedentary lifestyles?
6. What is the role of the home in preventing attention and learning problems?
7. What does attention have to do with our current crisis in "problem solving"?

A RISING TIDE OF DISABILITY

The problem of getting students to sit still, pay attention in class, and reflect thoughtfully on the task at hand figures prominently, along with reading difficulty, in an astonishing "epidemic" of "learning disability" in otherwise able children. Since the 1970s when the label, popularly referred to as "LD," became an accepted designation for problems not attributed to intelligence, physical, or emotional status, this loosely defined diagnostic category has grown geometrically. It now includes some children who might previously have been categorized as mentally deficient or emotionally disturbed as well as a large number who are having trouble in school for reasons that are often unclear.

Many students with specific difficulties in learning never make it into the maze of psycho-educational testing that leads to official diagnosis, but the number who do is rapidly becoming unmanageable. In the United States from 1976 to 1985, there was a 135% jump in diagnosed cases of learning disability from 796,596 to 1,868,447.[1] By 1988, Dr. Margaret C. Wang, a noted learning-disability educator, observed that up to 15,000 children nationwide per week were being referred for assessment. She warned that a "second system" of children with special learning needs was developing within the regular educational system.[2] This "second system," incidentally, is not an economic dumping ground; the diagnosis of "learning disability" has been a predominantly middle-class phenomenon.

Dr. Wang points out that up to 80% of American schoolchildren could now be diagnosed as learning disabled by one or more of the methods used, which may vary even between adjacent school districts. It is impossible to determine how much of the avalanche of new referrals is attributable to teachers' growing reliance on this method of extruding troublesome youngsters from classrooms. The only clear fact that can be derived from these statistics is that there is a serious misfit between large numbers of children and their schools.

"ATTENTION DEFICIT DISORDER"

In a great proportion of diagnosed cases, a subcategory of learning disability variously named "hyperactivity" or, more currently, "attention deficit disorder—with or without hyperactivity" is implicated, even when the primary difficulty lies in a specific academic territory such as reading. All "attention deficit disorder" cases have trouble focusing and maintaining attention appropriately; the term "hyperactivity" implies that the child's body, as well as mind, is bouncing off walls. One of the most invariable school symptoms of any form of attention disorder is difficulty listening attentively and remembering what the teacher says.

The exact relationship between "ADHD" (attention deficit with or without hyperactivity disorder) and other forms of "LD" is unclear, but experts estimate a 50% to 90% overlap between the two categories.[3] The impossibility of finding clear data is a frustrating testimony to the imprecision of educational diagnosis, but unquestionably, one of the main reasons the "LD" category is growing so large is because of a dramatic increase in the number of children with "attention disorders."

Flaky Kids and Pharmaceuticals

Currently in the United States, anywhere from one and one-half million to four and one-half million schoolchildren, mainly boys, bear the official diagnosis of ADHD. Incredibly, in some classrooms, more than 50% of students have been diagnosed as hyperactive, a fact rendered less surprising by a recent report that pointed out that one-third of all American boys meet some of the criteria.[4] Teachers say, however, that the identified cases represent only the most serious and unmanageable ones in an increasingly inattentive population of students. Girls are also more inattentive these days, but partially because they do not tend to cut up as much in class, they are referred for diagnosis less often.

In other parts of the world the incidence of ADHD is seen as being much lower, but rising numbers of cases have recently been reported from countries as widely separated as Finland and the People's Republic of China, to name just two examples.[5,6] A West German pediatrician specializing in the disorder recently published a study of a thousand children whom he had treated for attention disorders, many from upper-middle-class families.[7]

One controversial aspect of this problem is an increasing use of stimulant drugs to enable these children's brains to behave more attentively. As of this writing, an estimated 6% of American schoolchildren are being given a prescription drug, most commonly Ritalin, to render them sufficiently manageable to do their work in school. In some communities, where certain pediatricians have "specialized" in "hyperactivity"/attention deficits, the percentage is much higher. Some parents are also choosing to augment the prescribed daily dosage to counteract the drug's "rebound" effect and enable their offspring to manage themselves acceptably at home. A 1988 article in

Education Week entitled "Debate Grows on Classroom's 'Magic Pill' " pointed out that the production of Ritalin in the United States doubled between 1985 and 1987.[8] In the next chapter we will take an in-depth look at this whole issue. For now, let us explore the more general range of "learning disabilities."

"LD": MISFITTED BRAINS

Different Wiring Systems

I find that parents, and even teachers, are often confused by the term "learning disability." Contrary to what many have been led to believe, most children diagnosed as "LD" have not suffered any identifiable kind of brain "damage" either before or after birth. Moreover, they may be highly intelligent. Some nervous systems come into the world jumpy, clumsy, or otherwise ill-equipped for learning, but many children who wear the label "LD" do not have anything noticeably the matter with them. Even in neurological examination they may seem to be essentially "normal" children who function well in most settings—except for the classroom. It is especially hard for adults to understand why such a child should have difficulty with specific aspects of learning such as reading, math, memory, and paying attention.

Also contrary to popular belief, once a diagnosis is arrived at, professionals cannot simply "fix" the child just because they have put a label on the problem. Unfortunately, understanding of the vagaries of the learning brain is so tenuous that most treatment is still based more on "what works" than on a clear-cut neurological rationale.

The main reason diagnosis and treatment are so difficult is that all kids' brains are unique—the LD child's is just too unique for the school to handle. Even though all our brains are cut from the "Homo sapiens" template, each responds individually to different types of tasks, and each is potentially better at making synaptic connections for some kinds of learning than for others. The basic neuronal wiring diagram is determined both by the genetic blueprint and the environment in the womb; the postnatal environment helps determine how the connections get hooked up—according to how the child uses them. By definition, a specific "learning disability" occurs only when the child takes that special brain into a learning situation, batters his neuron assemblies against a certain kind of demand—and fails. In an extreme example, let us imagine that a child with a brain specifically ill-equipped for reading went to school in a society where all information was conveyed pictorially or by storytelling. The "learning disability" would never materialize!

Even in preschool years, a child's mental life and motivation interact with basic brain structure to shape specific talents for learning. By the time children enter school, each has a singular pattern of abilities, disabilities, and interests. Some children's patterns fit neatly into the classroom; others' talents show up more clearly on the playground, in the art or music room, in interpersonal politics, or when someone needs a friend. But these skills don't earn stars on the spelling chart— or many A's on the report card.

Some LD youngsters have wiring systems that must struggle harder with learning because of general difficulty with one or several of the following: memory, coordination of hands and eyes, rapid comprehension of new situations, language, visual-spatial reasoning, abstract thinking, or ability to focus attention quickly and appropriately. Even a problem that appears to be quite generalized, however, such as a memory problem, may actually show up only in particular (task specific) types of learning situations. Many times, when students come to me to complain about a "memory problem," it turns out they are really talking about *verbal memory* for things they read or hear; they may be terrific at remembering where Dad mislaid his car keys or how to put a Rubik's Cube together. The real "problem" is that brain systems are wired up better for some types of memory than for others, and the weak ones don't show up until they are called on to perform.

Sometimes I reflect ruefully, when I watch children trundled off to the "resource room" for tutoring in reading or spelling, that I, too, might have been LD. Like many who later chose teaching as a career, I was lucky that my brain's native abilities and my language-rich environment combined to fit me out quite nicely for my first-grade classroom. If at age six, however, I had suddenly been dropped into a society of visual artists, with a curriculum that consisted of drawing pictures and designing architectural blueprints instead of reading and spelling, I would shortly have been consigned to the "disabled" list. Wallowing messily in failed expectations, I would have waited for the weekly visit of the special reading teacher and my brief taste of success—that is, if the verbal "frills" hadn't already been cut from the school budget. Many children who face the opposite problem in our language-centered schools pine for the "frills" of art or music class but have little opportunity to be recognized for their talents. Are these students' brains "damaged"—or just disabled relative to that particular curriculum?

Should we change the curriculum? Must we alter teaching methods and the pace of instruction to accommodate growing numbers of "different" brains? These questions are increasingly being forced on teachers, who, even in the "best" schools, are discovering that giving students more of the usual types of instruction does not backfill the gaps. Meanwhile, the society clamors for higher standards—and our graduates can't compete in world markets.

Perhaps the American popular culture ought to take a hard look at its own curriculum. Because the kind of "coaching" provided by early environments has so much to do with a child's adjustment to school learning, everyone has an obligation to our children—and to their future teachers—to provide them with experiences likely to build the skills they will need in the classroom. This does not mean that parents should prepare lesson plans for infants, expect preschoolers to read, or drill kids on math facts when they are in their high chairs. It does mean someone must help them learn to listen, direct their own thinking, and use language effectively. I have already described the erosion of language stimulation for many children today; now let us explore more fully the ways in which environments are teaching them not to pay attention. These two problems are closely related and may account for much of this mysterious "epidemic" we are now experiencing.

Listening Skills and Learning Disabilities

By far the majority of learning disability referrals include difficulty listening to, understanding, or expressing verbal material, reading, writing, and spelling. These skills all rest on an underlying complex of "auditory processing abilities" and are mediated by language areas in the brain's left hemisphere. They include abilities to:

- listen carefully to the order of sounds in words or of words in sentences
- discriminate between similar sounds (e.g., *sh* and *ch*)
- remember things that have just been heard ("short-term auditory memory")

Problems with the above do not stem mainly from defects in the ears, but from the brain's processing centers. The sounds may get in, but they become scrambled or lost before they can be analyzed, understood, and remembered. One of the most prevalent symptoms of such problems is difficulty in recalling spoken directions. For example:

Parent: "Please go upstairs, get the soap out of the closet, and bring it to the laundry room."

Child: "Huh?"

Children with poor auditory skills—whatever the reason—have a difficult time learning to read, spelling accurately, remembering what they read long enough to understand it, or retaining the internal sound of a sentence they want to write down. They tend to tune out during class discussions and when the teacher lectures or gives directions. They respond much better to visual input, particularly if it is in pictorial rather than written form.

To compound the difficulty, children who do not *have* to listen can easily develop habits to avoid exercising (and thus building) these important auditory-processing connections. The very act of remembering lays down physical tracks in the brain, but children can quite easily avoid having to build these systems. When a teacher gives directions, they watch her for clues or look around to see what everyone else is doing (now that so many seem to have this problem, sometimes no one knows!). They say "Huh?" enough times to make frazzled parents either *show* them or do it themselves. When they don't hear the homework assignment in class, they call a friend. In reading they rely heavily on pictures in the text. Most children get the message more from the pictures than from "talk" when they watch TV, so extended viewing—particularly in early years when these brain connections are forming—compounds the problem. No wonder, when they have to read longer stories, math word problems, history books, etc., they can't hold the sound of the words inside their own heads long enough to understand what they're reading! Their brains have simply not been trained to understand and retain discourse.

What causes the basic weakness? Research suggests this type of problem may tend to run in some families. Nowadays, however, when most children's listening experiences are limited or attached to pictures, it is difficult to sort out who inherited the problem and who "caught" it from the environment. Whatever the cause, studies have shown that early experience with careful, analytic listening can dramatically improve auditory processing, listening comprehension, and in turn, reading ability—even in children with an inherited weakness.[9]

HEREDITY, ENVIRONMENT, AND "EXCEPTIONAL BRAINS"

Scientists are trying to get more specific about how nature and nurture affect patterns of learning ability. They have found that "exceptionality" (such as musical, mathematical, or linguistic talent, as well as some categories of learning disability) may be related to inherited differences in the way brains are constructed. Nevertheless, the effects of environments created by family members with particular interests can't be discounted, say Drs. Lorraine Obler and Deborah Fine in their fascinating book *The Exceptional Brain*. "Stating that a talent or disability is biologically or genetically based does not mean that it will necessarily develop or fail to develop regardless of the conditions under which a child grows up. Certain environmental factors are crucial for the manifestation of talent as they are for the manifestation of disability."[10]

Genes, Dyslexia, and the Fetal Brain

It is difficult and highly technical work to sort out the respective effects of genes and family habits, agrees Dr. Bruce Pennington of the University of Colorado. Dr. Pennington is director of a large study searching for specific genes by which language, reading, and learning disabilities can be transmitted from parent to child. Just because many members of a family have a certain trait, he says, we cannot assume it is necessarily genetic. After all, poor table manners can run in families!"[11] Likewise, parents who enjoy reading and conversation will tend to surround their children with a literacy-rich environment and extensive listening experiences, and vice versa.

Nevertheless, Pennington's research, the largest family learning-disability study ever conducted, has confirmed that some specific types of learning difficulties, including language disorders such as stuttering, speech, and some reading problems, are genetically influenced. Members of these families, interestingly enough, are often distinguished by talents in other areas. As researchers work to clarify definitions and probable causes, they are uncovering some fascinating clues about why this might be true.

The term "dyslexia" has often been used as a garbage can for any kind of problem with reading. Current research, however, has limited the use of the term to describe a brain-based disorder in putting together the sight and sound of printed language in reading, spelling, and writing (e.g., looking at a letter and saying its sound; remembering how to write *said*). Dyslexic children, who compose only one special segment of the entire LD population, may also have difficulty with some aspects of oral language, such as coming up quickly with the word they want to say or getting the order of the sounds and syllables straight. Because they tend to mix up the order of letters and words when they read (and sometimes the order of numerals when they do arithmetic), people used to think the problem was in their eyes. Now it is suspected that the culprits really are deficits in left-hemisphere systems responsible for analyzing and arranging things in sequential order and linking sound with written symbol.

Even with their genetically "different" brains, dyslexic children who come from homes where they have been exposed to books and good examples of language often learn to read reasonably well. Although their spelling is often "atrocious," these youngsters may escape diagnosis as they learn to compensate for or cover up their difficulties. They also prove that "disability" is a relative term, as they are often talented in more predominantly right-hemisphere skills, such as visual arts, mathematical reasoning, music, mechanical aptitude.[12]

Attention problems in school frequently accompany dyslexia, but dyslexics often have excellent visual attention for details of things they see (other than printed words!), and they can spend long hours in activities such as working on an engine or a design. They are youngsters who might be academic stars in a culture with a different set of intellectual priorities.

How are these brains different? Studies using new computerized pictures of brain areas in action show that dyslexic children seem to use different neural systems for reading than do "normal" readers.[13] A second line of evidence suggests that this mix-up takes place because certain brain areas developed differently before birth. Because the young brain is so plastic, it manages to reorganize itself around reading, but academic skills still suffer to some degree.

"A Terrible-Looking Brain"

Not long ago, the late Dr. Norman Geshwind and his colleague Dr. Albert Galaburda, of Harvard University, began intensive work on the brains of several dyslexics who had willed them for study. All of these brains differed in particular ways from the "normal" pattern of cell organization, especially in one general language area of the left hemisphere. Microscopic analysis pinpointed the origin of the differences at a certain period of prenatal cell migration. Instead of finding their intended homes, groups of neurons ended up in peculiar places and arrangements. Moreover, areas in the right hemisphere—the ones, in fact, that would probably underlie visual, mechanical, or other creative abilities—were proportionately larger in these people.[14]

Given the growing evidence that dyslexia tends to run in families and to be more evident in males, Dr. Geshwind decided to interview families of dyslexics. When he uncovered repeated prevalence of left-handed relatives and autoimmune, or allergic, disease, he developed a theory. He speculated that imbalances of hormones or antibodies secreted by the mother at different times during pregnancy might subtly rearrange the infant's brain in ways that would make it less adept at reading and language, more talented in visual-spatial skills, and more likely to be left-handed.[15,16]

No final answers are yet available, but this research is being continued by Dr. Albert Galaburda. Until more is known, these studies provide powerful evidence that even though baby brains are born with differences, they can eventually learn to accomplish a complex learning task (in this case, reading) with brain systems different—and perhaps geographically far removed—from the ones best suited for the job. The scientists working on these projects agree that *the way dyslexics—or anyone else—use their brains is a critical factor in modifying them.*

I had an opportunity to chat with Dr. Galaburda after a recent speech in which he emphasized "the Darwinian-like interaction" between the environment and the growing brain. Genes provide the environment with "a range of structures to choose from," he explained, "and the environment chooses from this range of possibilities. The structure of your brain determines that you can dance, but it doesn't permit you to fly," he said, smiling. "There are some things the genes just don't permit. But on the other hand, the brain is not prewired to act just one way; instead it gives the environment certain flexibility in selection. I think even if children have not quite the best wiring diagram for something, you can make it look better or less well depending on the environment.[17]

"Different kinds of environmental factors, from chemicals to societal pressures . . . are potentially capable of resulting in abnormal brain interactions," explained Dr. Galaburda. On the other hand, his studies of dyslexic brains have reminded him that we should never underestimate the ability of the brain, given the right kind of support, to compensate for innate difficulties. "If you change the brain [before birth] you probably change the range of possibilities that are available to this brain in some sense, but the range of possibilities is still very great. One of our dyslexics was a very distinguished, famous, brilliant psychologist and she had a *terrible-looking brain!*"[18]

The Flip Side of Dyslexia: Nonverbal Learning Disorders

Scientists are hot on the trail of brain differences that lie behind another difficulty, termed "nonverbal learning disorder," which seems to stem from the opposite problem: insufficient right-hemisphere power.

People with right-hemisphere disabilities may be quite competent at linear, sequential skills like spelling, reading out loud, or doing basic math equations, but have trouble when they must comprehend abstract ideas, relate to people socially, or reason in a visual-spatial format (e.g., maps, charts, three-dimensional puzzles, architectural drawings). They have trouble understanding the relationship of their bodies in space or the ideas in literature or social studies. They almost invariably run afoul of more advanced math courses. Their primary difficulty is one of seeing the "whole picture" of a situation: sizing up meaning when they read or when they deal with others, for example. They may have trouble interpreting the emotional quality of people's facial expressions and do or say inappropriate things in social situations.[19]

[**A Cautionary Note:** Most of us lean toward one "style" or another but are still well within the normal range; just because any of these descriptions sound like someone you know does not mean they have a brain disability, just that they are at a different point on a continuum than someone else. The fact that we all have unique patterns of talents keeps us supplied with people who want to be proofreaders as well as those who prefer architectural design.]

Serious cases of nonverbal learning disorder, in which the individual's abilities are obviously affected, are just now receiving professional attention. Little is known about causes or treatment, but researchers suggest early intervention to help the brain develop connections for manipulating the physical world and understanding other people's reactions and the principles behind ideas.

Children who show this type of learning profile may not look "disabled" in early grades and are often, in fact, viewed as quite advanced because of large vocabulary, facility on the computer, early reading of words, and good math computation skills. The tip-off is that they tend to pursue linear kinds of learning, like computer math or spelling drills, as obsessively as they avoid such visual-spatial challenges as video games, team sports, or mechanical puzzles.[20] Since the child's family may share some of the same characteristics, manual and interpersonal abilities may not have high priority at home.

Nonverbal learning disorders and dyslexia are just two of the many conditions that get lumped under the term "LD" (and which may or may not include "attention deficit" problems), but they are among the major ones for which specific, and possibly inherited, brain differences have been suggested. No one knows how many "learning disabilities" are caused by environments that interact with more "normal" brain patterns to make children unprepared for school learning. Most experts agree, however, that this number is probably growing. Because the types of technology needed to look, literally, at the learning brain are only now being developed and are expensive, it will be a long time before we fully understand the normal learning process, let alone all its variations. A few scientists have already begun the quest.

Looking Inside the Brain

At Michigan State University, Dr. E. James Potchen, chairman of the Department of Radiology, works at the forefront of these efforts. He directs a project in which magnetic resonance imaging, a method of seeing the working brain in "exquisite detail," as he says, is being used to probe the relationship of brain structure and learning disability.

Dr. Potchen has looked at 18,000 brains, and says that "we are all abnormal because all brains are so different. It's amazing we do as well as we do." Having brain differences should not necessarily be viewed as having a disease, he maintains, and there can be tremendous changes in the architecture of the brain from learning. He guesses the child's brain is always in the process of being rewired.

Dr. Potchen tells of both animal and human brains that have restructured themselves significantly on the basis of learning experiences. Some types of birds even develop new neurons when they learn to sing. In a human experiment he showed pictures of a stick figure to doctors and artists while their brain activity was being scanned. Different areas of the cortex would "light up" depending on the individual's profession. The artists, looking at the drawing, showed brain patterns indicating greater complexity of association and understanding.

This curious researcher has also been examining his own brain every four years to look for changes. "I haven't yet got to the point where I can see that if my golf swing got better, it would change my brain, but that may be coming—especially for children."[21]

FITTING BRAINS TO LEARNING—AND FITTING LEARNING TO BRAINS

Research like Dr. Potchen's has obvious promise for educators, but we are still a long way from being able to plan teaching on the basis of brain scans. In the meanwhile, this research should certainly sensitize us to the fact that learning environments—at home or school—can partially rearrange neural wiring diagrams. They can help the child overcome or compensate for innate differences or predispose to problems. In our schools, children who come with deficits in auditory attention and language processing are headed for trouble.

As I learn more about the wide variety of ways in which students' brains may differ from each other's—and from my own—I become increasingly aware of the importance of the "fit" between their brains' particular contours and the learning environment into which they have been injected. Now, when I walk into a classroom of twenty students, be they four- or forty-year-olds, I remind myself that I am trying to teach twenty individual brains that are probably as different in their learning patterns as my students' faces are in appearance. As a teacher, I must accept the fact that their level of success—and thus their motivation—will be directly related to the accommodation we mutually achieve between the subject matter and their particular pattern of abilities. I must encourage them to push themselves a little harder on things that do not come so easily, but I must also accept the necessity of supporting and working to develop each student's potential. Even with twenty students, which is fewer than the number found in most classrooms, this job requires skill, patience, and a lot of hard work.

If we could, as teachers, fill this awesome assignment, I venture to say both the number of "learning disabilities" and the dropout rate would decline precipitously. Our job is getting increasingly difficult, however, because we seem to be standing in the way of an avalanche of brains that are misfitted to our educational objectives. A teacher can easily become engulfed trying to reconcile administrators' demands for "achievement" with today's language and attention patterns. Unless the adult community decides to help us wrap these growing brains in the mental garments of language, reflection, and thought, I fear we will continue to see increasing numbers of children categorized as "educationally sick."

Why Can't They Pay Attention?

The reason our children don't follow directions is that they're tuned out. These children don't listen. They have so much stimulation—they're used to the TV blaring, the stereo, the household commotion. I'm not sure so many are ADHD; they're just restless because they don't have anything inside. They're so used to being entertained.

—Eighth-grade teacher,
suburban school, Georgia

They have a much better store of general information than children twenty years ago. If they listen, they can follow directions, but it is difficult to keep their attention long enough to explain what to do.

—Teacher,
ungraded rural school, Minnesota

The kids are sharp and intuitive, but—listening skills? Not as good as students in the past. Some seem to have forgotten how to learn without visual stimulation and affirmation of what they hear. Concentration and memory are just not as important to them. They seem to have their own agendas in life, and school gets in the way sometimes.

—Fifth-grade teacher,
urban school, Oregon

FIGURE 3

Courtesy of Dodie Corpening and *Gifted, Created and Talented Magazine.*

THE PROBLEM OF ATTENTION

Although "attention deficits" are involved in the vast majority of learning-disability referrals, teachers of all students complain more about diminished attention spans than about any other characteristic of their students. As soon as I began to talk with educators, I discovered that merely mentioning the word "attention" opened a floodgate of response. To my surprise, I also heard the same concerns expressed from abroad, although in other countries the diagnosis of "learning disability" and ADHD are much less prevalent.

In Tours, a large city southwest of Paris, the director of a primary school and an instructor in the highly esteemed École Normale (Teachers' College), told me, "The teachers here complain a lot; they say the children don't listen anymore, they are restless. This is only my personal opinion, but I think one learns not to listen when one watches television. I think the children get in the habit and then when the teacher talks, they don't hear her either." She went on to describe other concerns remarkably similar to those I was hearing at home about hurried lifestyles, overprogrammed children, and the decline of thoughtful conversations around the family dinner table. "Personally, I don't think the parents encourage calmness or listening," she mused.[1]

It is clear from the preceding comments that declining listening abilities are the main symptom, but most teachers sense that they also reflect students' problems with focusing and maintaining internal control of attention in any situation. Overall mental restlessness and inability to persist in solving problems, reading "hard" books, or doing work perceived as "boring" are even more serious symptoms. In the United States a national crisis in "problem-solving ability"—the ability to stay focused long enough to reason out and solve a mental challenge—has become the primary agenda item of the National Council of Teachers of Mathematics and the Association for Supervision and Curriculum Development.

Could these trends simply represent inevitable signs of progress? Will children be better off if they learn early to respond to the pace of the contemporary world? Certainly, to be adapted to today's surroundings, young brains need to deal with a lot of rapid-fire stimuli. To reason effectively and solve problems, however, growing minds also need to be able to retain and connect these "bits." Perhaps most important, they need to learn what it feels like to be in charge of one's own brain, actively pursuing a mental or physical trail, inhibiting response to the lure of distractions.

Attention determines how and what an individual learns.[2] It enables us to make choices and maintain control over what we notice, absorb, and remember. Children with attention problems fall into two general categories: some are too mentally active, with their focus jumping from one thing to another, while others behave as if their brains were underactive. Those in the latter group frequently are termed "spaced out," but they are much less frequently diagnosed than the "hyper" ones, who respond impulsively to whatever can be touched or seen in their environments and have particular difficulty internalizing personal controls.[3] Those with serious disorders often grow up to be impulsive adults; ADHD is statistically linked with delinquency and antisocial behavior. If our society wants citizens who can reflect as well as respond, who can come up with solutions to the problems of a complex world, it must teach its children to stop, listen, and think as well as to react.

How can we help children learn to direct their mental energies? How much can the environment affect patterns of attention, listening, and problem-solving? Let us consider first what is known about attention and why physicians prescribe drugs for some children who lack it. Then we will start to take a look at what environments, both physical and mental, have to do with the way it develops—or fails to—during childhood.

What Is an Attention Deficit?

Attention, like learning disability, is not a single measurable quantity. Although psychologists are far from agreeing on an exact definition, they have generally believed, as far as learning is concerned, that *selective attention*—the ability to concentrate and stay focused on a particular task—is the critical issue.[4] But selective attention has proven hard to measure. Like memory, it is "task specific," changing according to the job the brain is asked to do and the underlying motivation to do it. For example, many teachers who complain that students can't pay attention and listen in class also notice that the same children will concentrate on a computerized video game for long periods of time. In these two situations there are clear differences between both motivational and cognitive factors such as auditory or visual attention, saliency (attention-grabbing quality) of the stimulus, requirements for memory, physical involvement, and the pace of the activity, all of which affect attention.

For all learners, attention varies from situation to situation, and it is difficult to determine the fine line between normal restlessness and pathology. Now that so many children seem out of sync with the attentional demands of their classrooms, the problem is compounded. Even the extreme diagnosis of "ADHD"—which assumes that the child has some sort of organic brain dysfunction—depends on rather vague criteria, since there are no surefire neurological tests to prove its existence.

To diagnose a child as pathologically inattentive most doctors depend mainly on behavior checklists filled out by teachers and parents; the official diagnosis is often subjective. A certain proportion of items like the following must be checked:

- failure to finish things he or she starts
- failure to listen
- difficulty in concentrating or sticking to an activity
- acting before thinking
- shifting between one activity and another
- difficulty in organization
- calling out in class/difficulty awaiting turns

To earn the additional designation "hyperactive," the child must also show excessive physical activity (e.g., run or climb excessively).

Since all children exhibit these behaviors at times, the diagnosis is supposed to be restricted to problems that are unusually severe for the child's age and level of mental development. Curiously, however, doctors are told that the child may seem perfectly normal during the office visit, since ADHD children are often able to control themselves in novel or one-to-one situations.[5]

Controlling Attention: From Inside or Outside?

Ritalin and other drugs prescribed for ADHD are variations on the type of stimulants, or amphetamines, banned in over-the-counter diet pills. They help heighten and sharpen attention—even in many "normal" people. Some children with organic difficulties seem to benefit from carefully regulated doses that enable them to focus appropriately, listen more carefully to the teacher, and complete more work. In fact, moderate doses would have the same effect on almost anyone—at least for a while—and many doctors complain that the number of children treated is much larger than it should be. Some physicians, parents, and teachers are too eager, they say, to give children drugs with well-recognized negative side effects, instead of working to help them learn to manage their own behavior.

Many children diagnosed as having attention deficit disorder are extremely intelligent, but there is some reason to doubt the overall benefit of drug treatment alone in helping them use that intelligence productively. Students who take their medication do become more tractable, completing more repetitive "work" such as worksheets with fill-in answers and drills on math problems. In most studies conducted thus far, however, drugs per se do not make them score better on tests of academic achievement or of higher-level thinking and problem-solving.[6] Some studies have even shown that the level of dosage needed to make teachers approve a child's behavior is so high that it actually dulls reasoning ability. These findings raise questions, not only about the type of "work" dominating many classrooms, but also about the real source of the problem.[7]

Lasting improvement is generally not seen after the drug treatment is stopped. A few children appear spontaneously to "outgrow" attention problems around adolescence, probably because of nervous-system maturation, but many retain problems of self-control that persist into adulthood.

"Curing" attention problems seems to be close to impossible. Teaching students to talk through problems, thus developing conscious strategies for self-control, is the only therapy used thus far that appears to produce results lasting after drugs are discontinued.[8–10] In fact, this sort of "cognitive therapy"—using language to control behavior—has been shown to help even without drug treatment. Some professionals have gone so far as to suggest that the real disability is a lack of this type of teaching—both at home and at school.

Misfitted Attention: What Is the Real Problem?

Since most of the "epidemic" of inattention cannot be linked to proven organic dysfunction of the central nervous system, other factors that create a misfit between the children's development and the demands of the schools are being considered. According to the newest research, a small percentage of problems called ADHD may be covering up basic anxiety or depression.[11] Many more may be related to other, environmental causes. Overall a confusing picture emerges.

In her book, When Children Don't Learn, Dr. Diane McGuinness expresses skepticism about the validity of the diagnosis itself. "Problems in the control of attention could result from deficiencies in the central nervous system, which could produce distractibility, failure to sustain attention to a task, inability to plan actions, and a diminished attention span. However, similar difficulties could be created by an environment that is either *too overwhelming or insufficiently compelling* [emphasis added]," she states.[12] Dr. McGuinness, who confesses she is irate about the amount of Ritalin being prescribed today, believes that many children thought to be "hyperactive" are really normally vigorous children "who refuse to abide by adult admonitions to sit still and conform to rules set by adults for their own convenience." She makes the point that children's bodies are designed by nature to be active, and the overly wiggly ones may really know what is good for them more than the docile types "who are overly conforming and remain for hours in sedentary positions."

Under some circumstances (such as in the doctor's office), even children labeled ADHD are able to control their attention—but only if the situation is novel, one-on-one, and they get frequent and continuous rewards and reinforcement of some kind. For example, they can pay excellent attention to computer activities with frequent token rewards (e.g., a laser gun blows up a space invader every time the student gets a math problem correct), and their schoolwork improves noticeably when someone works individually with them. In one interesting study, children diagnosed ADHD were paid to respond quickly and accurately to a test on which they had previously scored quite poorly when no reward was offered. Much to the experimenter's surprise, promise of money brought their performance up to the level of a normal control group.[13]

These findings and others have led a number of professionals to begin rethinking their views. Dr. Russell Barkley, nationally noted authority and author of *Hyperactive Children*, recently told a large group of educators that he is changing his mind about what an "attention deficit" really is.[14] "If you have an attention deficit, shouldn't it show up everywhere? If language is impaired, we see language impairment anywhere the child needs to use language. How can this be an attention deficit? Don't we need to look for something else that explains this variation? Why do they do better with novel situations, with rich schedules of reinforcement [frequent rewards]? People are seriously questioning whether this is really an attention deficit."

One theory, according to Dr. Barkley, is that the ADHD children have particular trouble with what he calls "rule-governed behavior." When the environment demands adherence to a rule, especially one with few consequences, trouble begins. "So when a teacher says, 'He's not paying attention,' what she really means is he's not listening, he's not following the rule. 'I told him to go back to his desk, get out his math problems, and work on them, and he didn't do the rule.'

"It's been shown that when ADHD children are paying attention to what they like, they don't have an attention deficit," he emphasized. "So if they brought a car from home, or a transformer, or they're doodling war pictures on the corner of that reading workbook—their attention span for war pictures is phenomenal! But it isn't for the stuff you ask them to do. The problem, then, is not attention, it's a disability in rule-following."

However, even these children can follow rules if there is an immediate reward, Dr. Barkley has observed. "In adults, we are the only animal that operates on a very sparse schedule of reward; I only get a paycheck once a month, but I show up at work every day. There is something fascinating about the human brain that allows it to be exquisitely sensitive to extremely sparse schedules of reward, but that is something that has to develop. Young children can't do it. You can tell a young kid you'll take him to Disneyland in February, and that won't do it. These ADHD kids are like younger kids; they need immediate feedback and reinforcement."

Why might this be the case? Dr. Barkley suggests, for some children, underlying differences in the motivational-control systems of the brain may not be operating normally; thus they need a much stronger external impetus to concentrate on the task at hand. They simply don't respond as other children do to "social approval."

"Somehow, neurologically, these children have a threshold for what rewards them that is set too high; it takes a more powerful reinforcer to get them to do what they are told. That is why they require the money, food, bikes, toys, privileges, bribes—to work. Because the subtle rewards—love of learning, grades, teacher approval—don't motivate these kids at all. You can say 'good boy, good boy' all you want and that isn't going to work."

"They can understand what you say to them," he points out, "they just don't act on it. *It's really a problem with how language governs behavior*—the connections between the linguistic and the motor systems."[15]

Dr. Barkley suspects there is a genetic cause for these brain differences, possibly related to the way chemicals (neurotransmitters) help different parts of the brain work together. Children who develop the most severe forms of ADHD so that they become openly "oppositional" and often delinquent, tend to come from families with a history of alcohol abuse, delinquency, and antisocial behavior, which he thinks may reflect some overall type of inherited problem. We can't blame parents for the fact that they have a difficult child, he insists, but we must acknowledge that a child's environment helps determine how the problem is expressed. As with bad table manners that seem to run in families, no one has been able to measure exactly how much living with impulsive adults in poorly structured situations contributes to the problem.

Obviously, no clear-cut answers about the "why" of attention problems are available. Perhaps neurology is just struggling to catch up with common sense, for it seems foolish to deny that the way a child is taught and *shown to* behave has a lot to do with whether or not he learns to manage himself without an immediate reward. A number of practical, real-life studies show that children's adult models may be a significant, but frequently unappreciated, variable.[16]

FURNISHING THE EXECUTIVE SUITE: HOW BRAINS LEARN TO PAY ATTENTION

Both physical and mental environments help develop the ability to pay attention. Because attention requires the use of many different areas of the brain, any severe trauma, "insult," or biochemical abnormality may affect it. As we all know, even transient emotional states can knock this delicately balanced block off the tower of learning abilities.

Attention systems grow in several directions in the brain: side to side, bottom to top, and inside to outside. Here's a brief summary of how they are formed.

Activating the Hemispheres

The side-to-side connections are mainly in the *corpus callosum,* that tough and busy band of fibers that carries messages between the hemispheres and lets the two sides of the cortex work efficiently together. Several prominent neuropsychologists believe that brains with attention and learning problems have trouble getting an idea into the appropriate hemisphere and keeping it there long enough to be processed efficiently.

One recent study measured electrical brain waves in right and left hemispheres of LD (in this case, reading disabled) children when they were doing different types of learning tasks; the measurements were then compared with brain-wave recordings from a group of good students doing the same activities. The good students showed the expected changes in hemispheric activation depending on whether the task was a verbal or nonverbal one, although overall they tended to favor left-hemisphere strategies. The LD children showed different patterns: (1) they had less overall left-hemisphere activation, even in verbal tasks, and (2) they showed significantly smaller shifts from one hemisphere to the other when the tasks required different processing strategies.[17]

If children have not had a chance to develop strong connections between the two sides or enough practice using left-hemisphere systems for careful listening, they certainly might have more trouble concentrating, getting their brains quickly and efficiently into gear for school tasks, and finding the best way to study and remember things they are supposed to learn.[18]

Three Levels of Attention

The up-and-down axis of brain maturation, which is probably the major route by which children learn to pay attention, may be particularly at risk in today's environments. Although, technically, this "attention circuit" cannot be separated from the hemispheres, since it crosses through them, it is, in many respects, a separate apparatus. Imagine, if you will, a circuit that runs from the base of your skull at the back of your head all the way up through the middle of the brain to the front of your forehead and back down again. This is similar to the main route from which higher-level systems receive information about where and how attention should be focused. These higher centers, in turn, decide what is to be done and then instruct the rest of the brain in how the behavior (including learning) is to be directed.

This attention loop has three layers that develop from bottom to top and inside to outside the brain. The first, primitive stage of the circuit lies near the top of the spinal cord, where it joins the skull, in brain structures that closely resemble those of other animals. It is responsible for basic alertness (e.g., staying awake when it is appropriate), screening out or letting in various types of stimuli (e.g., focusing without being distracted by background sights or sounds), filtering information, and getting the higher centers of the cortex "in gear."

Second come centers for emotion and memory, which are located in the middle of the brain in an area technically called the *limbic system*. In these "subcortical" areas, the incoming stimuli are connected with motivation (how important is it for me to pay attention to this right now?) and some centers for memory. I find it particularly interesting, although not intuitively surprising, that attention, emotion, motivation, and memory have such a close physical link in the nervous system.

Developmental influences on the limbic system are one of the great, barely unfolded mysteries of the brain. How do children acquire the neural foundations of motivation? No one really knows, but the central role of these midbrain connections imply that they must be important indeed.

At the very top of the circuit lie the *frontal lobes of the cortex,* comprising the frontmost parts of both right and left hemispheres. This part of the brain, which is the human animal's unique neural possession, is often called the *executive of the brain* because it is responsible for planning and regulating behavior. It consists of the *motor cortex,* which helps plan and implement physical movement, and the *prefrontal* areas, which, when (and if) fully developed, become the "boss" of thinking. (The terms "frontal" and "prefrontal" are used interchangeably.)

The neural groundwork for attention abilities is laid early in prenatal life, when the bottom layer of primitive "alerting" areas are developing. After birth the child must collaborate with nature and the motivational system to build the connections that put the thinking brain in charge. Because the higher centers can't take over immediately, young children are notoriously "stimulus-bound"—at the mercy of any new sensory experience or idea. Thus they tend to be highly distractible.

During the years of childhood, especially between the ages of three and six, most youngsters work hard on learning to screen out both external and internal distractions and marshal their attention at will. Any environmental force that severely interferes with this important learning has the potential to disrupt the system. Sometime during adolescence, most brains are sufficiently mature to start to attend to future goals and use more complex forms of mental control (please notice, parents, I said "most"). It's a long process, indeed, and demands continued support from concerned and persistent (if often exasperated!) adults.

Attention and the Brain's Executive

Prefrontal development is not completed at least until late adolescence, or even adulthood. Thus, the way a child learns to use executive functions is doubtless highly dependent on the experiences the environment provides. Adults who show children how to put thought ahead of action, delay gratification, and use language as a tool for thinking and planning help provide the fundamental training ground for the brain's executive.

Curiously, this "highest" level of the brain's functioning does not seem to be measured by standard IQ tests. The rest of the cortex serves as the *storehouse* for taking in information, which it associates and connects into the intellectual data bank that constitutes a lifetime of learning. The frontal systems have a different responsibility: seeing that the data gets used effectively, the reason why they are referred to as the *executive*. When experts give advice about boosting mental skills, they are usually referring to the most efficient ways of filling up the storehouse. Unfortunately, they too often forget that merely trying to shovel in information will serve little purpose unless children also learn how to use their brains to stay mentally focused, put information into perspective, reflect on meaning, plan ahead, and follow through constructively—the fundamental components of problem-solving. For this reason, "competency tests" that measure only the accumulation of data may seriously mislead us about children's real learning abilities. Without an efficient "executive," real-life competency is jeopardized.

Despite its critical importance in learning—as well as in life—there is little research on the way prefrontal development can be influenced. It appears that the way the brain learns to talk to itself may be a major factor in building its internal connections and learning to control the workings of both mind and body.[19] I will expand on this extremely important point in the next chapter.

For now, let us consider some of the interrelated factors that can cause trouble at any of the three levels of the attention system. Outright trauma, either before or after birth, is probably responsible only for a relatively small percentage of attention problems, but increasing numbers of children are currently seen as being at risk because of greater loads of environmental toxins and better survival rates for low-birthweight infants. Other more subtle factors, from "noise pollution" to biochemical effects of junk food, may tip the brain's attentional balances either before or after birth.

Several types of hazards in contemporary life should be specifically mentioned:

1. Toxic substances and foods that may predispose children to attention problems.
2. "Noisy" environments that cause children to tune out rather than tune in.
3. Sedentary lifestyles.
4. Failure by adults to act as constructive, thoughtful "coaches" for children.

How Brains Get "Insulted": Environmental Hazards for Attention and Learning

Before birth, some children suffer specific types of damage or so-called "insult" to attention-regulating systems. As we saw in Chapter 2, brains are at risk both before and soon after birth by overt damage from illness, accident, or exposure to toxins (e.g., lead, solvents, medications, etc.). Anything that deprives the brain of oxygen, particularly during times of rapid development, can also subtly jeopardize attention abilities. For example, children whose mothers smoked during pregnancy, who were premature, or who suffered various types of birth trauma tend to have a higher rate of attention problems and related learning disabilities than other youngsters.

Even after the foundation systems are in place, the brain can be disrupted by anything that interferes with the proper workings of the limbic system or the higher centers in the cortex, particularly the frontal areas. Sometimes these effects are so subtle that no one connects the cause with the resulting learning problem. One reason is that the brain has built-in mechanisms to protect itself, which may work well until they become overtaxed.

A good example of a built-in protection system is the so-called *blood-brain barrier*, which screens out brain-damaging materials that may be circulating in the rest of the bloodstream. Some potentially injurious substances are able to sneak across this barrier, and it can also be weakened, or made more permeable, by environmental factors, such as prolonged exposure to toxins or an unbalanced or inadequate diet.

Once across the barrier, troublesome agents can affect brain functioning in at least two ways that are, as yet, only generally understood. First, they may be directly toxic and create overt, permanent damage, as in the impairments inflicted on the fetal brain by alcohol. More subtly, they may cause temporary changes in the fine chemical balance that makes thinking possible. Brains can be either intolerant or frankly allergic to certain substances, but it is difficult to pin down the culprits.

Alcohol and Drugs

Every prospective parent should by now be aware that alcohol use during pregnancy is clearly related to future learning problems, but it continues to be a significant issue. Exposure of growing brains to recreational drugs other than alcohol can also damage attention abilities. Yet, despite increased publicity about this problem, it seems to be getting larger. A recent article in the *New York Times* reported that "a frighteningly high number of babies—possibly 375,000 a year—are being exposed to cocaine, marijuana, amphetamines, or other illegal drugs in the womb . . . and face the possibility of health damage from their mothers' drug abuse." These findings, "not just an inner-city problem," span all levels of the socioeconomic spectrum and may significantly underestimate the extent of the problem, according to one expert quoted in the article.[20]

Toxic Environments

After birth, the growing brain remains highly susceptible. Lead is a particularly serious and ubiquitous threat to attention centers and can definitely lower children's IQs. Parents are well advised to screen their children's environments carefully for all possible sources, but educators are alarmed at recent reports that schools themselves may be physically hazardous in this respect. In Portsmouth, New Hampshire, school officials began testing water fountains after a local newspaper reporter discovered unusually high lead levels in one school. Ultimately, they disconnected thirty-one water fountains and faucets after finding lead levels that were more than twenty times above the current EPA standard.[21] The national PTA has recently issued an appeal to schools to check lead levels of water and adopt appropriate safety measures.[22]

In Mexico City, where airborne pollution from car exhaust causes inhabitants to have drastically elevated blood lead levels, authorities shut down the school system for the entire month of January 1989, to reduce children's exposure to polluted air as they went to school and played outside during recess. Some foreign embassies in Mexico have even advised their diplomats to leave young children at home and not to have a baby while residing there.[23]

Other metals such as aluminum, arsenic, manganese, and mercury can also be neurotoxic, especially if they are combined with lead. Because scientists are now beginning to pay serious attention to this issue, we may hope that current vague warnings will soon yield to clearer guidelines.

Many potential sources of neurotoxic substances can be found in today's culture of chemical convenience.[24] Professor James Croxton of the University of Santa Cruz recently shared with me his concerns about widespread spraying of pesticides in areas near schools and homes. Pesticides may weaken or cross the blood-brain barrier, particularly in children who are not well nourished, he says. In another example, some school boards came under fire recently for the prevalent use of pesticides in school buildings. Parents who cite evidence of adverse effects in some children who are sensitive to chemicals have demanded more careful monitoring of the use of such strong substances around young children. Although there is no absolutely conclusive evidence about the relationship of pesticides to long-term difficulties in attention, a number of school districts are starting to reconsider and change their policies on spraying in classrooms.[25,26] Since toxins may exacerbate each other's effects, any potential source of contamination should be a matter of serious concern. Intelligent societies do not poison—in a very literal sense—the minds of their young.

Junk Food and Jumpy Minds

Can fast food and soft drinks upset brain chemistry and thus be subtly poisonous to growing minds? In recent years a number of authorities have begun to investigate possible effects of dietary habits on brain function, but their disagreements are probably the prickliest in all of the research literature. While one responsible authority states with certainty that food does not cause attention or learning problems, in an adjoining room another insists that the diets of today's children— particularly additives, sugar, and "overprocessed" fare—play a major role.

As in most arguments, the truth appears to lie somewhere in between. Convincing evidence has been assembled to show that the chemistry of children's brains may be affected by what they eat or drink. Given the uniqueness of each individual's biochemical makeup, it is not surprising that offending substances may affect children quite differently. Moreover, since biochemical "insults" to the brain appear to be cumulative, some effects may not show up immediately or under some circumstances. For this reason, credible research findings have been hard to come by. I will summarize some of the newer findings.

The importance of a well-balanced diet is one of the few areas of professional agreement in this field. Such factors as iron deficiency and general malnutrition have negative effects on the brain and on learning abilities. The young brain is so plastic that the gross effects of severe early malnutrition can be reversed by changed environments, but authorities admit they cannot adequately assess more subtle forms of deprivation. Studies for many years have shown that children who eat breakfast or who are given nourishing snacks during school breaks show improved classroom performance.[27]

Increasing interest—and more controversy—has focused on effects of the modern diet, particularly excessive sugar or additives such as food dyes. Numerous studies have yielded a frustrating lack of firm conclusions; the best summary I can come up with is a rather unhelpful one: some things may be harmful for some children under some circumstances.[28] It does appear that several aspects of contemporary eating habits may be particularly dangerous. Children under three years of age may be most susceptible, but brains can be affected at any age.[29,30] Many of our youngsters are routinely exposed to these suspected hazards:

- diets high in refined sugar
- no breakfast or high-carbohydrate breakfasts (sugars, starches)
- "empty" snacking calories replacing nutritious ones (e.g., too many overprocessed, snack, fast-type foods)
- soft drinks and other foods containing aspartame (NutraSweet)

In her book, *Food Makes the Difference*, Dr. Patricia Kane makes a strong case for the causal role of nutrition in children's learning and behavior problems.[31] Unsuspected food allergies are often at fault, she maintains, although they are frequently difficult to identify. An even bigger problem is that modern diets in general predispose children to difficulty by weakening the brain's natural defenses. "The surge of refined carbohydrates [sugar, starch] into children's diets is appalling," she says. Convenience and fast foods and sugared cereal are only symptomatic of our neglect of basic nutritional priorities.

Carbohydrates may impair intellectual performance differently in different children, suggests MIT biochemist Dr. Judith Wurtman, because in large doses they may act more like drugs than like food. Depending on the biochemistry of the individual child, heavy doses of carbohydrates may cause a "sugar buzz"; more often, however, the aftermath is lethargy.

"A child who comes home, has potato chips and Coke in the afternoon, pizza with little or no cheese on it for dinner, and ice cream for dessert, has been priming himself with carbohydrates for several hours," Wurtman says. "When it comes time to do homework, that child will [have difficulty] because of sleepiness or lethargy." A little protein might make a big difference.[32]

One of the leading authorities in the field, Dr. Keith Conners, author of *Feeding the Brain*, has been particularly interested in the effects of sugar on learning.[33] In conducting extensive experiments with both "normal" and "hyperactive" children, he discovered that high-protein breakfasts (two eggs, in these experiments) could counteract sugar's negative effects and possibly even improve learning and memory in the brain's chemical transmission system. On the other hand, no breakfast or a high-carbohydrate one (two pieces of toast in this case) was a recipe for trouble in some children. (As a longtime parent, I should have asked Dr. Conners how he got the children to eat the two eggs, but I didn't.)

"Kids really ought to eat breakfast because there's a measurable decline in efficiency in all kids, not just hyperactive kids, when they don't," he concludes. "That breakfast probably ought to contain at least a minimum amount of protein." It's all right to eat cereal if it has milk on it, he explains, but children who only have dry cereal or things like doughnuts or potato chips may have trouble sustaining concentration through the morning. Stress makes the brain even more susceptible. "We may need to consider selective protein supplementation for kids under a lot of stress," he suggests.[34]

Dr. Conners also emphasizes that balanced nutrition can help the brain screen out undesirable substances, even toxins such as lead. Anemic, iron-deficient children, or those without other essential nutrients such as zinc, have brains more vulnerable to toxic assault. Vitamin pills probably aren't the answer, however, since combinations of essential nutrients may be less effectively taken up and used by the body than those in real food.

Dr. Conners is also concerned about a much less discussed but perhaps even more alarming trend. Along with many others, he deplores the growing use of aspartame by children despite warnings from physicians that extended usage may have unknown and potentially dangerous neurological consequences.

Aspartame, marketed under the trade name NutraSweet, and consumed by at least 100 million Americans in the form of soft drinks and other artificially sweetened foods (including some innocent-looking vitamin pills), is broken down by the body into compounds that can cross the blood-brain barrier. They have a proven potential to disrupt brain chemistry in some people. Small children may be particularly susceptible. One of these compounds is the same as the one that causes mental retardation in untreated victims of the inherited condition called PKU, for which all newborns are now routinely screened.

According to Dr. Richard Wurtman of MIT, the foremost researcher on aspartame's effects on the brain, some individuals may be genetically more susceptible than others. *But* the effects of consumption—which range from headaches and impaired learning performance all the way up to seizures—*may show up only after prolonged use of the sweetener*. The user, therefore, may not suspect the source of the problem. Researchers believe females are affected more often than males. Figure 4 presents a list of documented neurological effects of aspartame.

Dr. Wurtman convened a recent conference at which over one hundred scientists from all over the United States and Europe presented findings that should certainly make parents think twice about allowing their children access to this substance. A predominant opinion expressed by these experts was, manufacturers' reassurances notwithstanding, research to date is surprisingly "inadequate."[35]

"Some young kids do react very adversely to this artificial sweetener," says Keith Conners. "This is a real big concern since it is so widely spread out now in our food supply."

Having followed these reports, I find myself appalled that pregnant women and many young children, even toddlers, consume this controversial intrusion into the American diet. I also wonder, given the finding that depression may be one symptom resulting from use of aspartame, whether increased consumption has any bearing on some recent reports of increased incidence of depression in teenagers. It is easy to become impatient with a society that prates about the importance of mental ability and simultaneously feeds its children such substances.

The Brain of a Couch Potato

Unfortunately, "diet" soft drinks are partially a response to the fact that we seem to be raising a generation of sedentary, physically unfit children. A number of studies have shown that an alarming number of American kids are overweight and can't pass basic physical tests of strength, endurance, and agility. In 1984, only 2% of the 18 million children who took the Presidential Fitness Test received an award. The American Academy of Pediatrics recently issued a report declaring that up to 50% of the nation's schoolchildren are not getting enough exercise to develop healthy hearts and lungs, and 40% of youngsters between ages five and eight exhibit at least one risk factor for heart disease.[36]

As clear evidence of lifestyle changes in the last two decades, rates of obesity among children and adolescents jumped 45% between 1960 and the early 1980s. The United States Army was forced in 1989 to

FIGURE 4. Symptoms Reported by 405 Persons Susceptible to Aspartame

Symptom	NUMBER (% OF TOTAL)
Neurological	
Headaches	228 (45.1)
Dizziness, unsteadiness, or both	199 (39.4)
Confusion, memory loss, or both	144 (28.5)
Convulsions (grand mal epileptic attacks)	74 (14.7)
Petit mal attacks and "absences"	18 (3.6)
Severe drowsiness and sleepiness	83 (16.4)
Paresthesias ("pins and needles," "tingling") or numbness of the limbs	68 (13.5)
Severe slurring of speech	57 (11.3)
Severe "hyperactivity" and "restless legs"	39 (7.7)
Atypical facial pain	33 (6.5)
Severe tremors	43 (8.5)
Psychiatric and Behavioral	
Severe depression	128 (25.3)
"Extreme irritability"	113 (22.4)
"Severe anxiety attacks"	92 (18.2)
"Marked personality changes"	79 (15.6)
Recent "severe insomnia"	66 (13.1)
"Severe aggravation of phobias"	34 (6.7)
Visual and auditory	
Decreased vision and/or other eye problems (blurring, "bright flashes," tunnel vision)	121 (24.0)
Pain in one or both eyes	44 (8.7)
Blindness in one or both eyes	12 (2.4)
Tinnitus ("ringing," "buzzing")	65 (12.9)
Marked impairment of hearing	23 (4.6)
Myasthenia gravis (ptosis)	7 (1.4)

Source: Wurtman, R. & Ritter-Walker, E. *Dietary Phenylalanine and Brain Function*. Boston: Birkhauser, 1988, p. 374.

modify the physical requirements in basic training because so many enlistees were getting injured.

"It's our opinion that the young people coming into the military now have spent more time in front of the TV than on the tennis court or a softball field," commented Lt. Col. John Anderson, who says he can't remember recruits in worse condition in his twenty-year career.[37]

George Allen, chairman of the President's Council on Physical Fitness and Sports, expresses serious concern about our children's condition compared to that of their counterparts in other countries.

On a recent trip to the Soviet Union, he says, "I was amazed at how far ahead the Soviet youngsters are in fitness compared to American youth. . . . You don't find many of them watching television until midnight and eating junk food."[38]

If young bodies are in bad shape, what about the brains attached to them? Surprisingly, we know little about what poor levels of fitness imply for neural functioning. A moderate relationship has been shown between motor performance and school success, and exercise can improve both motivation and subsequent abilities to concentrate.[39] Yet no one has thoroughly explored the real effects of sedentary lifestyles on learning abilities. How many attention problems could be related to the fact that so many children nowadays have their natural energies bottled up in schedules and expectation—and few physical outlets? One survey of physical education classes even showed students getting only about ten minutes of active exercise because so much time was taken up by changing clothes and listening to the teacher talk. A mother of a third grader who just started taking Ritalin because he "can't concentrate" told me that her child comes home from a seven-hour "work" day (i.e., school), has a snack, and must then sit down and do homework until dinnertime so that he won't have to miss his favorite evening TV programs. "Does he have any time for free play?" I asked. "Well, not really"—she paused— "but he has his soccer practice on weekends and a swimming lesson once a week."

Small-muscle activity is also important for school success. One recent study of children aged five to thirteen surprised researchers by showing that "sensorimotor-perceptual skills" (e.g., solving pencil-and-paper mazes, putting pegs in holes quickly and efficiently, copying geometric shapes) were as closely related to academic achievement for the older children as they were for the younger.[40]

"Thought is constructed, not only out of perceiving objects, but also out of physical activities with them."[41] When a child plays and exercises large muscles or pursues games and hobbies that build fine-motor skills (e.g., constructing models, carpentry, sewing, playing jacks), he or she is strengthening motor synapses that are next-door neighbors to the neurons that manage mental behaviors— including attention. Some children with clearly organic learning problems are motorically clumsy; this may relate to a generalized difficulty organizing and managing what comes into and goes out of their brains (in this case messages to and from the muscles). It seems only reasonable to assume that learning to manage muscles teaches a child feelings of control. Whether or not specific neural connections for attention and more abstract types of learning are also being forged is an interesting research question.

A program of physical exercises, called Sensory Integration Therapy, was developed by California physical therapist Dr. Jean Ayres because of her conviction that movement is the foundation of many types of learning.[42,43] Many physical therapists and some teachers who work with children with learning disabilities have become convinced of the value of these techniques. Definitive proof has been hard to come by, but even professionals who are skeptical of claims about "sensory integration" are aware of the need to study the relationship of children's movement and learning.

Dr. Phyllis Weikart, associate professor in the Division of Physical Education at the University of Michigan and author of *Round the Circle: Key Experiences in Movement,* fears that lack of play and body movement is jeopardizing young children's potential learning abilities.[44] She thinks adults are too busy trying to sit children down and force learning, rather than letting them play naturally to build the motor-control centers of their brains.

"All this conversation is going on about cognitive development, but we've forgotten the child's body," she says. "The amount of physical activity since the turn of the century has declined seventy-five percent; children are not playing, and through play a great deal of active learning takes place. Children used to play in natural ways, with kids of different ages, outside, basically unsupervised by adults. Visual and auditory attention, body coordination—all were gained through that kind of play. This physical learning must take place before children start dealing with abstractions; it doesn't happen if children don't have those experiences."

Changing lifestyles may also be squelching the independent experiences by which children learn to manage their own brains, according to this expert on motor development. "We're providing care so the parents can work. We're creating homogeneity of age groups so children aren't learning in natural cross-age situations. There are so many issues that crop up for people who are caring for children; they have to keep the lid on so the child won't get hurt and they'll get sued. These issues didn't exist before, but they're not going to go away. Parents are going to work and these children have to be cared for, but we've got to be careful we don't negate all the naturalness that kids need in play."

Dr. Weikart has recently become fascinated by the question of how physical movement helps children develop an internal sense of "beat" that seems to correlate with reading and math abilities. She acknowledges she can not yet explain, in terms of the brain, what "beat" has to do with academic learning, but when we were talking, I remembered that several elementary physical-education teachers had shared with me their puzzlement about why so many more children today seem to be lacking this basic sense of internal rhythm. Dr. Weikart suggests that the reason may be they have not gotten in touch with the internal beat of their own bodies.

"It's frightening! They need beat, but rock music doesn't give them that because it's heard, they don't create it out of their own bodies," she insists. "Feeling has to be independent for the child; you can't make it loud and you can't make it visual as in the videos; *it has to be felt.* Unless the child is rocked, patted, stroked, danced with at the same time; unless adults are creating the feel of the beat for the child who is hearing it, that feel of beat does not develop."

If children are exposed to too much strong, external beat, they may become "disoriented" and develop attention problems because they are having difficulty reconciling their own inner beat with the outside stimulus, suggests Dr. Weikart. "That constant verbal, visual bombardment, all it's doing is tuning children out. If we want to improve their attention, we've got to get them up, get them physically involved, tune them back in."[45]

Noisy Brains

Nowadays when the parents bring these kids in the morning, we have to spend at least a half hour either waking them up or calming them down. They come from houses where the TV is going all the time, ride in cars with the music blaring—it's no wonder some have blocked it out and others are bouncing off walls. We used to be able to start our activities as soon as the children arrived, but now we always begin with a nice long transition period to get them tuned in.
                                        —Nursery school teacher, Texas

Could stereo headphones change children's brains? Obviously there's the potential for that. One could argue one of two things: either that it will make them more auditorily responsive or that it's going to produce some kind of weird dissociation between modalities [hearing and seeing] because they're chronically dissociated by the use of those things.
                                        —Dr. William T. Greenough

What does noise bombardment do to children's brains? How much may it account for kids who can't pay attention, listen to "talk," and tune in appropriately to learning? One line of research has centered on the irreplaceable structures in the ear that are especially vulnerable during early years. It has been proven that they can be damaged by certain loud noises, including music.

Another group of studies has shown that environments not considered particularly noisy by adults may interfere permanently with the development of language, listening, and even reading abilities.[46]

Other interesting avenues of speculation are also being discussed behind the closed doors of neuropsychological conferences. Three of these involve the effects of a preponderance of musical stimulation on the development of the hemispheres and the connections between them, some additional ideas about what heavy doses of "beat" might do to growing brains, and the effects of an overload of sensory input on a nervous system that has not yet developed effective mechanisms to defend itself.

Brain studies have repeatedly shown that music, for everyone but highly trained musicians, is processed predominantly in the right hemisphere—in areas directly opposite those responsible for most language processing. Most of us listen and respond primarily in a holistic, "feeling" way to melody (right hemisphere's specialty), while musicians are trained to listen analytically to the technical sequence of notes and other features that must be handled by the left hemisphere.[47,48] The relaxed state often induced by music is reflected in changes in brain-wave patterns: the more vigorous beta waves that characterize active mental processing yield to slower alpha waves, which are more commonly associated with relaxation. When parts of the brain are "in alpha," they are essentially switched off from active thinking or learning.

Why do some teenagers insist they can concentrate better on their homework with a background of music? We might speculate that music as background generates enough alpha in the right hemisphere to enable left hemisphere language areas to lead the attack on academic work. No one really understands all the ramifications of hemispheric byplay. Moreover, what works for one brain may be annoying or distracting for another. When music stops being background and becomes foreground, concentration probably suffers.

Increasing questions are being raised as to whether too much loud music might induce in a growing brain not real relaxation, but instead a habit of defensively "tuning out" to active thought ("going into alpha"). A related question is whether large quantities of uncritical listening may rob left-hemisphere language systems of the developmental time and space they need for fine-tuning. Certainly, the lyrics of much contemporary music are definitely not designed as linguistic models. "For every song that stands or falls by its words, there must be a hundred that thrive in spite of them . . . and sound often has the edge over sense," commented Jon Pareles, acerbic *New York Times* music critic.[49] Like other serious musicians, he expresses concern over declining interest by listeners in responding to more complex, analytic forms of the art. Much popular music, he says, "eliminates the most complex, time-consuming, mentally draining part of the musical experience—paying attention."[50]

No one would recommend depriving adults of badly needed relaxation and harmless—for them—pleasures. Yet there are many adult pleasures that are handled successfully only by the mature brain. For children, challenge is the stimulus for the hemispheres to get their act together by strengthening the physical connections between them. Anything that either forces or induces the brain into a non-learning state for extended periods of time could certainly interfere with this process.

Young brains are particularly sensitive because they haven't yet developed automatic screening devices. The normal human brain has built-in mechanisms for moderating incoming sensory stimulation to levels that keep it sufficiently "aroused" without becoming overwhelmed. Children's brains, however, have not had time to refine these filtering systems; when overwhelmed, they either "tune out" or their behavior becomes unmanageable. Even normal adults exposed long enough to abnormally high or low levels of sensory stimulation may start to act like hyperactive children![51] We all learn to screen out a great deal of background noise (e.g., canned music in stores, offices, etc.), but at some point the unconscious effort involved takes its toll and we become habitually stressed out without understanding why. For youngsters, it is even harder to sort out such effects.

Dr. Susan Luddington-Hoe, the authority on infant stimulation, points out that even before birth tender young brains show a distinctly negative response to certain kinds of noise. She cites one example of a professional pianist who, when pregnant, found she could no longer play Chopin because her infant started to thrash around so violently. This fetus, however, seemed to love Mozart. "The fetal heartbeat changes significantly to different types of music," says Dr. Luddington-Hoe. "Both before and after birth, babies are really bothered by strong beat and loud music—but they love soft music and are especially thrilled by Vivaldi." In another case, a fetus who was taken to a rock concert kicked so hard, apparently in consternation, that he broke one of his mother's ribs.[52]

"My guess is the biggest problem with learning-disabled children is that their sensory thresholds are so low because they've had such a history of bombardment," says Dr. Luddington-Hoe. "Their brains are letting in too much input because they're overwhelmed."

Hooked on Alpha?

When considering children whose attention problems seem to relate more to underactivity, some professionals wonder whether these children are learning to swaddle their brains in sensation-dulling music as an escape from excesses of stimulation in everyday life. Is it possible to be neurologically addicted to alpha rhythm? Certainly, headsets do seem to be on their way to replacing books and magazines for the young.

When I shared some of these questions with Dr. Jerre Levy, an expert on hemispheric development who teaches at the University of Chicago, she admitted she had been wondering about this issue herself. "It's the nature of the music they're listening to, this popular music," she said. It is different from other kinds of music in that the tempo is exactly like a metronome: beat, beat, beat. Studies have shown that flashing lights at a fixed frequency (flash, flash, flash) sets up a rhythm in the brain that interferes with normal processing. The same may be true of the auditory system, she suggests.

When a person is simply sitting doing nothing, Dr. Levy went on, brain waves are regularly synchronized: boom, boom, boom. (This is the case in relaxed states such as alpha.) If the person is given a mental problem to solve, the brain's rhythm becomes "desynchronized" because the rhythm is broken by being forced to think.

"Now, if in your waking hours you have something coming in that's going beat, beat, beat," she explained, "my own feeling is that you're going to make kids space out because it's putting the brain into a loop; if it's in the loop, it can't desynchronize and therefore it can't think. You're really *blocking the capacity for thinking*."[53]

Scientists have become sufficiently concerned to initiate animal studies of other kinds of rhythmic variables. Researchers at Fairleigh Dickinson University reared mice either in a quiet environment, one with soft classical background music, or one with equally soft but arrhythmic drumbeats. The first two groups developed normally, but the latter animals showed difficulty navigating a standard maze, hyperactive and vicious behavior, as well as significant abnormalities in growth of brain cells in centers for learning and memory. Thus, it appears that continual exposure to other kinds of rhythms may also irritate the brain, irrespective of volume.[54]

In summary, it does not seem unreasonable to suggest that the brain needs time and quiet space in which to develop the ability to manage itself. To gain enough inner control to enjoy the quality of its own mental life, a child's mind should be furnished with some pieces of quiet thought, not the tacky trappings of constant noise.

The Starving Executive

*It's the lifestyles. Kids have to learn to pay attention. But as far
as adults sitting down and doing tasks with a child, I don't think
our lifestyles encourage that.*

—NURSERY SCHOOL TEACHER,
SMALL TOWN, TENNESSEE

The growing brain, because it is so plastic, is a remarkably resilient
mechanism that can probably withstand a number of adverse factors
before it becomes overwhelmed. All the potential hazards in the
world may not account for the majority of the attention problems now
facing the schools. At least equally important, many experts believe,
is the way adults teach children habits of organization, reflection, and
internal control. These are important, not only for children at risk for
a clinical diagnosis of ADHD, but also for every child who will be
expected to pay sufficient attention to learn effectively.

According to a theory proposed by Dr. Michael Posner and Dr.
Frances Friedrich in a recent book on the brain and education,[1] it is
possible that training of attention in one type of learning—such as
how to do tasks at home—might make it easier for a child to learn to
use similar approaches in other situations—such as school.

Dr. Martha Bridge Denckla, a pediatric neurologist, director of the
Kennedy Institute Neurobehavioral Clinic, and professor at Johns
Hopkins School of Medicine, sees hundreds of children with learning
disabilities and attention problems each year. She says she is beginning
to wonder just how much of this growing phenomenon of inattention
might be attributable to a lack of basic organization in children's lives.

"I think clearly organic problems may account for about one-third of the cases," she told me, "but I'm beginning to think many of the others relate to changing environments for young children. I see an awful lot of parents with a lack of knowledge about child development who don't have the ability to provide the structure children need. I had a couple in the other day who thought their three-year-old was hyperactive, and when I asked them about their daily routines, I found out they expected, among other things, this three-year-old to take her own bath. There was no one to say to the child, 'Now we get up, now we get dressed.' There are families nowadays that never have a family meal; they literally leave food out on the counters. These are people living in $300,000 homes and both working in law offices."

Definite changes have occurred in the last five years, Dr. Denckla continued. "I'm worried about the parents who think they can just purchase goods and commodities without doing anything for the child. Simple things—mealtimes, bedtimes, who lays out your clothes. It would be like language deprivation—if you don't have organized 'tutoring' at home, you don't know what it feels like to have a rhythm to your day. Some parents' relationship with their children is almost all recreational. They view their child as someone to have fun with; they're the entertainment committee and the rest is up to the school or the day care. But I wonder if you can learn these general habits of self-regulation in day care. There will always be some survivors—some children will always survive—but how many are going to be in trouble?"

Could there be critical or sensitive periods for learning attention, just as there are for different aspects of language?

"No one knows," replied Dr. Denckla. "The whole developmental curve is a very long story. The steepest part of the curve is probably between ages three and six. The question not answered is whether at the very earliest part it needs one-on-one. Then, later, in a group, the underpinnings are already set."[2]

HOMES ARE IMPORTANT

Whether we want to admit it or not, the way parents and/or caregivers interact with children is critically important in teaching them how to pay attention. These interactions also communicate subtle messages about what is appropriate to pay attention to, the thing most children diagnosed as ADHD don't seem to understand.[3]

Although up to 40% of children show some specific symptoms that look like attention deficit during the preschool years,[4] many overcome these difficulties—as a result not only of maturation but of the way they are handled at home. Studies demonstrate: (1) for all but the most severely hyperactive or attention-disordered children, home environment variables are better predictors of educational outcomes and even later substance abuse and conduct problems (i.e., delinquency) than are innate biological factors;[5] (2) well-ordered, organized environments can compensate to a surprising extent even for the type of risk factors described in the last chapter; and (3) training of adult caregivers to teach children techniques of controlling behavior is at least as effective as and may be superior to the use of Ritalin.[6-8] Even when Ritalin is prescribed, its effects tend to be short-lived unless this kind of "behavioral" or "cognitive" therapy is included in the prescription.[9,10] These facts hold true at all levels of the socioeconomic scale, although the economically disadvantaged are more at risk for attention and conduct problems because of more disrupted home lives, fewer role models, less adequate health care, and a greater incidence of prematurity.[11]

The Magic Formula—Talk

In addition to helping a child with basic organization of daily routines, adults must be involved in showing children how to ask the right questions, talk through problems, plan ahead, and generally insert language (and some associated thought) between impulse and behavior.[12] In other words, adults must talk with children. Let me illustrate this point with an example. Traveling by plane, I was recently seated next to a mother with a four-year-old son and an infant daughter going from the East Coast to a western city that was to be their new home. The boy, an obviously bright and wiggly handful, had scarcely touched the seat before he began to spew forth questions. Despite her need to keep the baby under control, this mother patiently tried to answer each in terms the child could understand. I was struck with the advanced quality of both his language expression and his understanding—as well as the degree of maternal patience. Soon after we took off, the inevitable occurred.

"Mommy, I have to go to the bathroom!"

Long pause. "Are you *really* sure?"

"No, I really don't."

"Well, if you must go, I will take you, but I'll have to do something with the baby."

"We can leave the baby with this lady," he suggested, gesturing all too willingly at me.

"No, we can't," replied Mom with a wink in my direction.

"Why?"

"Because we don't leave babies with other people."

Momentarily satisfied, the child decided his needs were taking a different course.

"I'm thirsty!"

"The flight attendant will come around soon with a tray of drinks. Let's plan now what you would like to drink when he gets here."

After actively debating the relative merits of soft drinks and juice, he decided, "Orange juice. Why are you putting the table down?"

"So you'll have a place to put your drink when it comes. Now you're all ready."

"I'm going to ask him if he's going to serve lunch on this flight." This child was learning how to get mentally as well as physically prepared.

Eventually, the conversation turned to their new home. "Mom, show me again where we're going." Mom took a map from the seat pocket and juggling infant and bottle, pointed out their former home and their destination.

"And my dad's right there!" said the boy, tapping the map triumphantly.

"Yes, and tomorrow at three o'clock we're going to go to your new school and meet your new teacher. That will be fun because you'll get to meet lots of new children."

He mulled this over for a moment, and a shadow crossed his face. "Mommy!" he lamented. "I can't read!"

Mom smiled. "You're not supposed to be able to read—you're only four years old."

This seemingly unremarkable interchange struck me as important for several reasons. First, it seemed evident that the child's advanced language development stemmed, at least in part, from the time that his mother and other adults (she told me later she is a full-time student) have spent in conversation with him. Secondly, although he is obviously cut out of vigorous and distractible material, his energies have been directed into mental exploration of ideas rather than impulsive physical action. Third, his mother is teaching him the habit of using language to plan ahead and get prepared for things that will happen instead of responding impulsively. In this way, she is helping him get control over his own brain, his behavior—and his world. I am willing to bet this child will do well in school, not just because he is bright, but because his environment is preparing him for the kinds of sustained mental involvement and control that are so integral to learning.

I have also observed, less happily, other types of interaction: adults who abdicate the job of showing children what this type of thoughtful reasoning looks and sounds like, others who slap or jerk around children, responding impulsively to the exigencies of the moment themselves rather than taking the time to think and talk through a problem.

Even well-intentioned, loving parents sometimes teach children to respond in ways that don't build the type of attention- and problem-solving skills they will need for academic learning. On another flight not long after the one described above, I was dealt a father and his adorable two-year-old daughter, who were flying from Chicago to Los Angeles. This dad, clearly devoted to his little girl, got another prize for patience as he tried to amuse her with no toys or books and just a few snacks. She soon spied the instruction card and in-flight magazine in the seat pocket and started playing with them, putting the card in and out of the pocket, on her head, behind his back, etc. Dad cooperated, smiling, in the game, but there was no conversation. Anytime she wanted something, she would point or pull on his hand to attract his attention.

Eventually the game with the card became a bit too vigorous, so he opened the magazine in front of her, turning the pages as they regarded the pictures together. Again, almost no words were exchanged. The youngster would spy a picture and pound excitedly on it with her fingers; Dad would grunt an assent and then move on to another picture. Occasionally, he provided a simple label such as "flower" or "elephant." Once, at a picture of a tiger, the child held up her hands, pantomiming fear. "Oooooo—" she said, and Dad replied, "Ummmmmm."

Overall, it was clear, although this child was able to speak, she was being encouraged to respond more to color and interesting shapes than she was to the content of the pictures. Moreover, the "game" here soon began to focus on who could turn the page faster—and the action began to get out of hand, with the magazine now assuming the function of a manipulative toy. As the child got increasingly excited, father replaced the magazine in the seat pocket and without a word, offered her a packet of pretzels as distraction and struck up a conversation with me.

I feel guilty being critical of this devoted parent, and we certainly can't compare the verbal development of a two-year-old with that of a child two years older. Nevertheless, I was struck by the different styles these two parents were modeling. The first mother was showing her son how to think and plan ahead—to act rather than react. She was teaching him not only to express his needs, ask questions, understand and organize his world, but also to think and reason about situations far from the one at hand (the "decontextualized" thinking mentioned earlier as being so important in school). The father was encouraging his little girl, at a critical age for language foundations, to respond impulsively and almost exclusively to the physical, visual, and emotional aspects of each situation. A related message was that the text of reading material is secondary to the pictures.

Studies that we will explore fully in a later chapter have shown that children from homes that encourage these two different patterns tend to achieve—and to pay attention—very differently when they get to school. It is not a matter of intelligence, but rather a question of learning to use the planning functions of language to mediate personal thought and problem-solving.

Conversation Builds the Executive Brain

It is not intuitively surprising to learn that teaching children to talk through problems helps them with higher-level learning and mental organization—as well as with managing their behavior. It is more surprising to discover, in the writings of Russian neuropsychologist Alexander Luria, that conversing with one's own mind may have brain-altering physical effects. Luria believed, and many modern-day theorists agree, that using language can strengthen the brain's executive functions, with a shorthand system of communicating with oneself as the final and most critical stage of the process.

The term "inner speech" refers to this shorthand, an internal dialogue used, for example, to help us remember something ("Now, let's see, I was going to buy hamburger buns and mustard and something else for the picnic"), to plan ahead ("Since I'm going to meet him at noon, I'll have to leave home at eleven-thirty"), or to work out the steps in solving a problem ("If I start by trying . . . , then this might happen . . . and then I'd have to . . ."). As adults we don't *say* all these words to ourselves, we somehow *think* them almost instantaneously.

According to Luria, this ability develops slowly as a child's overall capacity to use language shapes growing powers of reasoning. He believed that both external and internal language partially account for the fact that the human species sports brains more complex and specialized than those of animals, mainly in the area of the executive prefrontal cortex. Language, he maintained, is a process that is "characteristic of the development of almost all the higher forms of mental activity" and can physically *"reorganize the cortical zones that underlie higher mental processes."*[13]

Luria drew many of his ideas about the way children learn to reason from the work of another Russian, Lev Vygotsky. Vygotsky's work is currently being rediscovered in Europe, Israel, and America and applied both by developmental psychologists and by therapists working with attention-disordered children. In an influential book entitled *Thought and Language,* Vygotsky described both the way in which inner speech develops and how interaction with adults helps children learn to use it to organize their mental processes.[14]

SPEECH THAT TURNS INTO THOUGHT

According to Vygotsky, inner speech develops as the child learns to use language, first to think out loud and then to reason inside his own mind. Eventually, it becomes an instinctive tool with which to think and also to communicate thoughts by speech and writing. I am convinced that a major reason so many students today have difficulty with problem solving, abstract reasoning, and writing coherently is that they have insufficiently developed mechanisms of inner speech. First of all, their brains may have been bombarded with too much noise and overprogramming (literally and figuratively!). How could they tune in to an inner voice if they are never allowed to experience quiet? Secondly, some adults are copping out on showing children how to use this tool for thinking. Third, schools that keep young children from talking much of the time—even to themselves—do not help the situation.

Inner speech starts with social experience in the earliest interactions of the infant and the caregiver. Children gradually absorb the methods that caregivers use to regulate them and then begin to use the same methods on themselves. Impulsive physical punishment or careless unconcern may cause the child to try to manage his world in the same manner. He may also adopt a similarly impulsive or diffident mental style—jumping at problems, striking out at them and then withdrawing, or else simply avoiding them. On the other hand, if adults show children that they themselves carefully evaluate, think, and talk through problems, the child receives a very different set of messages about the way the world—both physical and mental—should be approached.

Most parents talk to their infants. When they first begin, perhaps even before birth, speech has little if any meaning for the child. Soon, however, he or she begins to respond and gradually, as words spoken by adults begin to make sense, starts to use words on herself. A toddler may give himself or herself commands out loud, as when a two-year-old says "Susan, no!" when she knows she shouldn't touch something. At this point the system is still far from being internalized, so she may go ahead and touch it anyway! (Notably, adult patients who have suffered damage to frontal brain areas often behave in much the same way.) For the child, this step is an important one, which Vygotsky called "egocentric speech." "It does not merely accompany the child's activity . . . it is intimately and usefully connected with the child's thinking."[15]

Egocentric speech gradually starts to be absorbed. As prefrontal cortex matures, the regulatory "talk" goes underground between the ages of three and seven and becomes transformed into the ability to "think words" and use them to manage behavior. The ages of two to five years seem to be particularly important for this step,[16] and by the time a child is of elementary school age, the ability to reason within one's own brain should be off to a good start. It is probably no coincidence that this timetable appears to correspond with preliminary development of the executive control centers in the prefrontal cortex.

Examples from studies investigating the development of inner speech show how children learn it. Toddlers, when given a pegboard and instructed to hit a single peg, followed the directions better when they were shown how to say "one" at the same time they hit the peg. It was necessary for these little ones to say the word out loud. By upper-elementary school age, children should be able to use a silent cue with equal effectiveness.

School-aged children also tend to be more aware of the meaning of the words they use. In one ingenious series of studies, children aged three to seven were placed in a room containing highly attractive items such as food or toys. They were told that the longer they refrained from touching the tempting objects, the greater the prize they would earn. The experimenter then left the room while a hidden camera and a mike recorded the children's reactions. Children who mumbled or talked to themselves (e.g., "I won't touch, I won't touch") were more successful at waiting than those who didn't use language to help themselves. Then the experimenters tried teaching the children to use different types of verbal cues, either relevant (e.g., "I must not turn around and look at the toys") or irrelevant (e.g., "Hickory dickory dock"). Younger children were helped somewhat by being taught to say any words at all, whether they related to the situation or not, but older ones were more successful with instructions that had appropriate meaning. Experiments like these have shown that there is a definite developmental progression in the use of inner speech, and a "trend from externalized to internalized control."[17]

These forms of verbal self-regulation, as they are called, also help children with learning tasks. Children who use inner speech effectively can remember information and events better. They are better at problem-solving because they can "talk through" steps, evaluate alternatives, and speculate about possible outcomes. They can organize and apply information more effectively and develop better strategies when taking notes in class, studying for exams, and even understanding and remembering what they read.

Is it a complicated job to teach children verbal self-regulation? No, but it takes a long time and a lot of attention. When adults make the effort to sit down and work with a child, they not only automatically arouse the child's motivation, but they also tend instinctively to ask questions to clarify where the child's thinking "is coming from." Educational psychologist Eleanor Duckworth believes these natural interactions give children tools to refine their own inner dialogue. She says:

> To the extent that one carries on a conversation with a child as a way of trying to understand a child's understanding, the child's understanding increases "in the very process." The questions the interlocutor asks in an attempt to clarify for him/herself what the child is thinking oblige the child to think a little further also. . . . What do you mean? How did you do that? Why do you say that? How does that fit with what was just said? I don't really get that; could you explain it another way? Could you give me an example? How did you figure that?[18]

In today's parlance, Vygotsky's theory suggests that adults must act as coaches to show children how to internalize speech. As they do so, they also teach strategies for thinking. Parents instinctively model and help their children practice physical skills or speech patterns that are just one step above their current level of development; in similar ways they help them talk and think their way through problems. The adult, working with the child, structures the situation so that the child can reason at a level that would be impossible if he were left on his own.

When I reflect on this important view of adult roles in the learning process, I like to picture the child as perched somewhere on a long developmental ladder. Underneath are all the stages of mental development already mastered, far above are those yet unreachable. But directly above the child there is a lovely, ripe area that is attainable—but only with a leg up from adults who will provide physical and mental cues and clues. Vygotsky called this ripe area the *zone of proximal development*, now often referred to as the ZPD.

PROBLEM SOLVING, LIFESTYLES, AND THE ZPD

This type of adult support acts as a *scaffold* which surrounds children with competence as they move into new types of learning. Courtney Cazden describes a familiar scene in illustration of a basic physical type of scaffolding for a child who is just learning to walk:

> Imagine a picture of an adult holding the hand of a very young child. . . . The child does what he or she can and the adult does the rest; the child's practice occurs in the context of the full performance; and the adult's help is gradually withdrawn (from holding two hands to just one, then to offering only a finger, and then withdrawing that a few inches, and so on) as the child's competence grows.[19]

Intellectual reasoning and problem-solving are similarly guided. One of the adult's most important and difficult jobs, of course, is gradually to withdraw the supports until the child can succeed independently. Rather than fostering dependence, good scaffolding encourages independence. Caretakers who are overly anxious about their responsibility for a child, who end up doing everything for him and "picking up the pieces" of the problems he should clean up himself, are setting him up for later learning difficulties.

When a child learns along with an adult, special sorts of motivation and mastery infuse the experience. They mutually share the responsibility for the outcome; the child does what he can, and the adult fills in the gaps. Thus the child learns:

- how to do the task in question
- what it feels like to be successful at doing it
- the importance of persistence
- what it means to take personal responsibility for the outcome

These particular experiences are ones in which learning disabled and ADHD children tend to be deficient. The alarming news is that increasing numbers of "normal" children also seem to lack them. Poor learners are poor problem solvers; they have difficulty taking internal responsibility and coming up with effective strategies to cope with new or difficult types of learning. In classrooms now, the term "learned helplessness" is increasingly heard as a description of typical forms of behavior. One major theory even argues that "learned helplessness" and weakness in problem-solving strategies may be fundamental causes of learning disability.

Many children today spend a great deal of time in situations where competent adults are not available or involved in providing suitable scaffolding for inner speech and other problem-solving skills. These abilities are best learned in natural contexts, with real problems that have meaning to both adult and child—such as helping in the kitchen, the workshop, the garden, the store, or other forms of mutual activity. Watching television does *not* suffice, since it is not an interactive experience and tends to suppress any tendency to talk through problems or ask questions about why things are happening. It also tends to focus on "magical" solutions and visual effects that defy true logic.

One elementary school head in an affluent Midwestern suburb recently told me that children from "normal" households are now showing the types of language and impulse-control problems she used to see only in children who came from a home where a parent was "disturbed, depressed, or alcoholic.

"It's as if no one had taken the time to talk to these children, help them think through a process step by step. People used to say things like, 'Now we're going to clean the living room; what are we going to need? Let's see, we'll need a dustrag and the vacuum, etc. You go get the dustrag. Oh, I'd better put vacuum bags on the shopping list.'

"Simple things like that, so the child gets to make connections, classify, follow directions, learn to think ahead. Now our children don't so often help with the housework, the grocery shopping. The caregiver may be different from the housekeeper, and so the child isn't exposed to these kinds of experiences. Even when the parent does the chores, after they've been working all day they're tired, and it's easier to do it themselves.

"I'm worried," she added as I prepared to leave her office. "These parents are highly achieving people because of the input they received from their parents. They expect their children to be high achievers, too, but they're cheating them out of the same experiences."

A Generation of "Weak Reasoners"

Older students now in schools also have difficulty developing strategies to solve problems and sticking to the task until success is achieved. The startling national decline in reading comprehension, mathematics reasoning, and science ability in the United States has been attributed by many educators to a growing prevalence of this type of "weak reasoning"—and not just among the learning disabled. As an example, "dismal" was the term applied to student proficiency in mathematics by the National Assessment of Educational Progress on the basis of testing done in 1986. Although the amount of math homework and testing in schools has increased "dramatically" over the last few years, what little progress has occurred has come in lower-order skills (routine adding, multiplying, etc.). Students' abilities to answer questions requiring application of concepts and even elementary-level problem-solving strategies were alarmingly far off the levels required by future life and work settings.

Only 6.4% of the seventeen-year-olds could solve a multistep problem like the one in Figure 5 (which requires only simple knowledge of number facts, but which demands some persistence.)

One mathematics specialist recently told me she anticipates a growing "crisis" in analytic thought and problem-solving. As an example, she cited a group of "typical" middle school students who, she discovered, could multiply four-digit numbers with ease but were unable to deal with word problems like the following:

"A man bought four shirts at $19.95. How much did he spend?"

"They can compute, but they don't seem to be able to stop, think, and reason about the processes involved," she concluded.

Who should be teaching children the real-life basics of problem-solving? Adults need to be available—at home and at school—to act as models and guides at every stage of development. Jerome Bruner calls this "loaning children our consciousness."[20] But the models must themselves have the mental abilities in question. There are as many routes up the ladder—neural and mental—as there are different types of learning. When parents make decisions about who will have the job of caring for their children, they are signing up the intelligence and the consciousness that will shape those growing minds.

The Starving Executive: A Hypothesis

I believe the brain's executive systems and their links to lower centers for attention and motivation are particularly at risk for children

FIGURE 5

National Math Assessment:
Sample Question

Only 6.4% of the 17-year-olds could solve multi-step problems like this one:

R	S	40
35	25	15
T	V	W

In the figure above, R, S, T, V, and W represent numbers.
The figure is called a magic square because adding the numbers in any row or column or diagonal results in the same
sum. What is the value of R? 30; 40; 50; can't tell.

Source: "The Mathematics Report Card: Are We Measuring Up?"

today. These late-developing areas, which may be particularly sensitive to environmental deprivation, are responsible for many so-called
"control functions."[21]

Individuals who have suffered damage to prefrontal areas (depending somewhat on the location of the injury) behave much like children
with attention problems:[22,23]

- inattentiveness; distractibility; tendency to be "stimulus bound"
- lack of organization, planning, and programming of behavior
- difficulty delaying gratification and working toward future goals
- difficulty inhibiting inappropriate behavior
- dissociation between talk and follow-through
- problems with complex and conceptual verbal activities
- inability to regulate and sustain motivation

- difficulty controlling emotional responses
- deficits in selective attention

I am not implying here that children with attention problems are "brain damaged" in the same sense as adult frontal-lobe patients. I am suggesting that they may never have fully developed these abilities in the first place and thus may behave similarly to people who once had the functions but lost them through injury to the brain areas involved.

When Should Children Start to Learn Self-Control?

Researchers have been unsure when the various functions of the prefrontal lobes normally begin to mature. We know their growth continues into the twenties—and that they comprise the longest of the brain's developmental processes. One of the most important tasks of the adolescent brain, in fact, is to refine these control systems and learn to use them effectively.[24]

In a recent review, Dr. Pennington and his colleague Dr. Marilyn Welsh presented evidence that prefrontal abilities begin to emerge even earlier than anyone imagined, in the first year of life. According to these authors, even preschoolers may suffer from "subtle prefrontal dysfunction" that mainly takes the form of a lack of self-control, lack of "active information gathering" (e.g., systematically exploring the physical environment, asking questions). With older children, poor problem-solving is a prominent indicator of difficulty. These researchers call attention to the fact that "many childhood learning and behavior disorders are manifested in the context of normal IQ and some subset of these may be the result of a specific frontal dysfunction."[25]

If Luria was correct about inner speech being the mechanism that "feeds" the development of the frontal cortex, and if this area's development continues as long as researchers believe, it seems reasonable to assume that lifestyles that bombard children with noise, constant activity, and limited access to thoughtful adult models might certainly jeopardize its development. Many children today do not get much exposure to what reflective thought looks or feels like. Many live in homes or attend care centers where hurried, overworked, or undertrained adults don't have time to provide one-on-one scaffolding or to sense where that critical "zone of proximal development" lies. Others are tended by caretakers who do too much for the child and thus block the internalization of responsibility. Many attend schools that try to cram the storehouse full, while disregarding the necessity for internal motivation, talking—and thinking—to oneself, and personal coaching for problem-solving. A great deal of baby-sitting is done by a mesmerizing screen that reduces problems to two-minute "bits" in a generic "zone of proximal development." No wonder many of our children have trouble.

No one knows whether or when critical or sensitive periods occur for specific functions of the prefrontal cortex, but this principle may well apply here as well as to the rest of the brain. How long is the window open? Dr. Kenneth Klivington of the Salk Institute and an editor of *The Brain, Cognition, and Education*[26] says he thinks it is important for scientists to try to find out. "Attention is fundamental to any learning process, but no one knows if there is a critical period for attention. To my knowledge, there are no scientific studies of this fact, but there are so many capabilities that have critical periods in their development, it could also be that attention and logical thinking are the same. If so, once you pass that critical age, there's little likelihood of your being able to learn it," he told me recently.

"I wonder what that age would be," I replied.

"I don't know, but it's probably in the early teens—that's just guesswork on my part. It's important to raise those kinds of issues because the experiments need to be done, and unless those issues are spelled out and brought to people's attention, nobody's going to do the experiments," he continued. "They're hard experiments and may not even be possible to do, but it's important to try. We need to obtain further evidence if there are critical periods in attention or logical thinking."

"In the meanwhile, how would you advise parents?" I asked Dr. Klivington.

"I continue to place the emphasis on the need to generate language and thought, not just listen and watch," he answered immediately.[27] "If we consider the brain as the organ of thought, it has to be structured right to work right. If you don't wire up your computer right, it isn't going to work right."

SUMMARY: LIFESTYLES AND LEARNING

Attention and learning abilities depend both on the way the brains of the learners are innately structured and the uses for which they are trained. The success of any learning experience depends on the interaction between a brain's strengths and weaknesses and the demands of the learning situation. Some children's learning abilities are damaged by overt or subtle environmental impairment, but the term "learning disability" now often simply describes an unexplained misfit between child and school. Attention deficit disorder (ADHD) and dyslexia are examples of disabilities that may sometimes have a genetic component but that also reflect strong effects of environmental training.

The growing brain is resilient, but may eventually be compromised by combinations of factors ranging from exposure to toxic substances, over- or understimulation, or lack of availability of appropriate adults to provide scaffolds for intellectual growth. Particularly important are inner speech, attention, and problem-solving strategies attributed to prefrontal development in the brain.

Environments can cause problems if (1) the specific demands they place for learning are misfitted to the brains of the learners, or (2) if they fail to instill in developing minds the fundamental skills of attention and reasoning. Increasing numbers of children today show evidence of weakness in attention, language, and reasoning, yet teachers continue to assume the presence of these skills and tend to blame the students for their unwillingness to pay attention to content and method for which their brains have been poorly adapted.

If adults in a society have things they want children to pay attention to, they must make available the consciousness that will develop the habits of mind—and thus the structures of the brain—to make it possible.

Part Four

CLASHING CULTURES

TV, Video Games, and the Growing Brain

It turns kids into zombies!
Children are active while viewing.
Television shortens attention spans.
There is no evidence that television viewing affects children's
attention spans.
Video games make people right-brained.
Children today are smarter because of television.
Video use is killing off literacy.

Everyone has opinions about the effects on learning of television and other uses of video. What is the truth? What does viewing do to the developing brain? How much does growing up in the culture of visual immediacy affect a child's performance in the culture of academic learning?

When I began writing this book, one of my first questions was how much video use has played into the changes observed in children's learning habits. I soon found out: (1) good research on TV is hard to find, (2) much of what is purveyed as "fact" has not been thoroughly documented, (3) according to the most recent studies, television's effects may be more subtle, but also more powerful and pervasive than most people believe and (4) virtually no research is available on the effects of video tapes or computerized video games on children's mental development. Moreover, because more children now spend more hours with all video media than ever before, effects which might not have become apparent in previous decades may just now be showing up in schools.

Calling a Very Large Duck a Duck

All video has effects on mental activity; some of its uses are clearly more positive for academic learning than others. Good television programming has made a wealth of information available to children, although this benefit alone does *not* make them smarter if they lack the habits of mind to use it effectively. Good-quality videocassettes for children may also enhance cognitive and perhaps even language development if they encourage response from the child and if viewing is mediated by an adult. Many young children now use a familiar videotape as a sort of security blanket with which to relax. Rock videos, on the other hand, have aroused concern, not only about their effects on young brains, but on other aspects of development as well.

Let us first consider television. I was surprised to learn how much a part of young children's lives TV has become. American youngsters, on average, now spend more hours in front of the set than at any other activity except sleeping. *Sesame Street* has helped institutionalize the viewing habit for preschoolers, many of whom begin watching several hours a day of varied programming at about age two. By ages three to five—the height of the brain's critical period for cognitive and language development—estimates place viewing time of the average child at twenty-eight hours a week. For many children, extended hours in front of the set have drastically curtailed active playtime. Average viewing time for elementary students runs at about twenty-five hours a week, and for high schoolers, twenty-eight hours a week, approximately *six times the hours spent doing homework.*[1-4] No estimates are available on time spent with videotapes.

In many households, even infants are constantly exposed; programs replace family conversation that builds language and listening skills, reading aloud, and games and activities in which adults show children how to solve problems, talk out future plans, or deal with their own emotions. Many parents who would earnestly like to redirect their family time find the kids so "hooked" on viewing, says Marie Winn, that they "reject all those fine family alternatives"—mainly because watching television is *easier.*[5] Children from lower socioeconomic backgrounds watch the most of all.[6]

Where Is the Research?

Scientists are acutely aware that large doses of any type of experience have shaping power over the growing brain. Have they, therefore, been hotly researching the effects of large doses of television? No!

A relatively small number of studies have looked at TV's effects on learning, but when I initiated computer-assisted searches of all studies and articles ever published in the fields of medicine, psychology, child development, and education on TV's effects on brain development, I came up with a virtually empty net. As I queried experts and burrowed further into sources of professional information, I learned the truth: no sustained effort has been made to find out how TV might affect the basic neural foundations for learning. Moreover, many of the "facts" purveyed about television's effects—not only on brains but on learning in general—are based on wobbly research.

Appropriate, nonharmful technology for studying living brains while they are reading, learning, remembering—or watching the tube—has become increasingly accessible. For example, by pasting electrodes to the scalp and hooking them up to a computer, scientists can monitor brain waves and map mental activity in living color![7] Good research is admittedly hard to do, but I find it surprising that no effort has been made even to get it started. Since the scientific community's research proposals tend to cluster around any topic where funding is available, the obvious conclusion is that the interest—i.e., *money*—has not been there. Most of the few available studies, in fact, were done by advertisers who wanted to know how to grab and hold the brain's attention—whether the "subject" chose to be spellbound or not. (More about this later.) When some early results began to indicate that the actual physical act of viewing may cause the brain to enter a hypnotic, nonlearning state, the research trickle abruptly dried up.

One might certainly be tempted to conclude that no one is very eager to get the answers to the questions. And, of course, it is more comfortable to believe that TV's effects on learning are not particularly harmful. As I began writing this chapter, headlines throughout the United States were seized by a new, quasi-scientific "review of research" which seemed to suggest just that. Statements such as the following were quoted:

"There is little evidence to show that brain viewing reduces children's attention span. . . ."

"There is no evidence that television makes children cognitively passive."

Unfortunately, these articles were, in the words of the study's author, Dr. Daniel Anderson of the University of Massachusetts, "badly distorted." They failed to mention, first, the primary reason there is "little evidence" is that there has been little research! Moreover, some of the few reliable studies which have been done suggest just the opposite! Here are some other statements from that report that didn't make the headlines:

Television may indeed:

- overstimulate children and create passive withdrawal
- cause attention and listening problems (e.g., paying attention to an activity such as drawing pictures instead of to a teacher delivering instruction)
- make children need "the classroom equivalent of special effects" to maintain attention
- emphasize skills which do not transfer well to reading or listening[8]

"No, I am not at all satisfied with the quality of the research that has been done," Dr. Anderson told me. "There has been no agency willing to consistently fund research on the cognitive effects of television."[9]

"There is really no satisfactory data," agrees Yale's Dr. Jerome Singer, another of a handful of well-respected national authorities on children and television. "But it's amazing how we fail to appreciate the fact that children spend more time in front of TV than in school. Of course there are cumulative effects!"

Dr. Singer believes that it is best to withhold television completely until reading and learning habits are well established. He mentioned during the course of our conversation that his son, who has been a father himself for several years, delayed purchasing a television set as part of "an active decision" to significantly limit family viewing.[10]

Cognitive Consequences of TV Viewing

One problem with studies comparing viewers and nonviewers is that it is now impossible to find large numbers of American children who have not been exposed to the medium. Research clearly shows, however, that better students tend to watch less. Moreover, as viewing goes up, academic achievement scores eventually go down.

In a thoroughly documented and objective review article published in the *Reading Research Quarterly*, two scientists from Leiden University in the Netherlands culled the most reliable data on the relationship of viewing and reading, including some obtained when television first became available in several different countries. They found that television's negative effects on reading skills were particularly strong for the more advanced abilities needed for higher-level comprehension. Among other conclusions, they stated that television:

- displaces leisure reading and thus inhibits the growth of reading skills
- requires less mental effort than reading
- may shorten the time children are willing to spend on finding an answer to intellectual problems they are set to solve
- has particularly negative effects for heavy viewers, socially advantaged children, and intelligent children[11]

Curiously, these quotes never made the headlines either.

Much more research is needed to establish guidelines for the constructive use of this enormously influential medium. We know far too little about how media in general, and "educational" programming in particular, can aid literacy, school learning, and knowledge acquisition.

VIDEO AND THE BRAIN

Does viewing cause brains to become hyperactive? Passive? Tuned out? Can it change brain structure and function in ways that alter learning potential? Attempts to study brain activation and/or patterns of brain waves of viewers have been the main means by which studies—reliable or otherwise—have searched for answers to these questions. Babies', children's, and adults' brain waves change in response to television, but little has been proven about the types of changes that occur.[12] Three effects on learning abilities, all related to attention, have been suggested: (1) some television and videotape programming artificially manipulate the brain into paying attention by violating certain of its natural defenses with frequent visual and auditory changes (known as "saliency"); (2) television induces neural passivity and reduces "stick-to-it-iveness"; (3) television may have a hypnotic, and possibly neurologically addictive, effect on the brain by changing the frequency of its electrical impulses in ways that block active mental processing.

(1) Forcing the Brain to Pay Attention

Studies sponsored by advertisers have suggested the best way to get viewers to pay attention to their messages is to capitalize on the brain's instinctive responses to danger. First, sudden close-ups, pans, and zooms are effective in alerting the brain because they violate its reflex need to maintain a predictable "personal space"—a certain distance between oneself and others. Second, "salient" features such as bright colors, quick movements, or sudden noises get attention fast, since brains are programmed to be extremely sensitive to such changes that might signal danger.

Television advertisers and most children's programs, including *Sesame Street,* are planned with an eye to capitalizing on these involuntary responses. When the *Sesame Street* format was initially designed, pilot studies were conducted in which children were shown program segments alongside competing "distractors" such as colorful slides. Thus the programmers learned that the use of many "salient" effects would keep children watching—whether they wanted to or not.[13]

In a sense, these carefully planned manipulations separate the natural responses of brain and body; although the viewer's attention is alerted, there is no need for physical action. The brain registers specific changes after a camera zoom, for example, responding as if to real danger.[14] Yet the impulse has no outlet. Researchers soon began to suggest that children thus stimulated, without natural physical outlets for the pent-up response, might develop overactivity, frustration, or irritability.[15,16] In 1975, two Australian researchers predicted with increasing viewing time spent by children there would be a proportionate increase in disorders of attention.[17]

It has been hard to "prove" that this prophecy has come true, although virtually every teacher I interviewed is convinced that it has. Dr. Dan Anderson's review report summarizes several studies in which "there does appear to be some effect of TV on attention, although the importance, generality, and nature of the effect is unknown."[18]

One reasonably well-documented fact, also according to this report, is that children's attention to TV programs tends to be fragmented, in the sense that they are actually watching it only about two-thirds of the time they spend in viewing. They may simultaneously engage in other activities or simply look away for "reduction of stimulation"—until they are drawn back by another special effect.

Television is physiologically arousing, confirms Dr. Byron Reeves of the Department of Communication at Stanford, who conducted studies of viewers' electrical brain activity. Their brains did, indeed, respond to movement as if it were actually present, causing the nervous system to prepare for a physical response. Personally, Reeves told me he also believes these habits show up in school, as children become habituated to "surprise and circus-type" presentations.

"I see it with my college sophomores," he remarked wryly. "We all know a *Sesame Street* presentation gets more attention these days."[19]

Manipulations of "arousal mechanisms" that separate brain and body may be related to reports from psychologists and teachers that today's children are increasingly "touch starved." A heavy diet of vicarious viewing that replaces real sensory involvement is directly antagonistic to the most basic principles of a young child's learning. Much early development of physical and mental skills—and of their foundations in the brain—comes from experimenting and solving problems with real-world materials. The long-term outcomes of forcing children's attention unnaturally may have even more serious implications than we have realized.

Jerking children's attention around may cause a certain amount of emotional withdrawal, as well. Young children, while involuntarily captured by novelty, really need repetition and familiarity. Anchoring experience in this way helps them gain a sense of organization and mastery. Parents who laughingly complain about how tired they are of reading the same book ("Sometimes I think if I have to do *Goodnight Moon* one more time . . .") or seeing the same story on tape are the best witnesses to a child's overriding need for familiarity. Such predictability may be particularly necessary for learning to make sense out of a world that is already sufficiently confusing.

(2) Passive Brains?

Good learning and good problem-solving require active involvement and persistence. Failures at this level are related to many types of learning disabilities. Many people intuitively feel that exposure in early childhood to a great deal of television may create passive learners who give up too easily. Proof is now starting to emerge.

One prominent researcher, Dr. Jennings Bryant of the University of Alabama, is personally convinced that TV "certainly changes things" as far as active learning is concerned.

"One thing we do know," he explained recently, "is that it reduces what we call *vigilance* [the ability to remain actively focused on a task]. If they watch lots of fast-paced programs and then we give them things to do afterward such as reading or solving complex puzzles, their stick-to-it-iveness is diminished; they're not as willing to stay with the task. Over time, with lots of viewing, you're going to have less vigilant children. *This is especially critical with relatively young children—about three to five years seem to be particularly vulnerable times* [emphasis added]."

Dr. Bryant, who served on a research and planning committee for *Sesame Street's* sibling, *The Electric Company*, told me he now believes that choosing such a fast-paced format for both programs was a mistake.

"Unfortunately," he said, "I don't think *Sesame Street* is one of the good examples. We worked so hard to grab the child's attention in the competitive media environment that sometimes I'm afraid we forgot the learning. We may have been teaching the wrong thing—learning externally instead of internally. We may have created a child who was so reinforced to go after the excitement, the blazing stars, etc., that the learning was almost secondary."

Dr. Bryant says he decided, on the basis of his research, to sit down and watch with his own children to make them aware of "how this medium can manipulate." Now they're good students, active problem-solvers, and "very selective and cynical TV consumers."

Dr. Bryant also thinks that it is probably a mistake to let children do homework in front of the set. He says that his newest research shows how competing video messages get in the way of learning and cause homework to take longer and be done less well. Programs with many auditory-orienting devices to call attention to the screen make it especially hard to focus actively on learning.[20]

Research, overall, strongly suggests that fast pace and special effects can interfere with development of active learning habits. A few studies have shown that children try to organize meaning, follow plots, and make sense out of what is happening in programs or tapes that are of interest to them, but only if they are old enough and can understand the material presented. Studies show attention tends to wander when the material is seen either as "boring" or not readily understandable; then, when something salient happens, attention is drawn back. This conditioned pattern of sporadic, externally directed attention corresponds precisely with what teachers are reporting. In class or when doing homework, one can't just let the mind change channels or wander away when things become a bit difficult or "boring."

If "receptive" learning (e.g., reading, listening) is affected by TV-induced passivity, the more active "expressive" skills, such as organizing and getting ideas down in writing, are in even greater jeopardy. Even television's staunchest defenders admit that it is primarily a receptive medium that in itself provides little practice in expression of any kind.

Dr. Anderson, who has been accused by other authorities of interpreting the research too generously in favor of television (some of his work, in fact, has been commissioned by Children's Television Workshop, which produces *Sesame Street*[21]), himself admits that "television viewing probably does not require many of the self-generated cognitive processes required by writing; as receptive cognition it is likely different in many ways from productive cognition."[22] Moreover, he acknowledges, it is likely that it "reduces task perseverance and this affects reading comprehension."[23]

(3) The "Zombie" Effect

Does television suppress mental activity by putting viewers into a trance? The few studies made of the human brain in the process of viewing, while hardly definitive, suggest that it may, at least in some individuals and with some kinds of content.

In one early experiment, an electrode was pasted to the scalp of a woman while she first looked through a magazine and then watched television commercials. As she was reading the magazine, her brain registered active alertness, but switching to TV viewing "instantly produced a preponderance of slow (alpha) waves," which are classically associated with lack of mental activity.[24]

Unfortunately, little research followed. In 1980, researchers Merrelyn and Fred Emery, at the University of Australia, reviewed a meager crop of studies and found reason for concern that prolonged television viewing might cause a syndrome of mental inactivity that would interfere with thinking and concentrating. In an article titled "The Vacuous Vision," they suggested that as viewing time by youngsters increased "this prolonged idleness of the prefrontal cortex" would have serious consequences.[25]

Although it has been shown that alpha levels can be altered by training,[26] no one has conclusively proven that persistent viewing invariably changes basic brain patterns, although several other studies have also given loose support to slower brain activation (more alpha) from TV when compared with magazine advertisements. Only three can be found comparing brain waves during television viewing versus reading of regular text. Two of the three confirmed higher levels of more passive alpha while watching television and higher levels of fast-wave beta activity during reading.[27,28]

The third study, an unpublished doctoral dissertation, may be the most important of all: it suggested that active brain response depended more on the subject's involvement with the material than on the medium itself.[29] This researcher found that interesting, more complex (but still comprehensible) reading or television could be used to elicit fast brain activity, while more simple, uninteresting, or incomprehensible material induced more slow alpha activity, irrespective of the medium. It seems probable that if the subject "tunes out" because the content seems incomprehensible, brain waves would follow. Research to be examined in the next chapter suggests that even programs specifically directed at children may be largely incomprehensible to them, even when adults think they are understanding what they see.

Other studies have described a phenomenon apparently related to the "zombielike" responses of some viewers: "attentional inertia." The longer a look at TV continues, the greater the probability it will be maintained. For example, if a child gets "glued" to the set during a program, the more likely he is to remain fixated when the scene breaks to a commercial. Mothers who have trouble summoning their children to chores, homework, or even supper are already aware that the longer a child has been watching TV, the slower he is to respond when someone calls his name. While Dr. Anderson and colleagues take this only as a sign of "increased engagement with the TV," others fear that such nondiscriminating responses verge on "mindlessness."[30] Anecdotal reports suggest that this phenomenon is more severe in some individuals than in others.

"You raise kids on sweets, they become addicted to sweets. You raise kids on alpha, they get addicted to alpha, just like any hypnotic state," commented one neuropsychologist, himself a member of the TV generation and the father of a young child (who is allowed to watch TV in highly selected quantities). He recognizes that parents in high-stress jobs may crave a soothing dose of alpha for themselves after a hard day's work, but believes this habit is not desirable for immature brains that have not yet firmed up all their connections. "The brain is programmed to repeat the same experience; neurons learn to replicate a pattern, that's how people learn, but we don't realize that what we are really learning is habits. Whenever children are doing something for a lot of the time, we should ask: Is this a habit we want them to have?"[31]

Taken all together, this sorely limited research suggests that children may be physiologically compelled to "space out" when viewing fatuous, overly difficult, or confusing content. Since the brain builds its internal connections primarily in response to active mental effort, I am willing to make the leap and suggest, by inducing our children to habituate their brains to too much easy video pleasure, we may truly risk weakening their mental abilities. Studies have shown, when young animals are placed in an enclosure from which they can merely watch others playing, that their brain growth is proportionately reduced, no matter how stimulating the visual environment.

The Video Game Addiction

> If I didn't make him eat, sleep, and go to school, he would be at that thing twenty-four hours a day!
>
> —Mother of an eleven-year-old boy

Computerized video games appear to be even more addictive for many children than television. Why do they exert such a hypnotic force? What will happen to kids who spend every available moment seeking ever greater conquests in a fantasy microworld? Could this preoccupation possibly be educational? Will it build up imagination and nonverbal abilities—or will it limit them by keeping the child from normal play and human interaction? Will children learn new strategies of problem-solving—or will they lose the ability to initiate ideas unless prompted by a machine? Unfortunately, even less is known about the long-term implications of this new "addiction" in American life. The child-development experts I have queried have given only cautious responses—most of them negative. One of the main points they always mention is the issue of "transfer," that is, how much we can expect experiences with one type of input—such as video games—to build up abilities that can be used elsewhere—such as reading or more general types of reasoning.

The Problem of "Transfer"

One of the main problems with speculations on the effects of machines is that what may seem "obvious" about what children are learning from them may not be true at all. For example, we might reason that anything improving children's visual-spatial skills (e.g., playing fast-paced video games where objects coming from all directions at once must be shot at or avoided) should also improve their reading speed, or even their geometry abilities, which are known to call heavily on visual spatial reasoning. Many people have similarly reasoned that teaching children to program a computer, with its immutable demands for logical, linear thought, must certainly teach them to think more logically.

Unfortunately, however, the brain often seems to have difficulty applying skills it has learned in one specific arena to other kinds of problems. When teachers ask, "How well will this learning *transfer*?" they are referring to the fact that teaching children how to outline a story in English class does not necessarily mean they will automatically apply the same skills to their history textbook—unless someone specifically shows them how, and they practice the same outlining with the history book. Expecting some kinds of learning to transfer is a little bit like expecting jogging to build up finger dexterity; just because the body (or the brain) is exercised, we cannot assume that the activity will "take" other than in the specific area that receives the practice.

The brain has many millions of separate cell networks or "assemblies," and does not seem to generalize very readily from one set to another. For example, after hundreds of studies showing that eye exercises involving complex designs have little effect on reading ability for most children, experts concluded that reading is the best way to improve reading. There is no evidence that the general visual stimulation of watching TV improves visual reasoning abilities in other domains. Nor does listening to music improve auditory skills for language, because words and melody are processed by totally different cell networks.

Training in more fundamental "habits of mind," such as planning organized steps to reason through problems—at home, at school, or anywhere else—may well be more generalizable. Showing children how to apply critical analysis to both reading and video is a good example of "teaching for transfer" in today's world.

Another issue raised by video games is that children may be accomplishing higher-level tasks with low-level strategies. Just because a child appears to have "mastered" a game where he is required to work his way through various levels of decision-making does not necessarily mean he has learned any new mental operations. He may simply have mastered a routine through trial and error.

It seems fairly safe to say that much of children's experience with such games will have little, if any, transfer value to traditional school tasks. While the schools should think about how they might make use of skills learned outside the classroom to further learning, no one has figured out how to make intellectual capital out of "Space Invaders." On the other hand, we do know that lack of use can definitely affect potential for brain connections. If a child spends an inordinate amount of time on video games (or television, or even other types of computer use) instead of playing and experimenting with many different types of skills, the foundations for some kinds of abilities may be sacrificed. These losses may not show up until much later, when more complicated kinds of thinking and learning become necessary. Tender young brains need broad horizons, not overbuilt neural pathways in one specific skill area. This point is extremely important as we return to the topic that has many parents worried—for good reason.

Mania for Mastery

Video games such as "Nintendo" augment some of the most riveting aspects of television viewing with the built-in reward systems of computer games. These are many children's introduction to the computer's "artificial intelligence." Much like their elder counterparts termed "computer hackers," children enmeshed with this powerful alter ego seem to be hooked by lures that ordinary activities simply do not exert.[32] Here are the games' secret weapons:

- feelings of control and mastery by the players
- exact calibration of the level of difficulty to the player
- immediate and continual reinforcement
- escape from the unpredictability of human social/emotional relationships

As with television viewing, moreover, human brains are easy prey for the demanding, colorful, fast-paced visual formats.

Human nature drives us all to master problems. A golfer may think her life's goal is to break 100, but once she is consistently scoring in the high 90's, is she content—or, more likely, does she set a new goal to break 95? Video games are perfectly designed to promise mastery—in gradual degrees, which keep the player coming back for just a little more of this heady potion. The child is always presented with slightly greater challenges, individually calibrated and always tantalizingly within reach—with continued practice. Each effort, successful or unsuccessful, is promptly reinforced; the machine becomes a personalized tutor. Even children with attention problems in other settings respond to such immediacy.

Mastery leads to a sense of power, which feels especially good to a child in a world where things seem pretty much out of control, and where teachers order children around a lot of the time. Many of the games play directly on this need.

Can these games be educational? Some have suggested that they may be training children in skills which will be needed in the future but for which we don't yet know the uses. Many teachers comment, however, that frequent players have trouble readjusting from the microworld to that of a classroom, which offers much less sensory "saliency," not a whole lot of power, and less individual attention and gratification. Some, of course, suggest that what we really need to do is make school as personally rewarding as the games.

"If we could just convince children that learning to read, and do math would make them powerful, too . . ." one teacher wistfully suggested.

Although some preliminary research suggests that perceptual-motor (specifically, eye-hand) skills may be improved by the games, there is apparently little transfer to school tasks, including writing. In addition, although the player's attention is, indeed, riveted, there has been no evidence of transfer of attention to other kinds of learning.[33]

Do such games teach children to be better problem-solvers? After all, success in many is predicated on making a series of correct decisions. Dr. Linda Siegel, authority on child development and education, has wondered about this possibility. She suspects, however, that the ability to use logical thinking may actually be impaired rather than improved in children conditioned to this visual, holistic environment.

"We should be thinking hard about what these games really encourage. I'm not convinced they really promote decision-making," she told me. "I watch these kids playing and I wonder if those decisions are made on a rational basis, or if it is just chance. Are they developing systems of rules in their minds, or are they just responding intuitively? They seem to be in control, but how much control do they really have? And if it's intuitive rather than logical, is it thinking?"[34]

It would be nice if we had some answers to these questions. In the meanwhile, parents should remember that they are still in charge of the household. Aren't they?

BRAINS THAT READ VS. BRAINS THAT WATCH TV

One thing television does is it keeps kids from reading. Reading triggers certain experiences in the brain that just don't happen if you don't read. I think our brains are designed to symbolize and represent information in the way that we call language. If we don't exercise it, we lose it. Television, even *Sesame Street*, is not very symbolic. It makes things very tangible and easy to understand, but reading is the kind of exercise that causes the brain to develop differently because it uses that symbolic capability.

—Dr. M. Russell Harter[35]

Children's brains develop connections within and between areas depending on the type of exercise they get. A "good" brain for learning develops strong and widespread neural highways that can quickly and efficiently assign different aspects of a task to the most efficient system. Such a brain is able to "talk" to itself, instantly sending messages from one area to another. Such efficiency is developed only by active practice in thinking and learning which, in turn, builds increasingly stronger connections. A growing suspicion among brain researchers is that excessive television viewing may affect development of these kinds of connections. It may also induce habits of using the wrong systems for various types of learning.

The only sources of data—both direct and indirect—on this topic are studies comparing the effects of viewing with those of reading. Although, as always, the data are slim, they suggest that reading and watching TV make quite different demands on the brain and thus encourage different kinds of development. As with any activity, repeated exposure, particularly during sensitive periods, has the potential to cause lasting changes.

"If a certain part of the brain is available for reading and that part doesn't serve a reading function, a reorganization may take place that allows another function to become more developed," adds Dr. Harter, a major investigator in one of the first large-scale studies of reading and the developing brain, now being conducted at the University of North Carolina.

Intensive viewing has the potential for *at least* three effects on the growing brain, any of which could interfere with a child's natural potential for intelligence and creativity: (1) it may reduce stimulation to left-hemisphere systems critical for development of language, reading, and analytic thinking; (2) it may affect mental ability and attention by diminishing mental traffic between the hemispheres; (3) it may discourage development of "executive" systems that regulate attention, organization, and motivation. Without a solid research base, we can take only a speculative look at each of the three.

Does Television Unbalance the Brain?

The medium (at least in the United States), by maximizing quick cuts, which permit little critical analysis, and the visual presentation of violence or disaster, assures retention of global imagery content (right-brain functions?) at the cost of the more orderly and logical verbal and analytical processes (left brain?). Reading, by contrast, can present equally sensational information . . . but it requires a more active stance by the reader who must project his or her own imagery onto a more orderly array of verbal information.[36]

—Dr. Jerome Singer, Yale University

The fear most often expressed about extended television viewing is that it robs the left hemisphere of developmental time and space. Over a decade ago, Marie Winn speculated that television's "repeated and time-consuming nonverbal, primarily visual activity" and negative patterns of "nonverbal cognition"[37] might interfere with "left brain" functions, disrupting language and reading development. Two years later the Emerys suggested that non-verbal systems in the right hemisphere were being overstimulated by TV and that even "advantaged" children would be harmed if neural pathways essential to the development of spoken and written language and critical thought were not fully developed.[38]

Little credible research has been conducted to compare hemispheric activity during viewing vs. reading. What is available suggests that, relative to television, print media generate more left-brain than right-brain activity.[39]

Syntax vs. Saliency

While it is physically impossible to stimulate one side of a normal brain without engaging the other as well, it may be possible to "unbalance" development by neglecting certain types of input. Skilled reading depends heavily on (left-hemisphere) auditory language abilities.[40,41] (Many good readers may not even be aware that they "hear" sentences in their head as they read.) Children who lean too heavily on (right-hemisphere) visual, holistic strategies (they remember or guess what a word says only by the way it "looks"—first letter, shape, etc.) run into trouble when the text gets harder, when words get longer, and when they must read or spell accurately. Symptoms include inaccurate oral reading ("vacation" for "vacancy") and difficulty reading or spelling syllables in the right sequence ("renuramate" for "remunerate"). Children who never learn to process (understand and remember) language without pictures attached also have difficulty in school when they must listen to a teacher or to the author of a textbook. They keep looking around for meaning instead of creating it inside their own heads.

As we saw in Chapter 4, television is a poor teacher of language because it is not interactive and because it cannot tailor conversation, as can parents, to the needs of the individual child. Even seriously disadvantaged children do not seem to gain linguistic benefits from extended hours of TV. A number of studies have shown that children get information from television primarily through attention to visual action and nonverbal sounds (booms, crashes, music), not through following the dialogue.[42] To understand a complex plot or make sense of speech on television, they would have to overlook the highly salient features and focus instead on such "nonsalient" aspects as low action or normal human speech. Yet, as programs are increasingly designed to attract attention, the child viewer gains the habit of ignoring language in favor of visual and auditory gimmicks. Syntax is a very poor second to saliency.

As I watch children's programming, I am struck by the following (L or R indicates the hemisphere presumably more involved in each case):

- Holistic visual action (R) dominates oral language (L).
- Sound effects are mainly novel noises (R), not sequential speech (L).
- Language modeling consists primarily of vocabulary words— semantic (R and L) rather than grammatical—syntactic sequences of words or phrases (L).
- Rapid movement and novelty (R) are almost continual.
- Exaggerated emotional tone (R) characterizes many of the characters' responses.
- Color (R) is a predominant feature.
- Immediacy (R) dominates logical sequence (L) of episodes.
- There is little time for analysis (L) of anything, particularly what the characters say.
- Perception of the sounds (L) in the speech of the characters is very difficult, even for an adult brain.

Robbing left-hemisphere systems of valuable developmental exercise may tip the balance for brains constitutionally at risk for learning problems. Could it put more normal brains at risk? As the hours add up—who knows? Will minds schooled by television relinquish the special form of intellectual precision afforded our species by the evolution of language in the left hemisphere? No one can answer this question, either, but a lot of teachers have their own opinions.

Changing Brains: Neural Imprints of Literacy

While research has yet to show whether watching television permanently changes the brain, it has suggested that literacy does. Because reading and writing are skills not innate or even inevitable for the human brain, they require training and *practice*. The practice, in turn, seems to develop both brain and thought patterns in certain specialized ways.

Indeed, I am considering the possibility that the adoption of the alphabet by Western cultures has had a reordering effect on the brain
and the whole nervous system of literate people. . . .[43]
         —Derrick de Kerckhove in *The Alphabet and the Brain*

Scientists are having fun trying to find out how learning to use an
alphabet, particularly one that is read from left to right, might change
the way a human brain functions. Clues have come mainly from two
types of studies, as yet far from conclusive: some showing that illiterate people tend to have less strongly developed left-hemisphere
language-processing than people who can read, and some showing
that people who learn to read both a letter-type and a picture-type
script, as in Japan, tend to process language more equally between
the two sides of the brain than do people who read only letter-type
scripts.[44,45]

Good and poor readers commonly show up with differences in
brain function. Part of the reason may be that brains that read more
develop differently. "Good readers may spend more time reading
than poor readers, and this could conceivably affect brain lateralization," reports one noted team of researchers.[46]

Brains that read in unusual ways also develop differently. Studies
similar to those discussed in an earlier chapter show that deaf readers
use the two sides of their brain divergently. Deaf readers, we must
recall, rarely process beyond third- or fourth-grade-level reading ability in spite of intelligence and teaching; not surprisingly, they tend to
use right hemisphere (more visual) systems instead of left (more
auditory).[47] Is it only a coincidence that the reading abilities of today's
hearing students also begin to level off and then start to drop at about
the same point where most deaf readers get stuck?

Teaching That Changes Brains

Dr. Dirk Bakker, of the Free University and Paedological Institute in
Amsterdam, believes that the way children use their hemispheres can
be changed with surprisingly little effort. Using different methods of
reading instruction, he has altered brain function and also improved
reading scores.

Bakker insists that reading problems result when children use their
hemispheres inappropriately. Part of this "functional overdevelop-
ment" may be inherited, but experience can at least partially restore
the balance. To get these brains more effectively organized for read-

ing, Bakker uses training in which he tries to strengthen the weak system causing the problem.

Bakker's students improve their reading, but, more important, they also show "training-induced electrical changes in brain asymmetry" (changes in relative strength of brain waves over the two hemispheres) that correlate with the changes in their reading abilities. It is particularly notable—and a little frightening—that the teachers achieved these changes in hemispheric activity with only twenty-two weekly sessions of forty-five minutes each![48,49] Although it has not yet been shown that the brains were permanently altered in any major way by such brief training, these experiments offer hope that early elementary school years still provide an opening for reeducating underactive neurons.[50]

Most researchers are skeptical of what Marcel Kinsbourne terms "dichotomania"—the tendency to look at everything in terms of right versus left hemisphere. Children must learn to use—and thus help develop—both sides and the connections between them. Higher-order reasoning and putting *language meaning* together with the visual input are particularly important. In these respects skilled reading is a much better trainer than television.

Mental and Physical Effort—or Withered Brains?

> TV isn't tapping any higher-order integrative processes. It's much more dangerous than simply engaging children's right hemispheres. Both hemispheres can watch TV, but they do it with lower-level systems, mainly visual ones. The issue is not right or left, but the type of processing that gets stimulated.
>
> —Dr. Wendy Heller[51]

Authorities now suspect that the ability to activate and coordinate the work of both hemispheres may be even more important than developing individual systems in either side. They argue we should not allow viewing to replace physical play (e.g., running, kicking, climbing, throwing), handwork (e.g., building, working with clay, needlework, origami), doing puzzles, playing games, or other activities through which the two sides of the body—and their related connections in the brain—learn to coordinate with each other.

The *corpus callosum*, the thick bridge of fibers connecting the hemispheres, is one of the brain's latest-maturing parts. It ultimately makes possible important skills such as flexible manipulation of ideas, mature creative imagination, and effective interplay between analytic and intuitive thinking (e.g., seeing the way details fit inside the "big picture"; implementing an action plan for a creative idea). Poor development of this critical link between the hemispheres can result in learning and attention problems.[52]

Because of its late maturation, the corpus callosum may be extremely vulnerable to lack of practice. After an initial spurt of growth during the first two years of life, it probably continues to develop at a slow, relatively steady pace until somewhere between ages eight and fourteen. As the connections mature, the youngster must *practice using them*—through physical and mental activity. If the brain remains relatively passive during childhood and/or adolescence, it will be much more difficult to develop these skills later when the brain is less flexible.[53]

Dr. Jerre Levy, biopsychologist at the University of Chicago and an internationally known authority on hemispheric development, believes that *mental effort* of all kinds is what firms up these connections.

> I suspect that normal human brains are built to be challenged and that it is only in the face of an adequate challenge that normal bihemispheric brain operations are engaged.[54]

Dr. Levy insists that children need "a linguistic environment that is coordinated with the visual environment they're experiencing," not the "linguistically depleted" environment of TV. In other words, they need to pay attention to words as well as to pictures.

Dr. Levy feels that older children may actually be more affected by the low-level linguistic content of much television programming than little ones. "Furthermore," she added, "the main thing that worries me about TV is not even its intellectual level. To the extent that children commit time looking at TV, they're not spending time reading. When a child reads a novel, he has to self-create whole scenarios, he has to create images of who these people are, what their emotions are, what their tones of voice are, what the environment looks like, what the feeling of this environment is. These self-created scenarios are important, and television leaves no room for that creative process.

"I think brains are designed to meet cognitive challenges," she concluded. "It's just like muscles; if you don't exercise them they wither. If you don't exercise brains, they wither."[55]

Poor Scaffolding for the Brain's Executive

Equally troubling is the growing suspicion that the brain's executive centers may be compromised by too many hours in front of the tube. This concern was repeatedly expressed by neuropsychologists whom I informally polled at a recent conference, most of whom, incidentally, said they allow their children to watch—but on a limited and selective basis.

"It's too simple to say TV makes kids 'right-brained,' " commented Dr. Sid Segalowitz, an authority on children's hemispheric development. "It's important that parents realize how complex the brain is. They hear all this stuff about *stimulating* their child's brain; it's important to realize that you can't stimulate just one isolated part of it. Brain function is a system; we need to get away from this right and left idea. When we look at slides of blood flow in the brain when kids are reading, we can see so many different areas lighting up at once. Good readers tend to use both left and right hemispheres, including the prefrontal systems."

Spending time with something that doesn't challenge their brains much could impinge on development of prefrontal executive functions, such as control of thinking, attention, and general planning skills, said Dr. Segalowitz. "The frontal lobes are late enough developing that they can definitely be affected by environmental variables, but we still don't know how much is programmable hardware, and how much is not."[56] Like several colleagues, he would like to initiate research to find out more about how environmental influences affect this mysterious—and influential—brain area.

As reviewed in Chapter 8, frontal-lobe development continues throughout childhood and adolescence. It is closely related to the *vigilance* (persistent attention) that seems to be particularly affected by TV viewing. Growth in these executive systems probably accounts for the dramatic shift usually seen in children's control over their own reasoning abilities between ages five and seven.[57] During this period they become much better able to understand and plan strategies for what they are learning, as well as for controlling their own behavior. Parents don't need to be reminded, however, that many "control functions" don't become dependable until much later! How television may affect this course of development is unknown, although we may safely assume that extensive viewing has some effects.

Prefrontal development enables higher-level learning. Conversely, thoughtful, mentally challenging reading, reflecting, planning, and problem-solving nourishes these neural circuits. It is possible to *read words* without much help from these higher-level control centers, but comprehension and application—as well as motivation and persistence—require their use. These endangered skills appear to be the ones most related to our national crisis in learning. How much can be blamed on a generalized willingness to let TV "scaffold" children's development?

CONCLUSION: VIDEO CAN BE HAZARDOUS TO BRAINS AND LEARNING

The overall effects of television viewing and other forms of video on the growing brain are poorly understood, but research strongly indicates that it has the potential to affect both the brain itself and related learning abilities. Abilities to sustain attention independently, stick to problems actively, listen intelligently, read with understanding, and use language effectively may be particularly at risk. No one knows how much exposure is necessary to make a difference. Likewise, no information is available about the overall effects on intelligence of large amounts of time taken from physical exercise, social or independent play, pleasure reading, sustained conversation, or roaming quietly about in one's own imagination.

The notion that television overdevelops the right hemisphere is giving way to the much greater possibility that it underdevelops several areas and/or the connections between them. Not only left-hemisphere language systems, but also higher-order organizational abilities, including the all-important control, motivation, and planning functions of the prefrontal lobes, may be in jeopardy for children who watch without expending much mental effort. All these functions may have sensitive periods when they are particularly susceptible to variations in stimulation, but it is difficult to determine which age periods are more critical than others or how much exposure is needed to cause physical effects.

The fact that reports from teachers so precisely mirror the "symptoms" of these same deficits should give us all pause. Surely, with the amount of time children in this country spend in front of the screen, we should demand better research on its effects. There must be a great untapped teaching potential there somewhere. Meanwhile, the best advice to parents seems to be the usual caveats:

- Place firm limits on television and video use; encourage children to *plan* ahead for favorite shows and games.

- Participate with children whenever possible.
- Talk with the child about television content, methods of audience manipulation, point of view, etc.
- If you want children to become readers, *show* them how to turn off the tube and pick up a book.
- Remember, what is pleasantly relaxing to your brain may not be good for theirs.
- Give substitute caregivers strict guidelines regarding TV and video use.
- Read the next chapter before you encourage preschoolers to watch *Sesame Street*.

Sesame Street and the Death of Reading

With a small sigh, four-year-old Nancy settles her thumb in her mouth and herself next to her grandmother. The screen in front of them throbs into strident action. Blasts of music and color, brighter and louder than life, assail her consciousness. A confusing melee of animation churns forth as characters, seated around a dinner table, leap up and down shouting a harsh and hurried parody of human conversation. What are they yelling about? A winter storm rages violently on the sound track, doors slam, dishes crash; the overwhelming sound effects drown out the few words that might be intelligible.

"What is it? What is it? What is it?" whines two-year-old Peter, running to the screen and pointing anxiously at something. But Peter's question remains unanswered. Under his insistent finger the scene and characters alter, the action races relentlessly along, and Peter retreats to Grandmother's other side, also sucking a thumb.

From across the room I am stunned by *Sesame Street*'s sensory assault. I am equally unnerved by the transformation of these lively, curious children, who, five minutes earlier, had been chattering enthusiastically as they investigated the workings of my pocket tape recorder. Although some parents report that children who watch TV regularly become very active during the program, the response of Nancy and Peter is much more typical of novice viewers. We are all, in fact, overwhelmed as we sit, silent, engulfed by a cacophony of vignettes that change, literally, by the minute; *Sesame Street* segments run anywhere from thirty or forty-five seconds up to a rare maximum of three minutes. Muppets, people, objects, cartoons, cascade inexorably—each scene arrestingly novel and removed both visually and contextually from the last. Within twenty minutes we are propelled from Spain or Mexico (the pace is so rapid it is hard to tell) to the streets of New York, to a zoo, behind the set of a television studio, and to a game show. A cartoon history of the growing of peanuts and making of peanut butter is shown in fifty seconds, narrated by a voice mimicking an antebellum Southern accent. "It gr-ao-ws in the gr-ao-u-nd!" we are told. Nancy looks up, puzzled. Grandmother starts to explain, but the children's attention is instantly captured by numerals that leap onto the screen to dance, jump, metamorphose—appear, disappear, grow larger, smaller, in the flick of an eyelash.

"*One, two, three,*" shouts a disembodied voice. *H* floats by, suddenly experiencing an explosion of parts that transform it to *h*. "*H,*" the voice intones, but immediately *h* is gone and we are on a street in London where cartoon characters shout a slapstick routine that features rhyming sounds, unrelated in any discernible way to the previous "teaching." Unfortunately, their abrasively contrived dialects and the rapid pace of the jargon obscures both content and rhyme. Grandmother tries to repeat the rhyming words, but she is drowned out as we are swept into a new surge of music.

"Bu-bu-bu-bu-bu!" imitates Peter, picking up one intelligible sound from a character who sounds as if he is suffering from some sort of speech impediment.

A pulsating red numeral 3 appears, capering among a series of boxes. "Three," blasts the sound track amid more sounds of crashing and banging. Now 3 becomes a ball and leaps into the final box, which is immediately transformed (to an adult's eyes) into some sort of grinder; in a second, 3 is decomposed and pours out the spout as red powder.

"What happened to it?" asks Grandma.

"I don't know," says Nancy, registering surprise.

But there is no time to discuss this hidden machinery of cause and effect—to clarify the chimerical "magic" that transforms reality without human action or experience. Comprehension is superfluous.

CONFRONTING A SACRED COW

"*But at Least It's Educational . . .*"

The worst thing about *Sesame Street* is that people believe it is educationally valuable. It stands as a symbol of "good" programming, an institutionalized excuse for "boob tube" as baby-sitter. Well-intentioned parents earnestly swallow the dictum: "It helps children learn."

But what are they learning? First, that we expect them to enjoy this manipulative sensory assault. With habit, of course, they may indeed grow to "love" it, perhaps as smokers desire their prebreakfast cigarette. Human sensory organs—and the brains attached to them—grow accustomed to, even need, often repeated experiences. If children tell us they "love" *Sesame Street,* we should not decide it is *ipso facto* good for them; we should more likely be concerned about what has been done to their brains that enables them to tolerate—much less enjoy—it!

"Just because children do something willingly, even eagerly, is not sufficient reason to believe it engages their minds," cautions Dr. Lillian Katz, author of *Engaging Children's Minds.*[1] "And remember, enjoyment, per se, is not an appropriate goal for education."[2]

Yet children have also bought into the notion that *Sesame Street* is both "good" for them and educational. A typical platitude was recently expressed by a youngster interviewed for a national radio program.[3] "It teaches kids to read," he declared, confirming his adult-fostered delusions about the fundamental nature of the reading process. Like this little boy, who may be forgiven a certain degree of disillusionment when he gets to school, many children solemnly mouth the reassurances of their elders; yes, indeed, this is "education"!

Although *Sesame Street's* major raison d'être has been to improve the educational prognosis for the disadvantaged, the gulf between socioeconomic groups and the failure rate of poor school children grows daily to ever more frightening proportions. Clearly, a single program cannot be expected to reverse major societal changes. Poor children also tend to watch much more commercial television, with less supervision, than others, factors linked to poorer school performance. Yet, as we shall see, several aspects of *Sesame Street's* chosen format may be particularly damaging to the most needy of all.

Many hours of viewing *Sesame Street* have convinced me that adults who endorse it give children an erroneous message about what learning feels like. It is truly amazing that everyone seems to have bought the notion that this peripatetic carnival will somehow teach kids to *read*—despite the fact that the habits of the mind necessary to be a good reader are exactly what *Sesame Street* does not teach: language, active reflection, persistence, and internal control. The truth is that most adults have probably not taken the time to sit down and view this program objectively, from the perspective of tender young brains struggling to make the connections that will organize their intellects. They should.

Pervasive, Expensive, and Short on Research

Sesame Street is viewed by almost half of all American preschoolers on a weekly basis—over 5.8 million children between the ages of two and five watch an average of three episodes per week. Where I live, the program is broadcast three times a day for an hour each time. (In contrast, *Reading Rainbow*, which actually stimulates book circulation in libraries by engaging its audience with good children's books, is aired once a week at a time when children who can read are in school.) *Sesame Street*'s main influence, however, is not the proportion of total viewing time it occupies, but the messages it conveys—or fails to—about learning, about constructive children's programming, and about the responsibility of this overwhelmingly pervasive medium.

Sesame Street is expensive in every respect. Estimates have put the cost of producing each viewing hour anywhere from ninety-two thousand to one million dollars. [4,5] No one questions that this monumental product reflects good and earnest intentions on the part of its generators and producers, Children's Television Workshop. Yet when we encourage preschoolers to watch *Sesame Street*, we are programming them to "enjoy"—and perhaps even need—overstimulation, manipulation, and neural habits that are antagonistic to academic learning. In my opinion, it is a serious travesty of the educational enterprise particularly because it has assumed the mission and garnered parents' trust.

I am convinced it is not merely a coincidence that our faith in it has coincided with a major decline in reading and learning skills. Uncritical acceptance of *Sesame Street* as a model for "learning" has been part of a larger infatuation with expedient, product-oriented approaches that denigrate the essence of the educational enterprise. Its substitution of surface glitz for substance has started a generation of children in the seductive school of organized silliness, where their first lesson is that learning is something adults can be expected to make happen for them as quickly and pleasantly as possible. Thus prepared, they can hardly be blamed if they fail to discover for themselves the personal joys—time consuming as they are—of serious learning, mental effort, and mastery.

Despite its obviously large budget, the carefully crafted flagship of television's educational armada has not produced significant research by which the effects of its chosen format on either brains or learning abilities can be assessed. Although elaborate "instructional goals" for the program have been promulgated, little accountability for meeting them seems to be built into the system. Almost all of the research done by Children's Television Workshop, in fact, falls in the category of "formative evaluation": production research that mainly tests the program's appeal (i.e., how well it "sells").[6] "Summative" research, by which the attainment of those instructional goals might be evaluated, has mainly been left up for grabs—and for the twenty years of its life, few researchers have grabbed. The resulting studies have been piecemeal and inconclusive. Little documentation exists about the overall cognitive effects of *Sesame Street* despite all the money, time, effort, and good intentions that this program has consumed.

TEN REASONS WHY *SESAME STREET* IS BAD NEWS FOR READING

Studies showing how young children should be taught to read indicate that *Sesame Street* is going about the job the wrong way. Moreover, the show fosters inaccurate ideas about what and how preschoolers should be learning.

1. What Is "Brain-Appropriate" Learning for Preschoolers?

Sesame Street has popularized the erroneous belief that it is appropriate for most preschoolers to learn to read. In fact, it is a serious mistake to push reading skills at children before they have completed certain developmental tasks that will give them something to read about—and the ability to understand it when they do! Moreover, research shows that the correct way for very young children to start to read is not with structured lessons.

Misguided efforts to train preschoolers in skills more appropriate for kindergarten or first grade diverts valuable time and attention from their real learning needs. To become good readers children first need help in installing the cognitive and language furnishings that will make the brain a comfortable place for real literacy to dwell! During the early years these are best learned through active, hands-on experiences (e.g., playing, building, exploring, talking), imaginative social play, and listening with enjoyment to good children's literature, not from a medium which has made a science of taking control of the viewer's attention.

Preschoolers also need to practice the fine motor skills that will eventually enable them to write. New research indicates that the increase in *dysgraphia* (difficulty with handwriting) plaguing the schools may be related to the fact that children have spent so much more time in front of the TV than in free play and activities such as bead stringing, sewing cards, carpentry, sand and water play, crayoning designs, cutting out shapes, and other natural and appropriate learning activities.[7] *Sesame Street* could—and should—do much more to encourage them.

The mechanics of naming letters or "sounding out" words, as important as they will eventually be, are better saved for later—usually around age six. Many, perhaps even most, preschoolers' brains are not prepared to cope with connecting written symbols (letters) to sounds ("*B* says buh"). Some young brains can glue these together with remarkable ease; others, including many bright ones, do not. If well-meaning adults are encouraged to force the issue, they may create problems ranging from disaffection to disability.[8]

Many experts now believe that early pressure to remember letters and their sounds may cause learning problems for some children, especially those whose environments have not primed them for literacy. At the very least, youngsters who are mystified by the meaning of the dancing symbols on the screen may be picking up feelings of bewilderment about phonics—and about their own inability to understand something that everybody seems to think is so important. If teaching letter sounds to preschoolers really were important, it might be worth the risk. But it is not!

2. The Empty Alphabet vs. Language Meaning

> Reading is not walking on words. It's grasping the soul of them.
> —Paolo Freire

Sesame Street has overemphasized letters and numerals and underemphasized the language and thinking skills necessary to make them meaningful. Contrary to what most parents believe, learning the alphabet is only a minor part of learning to read. Overall language development is much more important. Yet back in the mists of reading research, some quite misleading studies "proved" that kindergarteners' ability to recognize alphabet letters was a good predictor of their reading success at the end of first grade. As is too often the case, people who did not understand that a correlation (relationship) of this kind does not necessarily imply causation decided that teaching alphabets would make children learn to read faster. The truth of the situation is somewhat different.

Alphabet (or "letter-sound") recognition by three-, four-, and five-year-olds might be viewed as a symptom, not a cause, of the type of brain that will acquire reading easily: (1) it comes from an environment with exposure to books and print; (2) it can, through a combination of nature and experiential stimulation, remember a sequence of spoken sounds and attach them to printed letters; (3) it is mature enough to make these connections with ease. This type of brain is likely to learn to read quite readily, whether someone drills it on the alphabet or not. Conversely, simply teaching the brain to have the surface "symptom" will not create the underlying abilities.

Children who buy *Sesame Street*'s implicit message that alphabet letters are the major key to reading are headed for trouble. When researchers ask groups of poor readers what reading is all about, they tend to say something like: "sounding out the words." When good readers are asked the same question, they give answers such as, "Understanding what the words and the sentences say." Somehow the poor readers have failed to pick up the idea that reading must take them far beyond the alphabet into an active search for meaning.

Children must have good language development before they can get the meaning. Ability to recognize printed letters and words gets children through early reading instruction. After grade 3, however, overall listening comprehension (e.g., the ability to understand and remember stories or reports they have heard) is much more closely related to students' reading comprehension than their ability to read the words themselves![9,10] Many long-term studies show that children superior in *oral* language in kindergarten and first grade are the ones who eventually excel in reading and writing in the middle grades.

When it comes to learning these uses of language, early environment is the critical factor. From the University of Umea in Sweden, Dr. Ingvar Lundberg, who has been working on a large study of children's reading development in all the Scandinavian countries, reports that even though Scandinavian children do not enter school until age seven, most pick up basic decoding (alphabet and word-reading) skills without difficulty. At that point, however, the effects of the preschool language environment become evident in the level of their reading comprehension.

"Right now we are in the process of looking at the effects on comprehension of a lot of early things happening," Lundberg reports. "If you have adequate teaching (in school), regardless of a lot of external circumstances, a majority of kids will certainly learn how to decode ["sound out" the words], but a majority of kids will certainly not have a guaranteed development of comprehension just by a reasonably good school environment. It seems that home factors play a very considerable role as far as comprehension is concerned."[11]

Given these well-recognized facts, it is disheartening to observe that *Sesame Street* itself provides such a poor language model. Although apologists for the program claim that its sentence length and grammatical complexity are appropriate for young children,[12] the only study I could locate on this topic failed to take into account the pace, clarity, or volume level of the characters' speech. Even a casual observer soon becomes aware that most of the characters talk too fast and shift topics too abruptly. Research on the development of auditory abilities shows that children of four, five, and even six years are still immature in their abilities to discriminate frequency and duration in human speech; they need slow, repetitive talk, with emphasis on word inflections.[13]

"You know," explained Dr. Janet Jensen, a prominent researcher in this field, "the way kindergarten teachers talk. Everyone makes jokes about it: 'Now—children—let's—look—at—the—bunny,' but they do that because the kids need and respond to it. Many children's programs, including *Sesame Street*, go much too fast for them."[14]

(Testimony to the fact that a children's program can follow sound development guidelines and still be enduringly popular comes from *Mister Rogers' Neighborhood*, whose slow, repetitive speech and invitations to the child to respond appeals instinctively to preschoolers—at least those whose sensibilities have not been dulled by raucous sideshows.)

Sesame Street also subordinates meaningful dialogue to brain-grabbing visual events, noises, and slapstick comedy. This emphasis is particularly troubling in view of the fact that both disadvantaged children and those with reading disabilities commonly show difficulty in using what are called "verbal strategies" for processing information.[15] This tendency to focus on the nonverbal aspects of a situation and disregard the language sets a child up for difficulty in school.

Although, to its credit, the program attempts to present both standard and nonstandard dialects and grammar, they too often appear in the form of poorly modeled and unclearly articulated parody. *Sesame Street* also sporadically attempts to teach vocabulary (e.g., names of ten baby animals in ninety seconds), but its format militates against sustained attention to the meaning of the grammar, sentences, or phrasal inflections that children will meet in books. And far too little effort is made to get the child to respond.

The few studies which suggest that *Sesame Street* teaches preschoolers to recognize a few more spoken vocabulary words provide very unconvincing evidence of overall language development. Although children who have watched *Sesame Street* get better at pointing to pictures in response to vocabulary words,[16] this type of recognition-level test cannot be taken to mean that the children can use the words in their own conversation.[17] Moreover, children in one study whose parents encouraged them to watch *Sesame Street* had the lowest overall vocabulary scores![18]

No one has convincingly demonstrated that *Sesame Street* actually succeeds in its fundamental goal of helping young brains learn to crack the alphabetic code. Well-publicized early claims that it had successfully taught disadvantaged children to recognize alphabet letters and numerals have subsequently been questioned on the basis that the money spent did not justify the small gains engendered.[19] Moreover, we now realize that empty word recognition is a meaningless exercise. Twenty years of throwing alphabet letters and dancing words at children is producing exactly what we might expect: students who, even after learning to read, lack the foundations for further progress; children who find reading "boring," who are satisfied with the superficial, who can't understand why meaning doesn't magically appear—like a visual effect—and who give up when it doesn't. The resulting failure and disenchantment are particularly tragic for those very children the program was primarily designed to serve.

3. *How Does Print Behave?*

The age of *Sesame Street*, optimistically crafted to narrow the chasms of disadvantage, has, in fact, seen those gaps widen. The facetious treatment of letters and other symbols gives children an erroneous idea of what to expect from the printed page. Words in books do not jump about, transform before one's eyes, or call attention to themselves. Children, particularly those disadvantaged by lack of experience with real books during the preschool years, are in for quite a shock when they get to school and discover that print stands still. No wonder they turn off when informed that they must bend their brains around the hard job of attacking the words, rather than having a barrage of letters, words, and pictures attacking them.

Even on the rare occasions when a real book slides through the cracks between *Sesame Street's* animation and agitation, the program may display only its illustrations (which, incidentally, tend to appear pallid and uninteresting by comparison to the program's vivid coloration). Thus, children miss one of their most important pieces of reading readiness, technically termed *metalinguistic awareness,* which is made up of knowledge that literate adults take for granted:

- understanding that letters make up words and that written words must be linked together into meaningful sentences
- knowing what a "word" is (i.e., that funny-looking bunch of squiggles with white space on all sides
- becoming familiar with the conventions of print (i.e., in English we read from left to right, observe punctuation marks, etc.)
- knowing firsthand the meaning of terms associated with books (i.e., "cover," "title," "author," "illustration," etc.)

Metalinguistic awareness is an important predictor of a child's success with early reading and is apt to be particularly deficient in *Sesame Street*'s target audience. Youngsters may be totally bewildered in school if the teacher says, "Now, Johnny, try to read this word," and the child has never learned to differentiate between letter, word, and sentence. Many children without book experiences or writing experiences with drawing and scribbling can't visually locate word boundaries or consistently follow a line of print from left to right. These skills require slow, careful, firsthand exposure, and the program should be placing more emphasis on this sort of learning for children who do not have access to such experiences.

4. Bits vs. Big Bites of Meaning

Sesame Street viewers are exposed to lots of incidental knowledge, but adults who think this kind of information automatically makes them "smarter" are fooling themselves. Apparent precocity can be deceptive; if the child has not also integrated good reasoning skills along with the data, the early promise will soon fade. Indeed, one of the biggest problems of older students today is making connections. "There now exists a large body of research that clearly shows that children of all ability levels in Grades 4–12 have considerable difficulty in studying and linking together the concepts presented in science and social studies texts," states a report from the International Reading Association.[20]

"They have all these little bits of information, but they can't seem to see relationships, make inferences, or draw conclusions," say teachers from kindergarten to college. Difficulties with understanding sequence in text and writing logically reflect identical problems with linking thoughts together meaningfully.

All television programming is increasingly predicated on the idea that rapidly changing scenes keep viewers watching. "Watching thinking is boring and slow," says Neil Postman, who quotes Robert MacNeil of *The MacNeil/Lehrer Newshour* on the fact that viewers are never required to pay attention for more than a few seconds at a time. "The idea is to keep everything brief, not to strain the attention of anyone but instead to provide constant stimulation through variety, novelty, action, and movement," said MacNeil.[21] *Sesame Street* has adopted the same format—only with more noise and more vivid color.

Watching *Sesame Street* with an adult brain that struggles to make connections can be a very frustrating experience. The rapid, minute-by-minute alterations in context—from a pirate ship to a city street, a barnyard to a cartoon of letter symbols—defy sequence or logic and make it impossible to see relationships, understand the sequence of cause and effect, or keep a train of thought in motion. Such brain-training is directly antagonistic to the active and sustained work on connecting ideas that is needed to understand written text.

5. Listening vs. Looking

Why doesn't *Sesame Street* make a much greater effort to teach listening skills? Not only are its "graduates" deficient overall in ability to pay attention to and understand oral language, but they also lack the skills of auditory analysis that underlie mastery of "phonics."

Many in our growing ranks of poor readers (and spellers!) can't listen carefully enough to discriminate individual sounds in words or identify the order in which they come (e.g., "Here is a word: *sun*. Now tell me what sound you hear first in the word *sun*. Which sound do you hear last?"). As was mentioned in an earlier chapter, these skills of "phonologic awareness" are fundamental for reading and spelling.

Sesame Street purports to teach children "phonics," and its statement of educational goals includes such elements of phonological awareness as rhyming words (which, unfortunately, are too often presented unclearly and far too rapidly).[22] Its demanding visual format belies the claim, however, since "phonics," by definition, is an *ear* skill, not an *eye* skill. These auditory systems are in a period of critical development during the very preschool years when so many youngsters are *watching* the tube. Researchers agree that when given both visual displays and dialogue, children attend to and remember the visual, not the "talk." (Even for most adults, listening can't compete with looking if the brain is given the chance to do both at the

same time.) Yet, as we saw in an earlier chapter, if auditory processing skills aren't embedded in the brain during the critical early years,
it is much harder, if it is even possible, to insert them later.

Research also shows that children process the same information
differently, depending on whether they look at it or listen to it. In one
study, clear differences were found between children who had seen a
televised folktale and those who heard the same dialogue read from a
storybook. Those who had watched the story on television described
the visual effects and what the characters did, whereas those in the
read-aloud group described more dialogue of the story and gave significantly more information about the content of the text and the
characters.[23]

What our children need is lots of good, slow, clear exposure to the
sounds that will become their armamentarium for attacking language
meaning as well as the written word. What a shame they are not
getting it from this program!

6. Perceptual Organization vs. Perceptual Defense

One of the brain's major learning tasks is to organize the confusing
array of sensory stimuli that start bombarding the infant at birth. For
this, children need an environment over which they feel some control.

Researchers investigating the brain's "sensitive periods" report that
the extent to which aspects of the inanimate environment change as
a result of the child's actions has been found to relate to overall later
intelligence and also to the ability to pursue a goal.[24] Unfortunately,
viewing *Sesame Street* presents quite the opposite situation; the
events are not only out of the child's control, but the noisy and
visually violent nature of many episodes may cause sensory
overload.[25]

The ability to organize a visual field is the entry point to reading.
Children with poor skills of visual organization have difficulty, for example, in distinguishing word boundaries and keeping their place in
the text. Yet, rather than encouraging children to develop *perceptual
organization*, such programming may actually force them to practice
habits of *perceptual defense* simply as a matter of neural self-
protection. When even an adult brain has difficulty organizing confusing action, abrupt changes, and inexplicable *deus ex machina* visual
effects, it should hardly be surprising if children become overwhelmed
by the perceptual chaos.

There is no good evidence (although it has been suggested) that television can create serious, organic, perceptual problems. We need some studies looking at possible subtle effects of noisy, visually demanding programming on a normal child's perceptual (auditory and visual) organization skills. The "tuned-out" viewing behavior that many parents report may simply be the immature nervous system's defense against too much stimulation. How much exposure is needed to have an effect? No one knows, but different children have different thresholds at which they become overloaded.

7. Active vs. Passive Brains

Poor readers—and poor problem-solvers in any domain—tend to be passive; they give up if they don't immediately "get it." Such habits of incomprehension may be exacerbated by programs which teach a young child that seeking understanding is either superfluous or impossible. While research suggests that most children instinctively try to comprehend the content they see on TV, they are too often prevented from doing so by overly confusing program formats. When this experience is repeated frequently, they soon learn they are neither required nor expected to grasp what is going on.

Studies by experts not commissioned by the program are beginning to show that much of *Sesame Street*'s content is incomprehensible to young children. Dr. Singer cites an example:

> One of the programs in the series we studied involved an attempt on the part of the producers of *Sesame Street* to demonstrate the notion of deafness to children. A group of deaf children were introduced and they engaged in a series of activities, including suggesting letters through their body postures. Despite the production effort and undeniable sensitivity of the show (at least from the perspective of an adult), only 1 of the preschoolers in our sample of 60 who viewed this program grasped that the children on the screen *could not hear*. In effect thousands of dollars went into the production which failed completely to communicate its major message to the preschooler target-viewing audience.[26]

Most parents assume children understand *Sesame Street* much better than they actually do, reports Dr. Singer after studying youngsters' responses to the program. The reason, he says, "is that too often the children simply failed to follow the material being presented from one sequence to the next. The necessary time for mental replay was not allotted, and there was insufficient repetition."[27]

No one has determined what effects continued noncomprehension has on brain function, but research cited in the last chapter suggest it may cause it to retreat into alpha—one of the "habits" we were warned about.

8. Good Readers Learn to Remember

Another related problem concerns children's ability to remember the meaning of what they read, a skill that requires, first, understanding the text, and second, use of active strategies for remembering it. Memory also demands mental perseverance, for it depends on maintaining information in what is called "working memory" long enough to "store" it in some sort of meaningful form, and "retrieve" it when needed. Passive brains retain sensations, not information.

Children who do not understand what they are seeing do not learn active memory strategies. Curiously, although *Mister Rogers' Neighborhood* does not rivet children to the set (research has shown they are much more inclined to walk and look around than during *Sesame Street*'s sensorially demanding format), they actually remember more from *Mister Rogers' Neighborhood*. In this regard, reports Dr. Singer, *those children who were less intelligent suffered more [i.e., remembered less] from exposure to* Sesame Street, *purportedly designed for the educationally disadvantaged* [emphasis added]."[28]

9. Good Readers Can Pay Attention

While young children watch television, their attention tends to wander unless it is continually pulled back. Researchers who cite studies "proving" that children "pay attention" to TV are usually referring to this type of *involuntary attention,* which is quite different from the sort of *voluntary attention* needed to do well in school in general and reading in particular. Likewise, when you hear that children "actively" watch programs like *Sesame Street,* you should know that this really means that the viewer is frequently tuning out, looking away from the screen, playing, eating, or doing other things. The average look at the screen is actually less than five seconds in duration.[29] The truth is that the viewer may indeed be active, but the viewing is not.

Ideas in a text do not seize the reader's mind as do Ernie and Big Bird. Reading demands sustained voluntary attention from a mind that can hold a train of thought long enough to reflect on it, not one accustomed to having its attention jerked around every few seconds.

10. Who Makes the Pictures?

One of the most serious charges leveled against television viewing in general is that it robs children of the chance to learn to make pictures in their own minds. This critical skill is a cornerstone of good reading, not only because it keeps the reader connected to the text, but also as a very practical way to keep track of and remember what has been read. When poor readers—and poor verbal problem-solvers—hear (or read) words, they have trouble projecting anything on the screen of imagination.

Not long ago I visited an advanced-placement English class in a fast-track high school. The first act of *Macbeth* had been assigned to students as homework the previous evening; as they arrived in class the teacher asked them to write a description of what they had "seen" as they read. With a classful of good readers, I anticipated some colorful and dramatic accounts, and I was not disappointed. For a handful of students, however, this assignment proved frustrating.

"I read this over and over, but I guess I just don't *see anything* when I read," lamented one girl.

"That must make it hard to understand what you're reading," I ventured.

"It sure does," she confessed. "Maybe that's why I really hate reading—but don't tell Mrs. ——!"

Later the teacher drew me aside to tell me that the same students who didn't see the pictures were the ones she was most worried about. "I knew they weren't as good readers as the others," she said. "Now I think I know one reason why!"

Visual imagery also helps with solving math and science problems. "If Tom has three baskets of apples with twelve apples in each, and he divides each basketful evenly into four small boxes, how many boxes will he have and how many apples will each box contain?" Many people use some sort of visual image to "see" the baskets and boxes and to keep track of each step in the problem. Interestingly, students of the *Sesame Street* generation have particular difficulty with such "story problems." It seems that a combination of poor reading skill, lack of persistence, and inability to visualize contribute to this difficulty. While this skill seems to come more naturally to some brains than to others, it can be developed with practice. In a few studies, after children had been taught to make mental pictures, their reading scores went up.[30]

Sesame Street is constrained by its medium in teaching visual imagery. Yet, with some research already available, it should not be too difficult to come up with activities to give "mind pictures" much more emphasis than they now get. The longer children are habituated to this externally demanding visual format, the less likely they will probably be to generate their own scenarios.

Only a few studies have looked at television's interaction with more general aspects of imagination. They have found that children tend to provide longer and more imaginative endings to audio (radio) than to audiovisual (TV) stories.[31] There are also many anecdotal reports from veteran preschool teachers who began to report changes in children's imaginative play soon after the inception of *Sesame Street*. Their principal concern is that frequent viewers are more likely to mimic characters and action from programs than to make up scenarios of their own. Jerre Levy has reminded us that the systems linking language and visual imagery are forming throughout childhood, but no one knows if—or when—there is a critical period for imagination.

ISN'T THERE ANYTHING GOOD ABOUT *SESAME STREET*?

During a famine, even a sacred cow may be required to yield some nourishment. During the two years I have watched *Sesame Street* for the purposes of writing this chapter, I have noticed the genesis of some encouraging change. The pace is slowing just a bit, although not nearly enough. Expansion of content has also occurred in an effort to broaden both conceptual and "pro-social" (positive effects on behavior) learning. The program exposes children to some important concepts (songs about "Same, Different" as just one example). It has provided a happy familiarity with new heroes of cultural literacy such as Ernie and Big Bird. (And sold a lot of products, too.) Although its sense of humor has accurately been described by Dr. Lillian Katz as "too arch and much too sassy," children do get a kick out of the slapstick routines once they learn to adapt their brains to the noisy pace (a questionable benefit!). Personally, I find some of the plays on words terribly clever (e.g., "Placido Flamingo" sings with the animal orchestra), but then, I already know how to read and I happen to know who Placido Domingo is.

The program has made a serious effort to give positive messages about cultural diversity, handicaps, and major emotional issues such as those surrounding death[32]—although, as we have seen, most of the message is missed by its young audience because of inappropriate modes of presentation. The material is arguably of better ethical quality than much other programming, and the statement of educational goals reflects current research (although it seems evident that they are poorly expressed in actual programming). If *Sesame Street* did not purport to be seriously educational, it might pass as clever and colorful light entertainment. But lauded as our major media effort to educate children, I believe it has failed and misled us at a time when we desperately need better models.

Children's Television Workshop has enjoyed a mandate to define good video "education" as well as appropriate academic methods and goals for preschoolers. They have not met their responsibility to provide sufficient summative research on their effects—either positive or negative—on learning. It can easily be argued that they have led an overly trusting public astray. The public, in turn, has been only too willing to cede them responsibility. And thus we reap the consequences.

One perceptive first-grader has summed up the situation quite neatly:

"*It doesn't teach me much. It makes me laugh.*"

As a reading teacher, however, I'm not laughing.

Conclusion: Teaching vs. Sensory Hucksterism

Reading is a complex intellectual act that cannot be peddled like an educational toy. The ability to read, and the related ability to write, are not hard-wired into the human brain. To make meaning out of printed text, the brain must be readied to *think* and to *understand language;* only then can it be trained to connect an internal mental life with written symbols that have no intrinsic meaning of their own. If reading is "sold" to unprepared children, they will soon discard it as worthless or uninteresting, because they lack the inner resources, both mental and physical, to bring life—and meaning—to the printed symbols.

Children immersed from birth in the spicy sensory bouillabaisse of visual immediacy will not become readers unless they have also soaked up the rich broth of language and reflection. Preschoolers who have been sold gimmicks in the name of learning and school-age children whose minds are habituated to the easy pleasures of viewing may well find the culture of the school an alien one. Their brains, shaped by visual novelty, may gradually lose the ability to bend themselves intelligently around the written word.

Who, then, will teach the next generation to read?

"Disadvantaged" Brains

Plasticity represents a double-edged sword: Processes available to be changed for the better may also be changed for the worse.

—RICHARD M. LERNER, PH.D.[1]

In the flossiest enclaves of New York's Upper East Side, an unusual child-care center serves the diverse needs of preschool children from two dramatically different constituencies. First to arrive each morning, the "neighborhood" children emerge from the sumptuous lobbies of their apartment buildings, accompanied by nannies or smartly clad parents. Chattering busily, they set about the activities of the morning as they await the arrival of their classmates, who come by bus from a welfare hotel. These youngsters started the morning in cramped rooms, usually without kitchen facilities, where as many as four children and a mother share two bunk beds. More silently, sometimes somberly, they enter the classrooms and begin the school day.

Lourdes Rivera, the energetic director of this venture in humanity, is a veteran teacher of children from severely deprived environments, but this is her first experience with such widely disparate groups. Like many visitors, I wondered how these children from opposite ends of the socioeconomic yardstick relate to each other.

"Kids are kids," stated Ms. Rivera emphatically. "They all learn from and help each other." To adults on the staff, however, the special needs of the homeless children are all too evident. Many come from brutalizing environments where even their most basic safety needs are in jeopardy. The simple learning experiences taken for granted in most families have not been available. For example, the children may never have eaten a meal at a table or helped (or even seen) anyone cook on a real stove. Because of their dangerous surroundings, both indoors and out, some have not been allowed to move freely about, so their motor development is often behind schedule. Some of the most serious gaps are in language and attention.

What is the prognosis for these youngsters, arguably the most disadvantaged group in our society? Can an enriched and caring environment make up for the appalling experiential abyss of their daily lives? "If we get them early enough," says Ms. Rivera, "I think we can make a big difference." Noticeable improvement usually begins as soon as they enter the preschool, she says.

"We've saved a lot of lives. I think of Matthew, a homeless child I worked with a couple of years ago. He was one who came from a loving family, but they had so many problems—both parents were in treatment for drug addiction. Matthew made fantastic gains when he was with us—he is in kindergarten now and I just heard he's being tested for the gifted program. We got him early, and his parents tried their best to help. When kids are older, though, or when the environment at home is too awful, it is so much harder."

The most difficult children to reach, she said, are those who have been physically abused or suffered severe emotional neglect from the adults in their lives. "Even when their mouths smile, their eyes don't," she reflected sadly.

Research on the long-term effects of early intervention programs confirm Ms. Rivera's observations. Although, as one researcher remarked, even the most enriched surroundings will not make every child into a Nobel Prize winner, environments can determine how well each one's inherited pattern of abilities is actualized. And while cognitive "stimulation" is important, so is the presence of caring adults in a child's life. Any teacher knows how important emotional as well as material support is for all children, and in this respect, at least, "disadvantage" does not always rest on economics. Even ostensibly "privileged" children may suffer in much more subtle, but still significant, ways if their emotional needs are neglected or if parental expectations are too demanding. Ms. Rivera reflected ruefully on one such case.

"We have a little boy here whose parents are very wealthy, but you might also call him 'disadvantaged' in a sense," she mused. "Paul has been in day care since birth; he's two and a half now and he's here from eight A.M. until six P.M. Then his parents hire our staff members to take him home and stay with him until they get home, which might be anywhere from seven until eleven that night. Unfortunately, it has to be a different person each day. He's a wonderful little boy, but he's just so weary and tired most of the time. Naturally, his parents have big expectations for him. He's still vastly better off than these homeless kids, of course, but . . ."

As we walked through the classrooms, I was impressed by the cheerful environment as well as the obvious attention by staff members and volunteers to the children's needs. Although some children required special help or comforting from adults, most were playing, learning, and interacting happily. To a practiced observer there were major variations in the maturation of language skills, but it was not always obvious to a casual eye which children were the "privileged" ones and which were the homeless.

As we entered the last classroom, I saw a small, sad-eyed child sitting alone, listlessly resting his head on the table in front of him. Stifling the urge to sit down and take him onto my lap, I whispered to Ms. Rivera, "One of the homeless?"

"No," she replied, "that's Paul."

DIMENSIONS OF DISADVANTAGE

Children are "disadvantaged" to the degree they do not receive adequate physical, social-emotional, or intellectual nurturing. Long-standing deprivation in any of these domains puts children at risk; when factors overlap and accumulate, learning, lives, and society are proportionately endangered.

In the United States the most seriously and dangerously disadvantaged are the children of poverty, a problem swept under the rug for so long that it has become a sizable lump that now threatens to trip up the progress of the body politic. A disgraceful number of American infants arrive each year into worlds of hunger, drug abuse, and neglect. Many are born to young teenagers whose own brains lack both a history of adequate nurturance and the final strokes of nature's maturational brush. These parents are ill equipped to provide for even their children's most basic physical needs, much less their intellects. This growing subculture of deprivation represents a growing threat to our institutions of education and inevitably, of law, despite demonstrated results from programs showing that it may be possible to repair and restructure, at least to some degree, both lives and intellects.

The physical, emotional, and cognitive events that transpire during the early years of a brain's development have a lifelong impact, not only on that brain itself but also on the society in which it will inevitably make its mark—for better or for worse. Children from economically disadvantaged families often come to school with brains poorly equipped for success there. The same is increasingly true for some of their more privileged counterparts. Let's examine the reasons why.

The Physically Deprived Brain

Many economically disadvantaged children start out with brains already compromised. Poor nutrition, substance abuse, or excessive stress for the pregnant mother can jeopardize its structural integrity. Pregnant women in lower class urban neighborhoods are more likely to be exposed to lead from car exhaust and to other pollutants that may harm the brain. Prematurity, often found in conjunction with poor health-care, can also put children at risk for learning disorders. Every year more and more preterm babies are being saved through technological advances, but without the enriched environments more common to middle class homes, these children are educationally at risk. Middle class preemies are more likely to recover or show milder forms of learning or attention disabilities. The prognosis depends on the severity of the initial problem and the infant's innate resilience, but also on the quality of the early learning environment.

For the children of poverty, nutrition may be inadequate, lead poisoning still a threat, and crowded quarters disruptive of free play, development of motor skills, and sleep patterns. Many poor children spend a great deal of time in front of a television set, which, unfortunately, does little to remedy perceptual, motor, cognitive, or interpersonal delays. They are much more likely to be targets of abuse and physical neglect. Most children living in poverty are never enrolled in any type of preschool; a large majority of the 253,000 children estimated to be homeless at this writing never attend school regularly.[2] Many more not classified as homeless suffer similar conditions.

Severe malnutrition takes a lasting toll on mental ability. The best-known study showing its long-term effects was conducted with a group of Korean children who grew up in conditions of extreme poverty, including malnutrition to the age of eighteen months, when they were adopted into American middle class homes. Although they rapidly regained much of the lost ground, the ill effects of the early experience on learning skills were never totally reversed.[3] No one has measured the effects of more subtle forms of dietary restriction, but there is good reason to suspect that it, too, can have lasting consequences for the brain, particularly if protein is inadequate.

No matter what its initial potential, a brain malnourished, assailed by toxic environments, or poorly nurtured has little chance of realizing its biological promise. Because risk factors are so interactive, youngsters higher up on the stack of environmental privilege are much better "buffered," but deprivation in one or more of the basic areas of need can have serious results for any child.

The Emotionally Deprived Brain

Children who do not receive interpersonal and emotional support during early years are harmed in less obvious but still devastating ways, although specific effects on the brain have not been well documented. Teachers are all too acutely aware that a mind preoccupied with worries or unmet emotional needs is a poor candidate for academic learning. The emotional centers of the brain (technically part of the *limbic system*, which underlies the cortex), are closely linked to more primitive systems whose job it is to "gate" the messages that pass into—or are kept out of—the thinking brain. If the "emotional" brain is preoccupied with fears or anxiety, it may fail to activate the proper cortical switches for attention, memory, motivation, and learning. High levels of stress can also change the fine chemical balance that enables messages to pass through all these systems; although the "good stress," generated by exciting and manageable challenges, may enhance learning, a child who is emotionally stressed may literally have trouble getting the brain's juices flowing for academics.

THE "ADVANTAGED" DEPRIVED BRAIN

Paradoxically, the same lack of respect for children's needs that causes the lump under the rug of poverty also threatens mental development at the other end of the socioeconomic continuum. Even materially "privileged" youngsters are put at emotional and intellectual risk when they become victims of a caretaker shuffle that exposes them to emotional neglect, inferior day care, or inadequate surrogate parenting. Habits of learning can also be compromised by inexperienced caretakers who overprotect their charges. Such oversolicitous attention may stem either from fear that children might get hurt or that they might complain to their parents if they don't get their own way.

It can foster both "learned helplessness" and habits of manipulating adults.

Victims of the Caretaker Shuffle

Many parents find the growing shortage of well-trained caregivers a source of frustration and anguish. Most parents naturally love their children and care deeply about their development. At the same time, with the majority of children in some sort of child care because either a single parent or both parents are working, adults who do not share their educational experience, conversational ability, cultural background, or academic values are being hired to mold the offsprings' brains. As a result, concerned observers report, the insidious tendrils of disadvantage are quietly inserting themselves across the socioeconomic spectrum.

Dr. Fred Hechinger, education editor of the *New York Times*, spoke at a recent meeting for teachers and administrators of the country's private schools to warn that their constituency is being profoundly influenced by changes in child-rearing habits among the middle and upper-middle class. The problems of children in poor and affluent families are becoming more and more similar, he explained, because the same people are taking care of the children.[4] No matter how loving or well-intentioned they may be, the environments they create for development of language and thought are quite often inconsonant with the parents' and the schools' expectations for the child.

Andree Brooks, author of *Children of Fast-Track Parents* and an outspoken critic of current trends in child rearing, warns of the potentially disastrous effects of a lack of nurturing by well-to-do parents who depend on an ever-changing stream of caregivers. A host of developmental problems, including "stunted language ability," may ensue, she maintains.[5,6]

"I hear this all over the country, and I'm hearing it more and more," she told me. "There's an increasing concern from the teachers of young children of the upper-middle class, which has traditionally been such a source of enormous educational and cultural enrichment, that the children are coming in without the same exposure. They're taking on some of the aspects of the disadvantaged. Upper-middle-class women are going back to work even sooner after their children are born than disadvantaged women, and all the traditional interactions we have assumed between them and their children are missing."

The practice of hiring surrogate caretakers is spreading, Ms. Brooks adds, as well-to-do nonworking mothers hire live-ins in order to keep up with the Joneses. And the mores of this fast track are now being copied by the less affluent. In countries abroad, she says, the same concerns are also beginning to surface.

"Do you think we have lost respect for children and their needs?" I asked.

"Absolutely," replied Ms. Brooks. "The child has been devalued."[7]

Reveta Bowers, director of a large early-childhood program in Los Angeles, has similar concerns that extend beyond the children of the wealthy. "You'd be surprised how many children are being raised by surrogates who don't speak English, and the parents don't care because they think the child will be bilingual," she says. But this rationalization, she points out, may put some children at risk for learning problems.

Insufficient research is available to quantify the effects of bilingual environments, but those that are inferior or not "natural" to the family itself may slow down overall language development and exacerbate potential learning problems. The quality of the language input, whatever it is, often varies according to the educational background of the speaker. While proficiency in more than one language is obviously an advantage, a child—particularly one who is not linguistically talented by nature—needs to interact with adequate syntax in at least one language to wire up the basis for development of the others.

Still, because of insufficient numbers of well-trained child-care providers, families at all socioeconomic levels feel pressed to compromise when they hire a caregiver. "It's a gamble," says Professor Edward Zigler of Yale University, a leading expert on early development. "If you get a wonderful one, it's like having a new valued family member. If you get an awful one, you and your child are in trouble." Zigler is acutely aware that even families who can afford good care for their children have great difficulty finding it. "Up and down the economic ladder, children are receiving care that may be compromising their optimal development."[8]

It is an unfortunate reality that the low pay scale for day-care workers has similarly tended to downgrade the level of skills in these facilities. Not many are lucky enough to have the able and dedicated corps of teachers and volunteers found in Ms. Rivera's center. Yet large numbers of children are in their care during the time when these developing brains are crafting the mental skills of a lifetime.

Children as Artifacts of Ambition

Parents who care about their children's success are vulnerable to false information about the best ways to get their children onto the academic fast track. A zeitgeist, fostered by dubious "experts" and seized upon by well-intentioned or guilty parents, now advocates an all-out campaign to "stimulate" mental ability. Parents, beware! Trying to force learning that may be all wrong for the child's level of development is dangerous, as are the inappropriate demands for performance—no matter how subtle—that usually accompany this kind of pressure. Even in the wealthiest of homes, a child who becomes an artifact of parental ego is at risk in a very real sense.

"Superbabies" of all ages are driven (quite literally, to an unremitting schedule of lessons, as well as more figuratively) to perform. These child "products" appear to be the polar opposite of the physically and intellectually neglected children of disadvantage, yet they, too, are deprived of important basic rights. I hear many tales like that of a young suburban mother who told me, "You would not believe the mothers in my neighborhood; they have flash cards for their kids before they're two and the children are in so many lessons and programs that they hardly have time to play! My neighbor insists her three-year-old sing the alphabet song; the other day the child was pleading, 'Please, Mommy, please, no more alphabet,' but the mother kept saying, 'Just one more time, sweetheart. Do it for Mommy.' "

Driving the cold spikes of inappropriate pressure into the malleable heart of a child's learning may seriously distort the unfolding of both intellect and motivation. This self-serving intellectual assault, increasingly condemned by teachers who see its warped products, reflects a more general ignorance of the essential needs of the growing brain. In a society that reveres the speed with which a product can be extruded from the system, that has become impatient with the essential processes of childhood, that measures children's mental growth like steaks on a butcher's scales, and that deifies test scores instead of taking the time to respect developmental needs, every child is potentially in jeopardy.

Wise adults do not impose demands for which development and experience have not yet primed the system. They take the time to listen to the child, to observe and enrich the environment accordingly. If they are too busy, lack the coping skills, or neglect their responsibility, the chances at each stage of development may be lost or diminished.

If a brain is jeopardized, what are the chances for "synaptic remodeling"? No one has yet been able to measure the long-term toll of too much pressure. Improved environments can make up to some degree for some experiential physical deprivation if it is "caught" early enough. The brutal truth, however, is that more acute forms of disadvantage leave indelible imprints. Their most serious consequences are probably for higher cognitive functions such as language and abstract reasoning. Emotional deprivation and stress take their toll in less measurable ways.

Research does not suggest bombarding children with high-powered brain-training or forcing overwhelming doses of "stimulation" on unready nervous systems. Prying open preschool minds and pouring in ersatz precocity is not the answer; realistically assessing—and then addressing—children's real intellectual needs is the way to improve their chances.

SOCIAL CLASS AND MENTAL DEVELOPMENT: THE PROBLEM NOBODY WANTS TO TALK ABOUT

It is an uneasy but incontrovertible fact that, on average, individuals from different social classes have widely different success in school. A close look suggests that learning patterns and brain organization may be shaped by certain types of environments in ways that make children's adjustment to academic learning more difficult.

Yet despite research that might help teachers understand and teach high-risk children more successfully, the issue of social class is one that many people prefer not to discuss. In an address to members of the American Psychological Association on the subject of "Race, Culture, Class, and Ethnicity," Dr. Richard Brislin pointed out that it has become easier and even more acceptable to talk about racial differences than about social class differences in America. The two should definitely not be confused.[9]

Race is determined by a person's genes. There is no convincing evidence of any genetic differences between races in learning potential. According to Dr. Brislin and other scholars, however, because people of the same race and ethnic background tend to grow up in communities where social class, cultural habits, and practices are similar, important differences caused by these variables may seem to be racial in origin.

"In classrooms, as in American life generally, ethnicity is confounded with social class," explains Harvard's Dr. Courtney Cazden. In her useful book, *Classroom Discourse*, she makes a realistic case for better education of teachers in understanding, accepting, and teaching children of different social classes, as well as those of differing cultural backgrounds.[10]

"Social class" or socioeconomic status (SES) is defined in research by several factors, primarily family income, parents' level of education, and occupations. The terms "lower class" or "underclass" are used by social scientists as an objective descriptor that includes both working class poor and the chronically unemployed. These terms sound blunt, but they are not meant to label individuals in a pejorative way, merely to describe a particular socioeconomic group. Any set of statistical generalizations about group differences has many exceptions; the main danger in reporting on this sort of research is in creating new stereotypes and unfair prejudices. But it is equally unfair to ignore data that may help us understand why some children have difficulty adjusting to school.

Members of different socioeconomic as well as different cultural groups tend to have differing values regarding children's learning and behavior. Overall, they rear children in different ways, have different ideas of what is important for learning, and may encourage different "habits of mind." Thus it is not surprising that children from these different types of environments arrive in school differently adapted to learning. It is unfortunate, in a country that claims to take pride in its heterogeneity, that educators have too often tried to cram all children into an unyielding curricular format. All children need a chance to participate equally in academic success, but unless policymakers start paying attention to the realities, they risk destroying both our children and our intellectual standards.

Separating Class Differences From Racial Differences

A growing number of studies confirm that irrespective of race, people develop different patterns of learning skills according to the social class in which they are reared.[11] Concerned researchers also point out that too many studies have tended to draw conclusions about blacks in general after studying only underclass black children. "In studies of black and white children and children from other ethnic groups, it's rare to find any race differences when class differences are carefully looked at," points out Dr. Brislin.

Dr. Sandra Graham of the Graduate School of Education at UCLA, one of a few scientists looking specifically at both racial and social-class differences, studied levels of school motivation among lower and middle class black and white seventh-grade students. She found significant differences between students from the different socioeconomic groups; the only racial differences were that the middle class black children displayed the highest persistence, more positive levels of self perception, and greater sustained achievement strivings.[12]

Teachers like myself, who have taught academically brilliant as well as not-so-brilliant students from various racial, cultural, and socioeconomic groups, realize how foolish it is to categorize youngsters intellectually on any basis. Still, in the classroom it also becomes clear that all students have tucked a myriad of formative learning experiences into their brains long before they started tucking notes and assignment sheets into their bookbags. The research shows, although there are always many exceptions, the most predictable variations in school success in most countries are found among families of different social classes.

Different SES, Different Learning

Children from families of different social classes may be prepared for and supported in learning differently. Even when not physically or emotionally disadvantaged, some children receive different types of cognitive and language stimulation because parents' level of education, perceptions of children's needs, and style of approaching problems may diverge from the "middle class norm." According to Dr. Brislin, middle and upper class families tend to emphasize verbal development, self-control, intellectual curiosity, and social skills, whereas values for many working class children are more likely to stress obedience, neatness, good manners, and quietness around adults. While this focus may have been more appropriate in an economy with a large number of factory jobs, it is maladaptive for the type of work increasingly available as a part of information technology. Moreover, because lower class children may not be as assertive around adult authority figures, teachers may expect less of them.

Social class is such a powerful predictor of "mainstream" test results that it can even override early risk factors. In one representative study, a group of researchers in Zurich, Switzerland, compared the long-term development of premature infants from higher- and lower-class families. These children were considered at high risk for language problems, learning disabilities, and "lower mental functioning" because of complications surrounding pregnancy and birth. Their course of development was also compared with that of a group of healthy full-term babies matched with the preemies according to social class. All the children in the study were carefully observed and tested for language development and intelligence at frequent intervals until they were five years old. As is almost invariably the case, socioeconomic status (SES) was highly correlated with tested ability in the normal, full-term children from the beginning of their lives. The at-risk children, however, all started out with below-average scores. Yet by age five the power of the environment over the biological problems had been demonstrated. The middle class high-risk group had narrowed the gap, while the lower SES children had not.[13]

Studies from all over the world demonstrate that children from higher SES groups have better language development and more mature cognitive skills.[14] Nevertheless, higher socioeconomic level alone does not offer a fail-safe guarantee of good progress, nor, certainly, are children raised in so-called "underclass" homes automatically destined to have difficulty in school. U.S. Education Department researcher Martin Orland, although acknowledging the high statistical correlations between poor academic achievement and "intense" poverty factors, points out that, even in poor homes, parents' attitudes have the most dominant influence. He claims that measures of "home atmosphere," such as parental aspirations for children, language stimulation, the amount of reading materials in the home, and family attitudes toward education, actually explain more of the variation in student achievement than parental income levels or other traditional socioeconomic measures.[15]

Families whose poverty has been long-standing and severe are much less likely to be able to provide a supportive home atmosphere, but some succeed despite the odds. It is clearly absurd to make assumptions about home quality only on the basis of an economic yardstick, and Dr. Brislin warns against letting class distinctions become a new source of discrimination. These differences should only be a "reminder variable," he points out, to lead us to more constructive opportunities for intervention.

In a large, longitudinal study conducted in England, researcher Gordon Wells was surprised when the expected correlation between class and educational attainment at age seven did not emerge. Carefully analyzing his results, Wells, too, developed "grave reservations" about any simple statements regarding this connection. Noting the close link between language development and school success, he concluded that certain kinds of interaction with adults, particularly a child's conversational experience, are mainly responsible for the difference.[16]

What Is the Problem?

Why, specifically, do so many "learning disadvantaged"[17] children have difficulty adapting to the demands of traditional schooling? Many become school dropouts during the first week of first grade—although they usually continue to occupy a desk (and a great deal of the teacher's physical and mental energy) for several more alienating and unproductive years. In the meanwhile, the growing dichotomy between their level of skills and the demands of the school interfere with the entire mechanism of teaching and learning, and their poorly suppressed rage may erupt in externally or personally destructive forms. Unsuccessful, "turned-off" children exist in every school, but they are endemic in areas housing the poor of our society, where over half of the five-year-olds who surge into the kindergarten each year may be doomed to failure.

These statistics are particularly tragic because poor parents often "have an especially high—even passionate regard for education and view it as the most promising means to improve their children's futures," asserts Lisbeth B. Schorr in her landmark book *Within Our Reach*.[18] They need help, however, in translating their yearning for their children's achievement into useful action.

PREPARING GROWING BRAINS FOR THE "CULTURE OF THE SCHOOL"

No one knows exactly what proportion of the ultimate differences between mental abilities come from differences in types of environmental input during the years when the brain is being encouraged—or not encouraged—to practice and master different types of skills. It is clear, however, that the closer the culture of the home (or the primary care center) is to that of the school, the easier the child's adjustment is likely to be.

Schooling, particularly beyond the elementary years, demands specific types of skills and even particular ways of looking at the world and of reasoning.[19] Such "scholastic thinking" involves analyzing experience, reasoning reflectively, using formal logic, and assimilating, storing, and recalling information. Because language development is so closely tied to these mental skills and to brain development as well, it assumes an especially pivotal role in preparing children for learning.

Many "learning disadvantaged" children are handicapped by lack of exposure to school-like ways of talking and thinking. Academically advantaged brains, in contrast, are well-girded for school learning because adults have provided models and given them time and encouragement to practice these basic ways of dealing with information.

Adult Models of Problem-Solving

The most frequently mentioned factors in the development of intelligence might include parental encouragement for achievement, exposure to intellectual models, and encouragement to rely on language. They are, in short, aspects of the upper-middle-class environment.
—Dr. Robert B. McCall[20]

Psychologists have spent a great deal of time studying the ways in which schooled and unschooled people typically go about solving problems and how they model these mental habits for their children. Homes influence several important dimensions of this "cognitive style":

1. Ways of Categorizing

Studies across many different cultures show that people who have been to school tend to group objects and ideas together in more abstract ways than do young children or unschooled adults, who tend to relate ideas on the basis of their physical attributes or use. For example, if asked whether an apple matches best with a pear, a red ball, or a knife, most schooled people, who tend to think more categorically, will respond "pear" because it is a member of the category "fruit." Unschooled individuals and young children may choose the ball "because they look alike" or the knife "because it is used to cut the apple." Although there is really no right or wrong answer here, schools tend to expect children to have the ability to deal with categorical modes of thought. A child who has not been exposed to them at home ("Johnny, let's put all the vegetables in this cupboard, and all the fruits in that one") may have difficulty understanding this type of reasoning.

2. Internalizing Understanding

"Many at-risk students have not internalized a cultural sense of what understanding is, probably because parents and teachers seldom hold 'understanding conversations' with them," suggests Dr. Stanley Pogrow, who has worked on ways to teach "thinking skills" to disadvantaged elementary school students.[21] Having "understanding conversations" means trying to get a child to reason through, evaluate, and express ideas ("How many different ways could this story end? Let's predict which one the author will choose . . ."). Dr. Pogrow says many of his students come to school not knowing how to use ideas to understand, generalize, or even talk about anything but "turfdom," because they have never been exposed to other types of thinking. Incidentally, he notes, *this problem is not limited to students from low SES homes.*

Parents and teachers who try to force high-level material on brains that have not been primed to accommodate it should be warned by Dr. Pogrow's finding that it is much better to converse intelligently about simple subjects than to have simple conversations about overly sophisticated content. "For example," he says, "teaching students Shakespeare will not develop general thinking skills if relatively few understanding conversations take place." Unfortunately, many of the "competency-based" teaching agendas that have been cantilevered into classrooms for disadvantaged children have fallen into this latter trap. Well-intentioned, they are essentially flawed by attempting to pour in information and drill children to repeat it at a superficial level rather than taking the time to give understanding—and synapses—a solid foundation.

It is possible to get almost any child deeply and constructively involved with important material, but the teacher must have the sensitivity—and above all, the time—to engage the students in activities or a dialogue that is meaningful to them. Dr. Robert Coles tells in his book *The Call of Stories* of his delight in "culturally disadvantaged" youngsters who "take to" a novel such as *Silas Marner,* often regarded as old-fashioned and boring. The reason? A skilled teacher spent time leading them into personally meaningful discussions of moral and spiritual issues in the novel that reflected many of their own life concerns.[22] Unfortunately, "competency," as it has too often been defined, has no time or space for this type of intellectual inquiry.

3. Reflectivity or Impulsivity

Unsuccessful students often tend to act without thinking. Research shows that impulsive youngsters fail to talk through problems in their own heads; they jump in without analyzing or planning the appropriate response. In research on problem-solving, students who use such an impulsive approach are seen as "weak reasoners" because they fail to apply what they already know to the new situation.[23] "Strong reasoners," on the other hand, are able to use previous examples to help reach conclusions.

The impulsive style (which overlaps with the problem now diagnosed as "attention deficit disorder") gets people into trouble outside of school, as well. There is a well-recognized link between this type of behavior, delinquency, and adult criminality.

Children who do not stop, reflect, and talk through situations often come from homes where adults never showed them how, irrespective of their economic advantages. I sometimes notice parents or caregivers who model widely different styles with children in public places such as the supermarket. Some are busy teaching the child to talk through alternatives ("No, we won't buy two boxes of cereal today because it will get stale before we eat it all. Tell me if you want Goops or Nuggets."). Others give in to the child's impulsive demands. Still others try to control behavior physically, with a minimum of conversation. They may even slap or jerk the child around as he reaches for desired treats. These parents undoubtedly are managing the situation in ways they think appropriate, and of course, we all tend to recreate the ways in which we ourselves were handled. The child who is being taught to stop and reflect is the one more likely to succeed in the culture of the school and perhaps, beyond it as well.

"Reflective" approaches are a useful adjunct to inspiration in nonverbal problem-solving such as in art work, geometry, or higher mathematical reasoning. One of the tests used to measure whether someone responds reflectively or impulsively requires picking the exact match for a drawing of a common object, such as a house, from several very close and confusing alternatives. To be scored "reflective," a child needs to take the time to compare carefully, analyze details, and weigh alternatives. Even in this visual task, however, many reflective children talk and analyze their way through the problem ("I think I'll start with the first one. Let's see, the chimney is different. Now, how about the second?" etc.).

An interesting cross-cultural study not long ago showed that American and Chinese-American children of comparable SES were similar in the way they developed the ability to solve the problems on this test. A comparable group of Japanese children, however, became more accurate much earlier in life in finding the matching picture. They outscored the American and Chinese youngsters, speculated the researchers, not because they were smarter, but because they were better able to manage their own patterns of thinking and responding.[24] These researchers did not hazard any guesses as to where they learned this mental control.

4. Scaffolding for Learning to Remember

Another major way in which parents who have been successful in school tend to differ from those with less schooling is in showing children ways to remember things. As they use and talk about their own memory strategies, their child becomes aware that remembering something doesn't just happen automatically but is something over which he or she has some control.

"I have five things I must buy at the hardware store this morning; let's see, I need two tools—a hammer and a big screwdriver—and three kinds of wire—thin, medium, and thick (categorizing). *I'll remember H,S,W,W,W* (forming active memory strategies)."

Or, *"I think I'd better make a list so I won't forget."* (Shows importance of writing and reading as well as planning ahead.)

5. Analytical vs. Relational Styles of Thinking

Traditional schooling also tends to teach people to approach problems analytically. This way of thinking calls on abstract logic rather than firsthand experience. For example, one of the cognitive skills learned in the culture of the school is to reason with syllogisms.

All of the women from Mexico City are beautiful.
I have a woman friend from Mexico City.
Is my friend beautiful?[25]

To most schooled people, the answer to this problem seems obvious, but adolescents and adults who have had little or no exposure to the institutions of formal schooling do not find it obvious at all. They tend to answer the question more pragmatically, on the basis of women they know personally ("My friend from Mexico City is very kind, but she is not beautiful"). The way questions like this are answered in different cultures are related to years of schooling, not to basic intelligence, conclude the researchers.

Parents Show Children How to Think

These are just a few of the many ways in which parents and caregivers directly influence the ways in which children learn to think. Does this mean that conscientious parents need to sit down and plan a course in problem-solving for their children? Or perhaps, if they are too busy to take the responsibility, sign them up for lessons? The fact is that these ways of thinking are learned and internalized because they are conveyed through everyday, emotionally cushioned and meaningful experiences with a close, respected adult.

Mealtime conversations, for example, have always been prime time for communication, not only for ways of thinking but also of values about what it is important to think about. Even such subtle attitudes as whether children are expected to ask questions of adults or whether people talk about ideas as well as about what they bought at the mall can make a big difference in the way children approach school activities. These days, though, thoughtful family dinner-table conversations are on their way to joining the dinosaur category even in many middle and upper middle class homes.

Other adult-child activities—cooking, relaxing, playing games, doing errands, working with tools, cleaning the house, visiting a parent's office, or pursuing real-life projects together—are also natural means through which these mental habits are learned. One of the reasons that school success, in all walks of life, is inversely related to the amount of time spent watching television may be that minimal TV viewing forces grown-ups and children to tune into each other's thoughts and activities. Children in severely disadvantaged homes, on the contrary, tend to watch more television; as we have seen, it offers precious little scaffolding for academic habits of mind.

Disadvantages in models of thinking are obviously not restricted to the children of the poor. Since I know this book is most likely to be read by parents of the middle or upper middle class, I would like to stretch this point with one personal experience.

This year I spent a lovely fall afternoon with some friends who live in a modest house in a rural area that has recently become the setting for a number of large, expensive new homes. The husband, a math teacher, had confided to me that he was beginning to feel self-conscious because he suddenly realized, observing his new neighbors, that he couldn't afford to give his son many of the advantages of their children. He admitted to particularly uneasy feelings when he watched his son's new friends being trundled off to their expensive schools, camps, computer and music lessons, etc.

On the day I visited, this dad and his son were heavily engaged in a tactical war with the family dog, an accomplished escape artist who had systematically broken out of every pen ever constructed for her. Armed with tool kit, boards, and wire mesh, they spent the entire afternoon contriving an escape-proof enclosure. As his wife and I sat in the yard, enjoying the autumn sun, I observed them reasoning together. "But Dad, if we . . . she might . . ." "What do you think will happen if . . . ?" "Why don't we try . . . because . . ."

As an unregenerate speculator about growing brains, I found myself having visions of pathways being forged between the hemispheres as parent and child talked about and physically manipulated the three-dimensional problem at hand. Their efforts inevitably linked verbal and visual-spatial systems in the way the brain learns best—with a firsthand problem. When one solution didn't work, the son got frustrated and wanted to give up, but his father patiently suggested they try yet another approach, while I fancied prefrontal neurons joyously reaching out to each other to strengthen systems for planning, attention, and problem-solving.

Meanwhile, on the large grounds next door, another youngster of about the same age amused himself for the entire afternoon zooming at top speed—and top volume—around house, stable, and swimming pool on a four-wheeled motorized vehicle that he propelled by pushing a pedal.

"Yeah," said my friend's son with just a trace of envy in his voice. "He rides it all year-round. His mom's usually at a meeting or something, but sometimes his dad takes him out to play golf with him on the weekends. Their maid doesn't speak much English, so she never even makes him do his homework."

"It's really a shame," my friend remarked. "His parents are so worried about that child. He's quite intelligent but they found out he has a learning disability. They have to send him to a special school because he got such poor grades and couldn't concentrate long enough to do his assignments."

"Learning disadvantaged" children are found everywhere.

SOCIAL CLASS, LANGUAGE, AND LITERACY

There is no solid evidence that the poor lack stimulation, except in the domain of language. It is accepted that the very poor everywhere use concrete, reduced vocabulary which takes away from communication the rich conceptual sharing that is taken for granted in the middle classes.

—Professor Gonzalo Alvarez, Santiago, Chile[26]

Sociolinguists tell us that the more stratified a society, the more variations there are in language,[27] and this variable alone seems to account for many of the social-class differences in academic achievement. Homes that offer substandard or unstimulating conditions for children's cognitive development tend to produce youngsters with language delays that ultimately translate into lower IQ and achievement scores.[28,29] Two aspects of the way children are exposed to language appear to be particularly important: ways in which they are talked to, and their contact with reading and written language.

Ways of Talking to Children

The types of questions the child learns to ask and answer are particularly important. Children trained mainly to be quiet, polite, and obedient have trouble at school when they need to talk in front of a group or speak up to ask an adult a question. The teacher may not understand that this behavior is considered "good" at home.

Children also have trouble in school if they are unaccustomed to answering questions asked by an adult, particularly ones to which they realize the adult (teacher) already knows the answer![30] Parents who have not themselves absorbed school-type talk tend to ask questions only when they really want information from the child ("What do you want for breakfast?"). Middle class parents are more likely to ask teacherlike questions, such as, "What is the girl in the picture doing?" (The most intelligent answer, actually, might be, "Why ask me? Can't you see for yourself?" But a polite child will only sit quietly and wonder how someone who asks such dumb questions could have become a teacher.) Eventually, experiential gaps in answering the "wh questions" (who, what, when, where, why—and how) translate into difficulty with analytic thinking.

Basic language skills alone do not assure school success. Later-developing abilities, such as understanding more complex sentence patterns, being able to "hold the floor," and possessing a more extensive vocabulary, gain increasing importance as students get older. Teachers may inadvertently use these criteria to judge students' abilities and may place lower-class students with more interactive, informal styles in lower "tracks."[31,32]

Dr. Jerome Bruner reminds us that language is also a major means by which a learner can "objectify" and get control of learning—instead of having the learning process in control.[33] When I visit a classroom where the children are reciting from memory and clearly do not understand (which, tragically, seems to be a situation foisted more frequently onto poor than privileged children), I am not surprised to hear they have "no initiative" for learning. If someone would take the time to make the learning, whatever it is, meaningful by coaching them in ways to talk about it, the turned-off faces might light up.

The type of coaching provided by home environments in uses of printed as well as spoken language may differ according to socioeconomic level. In an important recent study Dr. Shirley Brice Heath of Stanford University reported on her experiences observing both kinds of "literacy events" in homes of three different SES groups in a North Carolina town. She discovered that the two "non-mainstream" working class groups differed significantly from the "mainstream" homes, not only in the availability of books, magazines, and newspapers, but also the way they prepared their children for the type of thinking required in school. In one non-mainstream group, which Heath called "Trackton," parents demonstrated a great deal of love for their children, but their own lives contained few occasions for reading and writing. Books, magazines, or newspapers were not generally in evidence, and no priority was placed on story-reading. According to Dr. Heath, children's efforts to talk were generally ignored, and they got attention from adults by nonverbal behaviors such as bouncing up and down or tugging on a sleeve.

In contrast, the mainstream parents tended to reward children's verbal expression and "provide a running verbal commentary" on what they themselves were doing. They read often to their children, and showed them the uses of writing. For example, they followed written recipes, made lists, and wrote notes about chores to family members. Their children came to school ready to use and respond to traditional classroom language, materials, and expectations; when children from "Trackton" arrived in school, they entered an alien culture. Not surprisingly, they tended to do poorly from the outset and had often "given up" by sixth grade.

The second "non-mainstream" working-class community, dubbed "Roadville" by Dr. Heath, represents an interesting contrast to both other groups. These parents were overtly interested in education and tended to expose their children to alphabet books and other purchased "educational" materials such as workbooks. Yet, although the children mastered the "basics" in early grades, they tended to fall behind when deeper understanding of the material became necessary in later elementary years. The reason? Dr. Heath suggests that these well-intentioned homes had failed to show their children how to think. Unlike the parents from the higher SES group, they did not use questions to help children's reasoning develop. Their questions to their children tended to be more "directive or scolding in nature," and considerable emphasis was placed on *getting the right answer*. "Talk" as a means of solving problems had little priority; parents were much more likely to show, rather than tell, children how to do something. Reason-explanations such as, "If you twist the cutter, the cookies will be rough on the edge," were rarely given. Heath suggests that these "Roadville" children "do not know how to ask teachers to help them take apart the questions to figure out the answers."[34]

Although Heath's findings should not be over-generalized beyond these two communities, they do reinforce the point that even the most loving and well-intentioned caregivers can mold children's patterns of talking and thinking so as to put them at risk in "mainstream" classrooms. Educators have long been aware that environments which do not expose children to models of literacy impair their chances in school; we now realize that merely giving children books and pencils is not enough. Too many parents mistakenly believe that the purpose of reading to their children is to "teach" them to read rather than what it really is—showing them how to love and use the language and stories in books. Likewise, making preschoolers sit down and practice copying letters and words is poor preparation for higher-level thinking.

Parents don't need to—in fact, shouldn't—turn reading sessions into drills, emphasizes a researcher in the United States who discovered significant differences among middle class families in the effectiveness of their children's story times. In one of his studies, half of the parents were shown how to intersperse their reading with open-ended questions (e.g., "There's Eeyore. What's happening to him?") and to help the child elaborate on responses, while the other half were told just to read in their usual way. Later testing showed that children from the first group scored higher on both vocabulary and ability to express ideas, traditionally good predictors of later school abilities.[35]

DIFFERENT SES, DIFFERENT BRAINS?

How do these different cognitive and language backgrounds affect neural development? When considering this question, we should bear in mind that structural or functional variations that cause children to use different "learning strategies" do not necessarily imply lower overall intelligence. Brains less well adapted for certain types of verbal learning may still have many talents: creative, practical, or otherwise valuable.

There are several ways, both overt and subtle, in which the environmental differences found between different socioeconomic groups might be linked to brain differences. Dr. Gonzalo Alvarez, a neurologist on the medical faculty at the University of Chile in Santiago, who has studied the effects of severe physical deprivation on brain function in developing countries, is convinced that different patterns of child rearing also make their marks on the developing cortex.

Certain stages of cognitive development (i.e., the ability to understand the relationships of physical objects) are hard to change because they are "imbedded in the genetic code," maintains Dr. Alvarez. Although these relatively "hard-wired" abilities may be delayed in underdeveloped parts of the world, they will still eventually emerge, given even a minimum of stimulation. In children he has tested from such "opaque circumstances" of deprivation, however, he has also typically found "failure to perform adequately in tasks that involve complex abstract thinking and problem-solving" which he attributes in part to brain differences resulting from different levels of stimulation. Dr. Alvarez makes it clear that these children are not "mentally retarded" or even "neurologically damaged"; brains in the lower socioeconomic groups he has studied are not abnormal, he insists, but they may be delayed or incomplete in certain specific ways. When such children enter the educational system, these differences cause them to "miss the boat."

Dr. Alvarez contends that the "different levels of stimulation" go beyond basic differences in sensory (seeing, hearing, touching) input. He finds that different sets of cultural demands cause children to have particular difficulty with abstract, analytical thinking—because their brains are trained to work differently.

> The various strategies that brains elaborate in order to solve problems peculiar to that particular culture may depend on circuitry which varies from one culture to another. . . . *Whether or not sensory stimulation is lacking in early years amongst the poor, different modalities of rearing may lead to differential processing of information by brain structures* [emphasis added].[36]

Different Hemispheres: Different Learning Styles?

The parts of the brain in which scientists have looked for this sort of different neural circuitry are the two cerebral hemispheres. A few studies have, in fact, suggested that different ways of using the right and left hemispheres may account for some social-class differences in school success. Specifically, more successful students—and more middle class children—tend to use analytic "thinking styles" attributed to the left hemisphere, while less successful ones—and more economically disadvantaged children—rely more on the relational, holistic propensities of the right. As we have seen, many children raised in nonacademically oriented environments have little experience in using decontextualized, analytic language strategies for learning, and they may be more inclined to reason with visual, here-and-now, "hands-on" ("relational") strategies.

Thus far, most research on the use of these "styles" has not peered directly at the brain. Instead, children are tested on certain tasks that have been shown to reflect particular brain functions. In one such study, neuropsychologists looking at attention and memory skills of white kindergarteners from higher and lower socioeconomic levels found that children from the two groups used significantly different cognitive strategies for the same task. There were no differences in the amount of ability to pay attention overall, but the lower-SES group used more visual-spatial tactics (ordinarily mediated by right hemisphere) on a simple computer game, while the higher SES children were more likely to talk their way through the problem (calling on more left-hemisphere use).[37]

A few researchers have looked more directly at this issue in terms of the brain itself. Two early studies turned up differences in a standard listening test in which information is directed either into right or left hemispheres through the opposite ear. Results in both cases indicated different hemisphere use among children of different social classes. In an effort to control variables as carefully as possible, these studies used only right-handed youngsters because a small percentage of left-handers have a reversal of the usual left-hemisphere dominance for language. This study also suggested that children from lower SES were later in developing the usual left-hemisphere superiority for language, and that their left hemisphere did not appear to be as dominant for several types of tasks as that of the children from higher SES.[38,39]

One current study of part of a new generation of "disadvantaged"—a group of street kids in Toronto—found that 82% had reading problems. Overall, they were particularly poor in left-hemisphere language skills, including the "phonological awareness" so critical for reading success.[40] Their learning "styles" tended to be more "hands-on" and nonverbal.

Dr. Deborah Waber and her colleagues at Harvard University and Boston Children's Hospital, searching for reasons for such "stylistic differences between children from different socioeconomic backgrounds," studied 120 fifth and seventh graders from low- and high-SES backgrounds. All were Caucasian, right-handed, and spoke English as a first language; none had been identified as learning disabled. Using a machine (tachistoscope) that flashed words and numbers to right or left visual fields (which are connected to the opposite sides of the brain), they clearly showed that even though both groups got equal numbers of answers correct, the different SES groups used their brains differently to do so. Even when the effects of IQ were statistically controlled, the high-SES children showed a clear pattern of using their left hemispheres more effectively, while equally intelligent low-SES children tended to rely on the right. According to the researcher, these results reflected "SES-related variations in the nature of information processing in the two hemispheres." Boys' and girls' scores did not differ from each other.[41] Waber does not believe that her research implies that these differences are "immutable," but rather that they may have resulted from differing life experiences.[42]

These few studies are insufficient evidence on which to draw any conclusions on brain function and SES. Not all studies have even produced consistent patterns. "But if the differences are real, they suggest that environmental factors correlated with SES affect lateralization of function," suggests another team of researchers Drs. Sally Springer and Georg Deutsch, authors of the well-regarded book *Left Brain, Right Brain.*[43]

Culture and Brain Differences

A similar group of studies looking at variations in "cultural hemisphericity" (i.e., differences in development or use of brain hemispheres by different cultural groups) has produced other evidence that Springer and Deutsch term "scanty but intriguing."[44] This understandably controversial research has identified apparent hemisphere-associated differences in the responses of Navaho and Hopi as contrasted with English speakers. The scientists have suggested that some Native American languages, being more literal, concrete, and closely tied to visual experience, tend to engage the right hemisphere more than the left. Therefore, they reason, users of these languages may have an associated difference in the use of their brains that alters the usual specialization of left hemisphere for language.[45,46] Other researchers are in the process of investigating whether Native American children think about math problems and spatial relations differently from Anglo children.

Conclusions about hemispheric use are tricky, however. At the University of Northern Arizona, Dr. Walter McKeever administered a simple listening test to Navajo and Anglo fifth graders. Results of this typical experimental design can be analyzed to determine which side of the brain is most active for processing different types of syllables.

An outspoken skeptic about cultural differences in brain hemispheres, McKeever got some interesting results when he expanded this experiment so that the children were tested not just by an English (Anglo) speaker but also by a native Navajo speaker. When the person who spoke the syllables was Anglo, the Navajo children did, indeed, register a right hemisphere pattern. When the speaker was changed to a Navajo, however, the same children registered with their left hemispheres! The experimenters, initially baffled by these results, hypothesized that with the unfamiliar (Anglo) speaker, the Navajo children's right hemispheres may have been responding not primarily to the language, but to the novelty of the speaker's voice.[47] Thus their pattern, while appearing to be different, was actually what would have been expected from anyone (as the reader may recall, the right hemisphere tends to respond to novelty).

This experiment is a good illustration of the danger of premature generalizations. On the whole, a considerable amount of support has accumulated for the possibility that individual members of different groups may show differences in cognitive "style" that may be attributed to different patterns of upbringing and language that are inextricably related to brain function. But exactly how much of a lasting effect they have on the brain cannot presently be measured. Since the way any child learns to use the two sides of the brain depends on many factors, it may be a long time before any final answers are available.

Who's Interested

Perhaps an even more important focus of research on brain and learning in different SES groups will be on the behavior-regulating and planning functions of the prefrontal cortex. At least one study published in a well-respected professional journal has shown differences thought to be related to SES in the rate at which these abilities develop during childhood. In this study, children from lower SES groups, particularly boys, were immature at school entry in skills of self-regulation. Fortunately, they showed the potential to catch up to their middle class peers if given time and good teaching.[48] Since the self-management and attentional abilities that go along with prefrontal development go right along with language proficiency in earning children stars in first grade, this entire area of research should deserve some follow-up.

Yet little effort is being made to clarify this entire topic. According to Dr. Waber, whose hemisphere study, published in 1984, is the best known of those described, no one seems to be concerned.

"You're the first person who has even called me about it!" she exclaimed when I phoned her five years after the study was published. "I was actually a little worried about publishing those results because I felt they might be controversial; I was amazed that no one seemed to be interested."

Dr. Waber believes that environmentally created brain differences may indeed be responsible for some of the achievement discrepancies between children of different social classes. Some differences stem from environmental hazards such as lead, but others may represent differences in "neural software" resulting from different types of cognitive experiences.

"Of course different environments could make a difference in the way the brain functions. Any effect of experience on behavior must ipso facto be mediated by the brain. The fact that reading to kids must facilitate left-hemisphere development is one obvious example," she said. "If you want to help children, you have to start looking at the brain; after all, they don't read with their kidneys!"

Dr. Waber feels that neuropsychological study of children's cognitive functioning is critical because it adds the "structural constraints of brain function" to other models of learning. "The more accurate the model of cognition, the more likely one is to be able to build appropriate educational interventions," she says. This is the most constructive purpose that can be served by exploring the question of SES-related brain differences.

"The better you understand how the brain works, the better you know how to educate," she insists. "If anyone is really interested in educating these children, that is—and I'm not convinced anyone is. It ought certainly to change the way we start instruction, especially in early childhood education programs. For example, I've considered training lower class children on computers to try and help them become more focally oriented—to focus more and become more attentive. We're really talking about finding out how to teach them, not just how to unearth a wiring diagram."[49]

Dr. Waber now is directing more of her research toward prefrontal development related to attention and control because she feels that looking only at left-hemisphere differences oversimplifies the situation. Differences in control systems might even explain some of the variations now being attributed to the hemispheres, she suspects. Even if we decide it would be useful to try to change these chil-

dren's brains around somewhat, specific training programs will have
to await more definitive research. In the meanwhile, many researchers have been investigating the effects of more general types of "enrichment." In the process they are beginning to unearth some
interesting answers to an age-old question: How much can we change
tested intelligence by changing children's environments?

SYNAPSE REMODELING: HOW MUCH CAN INTELLIGENCE BE CHANGED?

> . . . aptitude is subject to change if the conditions are right—if . . . the
> cognitive training begins early in life and continues for an extended
> period through the formative years and beyond, and if it is carried out
> in a continuously supportive and motivating atmosphere.
> —Dr. William H. Angoff, Educational Testing Service[50]

Studies described earlier in this book showed measurable differences in the size of animals' brains as a result of living in "enriched"
or "impoverished" environments. These findings have naturally inspired interest in the potential of enriched human environments to
rebuild disadvantaged brains. The reader may recall that changes
were observed not only at a physical level but also in certain tests of
"intelligence," such as maze-running. In fact, several experimenters
feel that higher-level problem-solving abilities are doubtless most
susceptible of all to environmental effects.

Obviously, human environments are vastly more complex than experimental animal cages, and they cannot be similarly manipulated or
categorized. Two types of intervention, however, yield important
clues as to how much human intelligence can be changed. Adoption
studies look at children who have been brought up in environments
significantly different from those into which they were born, comparing them to both their blood relatives and their adoptive ones. Follow-
up studies of early-education programs are also used to evaluate
changes from an enriched setting. Both these types of studies have
demonstrated that "nature" is a powerful determinant of IQ. But
"nurture" also influences IQ and helps determine how that basic
intelligence gets utilized.

Repotting the Seedlings

A number of carefully controlled adoption studies have forced researchers to recognize that the elastic of nature's genetic program will

only stretch so far. IQ scores in particular seem to be constrained by genetic limits. Longitudinal studies have also shown surprising correspondence between variations in a child's intellectual skills, interests, and certain aspects of temperament (e.g., sociability, extroversion, level of activity) and those of the biological parents, even if the child has never lived with them. Curiously, the older the child gets, the more like the biological family he becomes, probably because he has more opportunity to follow his own predilections. No credible research has been completed on whether hemispheric "styles" have an appreciable genetic component.

Within this seemingly predetermined range, nurture takes over. Children who grow up in any type of deprived environment lack the opportunity to realize their potential and may not score well on an IQ test because they are unfamiliar with its expectations. A transracial adoption study looked at the IQ scores of ninety-nine black and interracial children who had previously been adopted by middle class white families and raised "in the culture of the tests and of the schools." Those adopted in the first year of life obtained an average IQ of 110, which is higher than the average for the white population and considerably higher than might have been expected had they stayed in their low-SES birth environments. Although the group as a whole was above average, relatively higher and lower scores still mirrored variations in the IQ level of their biological mothers more than it did those of the adopted mothers.[51] In other words, although the children, as a group, scored significantly better than did their mothers, the high scorers among the children's group had mothers who were the high scorers in the mothers' group, etc.

Dr. Sandra Scarr, who has produced the most blunt and realistic synthesis of the masses of information now available from early-intervention studies, confirms that children do benefit from "better-than-average home environments," but she is careful to point out "a genetic constraint on the degree to which individual differences in intelligence may be influenced."[52]

Other researchers believe that looking only at IQ scores is far too narrow a gauge of the influence of enriched environments. After all, it is a well-known fact that IQ scores are not terribly accurate predictors of success in adult life. A recent study conducted in Paris, France, looked instead at the incidence of grade failure in a group of eighty-seven children who were adopted before age three into homes of different social classes. By the time the adoptees were in late adolescence, there was a significant correlation between the social class of the adoptive fathers and the number of grades the children had been forced to repeat; children adopted into under class homes had repeated more grades. Their rate of school failure was also similar to that of biological children from the same social class. The one exception was that the biological children of upper class families tended to do slightly better than children adopted into upper class families. The author states that there is currently no way to tell whether genetic or environmental factors are responsible for this discrepancy.[53]

Overall, the experts continue to assign heredity and environment each about half of the responsibility for the final outcome of intellectual ability. Dr. Scarr points out that biological diversity is a fact of life, and individual differences add much to the richness of human experience. Nevertheless, while government policy cannot make an entire population into geniuses, the average level of an entire culture can be improved by social policy that raises the quality of early environments, schools, nutrition, and health care.[54] Some little-known research hints that such policies may have intellectual outcomes that extend farther beyond the present generation than anyone has yet realized.

An Intergenerational Shadow?

Can *intellectual* stimulation for parents have *physical* effects on the later learning abilities of their offspring? Recent studies have shown that enriching the cognitive environments—and thus enlarging the brains—of parent rats causes them to have smarter offspring, even when they don't raise the babies themselves.

In her book *Enriching Heredity*, Dr. Marian Diamond discusses the "lasting effects of both maternal care and enrichment in utero." As an example, she recounts some experiments in which parent rats lived in the sort of enriched cages described in Chapter 3 (in which food and water are kept constant and "enrichment" consists of cognitively stimulative toys and companionship). The parents were also trained in maze learning. Their babies were born with slightly larger brains than those of matched controls and also performed better on maze-running tests.

> To our knowledge, our experiments provide the first evidence that the dimensions of the cerebral cortex can be altered without directly enriching the offspring, i.e., *by enriching the parents before pregnancy and the female during pregnancy* [emphasis added].[55]

The Japanese have believed for centuries that "intrauterine education," "taikyo" (which consists mainly of maternal improvement, not prenatal pedagogy!), can have beneficial effects on the unborn child. In a recent set of experiments, Japanese researchers placed pregnant rats in either cognitively enriched or impoverished conditions. After their babies were born, some were separated from the biological mother, "cross-fostered," and raised in a standard, unenriched environment (i.e., pups from the enriched mothers were reared by the nonenriched mothers to eliminate any effects of maternal influences after birth). After weaning, the second generation was given a maze-running test; those whose real mothers had been enriched during pregnancy learned the maze significantly faster, despite the fact that their own environments after birth had contained no enrichment and some of them had never seen their real mothers. These results, say the researchers, "suggest that prenatal maternal enrichment has a beneficial effect on postnatal learning abilities of the offspring, although the mechanism remains to be solved."[56]

Extrapolating this limited data to humans is, of course, impossible. Most scientists would flatly deny that the intellectual "nurture" given one generation could become a part of the "nature" of the next. Nonetheless, these results do provide food for thought.

When the Iron Is Hot

Early is not the issue, timing is.

—Dr. Sandra Scarr[57]

Beginning with Head Start in the 1960s, many programs have attempted to better the chances of children at risk. Their successes and failures have been thoughtfully analyzed (see *Within Our Reach* by Lisbeth Schorr[58]); a careful look suggests that the most successful have respected nature's developmental pattern of plasticity. Different sets of neurons in the human brain get ready for different types of learning at different points in development. One key to future competency undoubtedly lies in making available the right kind of stimulation while each developmental iron is hot.

"There may be optimal periods or optimal amounts of stimulation depending on the organism's status, and too much or too early may be as detrimental as too little or too late," emphasizes researcher Dr. Ellin Scholnick.[59] Any kind of intervention may have varying effects on individual children at different ages. Some early-intervention programs, whose initial gains have not been as durable as educators had initially hoped, doubtless tried to paint on a veneer of skills rather than engaging the child's own need at the right time. For example, policymakers unfamiliar with the research on child development may think it is more desirable for children to learn to recite numbers to twenty than to engage in the type of structured play which builds cognitive skills for mathematical reasoning—but which takes longer and has less directly measurable gains.

Following the Brain's Curriculum

The key to planning experiences for young children is to make available a wide variety of mind-engaging experiences and allow the child some freedom in following her own internal promptings. Of course, adults need to provide firm structure because children do not always choose what is best for them (e.g., nutritional sugar, as in too much candy, or mind sugar, as in too much TV). Within these limits, however, each developmental period offers many natural opportunities for choice.

Infants need manageable levels of varied sensory experience, along with good nutrition, freedom to explore the physical world, safety, and security. Personal interaction with adults is critical. Programs for toddlers and older preschoolers should include problem-solving, listening skills, and oral language development along with such activities as interpreting pictures, active manipulation of physical materials, music, dance, art, experimenting with nature, and the ever-important emotional and social needs. Sitting little ones down with workbooks and trying to teach them to read and do math is simply antagonistic to the brain's needs during those years, and particularly for children from "learning disadvantaged" environments. Yet these activities are increasingly seen in early childhood programs; no wonder some of them fail to show lasting improvement! Enrichment programs that have emphasized language understanding and expression along with basic reasoning skills, interesting experiences, and positive attitudes toward learning have had far better long-range results.

Helping Families Help

No matter how much time a child spends in an enriched setting, studies show much better long-term outcomes when families are also involved. Parents need to be taught how to talk to and play with their children; many parents in disadvantaged homes do not understand that youngsters begin learning before they go to school. When they, often themselves school dropouts, can be helped to help their children break the cycle of failure, everyone's prognosis improves dramatically.

In Venezuela, Dr. Beatriz Manrique has headed a massive national effort to "invest in human development" by utilizing television and outreach programs to teach new parents about health, nutrition, and the importance of emotional bonding from the moment of conception. Simple lessons in prenatal care and in talking to the baby and stimulating sensory and motor development have paid remarkable dividends in higher levels of infant mental growth.[60] Dr. Manrique reports that treated babies were significantly better in developmental tests; the researchers are now looking at differences in head circumference, which, she believes, will demonstrate a physical basis for this improved performance.

"You should see these children! They are *so* beautiful!" she exclaims.[61]

Consistent with findings in the United States, however, the improvements from enrichment that ended soon after birth washed out after the children were one year old. Another intervention at age one is needed, she acknowledges, particularly to teach parents how to continue language stimulation as different stages are reached. This imperative for appropriate and changing types of input all the way up nature's developmental totem pole has profound implications to which many schools have yet to respond.

BRAIN-DAMAGING SCHOOLS

Putting already disadvantaged children into preschool intervention programs and then sending them off to inadequate schools is like giving the brain a midmorning snack while neglecting breakfast, lunch, and dinner. Successful intervention must start before birth and continue during the entire time of the brain's major development—well into adolescence. It is cruelly unrealistic to depend on early programs by themselves to effect significant changes in later learning. According to at least one authority, the years of eight to ten may represent a particularly crucial period when an "educational or psychological booster shot" is needed to sustain earlier gains.[62]

With older children, as with preschoolers, there is a strong temptation among adults who envision certain learning outcomes to try to "force" skills. Thus we have experienced cries for "competency" that are based on the idea that if everyone works hard enough at beating learning into children, and tests them often enough, we can "make" it happen. Of course it would be wonderful if all children could read at grade level or understand calculus when they are still in high school. But given the normal range of individual differences both in rate of development and in talents for different aspects of learning (true in "privileged" as well as underprivileged neighborhoods!), expecting all children to meet the same set of standards on the same schedule is absurd. At-risk children need more time and extra help to reach the same outcomes, and they can be badly harmed by assembly-line pedagogy.

Inappropriate expectations, however, may sound impressive, and curriculum dictators can misuse the whip of "standards" to flay tender intellects in any neighborhood. Advantaged brains are better buffered, however, and well-educated parents will only put up with so much nonsense. Studies comparing schools for upper- and lower-class children have shown that more privileged children are much less likely to be forced to subsist on the staples of what too often passes for "competency": a deadening diet of ditto sheets, workbooks, and rote-level memorization.

Misused "Standards": In the Inner City . . .

In a recent series of visits to an inner-city school, I witnessed the destructive effects of forcing learning on children without building the necessary foundations. Schools in this large Midwestern city have an unenviable, but not atypical, record of failure: a staggering drop-out rate, low achievement scores (half of last year's ninth graders failed the year), and little prospect of further education even for those who manage to stick it out. As of 1989, out of 3,146 students who had graduated from high school in 1984, only a single student had graduated from a four-year college, and 109 were still enrolled in one.

Taken to task for this lack-of-success rate, the school board and administrators imposed a series of "competency objectives" throughout the grades; each week a test would be given to see if specific material had been mastered. Teachers soon began to complain bitterly that the "skills" selected were neither worthy nor meaningful, that the goals could only be met by pushing students at a pace that precluded understanding, and that most classroom time must now be spent "teaching the test" by drilling students on material that they rarely understood.

"They could pass every skill on the test and still not have the foggiest idea of the meaning of what they read," one embittered fifth-grade teacher told me.

In my visits to the racially integrated classrooms, I saw discouraging confirmation of their concerns. In kindergarten, drill on recognizing and copying alphabet letters (even though many five-year-olds—in the suburbs as well as the inner city—are not developmentally ready for this task) superseded activities that enrich the classrooms of many "better" suburban schools: active social play and conversation, story-reading and storytelling, and the critical work on language and cognitive development that will later enable them to understand what they read and calculate.

The edges of my heart curled as I saw a lively, bright-eyed little boy disciplined (and embarrassed and angry) because he couldn't "pay attention" to the endless flash-card drill. How long, I wondered, will it take to turn this wiggly little mass of potential into an embittered "problem" child? The youngsters who retreated into their own boredom were deemed "good," but their silence was a clammy precursor of turned-off and tuned-out. Many were doubtless feeling "dumb" because they—like their age-mates at all levels of the socioeconomic scale—couldn't do tasks that are out of place in kindergarten.

"Why do you spend so much time on the alphabet when these children need so many other kinds of reading readiness?" I asked the teacher later.

"There's a big push for the kids to know it before they go to first grade," she replied. "We have to get it into them somehow."

The futility of these methods soon becomes apparent. In a third grade, twenty-five children, seated in orderly rows, were in their "reading" period. In this class, several children were still not reading as well as an average first grader, and few were at "grade level." Nevertheless, all the students were issued a worksheet on which they were given a list of quite advanced vocabulary words and asked to choose whether they were abstract or concrete. The teacher struggled to help them understand, but it was clear that only two or three were participating in the discussion. The rest sat, eyes glazed with boredom and incomprehension, waiting for the lesson to end. Even the active participants were puzzled. I, too, soon began to have trouble. Is *quiver* concrete or abstract?

"It's a concrete noun," said the teacher, consulting her study guide. "Just remember that until Friday."

This lesson took forty-five minutes. Reading time was now over.

Later, in the faculty room, I managed to express mild distress over what I had observed. "Do they ever read books?" I wondered.

"When we have time. But I have to cover these competency objectives for the Friday test," the teacher replied.

"Can they really pass the test? That's a difficult concept for third graders. And is it really important to spend time on this lesson when many of these kids need reading help so badly?" I ventured.

"Of course, it's ridiculous, and the math objectives are almost as unrealistic. Some of them memorize a clue like, it's concrete if you can feel it or touch it, but they don't really understand it. I always teach concrete/abstract on Thursday so it will be fresh in their minds. Of course, they forget it by the time they take the test at the end of the month, so we have to review again. There's not much time left for reading—and most of them hate it anyway. We mainly drill. The teachers have objected, but nobody seems to listen. Hey, I can't afford to lose my job!"

In a sixth grade, half the class was reading a story from a standard sixth-grade reading book. (The other half—those now reading at third-grade level or below—had gone down the hall for "remedial reading.") The story was a "tall tale" about a sea captain named Stormalong who sailed off the coast of Massachusetts during the eighteenth century. It featured not only concepts with which these children were massively unfamiliar but also words such as *Nantucket, Squibnocket, schooner, brigantine, sloop,* and *keel.* Although this particular selection is one with which I have seen many children get quite eagerly involved—if the time is taken to help them understand the context, the vocabulary, and the abstract notion of what a "tall tale" is—the teacher had so little time to cover this lesson that she acknowledged having done a sketchy job of preparing her class to understand it. The resulting struggle was not pleasant to watch.

The twelve children sat around a large round table, reading aloud in turn. These students had decent phonics skills, but inaccuracies in their oral reading betrayed a sad lack of understanding. One child read:

"These are all, um, ["sea-touched," supplied the teacher] places and since Storlong was a great season, he may have been bored in M . . . M . . . M ["Massachusetts," said the teacher]."

Another continued:

"Whatever it was, the ocean was right next door, booming and b—ou—n—cing against the store and sending salt spry over everything."

Teachers should know that when students make errors (e.g., *season* for *seaman; store* for *shore; bored* for *born*) that clearly denote lack of comprehension, it is time to stop and help the reader clarify understanding. ("What do you think that sentence means?" "Why would there be a 'store' in this story?" "Find something in the paragraph to prove Stormalong was 'bored.' ") But with the pressure of the lesson plan, the sudden noisy malfunction of one of the steam radiators in the room, and the necessity to reprimand several boys who were not shy about expressing their distaste for the activity ("This is stupid . . . who's this creep, anyway?") and started to throw paper wads, the teacher became distracted and the butchering of the text proceeded apace. By the time it had mercifully ground to its conclusion, we all breathed relief along with incomprehension. As the students returned to their seats, they took with them the fruits of the day's reading lesson: a renewed certainty that stories in books do not make sense and that expecting—or caring—to understand what one reads is not part of the game.

Why is this teacher required to use a text that few of her students can make sense of without intensive coaching—for which she is not allowed to take the time? Because, she told me, the "Board" insists that every child read at grade level. ("But it's really 'frustration level,' " added a colleague.) The only way out is to fall far enough behind to qualify for remediation, and of course, more and more do each year.

In another sixth grade, behind a closed door, a new teacher who confessed herself already "fed up with the system" had scrounged up several copies of a well-known children's classic from local libraries. The level of this story, both conceptually and linguistically, was actually more difficult than the "tall tale," but she had prepared her students to understand it. As she read it aloud to them, her class, three children to a book, bent eagerly over the dog-eared pages. The level of excitement rose as she expertly drew out their questions and helped them relate the story and its historical context to their own experiences. Several children begged to read out loud. Some "sneaked" time to read the book themselves during recess.

"I'll probably get fired," she sighed, "but I'm going to take a chance that by the end of the year they'll do better on the tests. I just wish I had enough books to go around."

I recalled a remedial reading lab I had seen down the hall, where, starting in fifth grade, students go to be plugged into reading drills on a dozen new computers with quantities of costly software (whose effectiveness in improving comprehension, incidentally, is not well established).

"But they've spent so much money on remedial materials. Why can't they buy you a few books?"

"Oh, that's different money," she sighed. "The federal government funds the remedial materials."

. . . and in the Suburbs

The perpetration of this sort of intellectual abuse is not confined to schools serving the underclass. It just gets called by different names elsewhere. One week after the above experience I visited an exclusive private school in a suburb of another large Midwestern city. There, in a first-grade classroom, I saw a teacher trying to force a small group of children to learn a rather complex mathematical concept from a workbook page (the missing addend and subtrahend), part of the curriculum they were expected to master.

This particular bit of learning is extremely confusing for most first graders, even bright ones, and many teachers either skip this part of the workbook (yes, the children will have another chance to learn it; all hope is not lost when they enter second grade!) or use countable objects, such as rods or cubes, to teach the principle in a way children can understand. During this lesson a pile of rods remained untouched in the middle of the table while the teacher belabored her earnestly struggling charges, much to our mutual discomfort. As the lesson ended and the children, totally bewildered by this session of "learning," put away their materials, the teacher caught my eye and mouthed over their heads (but within obvious view of the rest of the class),

"They're all l-ear-ning d-is-abled."

No wonder.

The Sad Truth About "Competency"

One of our favorite adult conceits is that just because we teach children something, they learn it. Perpetuation of this myth by people who have little contact with real life in the classroom puts the quality of our entire educational system at risk.

On the other hand, the fact that children can learn something does not necessarily make it worth teaching. Even when competency objectives are more skillfully applied than in the cases described above, they lean toward "window dressing" instead of substance. Test scores go up as charts replace student artwork on the walls of the superintendent's office, but students may have learned more about how to pass the test than about anything else.[63] One catalogue of educational materials now features *thirty-six workbooks on test-taking skills.* Is this our society's latest contribution to world culture?

We have yet to solve the problems presented by students who do not learn what we choose to teach them. Attention to "standards" must be a national imperative, but a "quick-fix" mentality militates against meaningful and lasting learning.

It is no accident that scores on tests of higher-order skills have been falling just as those for basic-skills tests have risen, emphasizes Gerald W. Bracey, director of evaluation for the Cherry Creek, Colorado, schools. "Scores on the higher-order tests have been falling precisely because we have been overteaching for [standardized achievement] tests at the expense of the other skills. Teachers say they no longer give essay exams—so they can prepare children for tests requiring them to respond to decontextualized, fragmentary bits of knowledge. . . . Teaching children in this way and hoping that they will learn to think is like teaching them when to slide into second base and hoping that they will get the general idea of how to play baseball. It won't work!"[64]

Bracey advocates what he calls the "zero-based" curriculum: start from scratch and justify everything you let back in. While this alternative is not likely to glean much support, it may not be such a bad idea. We certainly need to rethink old approaches that are frankly damaging to all children, and particularly to the children of disadvantage, the most vulnerable of all.

TAPPING INTO THE RESERVOIR

"There is a reservoir of unused intellect in many economically disadvantaged children," states Edward Zigler in pleading for programs that will liberate children's individual abilities and motivation to succeed.[65] The poor clearly represent our greatest challenge, but all children need good teaching to draw on their own deep pools of potential. Trying to cram children's intellectual raw material into shallow molds of ersatz "competency" will not make up for gaps in previous experience or for the emotional complications of adult neglect—at any socioeconomic level.

Schools cannot be expected to mend frayed social policy alone. Coordinated approaches to the overwhelming problems of disadvantage are clearly needed. Within their arena of intellectual development, however, schools must develop better means of responding to the new challenges of students in every community who come with new sets of needs, different patterns of learning, and perhaps, even brains that have been shaped in ways that require revised teaching approaches.

Yet educationally disadvantaged children also come with talents that we too often fail to notice. To maintain real standards of intellectual competence throughout our society, we must seek new ways of opening up the intellectual potential of the real kids who are sitting in the classrooms. Writing idealized prescriptions works only in fantasyland, and the schools of today are a long way from that. In the next chapter we will consider some real-world alternatives.

Part Five

MINDS OF THE FUTURE

New Brains: New Schools?

If we wish to remain a literate culture, someone is going to have to take the responsibility for teaching children at all socioeconomic levels how to talk, listen, and think. If we want high school graduates who can analyze, solve problems, and create new solutions, adults will have to devote the time to showing them how. And they had better get at it before the neural foundations for verbal expression, sustained attention, and analytic thought end up as piles of shavings under the workbench of plasticity.

It appears that schools will have to assume a larger share of this responsibility. Students from all walks of life now come with brains poorly adapted for the mental habits that teachers have traditionally assumed. In the past, deep wells of language and mental persistence had already been filled for most children by experiences at home; an educational priming of the pump made learning flow with relative ease. Now teachers must fill the gaps before attempting to draw "skills" from brains that lack the underlying cognitive and linguistic base.

We care deeply about the "smartness" of our children, but our culture lacks patience with the slow, time-consuming handwork by which intellects are woven. The quiet spaces of childhood have been disrupted by media assault and instant sensory gratification. Children have been yoked to hectic adult schedules and assailed by societal anxieties. Many have been deprived of time to play and the opportunity to pursue mental challenges that, though deemed trivial by distracted adults, are the real building blocks of intellect. Thus schools must lead the way, acknowledging children's developmental needs as they guide them firmly into personal involvement with the important skills and ideas that will empower them for the future.

What Doesn't Work

Schools, preschools, and day-care centers cannot slow the pace of adult life, alter changing family patterns, or eliminate media influences. Nor can they ignore these realities or the resulting differences in students. Kids today are no less intelligent than those of former years, but they don't fit the same academic molds. In many respects, children now come to school with more potential and a wider experiential background than children of a previous generation. At some level, the rapid pace of their lives may even prove to be adaptive for the constant scene changes of a new knowledge explosion. Yet this gloss of sophistication has been applied at the expense of important mental skills—and arguably, their underlying brain organization.

Comments on "Competency"

As I hope became obvious in earlier chapters, the simple cry *"Make them learn"* soon runs afoul of the developmental reality that brains learn in different ways and on different schedules. In olden days, those who did not fit the pattern dropped out and got good jobs in factories, shops, or on farms. Now these options have diminished. If we want almost everyone to achieve solid levels of academic competency, we must accept the need to diversify instruction for learners with different styles and timetables for mastery. Such sensitivity does not imply that some are "inferior" or that they cannot learn; it simply acknowledges that just as all adults should not be expected to enjoy and master sculpture, journalism, baseball, or eye surgery with equal facility, all children will not learn math or rope-climbing with comparable ease.

"Competency" is deceptive. When children must resort to memorizing "tricks" to pass tests (on material they don't understand), they soon "forget." Difficulties compound themselves as children who lack basic concepts of addition and subtraction are drilled to mouth algebraic formulae, or as they uncomprehendingly "read" the words from books or neatly copy "reports" from encyclopedias—without making mental contact with the content. Children who come from different linguistic and educational backgrounds are particularly at risk in this sort of curriculum.

Shallowly conceived "standards" also tend to fragment learning into inconsequential bits. Dr. Arthur Costa, who says he has "been through three back-to-basics movements" in his career as an educator, notes ruefully:

> What was educationally significant and hard to measure has been replaced by what is educationally insignificant and easy to measure. So now we measure how well we've taught what isn't worth learning![1]

Costa's personal vision of a school as "a home for the mind" is woefully different from current realities. He is convinced that we need change, and that education for workers of the future must emphasize more general thinking and problem-solving abilities along with the basic skills. People in an age of rapidly changing technology will have to keep on learning even after they graduate, but the outlook in the United States is not bright, he warns.

"We're facing a critical time in history. For our nation to survive we have to realize that what's coming up is the smallest work force we've had in a long time; we've had a big population dip and our industries have a much smaller pool of talent. The small group is one of the most undertrained with the largest number of dropouts. At the same time, industry has the greatest demand for problem-solvers and thinkers, entrepreneurs and craftsmen, creative people whose products are so excellent and whose thinking is so forward that we can match the other countries for survival."

Because of the ever-shrinking pool of talent, industries are being forced to economize, Costa continues.

"To do so they're cutting out middle management. This means that blue-collar workers will have to know how to think for themselves so industry won't have to hire management to solve problems for them. We're at a time of great competition for creativity and thinking— we've got to develop these skills in all our students. To do so we need a massive reorientation of what public education is about."[2]

No responsible critic denies that students—and their teachers— need to be held accountable for what is being learned. Tests are important, not only for determining the depth at which material is taught, but also in showing students what kinds of thought processes are important (e.g., simply memorizing facts vs. having to connect them together in higher-level thinking). In countries where thought and intellectual depth are esteemed, examinations consist mainly of having the students generate ideas, usually in writing, about the topic at hand. Someone recently observed that Europeans *examine,* while Americans only *test.* Examinations, in this sense, require students to have not only a thorough understanding of the facts but also a more general grasp of the subject and its important ideas as well as the ability to integrate and express them. It also means that someone has to read and grade the papers.

In the United States, the content of everything from English to algebra is currently being trivialized by machine-scored, multiple-choice tests. Why be surprised if students can't reason effectively—or if they emulate their elders in looking for the easy way out? Of course, if I have 150 English students every day . . .

"But the Japanese Seem to Be Doing Something Right"

Despite the apparent success of Japanese public education in extruding a dutiful and well-trained work force, aping a misconceived model of that country's system won't work in America. Nor will the rigid traditions believed to characterize Japanese secondary schools impart the innovation and mental flexibility Americans claim to prize.

Japanese and American schooling are predicated on different philosophical views of the individual in relationship to the society. They also have differing traditions regarding the purpose of schooling itself, particularly the balance between conformity and original thinking. While it would certainly be a step in the right direction to accord comparable respect (and expectations) to teachers and to the intellectual enterprise in general, we must recognize that Japanese pedagogy is designed for children from a very different tradition of upbringing.

In that country, mothers assume that their primary role is to provide a full-time training ground for their child. Children are expected to sail from home into school on an unbroken flow of expectations and support—not so much in terms of subject matter, as in the attitudes and mental habits for school success. Moreover, according to one careful observer, Japanese elementary schools (unlike those for older students) do not trade in the rote-level, robotic classroom scenes we imagine. Instead, their well-trained teachers (getting into this highly esteemed profession is a competitive business for which only the best are chosen) plan active, exploratory learning and take time to set the conceptual foundations in place. Whereas American second graders may spend thirty minutes on two or three pages of addition and subtraction equations, the Japanese are reported to be more likely, at this level, to use the same amount of time in examining two or three problems in depth, focusing on the reasoning process necessary to solve them.[3]

Ignoring the Reality . . . and Missing the Vision

While lessons can certainly be learned from the Japanese, our schools cannot succeed unless they are supported in confronting the reality of the children they are trying to teach. They cannot change society, but they can stand firm as advocates, not enemies, of mental growth. American children should learn to work hard, in fact considerably harder than most are working now. But they need to work on important, meaningful learning at which they can succeed.

Classrooms where students are enticed into involvement with content along with essential skills, where they experience each day the satisfaction of intellectual accomplishment gained by personal effort— such classrooms are a strong antidote to the anxieties and fragmentation that beset children in today's world. If schools direct their planning toward this goal, they have a much better chance to shore up shaky intellectual foundations while also infusing children with the ego-protective properties of well-earned success.

Is this simply more visionary claptrap? How can such lofty goals be accomplished in a practical classroom world? The first step is to take the pains to start where the children are. Another is to write the habits of mind, oral language usage, and thoughtful experience with important ideas into the curriculum along with reading, writing, math, history, and science. Instead of simply insisting that teachers stamp on the three R's in shallow transfer patterns, we must search for new ways to enrich young brains with the real "basics"—language and thought.

I do not propose, in one chapter, to outline a total new plan for restructuring American education. As must be clear by now, my main suggestions concern teaching and learning. To fill gray areas in kids' gray matter, however, structural as well as curricular changes are in order. Let me first skim over a few ideas that have been proposed in the name of the former before moving on to a consideration of some new (or rekindled) ideas about what we might start dishing out in the way of mental fare.

SOME OF THE NITTY-GRITTY

Changing the Way Schools Are Structured: Only Part of a Solution

The growing recognition that our schools are out of step with changing social patterns has inspired some rethinking about the way they are structured. Alternatives now on the table include adding early-childhood centers to the public schools, adapting the school calendar and/or length of the school day to schedules of working parents, and allowing students to stay with the same teacher for more than one year, as is done in some European countries, in hopes of gaining the sort of close relationship with an adult increasingly missing at home. These proposals all have potential merit—and potential problems. If what children get in school is ineffective or even damaging, simply adding more of the same will only exacerbate the problems.

Broader forms of restructuring, in which schools work closely with other social agencies, are also being proposed. Such teamwork appears to be necessary as increased needs for emotional and social support of even middle-class students drain instructional resources. Allan Shedlin, director of New York's Elementary School Center, feels strongly that schools should assume a more central role as "locus of advocacy" for all children. While not everyone agrees that they will be up to this task, most concur that some kind of coordination will be necessary. As we now stand, fragmentation of school time, facilities, and staff with nonacademic courses already threatens their basic role as academic institutions. Academic learning may well suffer when schools are compelled to add such extras as required courses in career, health, and nutrition education at all grade levels, as well as badly needed expedients such as group counseling for children with unsettled emotional environments at home (e.g., a course for children of divorce entitled "Who Gets Me for Christmas?").

It is indeed hard, perhaps even impossible, to teach well if students' nutritional or emotional agendas preempt their mental energy. But teachers' major obligation to students' emotional needs must remain to create classrooms and curricula where children are mentally as well as physically safe. This includes structuring academic demands so that students have a realistic chance of earning success as a buffer against other emotional stresses. Offering attainable academic goals and good teaching to reach them is the school's primary role in social service.

Changing the Way Children Are Taught

One potentially promising trend in this regard is a greater use of "collaborative learning" techniques, where more emphasis is placed on the types of cooperation and communication that will be needed in an "information age."[4] Inclusion of cooperation along with competition may have several effects: (1) making classrooms more success-oriented; (2) counteracting some of the social isolation experienced by children without old-fashioned "neighborhood" play experiences; (3) building oral language skills by teaching structured ways of talking together about what is being learned. Changes of this sort will not salvage academic learning, however, unless curricular goals are broadened to emphasize language and thinking skills. Since brains are shaped in classrooms as well as in homes, we cannot afford to overlook these growing needs during the hours children spend in school.

How Good Are the Teachers?

Another problem is how to stock classrooms with teachers who can—and do—read, write, and reason. Although none of the ideas to follow are revolutionary in scope, they all call for good teachers whose own intellects can be trusted, or at least developed. We cannot depend on workbooks and kits chosen because they are "teacher-proof" (a questionable, but all-too-common "attribute"). Such materials, by necessity, include little, if any, writing and reasoning.

It is beyond the scope of this book to solve the problem of where to find this band of angels who can simultaneously control twenty-five or thirty kids (someone very accurately compared it to trying to keep thirty corks under water all at the same time), inculcate the essential skills into a generation of unprepared brains, and also stimulate high-level reasoning and reflection. I would suggest, on the basis of school visits in many parts of the country, that many fine teachers are already in place. But they need encouragement, perhaps some additional training in language development and questioning strategies, and most often, smaller classes in order to do the job we demand of them.

Even (perhaps especially) elementary school teachers must be well grounded in the liberal arts and sciences as well as in the specific tools of their profession. They cannot expand minds to meet the demands of the next century if their own perspectives are foreshortened by pedagogical nonsense in place of substantive coursework. In my opinion, any teacher in a subject requiring students to read and write should be required to demonstrate the personal ability to read and reason intelligently, write coherently, and provide satisfactory models of oral language. The college years are not too late to effect changes in the habits of a human brain; it is certainly worth the considerable time and effort it would take to induce the ability to think in everyone to whom we delegate the charge of teaching it to our children.

Even the best teachers, however, can't do the foundation-building job alone. Many complain they now have to teach the parents as well as the children. Let us digress briefly to consider some issues surrounding this important division of responsibility.

The Changing Balance Between School and Home: Whose Responsibility?

If schools are to do a proper job, they cannot, with existing resources, also shoulder the major burden of their charges' personal, social, and emotional development. Yet school administrators and teachers are increasingly pressured to take on jobs they see as parental ones. Some assert quite vehemently that they are tired of spending so much time "parenting the parents"; even well-heeled professionals need frequent reminders of their responsibilities to their children. "I had to start sending notes home on Fridays asking parents to monitor the violent TV programs these kids were watching," went a typical comment from a kindergarten teacher in a middle class suburb. "I don't mind writing notes about a child's school progress, but do I also have to tell them how to be parents?"

"I wish I could sit down with every parent in America and emphasize how important they are to their children's education," stated Mary Hatwood Futrell, speaking for thousands of teachers nationwide.[5] Yet even filling a child's basic emotional needs is increasingly difficult for many families. Youngsters who have been caught in changing family patterns (e.g., divorce, single parenthood) have needs that may be difficult to meet. All children need consistent and realistic follow-through on standards for school achievement, but in the press of contemporary life, such consistency gets easily lost. Although many parents express concern about their children's progress, teachers also have trouble getting them to follow up on academic expectations at home. One of the reasons may be that parents feel alienated from the school.

Child psychiatrist Dr. James Comer, recounting his growing-up years in the 1940s, compares the informal neighborhood contacts between teachers and parents with the fragmented environments that now polarize parents and schools. "The positive relationship between my parents and school staff—and the probability of a weekly report [in a casual conversation in the store, or on the street]—made it difficult for me to do anything short of live up to the expressed expectations." Comer argues that too many children today are deprived of the "sense of trust, belonging, and place" so essential to learning.[6]

Helping Parents Parent

Parents themselves are pressured, tired, and unsure of how much they should interfere with schoolwork. Many complain that the only time they are wanted in school is when their child develops a problem. Dr. Futrell suggests that educators must start taking the initiative in inviting parents into school under more positive circumstances. Blaming parents and denying the reality of different lifestyles does not change social realities. Administrators who have accepted the facts and reached out by scheduling academic and social events at convenient times and encouraging working parents to attend (e.g., family potluck suppers, book fairs, etc.) have been gratified by the response. Others who had the funds to hire local psychologists to offer short courses in parent education have also reported positive results.

The principal of a nationally recognized elementary school in urban East Cleveland personally holds regular meetings with parents to discuss practical ways in which they can help their children do better in school. He says he has obtained excellent results from using a computerized dialing device that calls everyone with a child in the class to remind them of the meeting. Since the machine started recording the number of anyone who hangs up on his message, he reports that attendance has improved even more!

Broader efforts than schools can provide are needed, however, to teach parents about the needs of young children. Even middle class families may be able to profit by such courses as Dr. Burton White's "Missouri New Parents as Teachers Project (NPAT)." Emphasizing language development, social abilities, small and large muscle, vision, and hearing skills for a large group of children from birth through the first three years of life, Dr. White's curriculum for successful parenting places first priority on "the quality and quantity of adult input into the [child's] stream of experience." White advocates that a parent or grandparent be on hand virtually all the time during the first six to eight months of the child's life to provide "prompt response" to the child's needs or attempts to interact.

Children with parents in White's program consistently score significantly higher on measures of intelligence, achievement, auditory comprehension, and verbal ability than a comparable group whose parents were not enrolled.[7] Although other specialists insist a well-trained surrogate can provide equally responsive care, the initial success of this program appears to make a case for more realistic parental-leave policies.

While our society, as a whole, needs to be reminded of the critical nature of the infant and toddler years, some critics claim that programs like White's lead to too much pressure for early academic skills ("superbabying"). Parent educators must be cautious about implying to parents, particularly well-educated, "fast track" ones, that their main job is to "teach" school at home. Even in an information age, homes still need to provide personal guidance, love, and security. Worried parents need to be reassured that having children talk and participate with them in household and play activities is probably their most truly "educational" role. A spokesman for an important international educational association recently summed it up:

> If children are to become responsible members of society, they must not only be exposed to adults involved in meaningful and demanding tasks, but they must themselves begin to participate in such activities early in life. We need to involve children in undertaking genuine responsibilities that will give them a sense of purpose, dignity, and worth.[8]

Most parents have a natural instinct to "scaffold" their children's learning, but those who are sure of themselves and comfortable in their relationship with their child do a better job of it.[9] Parents need support systems; to the degree that schools must take on this extra job of providing them, they will need extra resources.

When children enter school, we have a chance to recast the die of early experience. The brain continues to grow and change throughout the school years. Even if the job is partially bungled in preschool years, much learning potential may be rescued. To do so, however, requires involving each child in meaningful, manageable experiences with language, listening, thinking, problem-solving, imagining, and creating.

LANGUAGE, LISTENING, AND LITERACY

Literacy and many other types of problem-solving demand more extended exposure to good uses of language than most children are now experiencing.

Tools of Language Meaning

Sorting Out the Sounds

> We all know these children can't listen, but we seem to be operating on the theory that they're just like us and they *ought* to be able to, instead of building up programs to teach them how.
> —Anna Jones, head, Charles River School, Massachusetts

One reason for declining reading and spelling abilities is that children now come to school with insufficiently developed abilities to listen to the sounds in words. Before reading instruction begins, teachers should be trained to determine a child's level of "phonological awareness," the ability to identify, remember, and sequence the sounds in words. Without this ability, common forms of "phonics" instruction are inefficient and may even be damaging, yet children do not necessarily "pick up" these skills without certain types of listening experiences. Children who have missed out during the sensitive period for auditory discrimination especially need concentrated training in these skills. Although lack of early experience may still result in gaps, a good training program can probably make up at least some of the lost ground.

Home and classroom activities promoting pure listening and sequencing of sounds should be a major part of prereading training. Such simple games as "Pig Latin" or rhyming words give children a chance to manipulate the sounds at the beginning, middle, and end of words. Unfortunately, structured oral training by itself is not a focus in most reading programs (which use workbooks and/or worksheets). When it is, new studies suggest it may be very effective. In one such program first graders did not even get reading textbooks until January. Doing exercises in pure sound awareness in a format designed by Dr. Patricia Lindamood, these students rapidly overtook and passed children in control groups when they finally got their reading books. According to Dr. Lindamood, schools in Idaho, California, Michigan, and Florida have had similar results. The Michigan program reduced intake to special-education classes by 60–75%. Even high-risk students in first through third grades achieved significantly better reading comprehension and spelling scores than a matched group of controls.[10] Dr. Lindamood adds, by the way, that approximately 20% of teachers need remedial training in the same auditory skills.[11]

Two researchers in Syracuse, New York, tried out a seven-week program of similar training in "phoneme segmentation" with a group of kindergarten nonreaders. Their scores on a word-reading test were then compared with comparable groups who received either traditional "phonics" training or no special intervention. At the end of the seven weeks those in the auditory training group significantly outscored both other groups. The authors of this study, who are working on ways in which kindergarten teachers can be taught to use these techniques, recommend that training "to focus the child's attention on the internal sound structure of the word" be included in every beginning reading program.[12]

If *Sesame Street* producers really want to teach children the foundations of reading, they should take all the pictures off the screen for a while and get the kids to *listen* to the sounds. Skills of phonological awareness are the entry point to reading. Once children have "cracked the code," however, they need other language skills to move forward with comprehension.

"Somebody Just Needs to Teach These Kids Grammar!"

"The main thing that's wrong with these kids is that somebody ought to teach them grammar!" opined my (highly literate) seat partner on a recent flight. He is right, of course. Understanding the syntax, or grammar, of the language is critical for reading comprehension, for writing, and for many types of reasoning. Nowadays, however, teaching grammar is not as simple as it was when this man was in school and his teachers and people on the radio (and in the early days of TV) tried to speak intelligently and expected him to follow suit.

When overwhelming numbers of students grow up with adult and media models (the distinction is not unintentional) who immerse them in misplaced ideas ("Having trapped the killer, gunshots rang out"); confusion of subject and object ("Him and myself agreed . . ."); mangled time sequence ("She had went . . ."); and stumbling modifiers ("Tastes good like it should"), a time-consuming rebuilding job is called for. It is hardly fair to expect teachers to single-handedly "cure" the casualties of a frontal assault on proper usage!

The resulting desperation to get "grammar" into kids has resulted in its being taught (just taught, not usually learned, by the way) badly. Most students regard this subject as if it were some sort of great, green, greasy monster waiting to gobble them up. They usually hate their grammar lessons so much that a sure guarantee of good deportment in most classrooms is to threaten students with a grammar worksheet if they don't behave.

Antagonism added to ignorance bodes poorly for survival of the logical structure of language, but one can hardly blame the children for detesting something that has been taught so poorly. Because pre-adolescent brains do not cope well with abstract rule systems, grammar is best learned initially through exposure to oral language and/or reading good books.

Children naturally start learning grammar (syntax) from the moment they are born; even in a linguistically depleted culture most five-year-olds are quite accomplished users of its basic rules. As we have seen, however, the brain will not generate refinements and extensions of this knowledge unless the culture follows up with the appropriate types of stimulation.

Meaningful real-life experience, however, is quite different from the teaching and testing of abstract rules that has become a stultifying commonplace in American classrooms. For example, children in elementary, or even middle school, who can say, write, read, and understand "The sunset was beautiful," and who can differentiate between a "naming word" and a "describing word" should not spend valuable time memorizing and being tested on "A predicate adjective is always preceded by a linking verb." They should, instead, spend a great deal of time listening to and generating—orally and in writing—the richness of nouns, verb tenses, sentence expansions, sentence combinations, dependent clauses, and all the other shades of complexity that will take them beyond the media's sandbox syntax.

Abstract rule systems for grammar and usage should be taught when most students are in high school. Then, if previously prepared, they may even enjoy the challenges of this kind of abstract, logical reasoning. Only, however, if the circuits are not already too cluttered up by bungled rule-teaching.

One ninth-grade student who came to me last year for help with grammar was hopelessly confused about the simplest parts of speech. Although she was intelligent and could, at her current age, have mastered this material in a week, she had been a victim of meaningless "grammar" drills since second grade. As Michelle and I struggled on the simple difference between adjectives and adverbs, I often wished I could take a neurological vacuum cleaner and just suck out all those mixed-up synapses that kept getting in our way. It took us six months to dispose of the underbrush, but finally one day the light dawned. "This is easy!" she exclaimed. It is, when brains are primed for the learning and the student has a reason to use it with real literary models.

Immersing children in good language from books and tapes, modeling patterns for their own speech and writing, and letting them enjoy their proficiency in using words to manipulate ideas are valid ways to embed "grammar" in growing brains. Working with them on their own writing is especially important. No amount of worksheets or rule learning will ever make up for deficits resulting from lack of experience with the structure of real, meaningful sentences.

The Oral Tradition

It is folly to ignore the importance of oral storytelling, oral history, and public speaking in a world that will communicate increasingly without the mediation of print. These skills build language competence in grammar, memory, attention, and visualization, among many other abilities. At least equally important, they can be used to tap the richness of cultural traditions outside the "mainstream"—and the talents of many children. Is it unreasonable to suggest that elementary teachers—and perhaps others, as well—take a course in storytelling? Many insist this training has made a big difference in their effectiveness in the classroom.

What's Wrong With Memorizing?

I personally believe, although I cannot cite any brain research to prove it, that helping students at all grade levels memorize some pieces of good writing—narrative, expository, and poetic—on a regular basis would provide good practice for language, listening, and attention. I do not mean reverting to a rote-level curriculum, but simply taking a little time each week to celebrate the sounds of literate thought. Memorizing can be done as a homework exercise so that not much classroom time is consumed.

Teaching Students to Listen

At the same time, schools must get into the business of teaching children to listen effectively because no one else seems to be doing it. Teachers cannot assume their students are attending to what they hear, because most are not. Unless we want to put on a three-dimensional, living-color dog-and-pony show every time we teach a lesson, listening training will have to start the minute they toddle into the school system.

Teaching kids to listen will probably consume a good bit of classroom time, but it will be time well spent. Good teaching of any of the basic learning and thinking processes slows down our relentless march through subject matter. But how much time is consumed by repeating directions, dealing with students who didn't do the homework because they didn't "hear" the assignment, and reteaching material that was not mastered because they did not understand what they heard—either from the teacher or from the author who spoke to them from the textbook?

A recent article in an influential educational journal advocated structured training in listening as a new part of the curriculum, teaching children "to participate in structured experiences that cause them to question, to sort, to organize, to evaluate, and to choose," so they may become "connoisseurs and rational consumers of auditory input."[13]

Programs have been designed to improve listening skills; although many of these were originally targeted for students with learning disabilities, they are now appropriate for almost everyone. Instead of adding still more worksheets, however, why not use daily lessons more effectively to accomplish the same purpose? Teachers continually tell me they have to repeat all directions at least three times; one reported she ends up giving separate directions to everyone in the class. And we wonder why students don't listen? Teachers should band together and agree to start—from the earliest grades—making reception of spoken language a priority. Examples:

"I am going to give two directions. I want you to listen carefully and then I will ask one of you to repeat them before we go on."

"I will start with a three-minute minilecture on the topic we will be studying in science class today. Listen carefully and then write down a summary of what you remember. I will not repeat anything. You can read your summaries out loud and compare what you remembered."

"Today we are going to play a game in which you work in teams to give each other directions and see if the other person can listen carefully enough to follow them."

Some children's learning styles make processing information through auditory channels more difficult, but research has shown that they, particularly, need practice in these skills. Adults who are sensitive to individual differences do not embarrass youngsters who have difficulty, but they continue to work toward high standards of attention.

Particularly important for today's students is making space for them to talk and listen effectively to each other. With more TV viewing, many youngsters lack skills for interacting positively with peers. Yet most teachers, sadly, do little to help the students learn to talk or listen. The classroom conversational ball gets tossed from teacher to student, then back to teacher, then back to another student, etc.

Teacher: "John, who was the main character of this story?"

John: "Samuel Adams."

Teacher: "Right. Ayesha, when was Samuel Adams born?"

Etc.

Meanwhile, the rest of the class is free to tune out until they hear their own names called. Alternate questioning techniques get all the students involved in group discussions where everyone asks and answers questions and discusses opinions and ideas within a structured format.

Teacher: "I want each of you to work with a partner and take fifteen minutes to list all the facts you can find in the text about Samuel Adams. Then we will compare your lists to classify important ideas and details. Then I will show you how to make some sample outlines to guide you in planning the one-page biography you have been assigned for tonight's homework." (This teacher slips in a lesson on categorization skills as the students determine the major and subordinate categories for the outlines.)

Do students start bouncing off walls if given this sort of freedom? Not if teachers are trained in establishing firm rules and classroom structures and if they take the time to teach the rules of constructive interaction. Even young children, in fact, can become very actively and productively engaged in this type of lesson. Professional journals and trade books feature more and more such ideas. Paradoxically, students in schools with the most rigid discipline may have the most difficulty with the self-discipline necessary for this type of interaction, so it helps to have teachers from the earliest grades trained to make active, constructive student participation—not robotic reception—an inevitable part of classroom life.

If parents want to help, they can first of all insist on careful listening at home. They can also repudiate the fiction that children learn best when they are silent—and support teachers who encourage active, but self-controlled, participation.

Battling "Um . . . Like, You Know"

I find it ironic that something called "communications" seems to have become one of the most popular college majors. Last winter, at the wedding reception of a young friend, I struck up a conversation with one of the bridesmaids, a delightful young lady who informed me that she was majoring in communications.

"Oh, that's interesting," I replied. "I have never exactly understood what a communications major entails. What are you learning about?"

Since I did not have my tape recorder, I can only try to recreate the essence of her response:

"Well, it's, well . . . we learn about, you know [hands grasping in the air for words], well, about how to *communicate*. It's like the kind of thing people need to know about these days—you know, like on TV and things."

How can we teach students to express their ideas effectively? Harvard's Dr. Courtney Cazden feels strongly that all students should be encouraged to talk together in school because they do not tend to talk outside of school about school topics.[14] Even when they do, they use the language of their peer culture rather than "forms of academic discourse—the special ways of talking expected in school."

Seating students in a circle so they can maintain eye contact with each other is helpful. Both at school and at home they can be encouraged to experiment with "exploratory talk" as they try to get their thoughts arranged.

Teachers and parents can help children clarify their thinking by asking questions:

- What do you mean?
- How did you do that?
- Why do you say that?
- How does that fit with what you just said?
- I don't really get that; could you explain it another way?
- Could you give me an example?

Cazden also emphasizes the importance of at least three seconds of "wait time" after a teacher or parent asks a question. This pause gives the child a chance to formulate an idea and the words to go with it. Most adults tend to wait only about one second after asking a question; few children can pick up their thoughts and tie them together with words in so short a time.

A New Hampshire middle-school teacher who finds her students have been conditioned to "linguistic passivity" writes:

It falls to me as a language arts instructor not merely to hone public speaking skills, but, even more challenging and difficult, to build an awareness of the demands of clear verbal communication on the most rudimentary interpersonal levels. My strategy is to counter the socio-cultural condoning of passivity by demanding extensive and precise verbal expression. Students have opportunities to experience a variety of uses of oral language and to feel the gratification that results from having clearly conveyed one's exact meaning.[15]

Attacking the problem "with a combination of verbal modeling and demand," she is careful about her own vocabulary and usage and encourages a great deal of discussion from everyone. When students use vague terms and slang, she tactfully helps them find more appro-priate words. Discussions are conducted in complete sentences only, a rule enforced from the first day of school in September. Often, particularly at the beginning, it is necessary to show them how.

Teacher: "How is Jody feeling in this part of the story?"

Student: "Sad."

Teacher: "Use a complete sentence, please. Jody is feeling . . ."

"By the end of the first quarter," she reports, "this prompting is seldom any longer necessary and we are already working on extend-ing the depth of answers to include reasons and verifications." Vo-cabulary and understanding grow as puns and plays on words are enjoyed and as meanings of words are examined and discussed.

How many verbs mean "to walk"?

Why is "a dirty old man" scary but a "soiled elderly gentleman" pathetic?

Many other teachers, including myself, have seen similar revital-ization of language skills, interest, and understanding in linguistically passive students. Youngsters with relatively full language back-grounds may pick up the skills more quickly, but persistence should pay off for almost everyone.

While it is heartening to know that such growth is still possible in the middle school years, we should be ashamed that a teacher at this level has to start the process. Children are in schools from the time they are five years old (or younger), when the language areas of the brain are still quite plastic. Teaching priorities—from preschool years on—must include setting standards and modeling effective use of oral language. Show-and-tell is not curricular fluff; used well, it is one of many opportunities to develop oral language, listening, and question-ing skills. But teachers, themselves, may need additional training in how to build youngsters' language skills, and they also need to ap-proach subjects in sufficient depth to have something meaningful to talk about. Those who are propelled by administrative fiat through a fill-in-the-blanks curriculum will not be able to make it happen.

Writing builds on oral expression. Writing practice offers a golden opportunity to build expressive language skills and vice versa. Although students cannot all *talk* at once, they can all *write* at once. When a teacher asks a question, instead of calling on one student to give the answer, he can ask everyone to write a sentence about it and then share some samples. This simple expedient immediately forces all brains in the classroom into engagement with the material, gives valuable practice, and also provides a good index of student understanding. Even in math classes, teachers have been astonished at students' improved understanding and memory when they are required to write regularly about what they are learning.

Ways of Questioning

> By engaging students only in a quest for the correct answer rather than for the interesting question, we condemn them to live inside other men's discoveries.
>
> —Priscilla Vail

Students—and their teachers—need to learn better ways of phrasing questions. Many children come to school today lacking experience with the "wh" questions (*who, what, when, where, why,* and *how*), with the related thinking skills, and with reflective habits of inquiry in general. Unfortunately, when educational objectives are defined too narrowly, these abilities continue to be neglected, since interesting questions represent more of a threat than a challenge.

The types of questions a teacher asks sets the intellectual tone of the classroom. Studies demonstrate that educating teachers in specific questioning techniques can improve their students' reading comprehension, among many other skills, by moving their thinking up from literal repetition of facts into the realms of comprehension, application, and inferential reasoning. Here are samples of some particular types of questions:

Fact: "What did Goldilocks do when she got to the three bears' house?"

Comprehension: "Why did Goldilocks like the little bear's chair best?"

Believe it or not, almost 90% of all teachers' questions come from these two categories, which require little, if any, higher-order thinking. No wonder students are so deficient in these skills! Consider the following:

Application: "If Goldilocks had come into your house, what are some of the things she might have used?"

Analysis: "How can we tell which things belong to each bear?"

Synthesis: "How might the story be different if Goldilocks had visited the three astronauts?"

Evaluation: "Do you think Goldilocks had a right to do what she did? Why or why not?"[16]

The idea of asking, even allowing, children to extend their thinking in these ways is alarming to some adults who like to see them sitting in rows and filling in blanks where there is always a right answer. Oddly enough, the same people also complain when students can't understand history, geometry, or Shakespeare. They also blame the kids when they rebel, become "hyperactive," or turn off completely from the educational process. Children need, of course, to master the factual "basics," but the most pressing questions in tomorrow's world will not be phrased at the literal level. At this writing, approximately sixty-three patent applications have been filed for new varieties of animals—genetically engineered by human scientists! Before they are approved, I, for one, hope someone will know how to ask the right kinds of questions!

Where will we get the time to implement all these ideas? First, we may have to sacrifice teaching some of the "data" we have cherished in the past—which computers will be handling anyway in the real world of the future. Second, we must explore ways to integrate and extend thinking and basic skills all at the same time. This focus has many educators excited about some new/old ideas called "whole language."

WHOLE LANGUAGE FOR WHOLE BRAINS

The idea of getting the learner personally involved in the questioning process is one aspect of a quiet revolution termed "whole language," which is sparking a major rethinking of the way we have been teaching (or more accurately, failing to teach) children to read, write, and reason. The "whole language movement," for, indeed, as the term implies, its advocates promote it with genuine missionary zeal, is a scheme of teaching derived from research on the way children naturally learn language. Adopted a few years ago in the United States by a few school districts, it now promises to have a significant educational impact as its use spreads.

As with any new trend, some of its implementations have been more effective than others. Its strongest advocates are teachers who have invested the time and effort necessary to use its ideas well. They report students "amazingly turned-on" to reading and good literature. Moreover, "I would never have believed it, but they *love* to *write!*" is a typical teacher comment.

What is the magical formula? The essence of "whole language" is threefold. First, in accordance with current research in cognitive psychology, the learner is viewed as an active "constructor of knowledge," not merely a passive recipient of information. Second, reading, writing, speaking, and listening are taught as integrated rather than separate disciplines. Third, the materials used for reading, and thus as a basis for many writing activities, include fine children's literature and examples of good language in a variety of narrative and expository forms. [17–20]

1. Learners Construct Knowledge

Research on learning has demonstrated that students understand best, remember ideas most effectively, and think most incisively when they feel personally responsible for getting meaning out of what they are learning instead of waiting for a teacher to shovel it into them. Many people believe that such ideas are merely pie-in-the-sky pronouncements from the groves of educational psychology, but any teacher who has tried it both ways knows it is true. Many have told me their delight at finding out that students who are working to find answers to questions that are important and meaningful to them do better work. If the situation is structured correctly, the students also present fewer discipline problems.

This finding has direct relevance to the teaching of reading. The passive and even mind-deadening nature of reading instruction has rightfully received a share of the blame for our new generation of disaffected readers. In the past, we got away with numbing children's brains for several hours a day because most of them came to school already imbued with the idea that reading and writing were something terribly important to learn; they understood that literacy skills were required for success in life, and many of them read at home— even if the favored materials were comic books. Having also learned

that hard work and boredom are standard lumps in the road to success, they—and their parents—were prepared to put up with some
bad pedagogy along the way.

The current generation of two-minute minds (don't blame them,
folks, we did it to them) are unschooled in persistence or reflection;
if they don't like something, they change the channel or persuade
their dad to sue the school. Surveying popular models of "success," as
well, I am not surprised that reading, writing, and oral expression do
not have quite the cachet they once did. If the school dishes out dross
in the name of reading instruction, today's young consumer simply
will not buy.

Research has shown that good readers actively pursue meaning,
carrying on an active mental dialogue with the writer. "What is this
saying?" "What will happen next?" "How does that fit with what I
already know . . . ?" To be a good reader, a child cannot be in the
habit of tuning out, either to the author's thinking or to her own. Poor
readers, on the other hand, respond as if they are waiting for the text
to give them the message; usually it doesn't. Many poor readers do
not even realize they have not understood something. Good teaching,
therefore, uses materials that students can understand (with some
mental effort) and then *always holds them accountable for the meaning of what they read.* If the material is of some intrinsic interest to
them, chances for a successful match increase.

In most American classrooms, children are issued a "basal" reading
text; they meet in "reading groups" where they read out loud in turn
and then return to their desks to write answers to questions and fill in
worksheets or workbooks. When students get older, more reading is
done silently, and sometimes "trade books" (children's fiction, biog-
raphies, etc.) supplement the basals. "Reading" time is carefully seg-
mented from other subjects, and as this exercise is repeated for each
of several groups in a class, most teachers have little time for extended discussion. Observational research in classrooms has un-
earthed the depressing fact that almost all reading instruction focuses
on lower-level skills; little time is spent discussing and teaching students to comprehend what they have read.

In many classrooms, particularly large ones, the teacher has few
opportunities to address the individual needs of students. I have been
in many private as well as public schools where students were working with reading texts that they clearly could not understand—and of
which there was no meaningful discussion. The inevitable result is a
habit of "reading" without understanding.

Students' reading abilities, in any normal classroom, usually span at least four years by the second grade and may span as many as ten or more by middle school (e.g., in a sixth grade, some students read more like average second graders and some like high school seniors). Unless materials are varied, some students are almost always baffled and others are frequently bored.

Even if all students in a class can read and comprehend the material, all still need to respond actively to it in order to become real readers. In one sixth-grade classroom in a suburban neighborhood, I saw a good example of how to turn kids off from the whole process. Eleven students (the "top group") sat around a large table, reading out loud in turn from *Johnny Tremaine,* a children's classic about a boy's adventures during the Revolutionary War. As each student finished reading a paragraph, the teacher said, "Good," or asked a question that could be answered in a word or a phrase. The turn then passed to the next reader. These kids were, in fact, proficient oral readers, rarely stumbling over a word, but their interest in the text was less than overwhelming. As each child read, the others sat passively, eyes wandering or glazed with the exaggerated ennui that is the forte of the preadolescent. When the bell rang, the teacher distributed a mimeographed list of questions to answer for homework.

As the students gratefully escaped into the hallway, I cornered several.

"How do you like this book?"

Shoulders shrugged. "Nyah, it's okay" was the most positive opinion expressed.

Whole-language teaching attempts to counter these trends by eliciting an active response from each child. Good children's literature is used, but instruction is aimed at understanding, discussion, and analysis, both oral and written.

"Skills" are taught in the context of meaningful prose. Sometimes each student selects his own book, for which he is then held accountable; at other times, groups of students read and discuss the same book. In kindergarten, teachers and children read and reread simple stories aloud, familiarizing students with the sounds and the meanings of the words and sentence patterns. Later, as language skills and reading vocabulary grow, the focus moves to independent silent reading, usually by second grade. Group lessons are usually an occasion for teaching phonics, reading mechanics, and comprehension skills in the context of the story that has been read. ("Can anyone tell me what the first sound of *slippery* is? How many syllables? What letters are used to spell that sound?" "What is this punctuation mark called? Why does this sentence need a question mark instead of a period?"

"Who can say the exact words that are inside the quotation marks?" "Who is meant by the word *you* in this sentence?" "What do you think the main idea of this chapter is?")

In whole-language programs, part of the time that would have been given to worksheets and drills is devoted to independent reading, and because all the so-called "language arts" are taught together, more time is available. *Teachers and theorists concur that children learn to read mainly by doing so. Since they are not doing it at home, they must have time to read in school.* Students enjoy selecting books from a large classroom library (teachers have the responsibility of directing students into materials that will challenge without baffling them). They vigorously discuss books with each other as well as with the teacher (young readers love debating about plot outcomes and authors' points of view). Inevitably, they exchange book reviews, even when not assigned. ("You've gotta read this mystery story, it's *so cool!* The ghost lives in this weird old house . . .")

Some experienced teachers prefer to keep some of the structured lessons of a "basal" text and supplement them with literature-based units of study; the teaching still focuses on the learner's understanding and the importance of building all language skills in a related form.

In a curriculum centered on "whole language," writing is a cornerstone, and the child's own interest and active thinking is enlisted in teaching it. Children are encouraged to begin writing in kindergarten through specific techniques adapted for young children. In later grades, a variety of methods, including computer word processing, are currently in use to get students involved in learning about mechanics, content, and style.

2. Linking Reading, Writing, Listening, and Speaking

Instruction that links, rather than separates, the components of language learning is a natural vehicle for making up gaps in children's language backgrounds. It can also be an effective means of engaging them in thinking, making mental connections, and expressing themselves clearly. For some reason, classroom instruction has tended to segregate "reading time" from "writing time" and "spelling time." In many schools, "English" and "reading" have been regarded as totally different subjects, with different textbooks (the publishers love this, of course), different lesson plans, and different teachers.

One of the biggest gaps in children's experience these days is in seeing connections between all the bits of information they have accumulated; teachers are frustrated because their students have difficulty linking ideas together meaningfully. A fragmented curriculum does nothing to remedy the situation. When larger blocks of classroom time are devoted to linking skills, children are asked to write about what they read, read what they have written, talk about both, and learn to listen to what others have to say.

In "whole language" classrooms the most commonly mentioned writing program is the "writing process," in which children work with classmates and teacher to plan, draft, revise, and edit their own writing. It has sparked renewed interest in writing—as well as in the refinements of language—where it has been well implemented. Since extensive personal writing improves reading abilities, double value is gained from the time spent.

I recently spent some time observing a fourth grade where the teacher was trying out some of these ideas. Since "whole language" is much more of an attitude than a prescription, each teacher uses the basic concepts according to the school's instructional goals. This class was engaged in a unit of study about Egypt. In addition to reading from many background sources, discussing, making projects, and collaborating on simple research reports, the students were also reading books of children's fiction related to the study at hand. One group was eagerly pursuing a story about some sixth graders involved in an Egyptian mystery; two other groups had tackled books of different levels of difficulty. Each group's homework assignments consisted of reading one or two chapters and writing a "response journal" in which they summarized the day's reading and then carried on a dialogue with the author about points of particular interest.

The teacher met with each group and listened to them read and discuss their journal entries. Meanwhile, the other two groups read silently. In the discussions, skillfully moderated by the teacher, the level of interest was high; each child had different views and different comments. I found myself astonished by the depth of understanding that these young students showed. Students presented opinions about characters, motivation, plot outcomes, etc. Occasionally, someone's point would be challenged, and pages quickly turned. "It says here . . ." "Yes, but on page twenty-four it also says . . ." (Observing this, I reflected ruefully on my own struggles to *make* eighth graders use evidence from a text to back up an argument!) Discipline was not a problem, since the children knew that if they were to continue this activity, which they enjoyed, they had to behave. When one child began to cut up, his classmates shushed him.

Clearly, this was a good teacher at work. To implement a philosophy that focuses on process as much as on product and that allows teacher and student to direct much of the learning, good training of teachers—who themselves appreciate reading and writing—is primary.

3. Using Real Books and Real Language

The "whole language" philosophy also implies the use of good models of written language from the earliest school years. It rejects many published "canned" materials. Children are, indeed, more motivated by real books than by many textbooks, as shown by the success of these programs in getting disaffected students turned back on to reading. (Interest in "whole language," incidentally, may get the credit for some of the recently growing market in children's fiction.) Good literature also readies students' brains for language and ideas that will be needed at higher grade levels.

Even if they do not choose to follow most of the ideas of "whole language," *teachers should read aloud to their students from "good" books every day—even through middle and high school years.*

4. "Whole Language" and Motivation

The handful of teachers in my survey who wrote that students' interest and comprehension in reading had improved instead of declined were all using some form of literature-based reading program. Comments like the following suggest that there is still hope for the written word:

> I am teaching reading by using novels as well as the basal reader. Reading comprehension is much better than it was when I first started teaching (thirty-three years ago). Children have a better background and storehouse of information that they bring to the written material. They also show greater interest in reading. In writing they share thoughts that children thirty years ago would never have shared.
>
> —Third-grade teacher, Tennessee

This lady also added that she has changed many of her teaching methods to accommodate shorter attention spans: adding more variety and challenge, allowing students to move more around the room, including many more writing activities, and using more games to convey information.

> In our district reading-comprehension skills remain strong. Our children are avid readers. "Drop Everything and Read" periods are used a great deal in our school. My students have trouble speaking in com-

plete sentences, but they have become more expressive since we started using the writing process.

I used to be a very teacher-directed lesson planner; now I let the students have a lot more input, and I try to make provisions for their different learning styles.

—Fifth-grade teacher, Connecticut

5. Misuses of "Whole Language"

As worthy as are its goals, these ideas have some implicit risks. It puts a great deal of responsibility in the hands of teachers, who may or may not be willing to invest the effort to do the job right. The difficulty in holding teachers or students accountable for important basic skills is a related concern. Some children, at least, will not master good word-attack skills unless they are taught more directly; children may learn to read initially "by sight," but have difficulty with accurate spelling or reading of long, unfamiliar words.

Children who have an inherited tendency toward reading and spelling problems ("dyslexia") are the most likely casualties of a system with no organized teaching of spelling rules. For this reason, many specialists recommend an approach that blends the demonstrated potential of whole language with good, systematic instruction in sounds and spelling patterns. For a generation with an overall weakness in listening skills, this is doubtless a sensible course—as long as the phonics tail is not allowed to wag the literary dog.

Perhaps the biggest challenge of "whole language," and indeed, of all teaching that focuses on the process as well as the products of knowledge acquisition, is the necessity for adults to trust the child's basic desire to learn—within a well-planned structure. Neuroanatomists who study the growing brain confirm two facts that bear on this point. First, the brain seems to have a fundamental instinct to seek the type of learning appropriate for its stage of growth; second, active curiosity and personal involvement may be the catalyst for increasing both the size and the power of the thinking apparatus. Animals who simply observe others pursuing mental challenges end up with smaller brains.

DISCOURSE AND DIFFERENCE

The forms of discourse internalized by children from different backgrounds may influence thought patterns and school success. Those who have absorbed verbal/analytic habits of thinking are often more successful in school, at least in early grades, than those who rely more on visual/holistic approaches. While the problem is greatest for children whose language backgrounds do not stress school-type reasoning, children from "traditional" backgrounds may also have linguistic deficits. It is a tragic error to believe, however, that these students cannot think effectively or that they cannot be taught to use verbal/ analytic strategies to help them cope with academic demands. Moreover, students with skills in more holistic uses of language are often skilled in poetry, storytelling, or dramatics—to which the classroom's more linear thinkers probably need exposure.

Many educationally "different" children are bright and potentially talented. Few, if any, are "unteachable," but there is ample proof that plunging them abruptly into the chilly, analytic waters of mainstream instructional practices is a prescription for failure, frustration, and a high dropout rate.

The schools appear to have three choices:

1. Keep the traditional "standards" and continue to cram children into them. Let prisons and the welfare system handle the overflow.
2. Throw out the standards.
3. Maintain the goals represented by the standards, but prepare students more effectively. Expand the schedule of expectation and the teaching methods to honor children's latent abilities.

The first two alternatives should be unthinkable. We are left with the third.

Prescriptions for the Linguistically Different

Obviously, culturally and linguistically different children require special approaches. Model programs so far showing the best results have tried to take into account both the children's "styles" of thinking and their own cultural backgrounds.[21] As a follow-up to her studies in Appalachia, Dr. Shirley Brice Heath was asked by parents and teachers to help them devise methods to give the "non-mainstream" children a better chance at school success. As she used her research to help teachers understand the social and language backgrounds of their students, they successfully altered some of their methods. First, they related lessons to content that was familiar to the children (e.g., starting a study of "community" in social studies with photographs of their own town). Secondly, they worked carefully to help them expand their language to include school-type questions and answers. The children responded enthusiastically to lessons and tapes that respected their own usage while modeling other patterns of response.[22]

Dr. Roland G. Tharp of the University of Hawaii has recorded the impressive results of two programs designed to help culturally and linguistically different children. The first of these, the Kamehameha Early Education Program (KEEP), was developed over the course of twenty years as a model of a "culturally compatible language arts program for kindergarten through third-grade children of Hawaiian ancestry." KEEP classrooms now serve over two thousand children each year.

Traditionally, Hawaiian children in ordinary schools have been among the lower-achieving minorities in the United States, says Dr. Tharp, but in the KEEP program they approach national norms on standard achievement tests. Perhaps even more important, they pay better attention, work more diligently, and have a much more positive relationship with the school.

The magic formula for this well-documented success is a threefold approach: first, language development activities focusing on verbal/analytic problem-solving; second, "contextualized instruction," in which teachers try to relate all learning to something that is personally meaningful to the child; and third, revision of classroom organization and student-teacher interactions to reflect the habits of the child's own culture. For example, because Hawaiian cultures value cooperation, collaboration, and close social interactions, KEEP classrooms are structured so that children work most of the time in small groups, helping and talking with each other. The teacher engages in "intense instructional conversation" with one group before moving on to another; meanwhile, the other children work on their small-group assignment.

A second KEEP program described by Dr. Tharp has been in place for six years on a Navajo reservation in Arizona. It, too, has shown notable success in reaching children whose prospects for success in school were formerly clouded. The researchers, however, soon discovered that the initial format of KEEP was not effective for children from this Native American culture, where individualism and self-sufficiency are strongly valued and where adults treat children with respectful reserve. In these schools, children are allowed to work alone or in very small groups, with the teacher moving from child to child for "lengthy, quiet individual discussions." Because of research suggesting that Native Americans, overall, score better on visual/

holistic as opposed to verbal/analytic/sequential skills, says Tharp, the
Navajo classrooms use more "observational learning." Teachers are
taught to present material in more holistic, visual contexts and then
let the children try it themselves. Tharp contends that "successive,"
or linear, abilities can also be strengthened by such approaches.

Minorities are not the only students who need broader approaches,
maintains Dr. Tharp, because conventional schooling is also failing to
satisfy many majority-culture members. He suggests that all students
in North America need new teaching strategies, including "varied
activity settings, language development activities, varied sensory modalities in instruction, responsive instructional conversations, increased cooperative and group activities, and a respectful and
accommodating sensitivity to students' knowledge, experience, values, and tastes."[23]

Discourse Against Delinquency

Between classes at a large urban high school in Manhattan, a youth
pushes through a group of four classmates who have gathered on a
stairway. Tempers flare, and suddenly, knives are drawn. Other students intercede and the dean is summoned. Who is to blame? What
can be done to forestall gang retaliation?

Normally, suspension or police action might result from such an
incident. In this school, however, the dean has an alternative. He
summons a student mediation team, whose members have each undergone a twenty-hour training course in how to listen, phrase questions, and get disputants to talk with each other to reach agreement
in a structured format. A mediator is chosen; after the disputants
meet with her and air their grievances, they sign an agreement stating that the matter is settled.

Similar programs are spreading rapidly in major metropolitan areas. New York City credits the mediation agreements, 95% of which
are kept, for cutting fight-related suspensions by 46–70% in the nine
schools where it is used. Because of the less violent atmosphere,
attendance by other students has also increased.[24]

In Chicago, "conflict resolution" has become a mandatory part of
the curriculum for ninth and tenth graders in all sixty-seven high
schools. A similar program developed in San Francisco has spread
into elementary schools in more than thirty states.[25] Acclaimed by
educators who have tried it, this technique accomplishes more than
reducing discipline problems. It teaches children the value of using
language and listening to manage themselves. In terms of the brain,

it may be no surprise that this technique is so effective, as this is thought to be one means by which prefrontal control centers are put in charge.

Another program called "Talents Unlimited" claims similar success in teaching younger children the values of talking through problems and planning ahead. In one classroom, for example, kindergarteners eagerly participated in planning a class party.

"First we told about our plan," explains an eager five-year-old, pointing to a bulletin board on which the teacher has listed the four parts of the plan. "Then we thought of all the things we would need and put them in a list. Then we had to think of what we're going to do and put down the steps of our plan. And then we had to think of things that might spoil our plan, like if people didn't behave."[26]

Organized extensions of similar ideas into suburban as well as urban classrooms are showing students how to use verbal strategies to generate ideas, make decisions, plan, forecast, and communicate. Sponsors claim such programs can not only improve student behavior but also integrate verbal and thinking skills into the academic curriculum. Some are convinced that practicing the techniques significantly increases students' higher-order reasoning abilities.

Dozens of similar programs are being discussed. Although everyone agrees that children need to learn to think better, educators nevertheless argue about how—and even whether—this goal can be accomplished. Let's continue our look at some of the alternatives.

Teaching the New Generation to Think: Human and Computer Models at School and at Home

CAN WE TEACH CHILDREN TO THINK?

"Teaching thinking skills," another "movement" currently passing through the educational system, is a response to a growing concern that Johnny can't think any better than he can read. Programs attempting to teach thinking skills are selling like hotcakes at teachers' conferences and workshops. Yet critics scornfully point out it is a contradiction in terms to rely on packets, workbooks, computer drills, and worksheets to engage students' higher cognitive abilities. On this question lies the crux of the argument: Are so-called "thinking skills" best taught by setting aside a special time for mental calisthenics and then hoping they will transfer to other sorts of learning? Or are "thinking skills" better served by teaching all subjects in ways that draw students toward higher-level reasoning by the nature of the materials and the problems presented? The most generally prevailing opinion (aside from the purveyors of "thinking skills" programs) is that persistence and flexibility in problem-solving should be incorporated into overall teaching goals, modeled and supported in every discipline—provided, of course, that the teacher's own thinking skills are up to the task. Some educators also have hopes for computer programs that expand and may be able to challenge reasoning skills.

"Critical thinking," a primary goal of all such programs, is hard to pin down. How can it be measured? How does it develop? "Slickly packaged materials do not necessarily create good critical thinkers," says Dr. Marilyn Wilson of Michigan State University in a recent article that also raises several important questions. Is critical thinking out of place in a traditionally structured classroom? Is society ready for critically thinking students?[1]

Many educators have trouble with the idea of upsetting traditional ways of teaching and encouraging mental autonomy in their students. Yet true critical thinking cannot simply be added to the curriculum like driver training.

A Superficial "Fix"

Not long ago I had a disheartening look at an attempt to lay a superficial "fix" on students' thinking. I was leading a graduate course on the teaching of reading. My students, reading teachers from inner-city high schools, had been required to teach a nationally heralded program of "thinking skills." On the first night of class, they made their opinions clear. They thought this program was terrible. It was true, they acknowledged, that many of their students were extremely poor readers with comprehension scores considerably below grade level, but the teachers were required to spend class time on "thinking skills" instead of what they saw as badly needed reading instruction. Their major beef was that the program consisted of an extensive (and expensive) series of workbooks and worksheets that the students often did not understand—but that they were required to cover.

I was skeptical. What could be so bad about teaching poor comprehenders to reason more effectively? As soon as I asked the question, I was besieged with invitations to visit their classrooms. "Come and see for yourself," they said.

I began with a teacher who was clearly one of the most lively, turned-on, and thoughtful of the group. Arriving in the high school where she taught, I was escorted by a guard to her room, where she was about to begin her first class of the day. Her twenty-eight juniors were among the statistical survivors of a system where over half their classmates had already dropped out. As the bell rang, she took a large key from her belt and locked her classroom door—standard practice while in session. I noticed that she swung a baton resembling a small billy club—also standard issue—during the class period, but there was never a reason to use it. Her students were courteous, friendly, and their affection and respect were obviously returned in kind.

The day's worksheets were distributed. Each day brought a new lesson, whether or not the students had understood the last one. This lesson consisted of a long list of complex analogies calling heavily on abstract verbal categorization skills. They were phrased in high school to college level vocabulary. The teacher demonstrated solving two problems on the board, then the students started to work. I joined her as she circulated among the desks, trying to answer individual questions. It soon became clear that most of the kids, whose tested reading abilities ranged mainly between third- and eighth-grade level, could not understand this assignment at all. Indeed, as I puzzled over some of the problems, I decided they would make challenging work for a group of graduate students.

Of the class, eight or ten noble souls persisted in trying to make some sense out of this thing (the rest just filled in the blanks with any old word and then sat staring out the window or making faces at each other). Some of their reasoning was extremely sophisticated, although not of the type demanded here. One boy kept saying, "I know there's a trick, if I can only figure it out." I could not explain to him that the "trick" had already been played—by administrators who thought they could "make" certain types of thinking happen by decree.

Soon the bell rang, the teacher unlocked her door, and the students left, convinced once again by their loving school system that learning was a mystery and they were all inadequate. I found myself admiring them for hanging in there for so long—and feeling within myself the rage that must impel violent acts.

Of course this program's creators did not intend for it to be implemented this way. Of course the administration of this school district thought they were helping students learn better. Of course the teacher would have preferred to engage her students' interest and their genuine thinking skills with some of the many good books that would be readable, accessible, and meaningful to them. Of course, in a different context, such exercises may be useful, even enjoyable. But trying to teach the art of reasoning or problem-solving as if it were one more bit of content to be covered in a forty-minute period is clearly not the answer. The most frustrating thing for me is knowing that, with time and good teaching, many—if not most—of these students could learn successfully and become productive to themselves and to their community.

"Mindware"

Dr. David Perkins of Harvard believes we must take a much broader view of thinking for all children. Describing "a new science of learnable intelligence," Perkins advocates helping children and young people build flexible "mindware": abilities to organize and reorganize their patterns of thinking. He recommends getting them personally engaged—at school and at home, when it is possible—in mental challenges such as decision-making or inventive thinking about open-ended questions ("How are automobiles like books?" "How are rules for society like the rules for fractions?"). Clearly, the level of the challenges must fit the students, who will need guidance in developing and clarifying their ideas for more abstract questions.

Can some students just naturally reason more effectively than others? Every brain has an individual neurological basis for efficiency and effectiveness, says Perkins, but human beings are not "boxed in by neurology." His "triarchic" model of intelligence starts with inborn physical foundations in the neural system, but also includes two other layers: mastery of content (e.g., the multiplication tables, how to play chess, how to make cookies) and the development of patterns of thought. Although most current teaching concentrates on content (much of it "lower-order," he suggests), patterns of thought are, perhaps, the most important of all. Students must be shown how to use thinking in broader and more flexible ways.

"Don't assume that by getting kids just to think more, they'll get better at it," he cautions. They particularly need exposure to "metacognitive" models that enable them to use verbal skills to interpret and plan, to "mediate" experience. These skills are the foundation of good "mindware."[2]

Other leading educators urge broadened views for preparing students to think and reason effectively in tomorrow's world. Grant Wiggins, of the Coalition of Essential Schools, agrees we must stop focusing on limited goals of "content" and start thinking of education in terms of "intellectual habits."

"We don't teach kids intelligent strategies, we assume them—but even kids in the best schools don't have them," he told me. Students soon forget three-quarters of what is commonly taught and tested. Careful reading, mathematical reasoning, note-taking skills, understanding abstract concepts such as irony or inertia—all are habits, he says, that require extended practice throughout the school years.[3] These skills are the ones we internalize, use, and will increasingly need in the future.

In an era when more children come to schools less equipped with essential habits of mind to master "intelligent strategies," schools must reset their priorities to include them. Habits of mind, however, should not be separated from significant content. The challenge—too often unmet—is to infuse intellectual habits into the teaching of reading, writing, science, history, and math.

Members of a National Academy of Sciences committee recently declared current teaching to be an anachronism in an information age. Cramming children full of "factlets" and forgetting to focus on understanding is a problem exacerbated by the use of standardized tests, they point out. Citing most biology teaching as an example of an "outdated failure" that promotes memorization without understanding, this group is rewriting the entire science curriculum to include more in-depth laboratory work (another opportunity for "contextualized learning," by the way) and exploration of important concepts.[4] Computer simulations, in which students get first-hand experience solving real scientific problems, may ultimately provide one avenue to this goal.

Continuity and Meaning for the Two-Minute Mind

To develop strategic thinking, victims of the two-minute episode need help in seeing connections between ideas. Their courses should stress coherence rather than fragmentation, not only within each discipline, but across them as well (e.g., How are the trends you're studying in history related to ideas from English, art, physics, or music class?). At home, parents should keep this same principle in mind (e.g., "Have you noticed the tigers we saw in the zoo look a lot like your kitten?" "Do you think this story is anything like the one we read last week?"). But many families do not—or cannot—take the time to model this type of reasoning.

In previous times, points out Stanford's Dr. Eliot Eisner, many sources in children's lives outside of school provided continuity and meaning. This is no longer the case for many students where schools may provide their only opportunity for a "connected experience." Yet, most high school students he interviewed said they don't expect to encounter connections between one subject and another. "We must move away from programs and methods and incentives that breed short-term compliance and short-term memory," he insists.[5]

One way in which many teachers have already started helping students see connections and develop "intelligent strategies" is by including more "hands-on" activities. For a generation with short attention spans for listening, most successful teachers today also stress the necessity of including more visual types of presentations along with "talk." Projects and problem-solving situations in which children work alone or in groups with materials they can see and manipulate are particularly effective in math and science, but other "hands-on" activities such as dramatizations and debates can make learning real while maintaining a high level of intellectual discourse in English, history, and foreign language classes. While this type of learning has long been validated for younger children, educators have tended to forget that even adults may need to learn something for the first time by *doing* rather than simply hearing about it. Parents often believe that projects are only "busy work," but they, too, should recognize their value and encourage their child to work through the problem with a minimum of help—even if the results aren't perfect! One of the most important things all parents can do, even if they are themselves very busy, is to realize that schools (or children) should not be judged merely on the basis of the number of completed worksheets that come home. Potentially great minds are also encouraged to "mess around" with real-life challenges—and with great ideas. Neither have neat, tidy edges.

Metacognition: The Art of Knowing Your Own Mind

The human brain is unique in its abilities to reflect on its own thinking. Homes where children do not spend much time with reflective adults and schools where they are "trained" to learn mainly by memorizing data neglect this special asset. They also put children at risk for attention problems.

For metacognition, the key word is *strategies*, the mental processes that learners can deliberately recruit to help themselves learn or understand something new.[6] Examples of ineffective strategy use can be seen in every classroom: children who race through math papers without stopping to think about whether the answers are right or wrong, readers who absorb the words with their eyes but never ask themselves if their brain understands, students in art class who start slapping on paint before they think about the space on the paper, problem-solvers who give up after the first solution doesn't work.

Programs developed for parents and teachers in "strategy training" primarily involve recruiting the child's inner speech for thoughtful mental processing. For example, a typical training program teaches children first to "talk aloud," then to "whisper aloud," then to "whisper inside your head" in an effort to build that inner voice so frequently missing in today's distracting environments. When confronted with a problem, children may be taught to follow a four- or five-step plan such as the following:

1. Stop. Think. What is my task? (identify the problem in words)
2. What is my plan? (talk through possible steps to solution)
3. How should I begin? (analyze first step)
4. How am I doing? (keep on task)
5. Stop. Look back. How did I do? (analyze the result)

Practice with these steps is surprisingly effective in helping children with attention problems manage their behavior more effectively. Similar techniques applied to reading comprehension ("Am I understanding this? What don't I understand?") have also shown good results. It is important to note that all these successes result from using language to direct thoughts and impulses. Research shows that even some students with so-called "memory problems" have a more fundamental difficulty in managing their own thinking.[7]

Israeli Dr. Reuven Feuerstein, perhaps our most perennial optimist about the modifiability of human intelligence ("Heredity, shmeridity!" is one of his favorite lines), is convinced that the brain itself can be improved by "metacognitive strategy training" that makes human beings more resistant and adaptable to changing circumstances. "The brain can be modified or changed in a structured way to enable individuals to self-perpetuate," he maintains. "Human beings are unique in their capacity to modify themselves. I call this 'autoplasticity.'" But even before they get to school, children need adults to impose meaning on them or they will always go around the world searching for meaning," he states flatly.[8]

In the absence of this sort of experience, which he terms "mediated learning," Feuerstein believes children do not develop adequate thinking skills. As an example of nonmediated learning, he describes a parent putting toys around a room and expecting a child to play. In mediated learning, the parent would place a building toy in front of a child and then sit down and demonstrate several ways to use it, talking about each alternative and allowing the child to experiment while still feeling the support of the adult.

Although Feuerstein holds parents largely responsible for this kind of training in early years, he also tells teachers they must help structure meaning for the child. Instead of simply handing a child a book to read, for example, a mediating teacher might help the student make some predictions about the plot, clarify the meaning of certain vocabulary words, and check out familiarity with necessary background information. The trick is to keep the assistance strictly within the limits of what is necessary for the child to succeed, not to offer so much help that the parent's brain does most of the growing and the child becomes overly dependent.

Although Feuerstein believes firmly in human mediation, others have suggested that computers which can be programmed to respond directly to each child's needs and ability level may eventually be able to do at least part of this job. Thus far, such electronic scaffolds are mainly used to drill on specific subject matter (e.g., multiplication tables, spelling, foreign language vocabulary), but new programs are constantly being developed.

In the meanwhile, this research has profound implications for the content of early childhood programs, especially for children disadvantaged by the absence of mediating adults in their lives. In fact, it has an important message for educational policymakers at all levels. Now that so many children lack these models, *helping children structure meaning* must become a priority in schools.

Speaking to a group of teachers not long ago, Feuerstein challenged them to reconsider their definition of appropriate goals for education.

"Should it be more data, units, tests? Let me remind you that many of the things you teach today will soon be obsolete! Only brains that can adapt and change themselves will ensure the continuation of our culture."[9]

What About Creativity and Imagination?

Feuerstein's concept of "imposing" meaning through helping a child structure understanding is very different from imposing a list of "thinking skills" on an already bite-sized curriculum. Trying to over-analyze "thinking," in fact, may result in sacrificing its inherent creativity.

Good thinking requires good analytic skills, but it also depends on imagination. Both halves of the brain, not simply the linear, analytic-verbal left hemisphere, contribute to it. The more visual, intuitive right hemisphere probably provides much of the inspiration, while the left marches along in its dutiful role as timekeeper and realist.

While verbal mediation strategies are clearly effective for directing thought, they should not preclude opportunities for children to practice open-ended thinking, artistic, and nonverbal problem-solving.

Some observers, concerned about declines in creative thinking, as well as in imagination, have advocated teaching methods and classroom experiences to stimulate the right hemisphere. Although some of these so-called "right-brain" activities are fun, their specific neurological merit is viewed by scientists with considerable skepticism. Moreover, it is increasingly clear that genuine creative imagination springs from much deeper developmental roots—which can easily get short-changed both in homes and in schools.

Children Without Their Own Visions

Do television-raised children, or hurried children who lack the time to sit and dream, grow up with poorer imaginations? Is lack of imagination one of the causes of indifferent problem-solving in today's students? One of the most troubling reports to come out of interviews with preschool teachers is that children today don't make up their own "scripts" for playing. Instead of spontaneously creating open-ended settings and actions ("You be a daddy and I'll be a mommy"; "You be a bad guy and I'll be a hero"), they reenact those they have already seen, even to repeating the dialogue ("You be Bill Cosby in the one where . . ." "Let's be the Mario Brothers when they chase the . . .").

In my survey, teachers were more divided than on any other issue when asked whether students' visual imagery and/or imagination had changed. While about half stated categorically that children today have less imagination, other responses were mixed. To my surprise (and dismay) this item was the only one frequently left blank or frankly answered as "I don't know" (or care?). Others acknowledged that their students' demonstration of imagination and creative thinking depended a lot on their own attitudes and skill as teachers. Some examples:

> TV and computers seem to have blurred distinctions between the real and the imaginary; they still visualize (with luck?) but it's hard to rigorously define the images (e.g., in geometry and on maps).
> —Computer instructor, Massachusetts

> Just as sharp and intuitive as always. (When allowed to be!) I have integrated subject matter, added the arts, provided kinesthetic in-

volvement, relaxation exercises, and used cooperative learning groups with the purpose of teaching social skills and addressing learning styles. The result has been renewed enthusiasm for teaching for me, and more connectedness between my students with each other and with me. It's become fun!!! again.

—Fifth-grade teacher, Oregon

Imagination is disappearing with our structured childhood lives. Parents plan the total child day leaving little free time for playing alone or free play with groups. Leisure time is almost a thing of the past.

—Elementary-school teacher, Wisconsin

I find that my children still have wonderful imaginations!

—Third-grade teacher, Texas

They are very restless and their attention span is short, but in the arts, when you can establish an atmosphere in class that helps them tap in, all the richness is still there, the imagination. No, in the arts I don't think it's ever too late.

—Director, arts integration program, Minnesota

Many books have been written to help teachers wed creative thinking and open-ended problem-solving to daily mastery of content. Suffice it to say here that if we wish to flourish technologically as well as aesthetically, it may be time to rethink priorities that have viewed creativity and imagination as "the art (or music) teacher's responsibility." Mature creativity stems from an inquiring mind with solid foundations in the major intellectual, spiritual, artistic, or aesthetic domains of human achievement, not from gimmicky "right-brain training." Habits of mind that enable a lively interchange between a student and the great thinkers, artists, and technicians of past and present are most appropriately, and indeed, most elegantly, attired in the important content of global cultures.

If we encourage our teachers to be thoughtful, well-informed, and curious themselves, we may more likely expect them to infuse the entire curriculum with creative as well as critical thinking. Otherwise, we will be forced to abandon our children—who now, more than ever before, need good models of imaginative intellectual engagement—to machines or "teacher-proof" kits and workbooks. Why spend time on activities such as "write an essay from the point of view of your pencil eraser" while leaving untouched the significant mental challenges of a child's world? This is about as silly as teaching children to "think" by dropping "factlets" into an intellectual abyss in the name of something called "cultural literacy."

On "Cultural Literacy"

In 1987 Dr. E. D. Hirsch published a book entitled *Cultural Literacy: What Every American Needs to Know* which caused many parents to wonder if they should march on schools, insisting that their children be forced to memorize more terms, names, and dates. Maintaining that one of the major reasons for lagging achievement is that students today lack a basic core of background knowledge to help them understand what they read, Hirsch and a colleague, Dr. Joseph Kett, developed a list of everything a decently educated person should know.[10] While I would not argue that growing numbers of citizens' brains have barely been grazed by the knowledge base on which our civilization rests, I have serious reservations about the implications that have been drawn from this arguably superficial concept.

Educators who spend their time with real children in real class-rooms are only too acutely aware that passing something in front of (or even temporarily through) them in the name of teaching guarantees nothing in the name of learning. Unfortunately, the mere existence of such a "list" is an invitation to simple-mindedness. Although cursory exposure to bits and bites of learning is the exact opposite of the authors' stated intent, our country's current reductionist mentality (inspired, as we have seen, by legitimate panic over the state of learning) has interpreted it to mean that simply mastering—read "memorizing"—the items will get us intellectual standing room.

Ironically, Dr. Kett told me that a major change he has noted in the writing of his freshmen students at the University of Virginia is a "lack of coherence."

"These kids are bright," he said. "This is a seminar that they know is hard, but their writing is more jumbled than what I used to get from students. They enumerate facts rather than summarizing. They have difficulty discriminating thoughts and there is no transition be-tween paragraphs."[11]

Who Should Teach "Cultural Literacy"?

Real access to the great concepts of any cultural heritage comes from extended, personally meaningful contact. In the past, this exposure came mainly from conversations with adults and two other sources:

books, which were read out loud at home, personally perused for pleasure, or read as part of schoolwork; and lessons that were understood and internalized. Nowadays, these methods of transmission are in short supply. Many students do not read what they are supposed to, much less for pleasure, and few teachers require much essay writing. Often they are not given (or do not choose to take) sufficient time to cover a topic in depth,. There is simply more to learn than there is time available. Without associations with meaning, however, items from a list don't stick well to memory.

Perhaps Dr. Hirsch's most important point is that the reading children do in school should be an important vehicle for cultural transmission. It is inexcusable for youngsters to be reading pap when research has clearly demonstrated that even first graders enjoy, remember, and understand good literature better. If we engage children's minds, in Dr. Lillian Katz's words, by integrating reading instruction with in-depth studies of historical periods, scientific ideas, etc., they will learn and remember even more.

Another point: Has no one noticed that children are very culturally literate—except that it's for a different culture? Just make up a list of any details from *Roseanne, Family Ties, Sesame Street*, etc. and most kids would come out looking as smart as they really are. The problem is that our children have exposed us to ourselves, and we don't like what we see. We have shown them what is really valued in our society, and those little cultural apprentices have happily soaked it up.

If we are serious about wanting them prepared by a knowledge base to gather the intellectual fruits of world cultures, the obvious expedient is to change the content of children's television programming and use other video as enrichment. In my opinion, this should be a major responsibility of both educational and commercial networks. Otherwise, we will soon be forced to revise university-level curricula to include in-depth studies of talking animals and human buffoons.

Schools cannot plaster children with a paste of "cultural literacy" that the culture itself repudiates. Nor can schools completely counteract the powerful effects of television programming that works at direct cross-purposes with our efforts to teach children to think.

TEACHING CRITICAL THINKING—ELECTRONICALLY

This dilemma was put into sharp relief when a recent *New York Times* "Education Life" supplement happened to juxtapose these two reports:

1. A major life insurance company flies their claim forms to Ireland where "a surplus of well-educated white collar workers" are eager to process them. The reason? American workers lack the educational skills as well as the motivation.

2. Because of poor habits of nutrition in American schoolchildren, the government has set a new goal to make nutrition a requirement in the school curriculum of all fifty states.[12]

People seem only too happy to blame the schools for the fact that our work force is so undereducated. At the same time, however, they insist badly needed instructional hours be used to undo the effects of television commercials that have systematically trained children in poor nutritional habits. What a preposterous situation! The first place where critical thinking should be applied is to the content of television, but if adults can't do it, why should children? Moreover, how can we lambast kids for their lack of "responsibility" at the same time we unload all of our own onto the schools? No wonder many children expect to have learning pumped into them without any reciprocal obligation.

Few dispute the fecklessness of American network programming for children. In his book *Television and America's Children: A Crisis of Neglect*, Edward Palmer details its inadequacies.[13] Yet no major effort has been made to train children to be critical viewers. Suffice it to repeat here that the brain tends to be deeply imprinted by repeated experience, particularly in early years. If teachers are required to reverse attitudes and values carefully inculcated by the media, they will have little time to bind up its intellectual casualties.

Yet the reality of the tube in the lives of the current generation is undeniable. Schools will have to assume a more positive—and educational—role in guiding children, who are by nature "visually vulnerable," into analysis and evaluation of its content. "The potential of our new electronic teachers is awesome," states Ernest Boyer in his introduction to Palmer's book. "Educators would be naive to ignore these influences, which have become, in effect, a new curriculum."[14]

In her book, *Mind and Media*, Patricia Greenfield points out that visual literacy must now be taught in addition to print literacy.[15] She recommends specific programs to turn children from passive into active consumers of all kinds of visual material. Using network programs to teach questioning techniques, studying the effects of devices such as zooms and pans, analyzing plot structures and comparing them to those of literature, and leading critical discussions of the art of persuasion are all ideas that might be applied in homes as well as in schools. Classroom production of videotapes that children plan, write scripts for, and then analyze can help put them in control of the medium instead of vice versa.

Greenfield also advocates more effective uses of television to reduce the educational gaps between advantaged and disadvantaged children, citing successful experiments in Third World countries with video designed to make children interactive participants in learning. In Niger, for example, children were successfully taught French by programs that incorporated interactive language instruction. As they engaged in structured follow-up exercises with classroom aides, they became "more actors than spectators," and learning proceeded apace.

A New Curriculum

Cognitive psychologist Dr. Michael Posner believes that schools may have to change in even more fundamental ways in response to an electronic age. Children soon observe, he suggests, that a school with a rigid schedule is very different from the more flexible environments in the real world of work. Children see adults looking at television and working at computer displays more than they see them reading and writing. "But we still act as if the only important skills were reading and writing," he points out.[16]

"We remain myopically obsessed with print literacies while our pupils continue living in a world that is increasingly high-tech and electronically visual and auditory," wrote an editor of *Language Arts*, published by the National Council for Teachers of English. Instead of avoiding questions of how "computer literacy" or "visual literacy" relate to critical thinking and learning, educators must broaden their research and include their constructive uses.

THE COMPUTERIZED BRAIN

As we turn now to consider future definitions of "thinking," we move into an area where there are some rather unsettling questions and no answers. One of the most important is how adaptive our children's "new brains" will prove to be in a culture that may be in the process of evolution away from print-based representations of knowledge.

Asking "experts" what they think computers will do to children's brains elicits little agreement.

1. "A computer is simply a caricature of the left hemisphere, just as video games are a caricature of the right. I think that working

with computers will definitely make kids more left-brained."
2. "Computers can do all the detail work, but humans have to have the 'big picture' of what they want the machine to do. And they have to 'see' and plan an overall strategy. When kids are freed of the details, I think working with computers may enable them to be more right-brained!"

The answer I like best was suggested by Dr. Jeannine Herron, director of California Neuropsychology Services, who works on developing computer software as an educational tool.

"I think computers are going to enable us to stretch the limits of both global and linear. If they want detail, they can get very fine detail, but they can also get a wider, very global perspective. A child who can browse through great photographs of the dust-bowl era is certainly getting an overall concept of that historical period. But I don't think we'll be able to build the linkages between those two kinds of systems unless the experience is meaningful for the child."[17]

In order to understand the effects computers may have on the user's thinking skills, we must start with the major difference between artificial and "real" intelligence.

Sequential and Parallel Processing

Normal human brains have at their disposal two complementary methods of processing information: sequential and simultaneous (often called parallel). Sequential processing takes one bite at a time: A, then B, therefore C, etc. ("If the suspect entered the office at 2:30, then the secretary would have just returned from her coffee break, and therefore she would have seen him." "If $x = 3$ and $y = 5$, then $x + y = 8$") and is primarily associated with the left hemisphere.

The opposite—but, for us, interlocking way of solving problems is called parallel, or simultaneous, processing because many associations become activated at the same time. This sort of thinking has been compared to a "ripple" effect, in which A elicits a wide network of connections with other sets of associations and ideas, often represented in images. The linkages may be well learned or spontaneous and unique, as in the process of first feeling, then "seeing," then articulating a metaphor. Artists, inventors, writers, and other creative thinkers depend heavily on simultaneous processing, which is more often associated with the right hemisphere. Of course, at the point where it becomes necessary to articulate the image, hypothesis, or general principle on a typewriter, canvas, musical score, or graph paper, sequential skills assume their own value.

Human brains continually blend simultaneous and sequential processing, although, as with learning "styles," different individuals may tend to favor one form over another. The way the brain is trained probably helps determine the balance. The demands of the task may also nudge the brain into one mode or another.

The "artificial intelligence" (AI) of most present-day computers represents sequential processing carried to an extreme. Traditional AI can deal only with one piece of data at a time, and computers act irritable if items and instructions don't arrive in the proper order, as anyone who has responded to the cybernetic cry of anguish—"syntax error"—can attest. Until new prototypes of artificial intelligence are widespread (some which use parallel processing are even now becoming available), computers are locked into a mentality that makes even the most unimaginative human number-cruncher look like a creative genius. The reason, of course, is that the human has two hemispheres cushioned by some nice soft emotional centers; the machine has, in essence, only part of a left hemisphere and no feelings that we know of.

I find it interesting to speculate—because there is little research available—on the physical effects of interactions between the human and this machine brain. As of now, when children meet up with AI, they are usually involved in one of the following types of applications:

1. Drill and practice programs (e.g., games to learn the multiplication tables, practice a spelling list, place the state capitals on a map)
2. Programming (e.g., giving the machine a series of commands to make it draw a square or compute gas mileage; these must be presented to the machine in its own language and its own one-step-at-a-time logic)
3. Working with data bases (e.g., accessing a list and selected summaries of all the articles on parakeets published since 1973; creating a data base in which all the local birds from your area are listed and categorized according to type of beak, feathers, color, etc.)
4. Simulations (e.g., You are a pioneer about to set out on the Oregon Trail. You are given a budget and must choose from a "menu" of supplies; as the trip progresses, you undergo various hardships and must make decisions along the trail. You may or

may not make it to Oregon. It is assumed you will learn some history and some decision-making skills in the process. Video games are also simulations.)

5. Word processing (e.g., the computer as an advanced form of memory typewriter)

These different uses call on very different types of mental processing, the implications of which have barely been tapped. I will touch here on just a few of the most relevant issues in terms of the development of thinking skills.

Learning to Talk to Machines: Accurately!

Teaching children to program a present-day computer virtually demands they use precise, analytic-sequential reasoning (e.g., If . . . then . . .). I have seen many youngsters whose minds do not naturally tend to work this way (and little children's, particularly, do not) become extremely frustrated because they can't just "make it understand" by telling it, "You know . . ."

Other uses of the computer also require precision of language. Dr. Judah Schwartz of the Education Department at MIT points out that getting the computer to work properly with data bases does not permit "sloppy" understanding of words such as *and, or,* or *not.* Try to figure out this one:

> I have watched youngsters not understand why a data base on United States presidents, when queried about the number of presidents born in Massachusetts and Vermont, insisted on claiming that no presidents were born in Massachusetts and Vermont [if you didn't get it the first time, neither did I!]. Clearly the problem has nothing to do with the technology. Rather we need to educate people to use the language with much greater precision than they are presently accustomed to using.[18]

Schwartz emphasizes that similar "analytic barbarism" causes most of people's trouble with spreadsheets (where they may try to add months to dollars, etc.). Computers simply won't buy slushy language or slushy thought, at least as the machine has been programmed to define it.

Will working with computers teach children better habits of orderly thinking? Thus far, research offers contradictory views. On one hand, programming a computer requires that a student be able to break a problem down into logical, sequential units and then accurately give this information to the machine. We are beginning to learn, however, that students whose brains do not take naturally to this way of thinking usually avoid programming in the same way people who think they lack drawing ability flee from art classes.

"Watching students try to program teaches me a great deal about the way they think, but I don't believe it makes them better thinkers—at least not the way we're teaching it now," one experienced teacher told me.

On the other hand, computer programming might encourage those who are already too focused on details to obsess even more. Some theorists fear that too much interaction with artificial intelligence will magnify the role of linearity, logic, and rule-governed thinking in our culture to the point where we might be in danger of retreating into a "flattened, mechanical view of human nature."[19] Most agree that computers are a tool with almost unlimited potential, but until they can engage in parallel as well as simultaneous processing, they will not only be a poor match, but also a poor model for most forms of human reasoning.[20]

At this point, computers can perform many functions of the brain's storehouse. Nonetheless, they still have to depend on the executive and general reasoning abilities of the human brain. I venture to say it will be a long time, if ever, before prefrontal, emotional, and motivational centers can be attached to a hard disc. Thus it may be especially important to make sure our children retain these capabilities themselves.

Computer as Scribe

Children who learn to use word processing programs become more fluent writers and are more willing to revise what they write. Many who have trouble with mechanical aspects of handwriting and spelling find they can express their ideas successfully for the first time. Word processing programs are, without doubt, one of the most commonly used and appreciated computer uses in the classroom.

As a dedicated fan of my own electronic amanuensis, however, I must acknowledge that writing on a screen changes, not only the experience itself, but also the resulting prose. In addition to the danger of prolixity, many writers feel they tend to lose a sense of the "gestalt" of the piece and find it necessary to revert frequently to "hard copy" (paper printouts) to understand their own line of reasoning and see how the parts fit together. Perhaps this is because we initially programmed our brains to read and write on paper; perhaps it is an inherent problem in the technology.

An outstanding English teacher commented that she has no trouble telling which of her students' essays started life on the computer. "They don't link ideas—they just write one thing, and then they write another one, and they don't seem to see or develop the relationships between them."

Assuredly, we must encourage students to use the computer as a tool, but also teach them to rise above its ineluctable linearity and use the parallel processing capabilities of their own human brains.

The Electronic ZPD

Computers make good "coaches" for specific sorts of skills because they can be programmed to operate directly within the "zone of proximal development" described earlier. Schoolchildren already show success working with individual machine "tutors" to perfect routine skills. It must be remembered, however, that interaction with any kind of computer software really boils down to interacting with the intelligence of the person who programmed the software. Naturally, some are better than others.

With perfection of machines that can process human speaking and "listening," children may someday have personally responsive tutors for oral language. (But how about the melody, the inflection, the "body language"?) Spelling "checkers" that now act simply as correcting devices might be programmed to notice patterns of errors, diagnose the types of help a poor speller needs, and develop drills for a personal tutoring session on spelling rules needed by that particular individual. Grammar "readers" may ultimately be able to extend learning as well as correct and reshape usage. The ones so far available for written text, unfortunately, are singularly pedantic and may actually strip a manuscript of style and complex usage, nuance not being a forte of the machine's intelligence.

The possibilities are limitless, but they must be wisely sifted and monitored. Even simulation games that are apparently quite educational (e.g., "Oregon Trail") require a good teacher nearby. Otherwise, it often gets treated by the youngsters simply as a game of chance, with little attention to the educational context.

Programs to teach children—or even graduate students—to reason logically have similarly earned mixed reviews. Although we will see increased attention to this important potential application, programs now available are not capable of making "fuzzy" thinkers into logicians.[21] Nor has anyone yet demonstrated exactly what kinds of global, "big picture" skills computer uses may engender. Getting a "view" of the way steps might fit together to produce a desired result when writing a program, deciding which combination of statistical programs to use to analyze a varied set of data, or seeing categorical relationships between items in a data base all tap aspects of this ability. There is some evidence that extensive work with programs that relate visual-spatial activity on the screen to the child's own physical movements in space (e.g., LOGO) may improve at least some types of visual-spatial reasoning, but overall, the jury is still out.

Computer scaffolding offers wonderful possibilities for the disabled. It can help children who have orthopedic or learning handicaps express their intelligence in ways heretofore unavailable. It may also hold potential for more intensive, individual work with disadvantaged children who are, unfortunately, placed in classrooms without enough teachers to meet their particular learning needs. The attention-getting format of computer programs has been shown to be appealing even to children who have acquired a basic mistrust of school learning. One observer cautioned, however, that cozying up to software can never completely replace rubbing up against good teachers.

"In the end it is the poor who will be chained to the computer; the rich will get teachers."[22]

As always, too, the problem of "transfer" emerges. Can reading from a screen or learning to hunt and peck on a keyboard be used to improve proficiency and pleasure in real reading and writing? Or will machine analogues become the "real" processes? With electronic books now available, it may soon be hard to tell.

For Young Children: Artificial or Real Intelligence?

While dining not long ago with a scientist who probes the workings of the brain, I enjoyed hearing about the intellectual exploits of his three-year-old daughter, clearly the apple of her Daddy's eye. I enjoyed his stories, that is, until we got to dinosaurs.

"She can recognize all the names when she sees them on the computer screen: Tyrannosaurus Rex, Brontosaurus, whatever—and she matches them right up to the pictures!" he said happily. "The program we got her even teaches about what each one ate, and whether they could fly, and all kinds of stuff. It's amazing!"

I didn't say what was really on my mind at that point . . . something like, "I'm sure that will be really useful for her when she takes her first course in paleontology." Being something of a wimp in the presence of those who spend their days rooting around in other people's brains, I only said,

"And how long did it take her to learn all this?"

"Oh, she loves her computer. She spends a lot of time at it. When my wife and I are busy we would much rather see her there than watching TV. At least we know she's doing something educational."

"Does your little girl ever just play—by herself, or with other little kids?"

"Oh, sure." He thought for a moment. "But she really loves that computer! Isn't it wonderful how much they can learn at this age?"

"What do you think that computer is doing to her brain?" I asked.

He paused. "You know," he said slowly, "I never thought about it. I really haven't a clue."

Many parents with far less scientific sophistication than this man also don't have a clue as to what early use of computers can do to children's brains. The long-term neurological effects of this type of experience are unknown—and, very likely, unknowable. We do know that short-changing real-life social and fantasy play is a big mistake. Yet many adults understandably believe that if a child looks as if she's mastering something that they themselves view as complicated, it must mean the kid is getting really smart. But does it?

Many child development authorities question how much, if any, of preschoolers' time should be spent sitting at a computer terminal. "Young children who will grow up in a high-tech world need a low-tech, high-touch environment," insists Dr. Lillian Katz.[23] Early childhood is a special time for brain development of special systems that will underlie many different kinds of learning; even executive centers have already begun to develop by age two. While many types of computer programs sold for young children may be useful to get specific kinds of learning into older brains, research has not yet supported their value for preschoolers.

What might be wrong with giving children a leg up on all the interesting facts in our cultural data base? First of all, many programs of this sort use paired associate learning (e.g., matching names, letters, or numerals with pictures), which is not a high-level skill and not one that builds many widespread neural connections. For some children, a preoccupation with memorizing bits of information may even herald a serious learning disorder.[24] Even when the programs call on more complex skills (e.g., categorizing attributes of dinosaurs), feeding the brain with too much vicarious experience (e.g., words and pictures on a computer monitor) instead of real ones (e.g., investigating the behaviors of actual kittens, goldfish, ants, salamanders or whatever) or with feelable, manipulable objects (e.g., dolls, stuffed animals, making dinosaur models out of clay, if the child is genuinely interested in dinosaurs) could place artificial constraints on its natural developmental needs. The preschool brain's main job is to learn the principles by which the real world operates and to organize and integrate sensory information with body movement, "touch," and "feel." It needs much more emphasis on laying the foundations of control systems for attention and motivation than on jamming the storehouse full of data that makes it look "smart" to adults.

The child's need to initiate and feel "in charge" of her own brain's learning is another issue to consider. Commercial computer programs are designed to attract and hold attention, but programming a youngster to expect to receive information without independent mental exploration and organization may be a grave error—which won't become apparent until she can't organize herself around a homework assignment or a job that requires initiative. More commonplace activities, such as figuring out how to nail two boards together, organizing a game, or creating a doll house out of a shoebox may actually form a better basis for real-world intelligence.

The last thing today's children need is more bits of learning without the underlying experiential frameworks to hang them onto. In tomorrow's world of instant information access, activities like memorizing the names and characteristics of dinosaurs could be as anachronistic as the creatures in question. Moreover, children who have concentrated on getting the right answer rather than on building the independent reasoning to ask the right question, or who, by replacing playtime with too much computer time have failed to develop "big picture" frameworks from self-initiated experience, may become dinosaurs themselves.

Looking Ahead

Computers offer extraordinary potential as brain accessories, coaches for certain types of skills, and motivators. Their greatest asset may ultimately lie in their limitations—which will force the human brain to stand back and reflect on the issues beyond the data—if it has developed that ability.

Expanding Minds

When cultures change and new cultural tasks give rise to new demands for cognitive competence, human plasticity makes it possible for the new outcomes to be reached.

—JOHN U. OGBU[1]

Technology is here to stay. We have to be damn sure we do it right—whatever "right" means. Therein lies the vision—and the challenge.

—GARY PETERSON, SUPERINTENDENT,
LEARNERS' MODEL TECHNOLOGY
PROJECT, CA

In a large classroom, groups of teachers cluster around computer monitors. Their charged intensity belies the summer heat that presses against the air-conditioned building, a contemporary anachronism on a quiet, white-pillared campus whose traditions reach back well over a century. But no one is gazing out the window at the green lawns, white clapboard buildings, and gracious, overarching trees. As their instructor walks to the center of the room, some remain engrossed; others look up with an expression that can best be described as dazed.

"Well," he says. "You came to this workshop to learn the newest methods for teaching math, and I've just shown you a forty-five-dollar computer program that can do all the operations of algebra, trig, and calculus. This afternoon I will demonstrate a pocket calculator that will soon be available which can do graphing and geometry. Many of you spend up to eighty percent of your class time teaching kids to do these calculations that a simple program can now perform almost instantly. So, I've only got one question. What do you plan to do for the rest of your life?"

"Retire!" says one man, obviously eager to head back to his green-shuttered dormitory.

"Wait! This is exciting!" exclaims another. "Think of the problems we'll be able to work on. We'll have to teach the kids to understand the questions. Even if the machines know *how*, somebody's going to have to know *why*. Students can't plug in the right data and know what operations to use unless they understand the problem."

As the group adjourns for lunch, I approach the leader, Lew Romagnano, to thank him for allowing me to sit in on this impressive demonstration.

"What sort of impact do you think computers will have on the human brain?" I ask him.

"Who knows. You're the brain person, not me! Probably brains will get lots bigger because we won't have all this computation nonsense to worry about anymore. Seriously, you're talking about real mathematical thinking—patterns you can *see*—without doing hours of arithmetic. If we didn't have to teach long division for six months in the fifth grade, think what else we could teach—probability, statistics, geometry, mathematical reasoning. It's sure to have some sort of effect on the brain."

MINDS IN AN "INFORMATION AGE"

As I have worked on this book, my file optimistically labeled "Future Minds" has overflowed and been expanded until it has finally assumed book-length proportions of its own. I search it to discover what may happen to a human brain that takes on machines as intellectual boonfellows, but I don't find any answers. Even the dimensions of the question, in fact, aren't totally clear. The first is doubtless what new demands will be placed on the human mind as a function of the "information age."

With a proliferation of new technology, occupational demands on the human brain are shifting from direct manipulation of the physical universe (e.g., putting parts together on an assembly line, driving a tractor, going to a library to look up research articles, mixing chemicals in a lab, making change from a cash register) to managing machines that perform these functions. The machines, in turn, churn forth and instantly transmit inhuman quantities of data. The amount of available information is now estimated to double every two years—an astounding harbinger of future possibilities, but an alarming reminder that we now need machines to manage our knowledge as well as our commerce.

It is estimated that 40% of new investment in plant and equipment is for electronic data-shufflers. A proliferation of computers, video, telecommunications, copying and FAX machines, and various permutations among them, encapsulate and speed the pace of human discourse.

These changes inevitably cause fundamental shifts in mental activity. Machines become extensions of our brains. Thinking is referred to as "information processing"; working requires more and more ability to access, manipulate, and use data. The worker of the future, we are told, must be prepared to act as an individual manager of both the information and the technological tools by which it is assembled: computer memory banks and data bases, electronic libraries, video encyclopedias, etc. Meanwhile, with instantaneous transmission of written as well as oral communication all over the world, the human "patience curve" wavers perceptibly.

But someone has to "see the patterns," figure out the purpose and the plan for this frenetic fact-factory. One might also hope that people will retain enough control to reflect on where it is all taking us—and why.

Subtle shifts in what the human brain is required to do will eventually cause it to modify itself for new uses, at least in those who are either young or sufficiently motivated. Speculations naturally abound as to what these effects may be, but if I restricted this chapter to what has been proven about technology's ultimate impact on brains, it would end right here.

Nevertheless, since these electronic developers are lining up to stake out a claim in the brains of today's children, I believe we should try to figure out a few more questions to ask before we sign the contract. We have already witnessed clear changes in children's habits of mind: declining verbal skills, changing patterns of attention, a less reflective approach to problem-solving. How might they fit with our conjectures about the future? Are human brains about to get caught in the experiential fragmentation of machine technology, or will they gain broader abilities to stand back and understand what is happening?

EVOLVING BRAINS?

One of the questions I often get after presenting the ideas set forth in this book is whether the changes so consistently observed in students may represent some sort of evolutionary trend. Is it possible that print literacy and/or the process of extended mental reflection are merely evolutionary way stations for a species en route to bigger and better things? As we saw in Chapter 3, neuroscientists have proposed that the inner workings of the brain itself adapt themselves to new environments through a Darwinian model of competitive selection.

Scientists agree that generational changes in cognitive abilities are probably part of an evolutionary process. Dr. Steven Jay Gould, noted evolutionary biologist and authority on Darwinian theory, believes such changes are primarily associated with a dynamic process of "cultural evolution." Gould believes that genetic changes, in the strict Darwinian sense, take far too long to be so readily noticed, although they, too, are doubtless occurring over the long march of human mental development.

Most geneticists, of course, do not believe that simply using the organs of one's body differently can cause heritable changes in the underlying genes. If some motor neurons in a monkey's brain wither because he lost the use of two fingers, his offspring will not be born with either the fingers or the neurons missing.

For humans, however, so-called "inheritance" of intellectual traits and habits is possible, because it happens differently, says Gould. Even Darwin believed that "cultural evolution," which occurs only in human societies, causes changes in knowledge and behavior that can then be transmitted across the generations. As Gould explains it,

> Human uniqueness resides primarily in our brains. It is expressed in the culture built upon our intelligence and the power it gives us to manipulate the world. Cultural evolution can proceed so quickly because it operates, as biological evolution does not, in the "Lamarckian" mode—by the inheritance of acquired characters. Whatever one generation learns it can pass on to the next by writing, instruction, inculcation, ritual, tradition, and a host of methods that humans have developed to assure continuity in culture.[2]

Cultural evolution is not only rapid, he says, but also readily reversible from generation to generation because it is not coded in the genes. Other scientists agree that human gray matter is "capable of meeting widely varying cultural assumptions" and thus may change rather rapidly. Each generation of human brains seems to have the potential to develop new types of neural networks or find new combinations for old ones that haven't been fully tapped.

Another expert told me he explains the mental flexibility of our species as somewhat analogous to a pitcher of martinis at a cocktail party. The same (genetic) ingredients are always there—gin and vermouth—but over the course of the evening the hostess may add more of one or the other and the mixture will change slightly, although it's still a martini. The genetic basis of the human brain may be similarly constant, but its ingredients can get mixed and matched differently during the process of adaptation.

One reason inherited forms of intelligence or behavior may shift, say some scientists, is that genes can be either turned on or turned off to varying degrees by environmental demand. As a species, we have talents we probably haven't even used yet. According to Gould, human brains are "enormously complex computers" that can perform a wide variety of tasks in addition to the ones they first evolved to perform:

> I do not doubt that natural selection acted in building our oversized brains—and I am equally confident that our brains became large as an adaptation for definite roles. . . . [These complex brain] computers were built for reasons, but possess an almost terrifying array of additional capacities.[3]

Gould adds, incidentally, that evolutionary design can degenerate as well as improve.[4] Apparently, as another authority opined, our current state represents "not a package of perfection, but a package of compromises."[5] Will we continue to "improve"? By what standards can we judge?

Dr. Jerome Bruner offered a thoughtful commentary to my questions about changing brains in a technological age. "The only thing I can say with some degree of certainty," he wrote, "is that the evolution of human brain function has changed principally in response to the linkage between human beings and different tool systems. It would seem as if technology and its development leads to a new basis of selection . . . surely there must be a variety of changes in progress that resulted from writing systems, even though writing systems were introduced only a short time ago as far as we reckon evolutionary time. And now, of course, we have computers and video systems, and how long before the selection pattern changes as a result of these?"

But, he advised, we should first worry about more practical issues. "The fact of the matter is that we need a much broader distribution of high skills to run this culture than ever was needed before, and the failure to produce that distribution has been the cause of serious alienation. If we produce a two-tier society, it means in effect that we have two separate sets of evolutionary pressures operating—one within the elite group that calls for an acceleration of ability, and one within an underclass where no such pressure operates.

"See what you can make of that," he concluded.[6]

What kinds of intelligence will be most likely to produce these new forms of "high skills"? That must be the next question.

NEW INTELLIGENCES?

The cognitive skills required by the new computer technology require precise definitions, linear thinking, precise rules and algorithms for thinking and acting.

—Committee on Correspondence on the Future of Public Education[7]

We're going to have to get out of this linear model of thinking. I suppose major change is the only way we are going to break loose from the formal mind and become general systems thinkers in time for species preservation to occur. We've pretty much, for the time being, exhausted the scientific method. We've objectified life about as far as it can be objectified—and it hasn't worked. You can only go so far with the right leg, now it's time to move the left leg forward for a while.

—Dr. Dee Coulter, Naropa Institute

Obviously, no agreement exists on the nature of the "new intelligences." Many claim that mental abilities for the future must include widened perspectives, a broader range of mental skills, and a great deal of open-ended imagination to come up with solutions to the world's big problems. On the other hand, some believe we should adapt our human mentalities more closely to the precision of the machines.

One issue concerns the kinds of intelligence we should encourage in children who will live in a world where machines can do most of the mental scut work. What should we be teaching if the human brain will soon be relieved of the responsibility for doing arithmetic problems, spelling accurately, writing by hand, and memorizing data? At some time in the not-too-distant future, every student—at least in districts where funding is available—may work at a computer station where all these operations will be performed by a machine. Computerized data bases will instantly access any type of information, sort and summarize it. Word processing programs, perhaps with the aid of spelling, grammar, and punctuation checkers, and outlining programs designed to help the writer organize ideas, will enable rapid note-taking and report writing.

At some point, this equipment may become pocket-sized—a portable, permanent adjunct to the brain's memory systems. What will be important to learn then? Probably not the names and dates of the kings of England or the formula for the area of a parallelogram.

Glimpses of Electronic Learning

Some of the applications already available or on the drawing boards open astonishing windows onto future learning. If a student wants to learn about the French Revolution, for instance, here is a not-so-imaginary scenario: A program will project on her monitor screen a written and/or narrated summary of facts and events, lists and/or abstracts of relevant historical research, an animated time line of key events with a visual enactment of important scenes, set to the music of the period. She may choose to drill herself on the words of the "La Marseillaise" or some French verb tenses, or she may choose a program that lets her wander through the Louvre, browsing among relevant paintings. She might participate in a mock interview with Marat or visit the prisoners in the Bastille—in French with English translation, or vice versa. She may then choose to perfect her French vocabulary and spelling by playing a game; each time she gets an answer correct, she saves one aristocrat from the guillotine. She will then visit a French street market to use the words she has just learned in a conversation on interactive video that will also check out her accent and idioms (computers that can accurately hear and "understand" children's voices are not yet available, but there is every reason to believe they will be before too long). Or she may boot up a "simulation" in which she assumes the role of a leader on either side of the dispute, sits in on planning sessions where she makes decisions about key turning points in the Revolution, and then learns the historical consequences of her choices.

These activities, prototypes for most of which are already available, assuredly understate the possibilities of the next decade. Defining the "basics" that children will still need to master in such a world will get you a good argument among any group of educators. Maximizing the effectiveness of such technology may require well-reasoned reconsideration of some long-cherished ideas about who teaches what to whom, when, and how.

Technology will enable radical changes in teaching formats. Whether or not children will still need classrooms—or even human teachers—in the new age of instant communication is also a nice discussion-starter. With equipment developed by IBM, students even now can sit at home—or in different parts of the country (world?)—with computerized video monitors through which they communicate instantaneously with classmates and instructor. The teacher can ask a question and see an immediate tally on his screen of every student's response, so he knows immediately who is understanding and who is not. Of course, such questions tend, at least so far, to be of the multiple-choice variety. Will we still need oral language when we spend most of our time on keyboards or pushing buttons? What new sorts of perceptual or mental skills will be required? And what will happen to some of the old ones—not the least of which is interpersonal/emotional development—as the brain devotes its time and connectivity to different challenges?

Forward to the "Basics": What Will They Be?

The computer age may also promote different types of learning abilities than the ones traditionally valued and rewarded. Facility for memorization, spelling, or good handwriting may not seem all that important anymore. Some people believe these basic disciplines should still be stressed because they build up children's brains for other types of thinking, but psychologists are unsure about the generalizability of specific types of "mental exercise." It may be better, they say, to work on general reasoning ability so the child will be able to learn all types of new skills, since many—perhaps most—of the occupations they may eventually pursue haven't even been invented yet! Children clearly need to be taught habits of mental self-discipline, but no one has clearly established the best way to do so.

Will children still need oral language skills? Very likely, both for personal communication and as a foundation for reading and writing—even if it is connected with a computer screen. A recent government report entitled "Technology and the American Transition" acknowledged that all workers will need more mental flexibility than has previously been the case. Yet the "protean" mentality that will prosper in the new work force must still possess sophisticated verbal skills. "The talents needed are not clever hands or a strong back," the report concludes, "but rather the ability to understand instructions and poorly written manuals, ask questions, assimilate unfamiliar information and work with unfamiliar teams."[8]

Overall, most thoughtful people who have considered the skills that will be needed—and reinforced—in brains of the future agree that higher-level abilities will be required from everyone. Yet, according to Priscilla Vail, common definitions of what constitutes "higher-level" skills may also change. She points out that the educated person used to be one who could find information; now, with a flood of data available, the educated mind is not the one that can master the facts, but the one able to ask the "winnowing question."

"The ones who have kept alive their ability to play with patterns, to experiment—they will be the ones who can make use of what technology has to offer. Those whose focus has been on getting the correct answers to get a high score will be obsolete!"[9]

Dr. Howard Gardner has reminded us that intelligence usually gets defined in terms of which individuals can solve the problems or create the products that are valued in the culture at any given time. Brain systems for different types of intelligence are relatively discrete; improving one will not necessarily improve others (e.g., playing video games will not make children faster readers; learning the organization needed to write computer programs will probably not improve their skills in cleaning up their rooms). Moreover, when time and practice are devoted to one set of skills, space for others may be preempted. It appears as if minds that will be most valued in the future will need to have a remarkable combination of "big picture" reasoning and analytic acuity. They will be able to "see" patterns, but also communicate and interpret language accurately. Yet some believe that these two types of abilities are fundamentally at odds with each other.

DUAL ABILITIES IN THE UNIFIED MIND

It is quite possible that linear thinking, as opposed to imagery thinking, has been one of our handicaps in trying to solve [many of our] pressing worldwide problems. The mode of thinking we need . . . must help us to visualize the connections among all parts of the problem. This is where imagery is a powerful thinking tool, as it has been for scientists, including Einstein.

—Mary Alice White, Teachers College, Columbia[10]

In general the competent uses of data bases requires a careful, rather than a sloppy understanding of . . . words. We need to educate people to use the language with much greater precision than they are presently accustomed to using.

—Judah L. Schwartz, MIT[11]

Visual Literacy

A sixth-grade student nervously walks to the front of the classroom to present his research report on different types of aircraft. Inserting a video cassette into a monitor, he presses a button and the presentation begins. A series of film clips illustrates aviation scenes. As each type of plane is shown, the student reads a brief sentence introducing it, then remains silent as his classmates watch the remainder of the clip. As the video ends, a plane explodes in midair. The audience cheers. The teacher compliments the "author" on his creativity.

This "demonstration lesson" of uses of video in the classroom elicits a mixed response from school principals invited to view it. Some are delighted. "The boy showed a lot of imagination." "Endless possibilities" "Look how intent those kids were . . . they rarely listen that well!"

Others are more skeptical, particularly about the absence of extended narrative. The pictures, indeed, tell the story, but what happened to reading, writing, and reasoning? The rapt attention of the child's classmates is questioned. Is their response to the screen merely conditioned—but uncritical? Is this the shadow of the future? Should we be worried?

Excerpts from a "video encyclopedia" are shown. In one "entry" a contemporary demagogue is seen delivering a segment of an emotionally charged oration. This man is a persuader and his delivery capitalizes on body language; his views are also controversial. But no analysis accompanies this "entry"; encyclopedias are, after all, compilations of fact. This film is an accurate record of what occurred—but is it "fact"? Who can guarantee students access to opposing views? Who will show them how to ask the winnowing questions?

Video is persuasive. For immature viewers—and perhaps for mature ones as well—it pulls on emotions and evokes mood more readily than does print. Visual media are often accused of being more subjective. Their immediacy may bias against thoughtful analysis, at least for people untrained in critical viewing. A series of images may also tell a more fragmented story than the linked ideas that follow each other in a text. Certain types of visual information (e.g., television) may require less effortful processing than print media. Yet visual media are effective conveyers of some aspects of experience. Seeing film clips from a war can amplify and add perspective to reading about it in a history book. Visual images encourage intuitive response. Video presentations also have unlimited boundaries of time and space; they are free from the narrative chronology of text. Moreover, most brains tend to retain colorful visual images more readily than what they have heard or seen in print.

The growing question, of course, is whether so-called "visual literacies" could replace print. Will instruction manuals of the future rely on pictures and diagrams instead of words? Will holistic/emotional responses blot out more precise verbal/analytic forms of reasoning? Might human reasoning actually rise to higher levels if we were unencumbered by the constraints of syntax and paragraph structure? Are we on the cusp of a major alteration in the way the human brain processes information? After all, human beings have been receiving information from visual and interpersonal communication for over ten thousand years; they have only been getting it from readily available print during the last five hundred.

Thought Without Language

Should we regard rock videos replacing Shakespeare as an evolutionary advance? Does language place artificial constraints on ideas that might be liberated by nonverbal reasoning? Is thought possible without any sort of symbol system? In *The Dancing Wu Li Masters*, Gary Zukav explains how he thinks reality gets fragmented by the use of symbols—particularly words. As an example he uses *happiness*, a global state of being that cannot fairly be boiled down to a symbol. Pinning a word onto this indescribable state changes it to an abstraction, a concept, rather than a real experience. "Symbols and experience do not follow the same rules," states Zukav. "Undifferentiated reality is inexpressible." The goal of "pure awareness" sought by Eastern religions is presumably an example of transcending the need to distort understanding by trying to communicate it.

Zukav's main point is that holistic approaches to reality, which he relates to the right hemisphere of the brain, more accurately represent the principles of our physical world, exemplified in physics and mathematics. Their reality, he claims, is actually distorted by forcing them into symbols. Although he does not solve the problem of how to communicate ideas "which the poetic intuition may apprehend, but which the intellect can never fully grasp," he recommends broadening our outlook into the "higher dimensions of human experience."[12]

So-called "nonverbal thought," freed from the constraints of language, is a recognized vehicle for artists, musicians, inventors, engineers, mathematicians, and athletes.[13] Nonverbal thought is not always a poetic and undifferentiated whole, but can also relate to much more mundane matters and proceed sequentially (e.g., picturing the steps in assembling a machine or turning it over in one's mind and examining the parts or mentally rehearsing the sequence of body movements in a tennis serve). Much important experience can't be reduced to verbal descriptions. Yet in schools, traditionally, the senses have had little status after kindergarten.

"Even in engineering school, a course in 'visual thinking' is considered an aberration," says one critic who believes that too much emphasis on verbal learning places conceptual limits on inventiveness. By neglecting such studies as mechanical drawing for all students, he insists, we are cutting out a big portion of an important, and valid, form of reasoning.[14]

Can computers guide people in nonverbal reasoning? Dr. Ralph Grubb of IBM is an enthusiastic advocate of this idea. Computerized simulations of math, engineering, architectural, and scientific problems will help us get away from our "tyranny of text" and move into more visual thinking, he claims. For example, computers can now produce three-dimensional models of scientific data, graphs or representations that can enable a manager to "see" all the aspects of a complex financial situation, or simulations that allow an architect to take a visual "walk" through a building she is designing. Although, to the uninitiated, some of these simulations are totally baffling, they are doubtless the mode through which much information will be represented in the future. "Visual metaphors will strip away needless complexity and get right down to the idea," he said. "Flexibility is the key—you have to be able to shift between perspectives."[15]

When I was talking with Dr. Grubb, however, I noticed that all his examples involved mathematical, mechanical, or artistic fields. Can nonverbal metaphors also mediate the study of history? Is body language a good criterion for judging a political candidate? Perhaps we should make sure the "tyranny of text" gets supplemented rather than replaced.

Some thought certainly needs to move beyond (or remain before) words. Most people who have studied this question, however, insist that written language and the symbol systems (e.g., mathematics) should remain an important vehicle for organizing, thinking abstractly, reasoning about future as well as present, and communicating some types of information more precisely. While mathematical ideas may best be apprehended holistically, the process of thinking through a problem in a step-by-step sequence to get it down on paper confers additional advantages, not the least of which is the ability to communicate the procedures to someone else.[16]

Since much nonverbal reasoning depends on visual imagery, many people wonder what more exposure to video will do to children's abilities to gain these "higher dimensions of human experience." Although I haven't heard anyone suggest that TV has improved kids' spiritual natures, one noted drama teacher told me she sees children of the video generation as better able to handle a "multiplicity of images, less stuck in narrative chronology." "The camera is a dreamer," she pointed out, that encourages their imaginations.[17] Other teachers say just the opposite. "They have lost the ability to visualize—all their pictures have been created for them by someone else, and their thinking is limited as a result."

Curiously enough, however, visual stimulation is probably not the main access route to nonverbal reasoning. Body movements, the ability to touch, feel, manipulate, and build sensory awareness of relationships in the physical world, are its main foundations. A serious question now becomes whether children who lack spontaneous physical play and time to experiment with the world's original thought builders (e.g., sand, water, blocks, mom's measuring spoons, tree-climbing, rock-sorting, examining a seashell or the leaf of a maple tree, etc.) will be short-circuited in experimentation with nonverbal reasoning. Children who are rarely alone may well miss out on some important explorations with the "mind's eye." Frantic lifestyles do not lend themselves to imagination and reflection any more than aerobics classes for toddlers encourage manipulation of life's mysteries. Inept language usage is a serious problem, but inept insights might well be an even greater disaster.

Alphabets and Changing Brains

If (or as . . . ?) we shift our major modes of communication from books to video, handwriting to computer word processors, what happens to the evolution of the brain? Such shifts, along with changes in the related patterns of thought, have both prehistoric and historic precedent. It is generally assumed that when humans learned to speak to each other, not only habits but brains changed. The development of written language is also believed to have had cognitive consequences—or at least accompaniments. Not only does literacy, itself, change thinking, but the brain is apparently so sensitive to the input it learns to process that even different forms of the alphabet may have different effects.

The Western alphabet, in particular, has been linked to (or blamed for, as you will) our form of scientific thought and our system of formal logic. In *The Alphabet Effect*, Robert Logan points out that Eastern alphabets such as Chinese ideographs ("picture writing") and the more linear, alphabetic-phonetic patterns of the West show differences that he relates to "right-brained" and "left-brained" modes of thought. Logan suggests that while alphabetic systems cannot cause social changes, their usage encourages different types of cultural—and perhaps neural—patterns.

During the so-called Dark Ages in the West, when reading and writing diminished, many major advances in inventions and manual technologies took place. Logan implies that liberation from the written alphabet may have enabled relatively more progress in the fields of practical arts, mechanical and agricultural inventions, and the establishment of the framework of Western democracy in the Magna Carta. These, he suggests, are related to more holistic functions of the brain that were freed-up by lessened demands to process the printed word.[18]

After the invention of the printing press, academic learning was revived, and a new infatuation with the objective empiricism of the scientific method took hold. As we saw above, some now dare to question the enduring utility of this stage of the progression. Is it time for another change?

Certain specific features of alphabets may be responsible for differences in the way the brain processes them. Dr. Derrick de Kerckhove of the McLuhan program in Culture and Technology at the University of Toronto has presented evidence that Indo-European alphabets (like ours), in particular, "have promoted and reinforced reliance on left-hemisphere strategies for other aspects of psychological and social information processing." The relevant features include left-to-right progression of print, precise differentiation of vowel patterns, which tap left-hemisphere auditory areas; and linear, speech-like order of sounds. These forms may have a "reordering effect" on mental organization and even brain structure, suggests de Kerckhove.[19]

De Kerckhove, who works at the McLuhan Institute in Ontario, Canada, points out that our more abstract ways of thinking—which, he believes, do not come "naturally" to the human brain—were probably imposed, at least in part, by this particular system of writing.

The exact rendering of the writer's language afforded by our alphabet (in contrast to more open-ended symbol systems such as pictorial scripts, which allow a wider range of personal interpretation of what was said) takes the reader away from his own associations and interpretations and enables him to reach into the more abstract logic behind the writer's thinking.

If such fine-grained differences between writing systems might be able to change thinking and even the related brain structures, it seems evident that a major shift in "the ratio of the senses"(in McLuhan's words), from print to visual processing, could have even more dramatic effects.

Some observers find this possibility troubling. If print literacies get trampled under the hooves of technological innovation, what will happen to our thinking? Will we lose precision of thought along with precision of expression? Will our ability to communicate outside a face-to-face context become limited? What will happen to the disciplined analytical and inductive thinking that serve creative intuition?[20] While purely verbal thinking may, indeed, be "sterile," it is doubtless an important adjunct to higher-level reasoning and creativity.

> . . .while nonlinguistic symbol systems such as those of mathematics and art are sophisticated, they are extremely narrow. Language, in contrast, is a virtually unbounded symbol system . . . the prerequisite of culture. In sum, we do not always think in words, but we do little thinking without them.[21]

Dr. Diane Ravitch, noted scholar and educational theorist, is worried about current attitudes that imply "a longing to get away from language, as though we would all be more primitive, more spontaneous, and more joyful. Then we could read each other's body language rather than have to communicate through written devices.

"Enemies of print literacy," she admonishes, are all too ready to say, "Well, man, this is where it's happening, let's go with the flow." But blind faith that change inevitably implies progress is just as foolish as refusing to accept new ideas at all. Throwing out the precision of language would be particularly dangerous at a time when balance is badly needed. Print and visual literacies can and should complement each other; visual images open doors to new modes of understanding, but print is still necessary for thoughtful analysis.[22]

This argument will probably assume greater urgency as the computer age forces us toward more analytic precision at the same time it demands visualization of new technological applications. Tension between visual and verbal reasoning, in fact, is a major kernel of the information-age paradox. Our children will need both.

THE CHALLENGE: EXPANDING MINDS

Technology has not yet reached the point where it can guide our children's mental development—if it ever will, or should. Nor can children, without good models, shape their own brains around the intellectual habits that can make comfortable companions either of machines or their own minds in a rapidly changing world. Adults in a society have a responsibility to children—all children—to impart the habits of mental discipline and the special skills refined through centuries of cultural evolution. It is foolish to send forth unshaped mentalities to grapple with the new without equipping them with what has proven itself to be worthwhile of the old.

A prudent society controls its own infatuation with "progress" when planning for its young. Unproven technologies and changing modes of living may offer lively visions, but they can also be detrimental to the development of the young plastic brain. The cerebral cortex is a wondrously well-buffered mechanism that can withstand a good bit of well-intentioned bungling. Yet there is a point at which fundamental neural substrates for reasoning may be jeopardized for children who lack proper physical, intellectual, or emotional nurturance. Childhood—and the brain—have their own imperatives. In development, missed opportunities may be difficult to recapture.

The growing brain is vulnerable to societal as well as personal neglect. The immediate effects of ecological folly and misdirected social planning are already swelling the rolls of physically endangered brains. The more subtle legacies of television and adult expediency are being manifested in an erosion of academic and personal development for children from all walks of life. Their needs press heavily on our visions of the future.

While "progress" must be judiciously assessed, new developments are both needed and inevitable. Parents and teachers will need to broaden, perhaps even redefine, traditional parameters of intelligence and learning, not simply because of the changing priorities of future technologies but also because of present realities. This book has depicted a growing crisis in academic learning, created in large part by an alienation of children's worlds—and the mental habits engendered by them—from the traditional culture of academia.

Young brains have been modeled around skills maladaptive for learning. Merely lamenting this fact, however, does not alter the reality or rebuild the brains. Nor does choking our young with more didacticism make them learn to think.

Closing the gap between wayward synapses and intellectual imperatives will not be easy. It will certainly not be accomplished by low-level objectives, such as memorization of information, that can now be accomplished far more efficiently by even the least intelligent computer. Human brains are not only capable of acquiring knowledge; they also hold the potential for wisdom. But wisdom has its own curriculum: conversation, thought, imagination, empathy, reflection. Youth who lack these "basics," who cannot ponder what they have learned, are poorly equipped to become managers of the human enterprise in any era.

The final lesson of plasticity is that a human brain, given good foundations, can continue to adapt and expand for a lifetime. Its vast synaptic potential at birth can bend itself around what is important of the "old" and still have room for new skills demanded by a new century. A well-nourished mind, well-grounded in the precursors of wisdom as well as of knowledge, will continue to grow, learn, develop—as long as it responds to the prickling of curiosity. Perhaps this quality, above all, is the one we should strive to preserve in all our children. With it, supported by language, thought, and imagination, minds of the future will shape themselves around new challenges—whatever they may be. But if we continue to neglect either these foundations or the curiosity that sets them in motion, we will truly all be endangered.

Notes

Chapter 1: "Kid's Brains Must Be Different . . ."

1. Jackson, A., and D. Hornbeck. "Educating young adolescents." *American Psychologist* 44 (5), 1988, p. 831.
2. *Fortune*, November 7, 1988.
3. Lopez, J. "System failure." *Wall Street Journal*, March 31, 1989, p. R13.
4. Source of all SAT and GRE scores: The College Board, Educational Testing Service, Princeton, NJ.
5. Venezky, R., et al. *The Subtle Danger.* Center for the Assessment of Educational Progress, Educational Testing Service, January 1987.
6. *New York Times*, April 26, 1988.
7. Barrow, K., et al. "Achievement and the three R's: A synopsis of National Assessment findings in reading, writing, and mathematics." NAEP-SY-RWM-50, 1982 (ED 223 658).
8. Munday, L. "Changing test scores." *Phi Delta Kappan* 60, 1979, pp. 670–71.
9. *New York Times*, March 28, 1988.
10. Lapointe, A. "Is there really a national literacy crisis?" *Curriculum Review*, September/October 1987.
11. Carroll, J. "The National Assessments in reading: Are we misreading the findings?" *Phi Delta Kappan*, February 1987.
12. Manna, A., and S. Misheff. "What teachers say about their own reading development." *Journal of Reading*, November 1987, pp. 160–68.
13. Cullinan, B. *Children's Literature in the Reading Program.* Newark, DE: IRA, 1987.
14. *New York Times*, January 2, 1989.
15. Shuchman, L. "Books on tape: the latest best-sellers in Tokyo." *New York Times*, September 10, 1988.
16. Kozol, J. *Illiterate America.* New York: NAL, 1986.
17. Reed, K. "Expectation vs. ability: Junior college reading skills." *Journal of Reading*, March 1989.
18. Hechinger, F. "About education." *New York Times*, March 16, 1988.
19. Rothman, R. "NAEP releases delayed report on reading test." *Education Week*, March 2, 1988.
20. *New York Times*, December 30, 1987.
21. Eurich, A. "The reading abilities of college students—after fifty years." New York: New York Times Foundation, 1980 (ED 182 742).

22. *Education Week,* April 5, 1989, p. 1.
23. *Stanford Achievement Test,* Eighth Edition. New York: Harcourt Brace Jovanovich, 1988.
24. Cannell, J. *Nationally Normed Elementary Achievement Testing in America's Public Schools: How All Fifty States Are Above the National Average.* Daniels, WV: Friends of Education, 1987.
25. *Education Week,* April 20, 1988.
26. Valenti, J. "About historians who can't write." *New York Times,* December 11, 1987.
27. Woodward, A. "Stress on visuals weakens texts." Commentary, *Education Week,* March 9, 1988, p. 19
28. *New York Times,* April 26, 1987.
29. Flynn, J. R. "Massie IQ gains in 14 nations: What IQ tests really measure." *Psychological Bulletin* 101 (2), 1987, pp. 171–91.
30. Emanuelsson, I., and A. Svenson. "Does the level of intelligence decrease?" National Swedish Board of Education, Stockholm, 1985 (ED 262 094).
31. Lynn, R., and S. Hampson. "The rise of national intelligence." *Personality and Individual Differences* 7 (1), pp. 23–32.
32. Parker, K. "Changes with age, year-of-birth cohort, age by year-of-birth cohort interaction, and standardization of the Wechsler Adult Intelligence Tests." *Human Development* 29, 1986, pp. 209–22.
33. Franke, R. "A nation at risk? IQ and environment in the 20th century." Paper presented at the Annual Convention of the American Psychological Association, Washington, D.C., August 1986.
34. Flynn, ibid.
35. Flynn, J. R. "Sociobiology and IQ trends over time." *Behavioral and Brain Sciences* 9 (1), 1986, p. 192.
36. O'Rourke, S. Personal communication. September 1988.
37. Kirk-Alpern, P. Personal communication. September 1988.
38. Costa, A. Personal communication. June 1988.
39. Gulick, R. Personal communication. April 1988.
40. Brazelton, T. B. "First steps." *The World,* March/April 1989.
41. Luddington-Hoe, S. Personal communication. September 1989.
42. Coulter, D. Personal communication. February 1989.

CHAPTER 2: NEURAL PLASTICITY: NATURE'S DOUBLE-EDGED SWORD

1. Diamond, M. *Enriching Heredity.* New York: Free Press, 1988.
2. Diamond, M. "Enriching heredity." Address given at conference: The Education Summit. Fairfax, VA, 1988.
3. Diamond, M. Personal communication. June 1988.
4. Denenberg, V. H. "Animal models and plasticity." In Gallagher, J., and C. Ramey, eds., *The Malleability of Children.* Baltimore: Paul H. Brookes, 1987.
5. Lerner, R. *On the Nature of Human Plasticity.* New York: Cambridge University Press, 1984.
6. Lerner, R. Personal communication.
7. Scott, J. P. "Critical periods in behavioral development." *Science,* 1972, p. 957.
8. Scheibel, Arnold. "The rise of the human brain." Paper presented at symposium, "The Ever-Changing Brain." San Rafael, CA, August 1985.

9. Greenough, W. T., J. E. Black, and C. S. Wallace. "Experience and brain development." *Child Development* 58, 1987, pp. 555–67.

10. Greenough, W. T. Personal communication.

11. Bernstein, Jane Holmes. Personal communication. October 1988.

12. Bernstein, Jane Holmes. Neurological Development: Brain Maturation and Psychological Development. Unpublished manuscript.

13. Diamond, M. Personal communication. March 1989.

14. Krasnegor, N., D. Gray, and T. Thompson. *Developmental Behavioral Pharmacology.* Hillsdale, NJ: Lawrence Erlbaum Associates, 1986.

15. Elkington, John. *The Poisoned Womb.* New York: Viking Penguin, 1985.

16. Eskenazi, B. "Behavioral teratology: Toxic chemicals and the developing brain." Address given at "The Ever-Changing Brain." San Rafael, CA, 1985.

17. Eskenazi, B. Personal communication. 1987.

18. Needleman, H. "Exposure to lead at low dose in early childhood and before birth." In Krasnegor, N., D. Gray, and T. Thompson, eds., *Developmental Behavioral Pharmacology.* Hillsdale, NJ: Lawrence Erlbaum Associates, 1986, p. 169.

19. Riley, E. P., and C. V. Vorhees. *Handbook of Behavioral Teratology.* New York: Plenum Press, 1986.

20. *USA Today,* August 29, 1988, p. 1.

21. Healy, J. M. "Birth defects of the mind." *Parents,* March 1989.

22. Eskenazi, B. Personal communication. August 1987.

23. Dr. med. H. Pomp: Ev. Bethesda-Krankenhaus GmbH. Personal communication. January 1987.

24. Erik Jansson, co-ordinator of the National Network to Prevent Birth Defects. Personal communication. 1987.

25. Lauder, J., and H. Krebs. "Critical periods and neurohumors." In Greenough, W. and J. Juraska, eds., *Developmental Neuropsychobiology.* San Diego: Academic Press, 1986.

26. Fride, E., and M. Weinstock. "Prenatal stress increases anxiety-related behavior and alters cerebral lateralization of dopamine activity." *Life Sciences* 42, 1988, pp. 1059–65.

27. Kelley-Buchanan, C. *Peace of Mind During Pregnancy.* New York: Facts on File, 1988.

28. Rapin, I. "Disorders of higher cerebral function in children: New investigative techniques." *Bulletin of the Orton Society* 31, 1981, pp. 47–63.

29. Gardner, H. *Frames of Mind: The Theory of Multiple Intelligences.* New York: Basic Books, 1983.

30. Healy, J. *Your Child's Growing Mind: A Guide to Learning and Brain Development from Birth to Adolescence.* New York: Doubleday, 1987.

31. Luddington, S. "Infant developmental care." Address given at Symposium Medicus. Cleveland, OH, September 1988.

32. Smotherman, W. P. "Fetal learning in utero." Paper presented at the meeting of the International Society for Developmental Psychobiology. Baltimore, 1984.

33. De Casper, T. "Do human fetuses eavesdrop in the womb?" Paper presented at the meeting of the International Society for Developmental Psychobiology. Baltimore, 1984.

Chapter 3: Malleable Minds: Environment Shapes Intelligence

1. Kaas, J. H., M. Merzenich, and H. Killackey. "The reorganization of somatosensory cortex following peripheral nerve damage in adult and developing mammals." *Annual Review of Neuroscience* 6, 1983, pp. 325–56.
2. Epstein, H. "Growth spurts during brain development: Implications for educational policy and practice." In J. Chall and H. Mirsky, eds., *Education and the Brain.* Seventy-fifth Yearbook of the National Society for the Study of Education (Part 11). Chicago: NSSE, 1978.
3. Yakovlev, P., and A. Lecours. "The myelogenetic cycles of regional maturation of the brain." In A. Minkowski, ed., *Regional Development of the Brain in Early Life.* Oxford: Blackwell Scientific Publications, 1967.
4. Renner, M., and M. Rosenzweig. *Enriched and Impoverished Environments: Effects on Brain and Behavior.* New York: Springer Verlag, 1987, p. 13.
5. Globus, A., et al. "Effects of differential experience on dendritic spine counts in rat cerebral cortex." *Journal of Comparative and Physiological Psychology* 82, 1972, pp. 175–81.
6. Greenough, W. T., Black, J. E., and C. S. Wallace. "Experience and brain development." *Child Development* 58, 1987, p. 547.
7. Diamond, M. *Enriching Heredity.* New York: The Free Press, 1988.
8. Diamond, M., et al. "On the brain of a scientist: Albert Einstein." *Experimental Neurology* 88, 1985, pp. 198–204.
9. Bernstein, Jane Holmes. Personal communication. October 1988.
10. Scheibel, A. Personal communication. August 1984.
11. Bornstein, M. H., ed. *Sensitive Periods in Development.* Hillsdale, NJ: Lawrence Erlbaum Associates, 1987.
12. Hirsch, H., and S. Tieman. "Perceptual development and experience-dependent changes in cat visual cortex." In Bornstein, M. H., ed., *Sensitive Periods in Development.* Hillsdale, NJ: Lawrence Erlbaum Associates, 1987, p. 70.
13. Bornstein, M. H. Op. cit.
14. Buchwald, J. S. "A comparison of plasticity in sensory and cognitive processing systems." In N. Gunzenhauser, ed., *Infant Stimulation.* Somerville, NJ: Johnson & Johnson, 1987, p. 9.
15. Ibid., p. 27.
16. Bornstein, M. H., ed. Op. cit., p. 169.
17. Edelman, G. M. *Neural Darwinism.* New York: Basic Books, 1987.
18. Ibid., p. 165.

Chapter 4: Who's Teaching the Children to Talk?

1. Luria, A. "The role of speech in the formation of temporary connections and the regulation of behavior in the normal and oligophrenic child." In B. Simon and J. Simon, eds., *Educational Psychology in the USSR.* Stanford: Stanford University Press, 1968, p. 85.
2. Bruner, J. *Actual Minds, Possible Worlds.* Cambridge: Harvard University Press, 1986, p. 8.
3. Hamilton, A. J. "Challenging verbal passivity." *NEATE Leaflet* 85 (1), 1986, p. 22.
4. Gigioli, P., ed. *Language and Social Context.* Baltimore: Penguin Books, 1972.

5. Postman, N. *Amusing Ourselves to Death*. New York: Elizabeth Sifton Viking, 1985, p. 112.
6. Geyer, G. "Words bounce blame." *Cleveland Plain Dealer*, September 17, 1988.
7. Wells, G. *Language, Learning, and Education*. Windsor, Berkshire, England: NFER-NELSON, 1985, pp. 102–3.
8. Schieffelin, B., and E. Ochs. "Language socialization." *Annual Review of Anthropology* 15, 1986, pp. 163–91.
9. Schieffelin, B. Personal communication. August 1988.
10. Olson, S., et al. "Mother-child interaction and children's speech progress: A longitudinal study of the first two years." *Merrill Palmer Quarterly* 32 (1), 1986, pp. 1–20.
11. Rinders, J., and M. Horrobin. "To give an EDGE: A guide for new parents of children with Down Syndrome." Minneapolis: Colwell Industries, 1984.
12. Wells, G. Op. cit., p. 135.
13. Squire, J. *The Dynamics of Language Learning*. NCRE/ERIC, 1987.
14. Kuczaj, S. A. "On the nature of syntactic development." In Kuczaj, S. A., ed., *Language Development* (vol. 1). Hillsdale, NJ: Lawrence Erlbaum Associates, 1982.
15. Bohannon, J., and L. Stanowicz. "The issue of negative evidence: Adult responses to children's language errors. *Developmental Psychology* 24 (5), 1988.
16. Zigler, E., and M. Frank, eds. *The Parental Leave Crisis*. New Haven: Yale University Press, 1988.
17. Dumtschin, J. "Recognize language development and delay in early childhood." *Young Children*, March 1988, p. 20.
18. Schieffelin, B. Personal communication. September 1988.
19. Wells, G., op. cit., p. 117.
20. Dunning, B. "Doesn't anybody here talk English any more?" *Cleveland Plain Dealer*, January 28, 1988.
21. Vail, P. *Clear and Lively Writing*. New York: Walker & Co., 1981.
22. Vail, P. *Smart Kids With School Problems*. New York: NAL, 1989.
23. Pratt, A., and S. Brady. "Phonological awareness and reading disability." *Journal of Educational Psychology* 80 (3), 1988, pp. 319–23.

CHAPTER 5: SAGGING SYNTAX, SLOPPY SEMANTICS, AND FUZZY THINKING

1. Mandelbaum, D. G. *Selected Writings of Edward Sapir in Language, Culture and Personality*. Berkeley: University of California Press, 1958.
2. Whorf, B. *Language, Thought and Reality*. Cambridge: MIT Press, 1956.
3. Tyler, S. *The Said and the Unsaid*. New York: Academic Press, 1978.
4. Blount, B., and M. Sanches. *Sociocultural Dimensions of Language Change*. New York: Academic Press, 1977.
5. Luria, A. *Language and Cognition*. New York: Wiley, 1982.
6. Vocate, D. *The Theory of A. R. Luria*. Hillsdale, NJ: Lawrence Erlbaum Associates, 1987, p. 29.
7. Premack, D. "Minds with and without language." In L. Weiskrantz, ed., *Thought Without Language*. Oxford: Clarendon Press, 1988.
8. Cohen, M., and S. Grossberg. "Neural dynamics of speech and language coding." *Human Neurobiology* 5 (1), 1986, pp. 1–22.
9. Siegel, L., and E. Ryan. "Development of grammatical-sensitivity, phonological

and short-term memory skills in normally achieving and learning disabled children." *Developmental Psychology* 24 (1), 1988, pp. 28–37.

10. Dennis, M. "Using language to parse the young damaged brain."*Journal of Clinical and Experimental Neuropsychology* 9 (6), 1987, pp. 723–53.

11. "Students said to lack writing skills." *New York Times*, December 4, 1986.

12. Benbow, C. "Neuropsychological perspectives on mathematical talent." In L. Obler and D. Fine, eds., *The Exceptional Brain*. New York: Guilford Press, 1988.

13. Orr, E. W. *Twice as Less*. New York: Norton, 1987.

14. Miura, I., and Y. Okamoto. "Comparisons of US and Japanese first graders' cognitive representation of number and understanding of place value." *Journal of Educational Psychology* 81 (1), 1989, pp. 109–13.

15. Sachs, J., Bard, B., and M. Johnson. "Language learning with restricted input." *Applied Psycholinguistics* 2, 1981, pp. 33–54.

16. Newport, E. "Maturation and language acquisition: Contrasting conceptualizations of critical periods for learning." Address given at annual conference: Jean Piaget Society. Philadelphia, June 1988.

17. Kay, P. "Language evolution and speech style." In Blount, B., and M. Sanches, eds., *Sociocultural Dimensions of Language Change*. New York: Academic Press, 1977.

18. Vocate, D. Op. cit., p. 19.

19. Gleitman, L. "Biological preprogramming for language learning?" In S. Friedman, K. Klivingdon, and R. Peterson, eds., *The Brain, Cognition, and Education*. New York: Academic Press, 1986.

20. Baker, R. "Swine by design." *New York Times*, October 2, 1988.

21. "Sassy: Like, you know, for kids." *New York Times*, September 18, 1988.

CHAPTER 6: LANGUAGE CHANGES BRAINS

1. Readers who may wish more amplification of hemispheric research as it relates to children may consult: Best, C. *Hemispheric Function and Collaboration in the Child*. New York: Academic Press, 1985. Molfese, D., and S. Segalowitz. *Brain Lateralization in Children: Developmental Implications*. New York: Guilford Press, 1988.

2. Snow, C. "Relevance of the notion of a critical period to language acquisition." In M. H. Bornstein, ed., *Sensitive Periods in Development*. Hillsdale, NJ: Lawrence Erlbaum Associates, 1987.

3. Witelson, S. "Neurobiologic aspects of language in children." *Child Development* 58, 1988, pp. 653–88.

4. Dennis, M., and H. Whitaker. "Language acquisition following hemidecortication: Linguistic superiority of left over the right hemisphere." *Brain and Language* 3, 1976, pp. 404–33.

5. Curtiss, S. "The special talent of grammar acquisition." In Obler, L., and D. Fine, eds., *The Exceptional Brain*. New York: Guilford Press, 1988.

6. Levine, S. "Hemispheric specialization and implications for the education of the hearing impaired." *American Annals of the Deaf* 131 (3), 1986, pp. 238–42.

7. Marcotte, A., and R. La Barba. "The effects of linguistic experience on cerebral lateralization for speech production in normal hearing and deaf adolescents. *Brain and Language* 31, 1987, pp. 276–300.

8. Neville, H., et al. "Altered visual-evoked potentials in congenitally deaf adults." *Brain Research* 226, 1983, pp. 127–32.

9. Neville, H. Personal communication. March 1989.

10. Simonds, R., and A. Scheibel. "The postnatal development of the motor speech area: A preliminary study." *Brain and Language*. In press.

11. Scheibel, A. Personal communication. June 1989.

12. Almli, C. R., and S. Finger. "Neural insult and critical period concepts." In M. H. Bornstein, ed., *Sensitive Periods in Development*. Hillsdale, NJ: Lawrence Erlbaum Associates, 1987.

13. Witelson, S. Personal communication. November 1988.

Chapter 7: Learning Disabilities: Neural Wiring Goes to School

1. Ohio ACLD Newsletter. Spring 1988.

2. Wang, M. C. "Commentary." *Education Week,* May 4, 1988.

3. *ACLD Newsbriefs* 24 (1), January 1989, p. 12.

4. McGuinness, D. "Attention deficit disorder: The emperor's clothes, animal farm and other fiction." In S. Fisher and R. P. Greenberg, eds., *How Effective Are Somatic Treatments for Psychological Problems?* New York: Erlbaum. In press.

5. Lyytinen, H. "Attentional problems in children: Review of psychophysiological findings relevant to explaining their nature." Paper given at Annual Meeting, International Neuropsychological Society. Lahti, Finland, July 1988.

6. Yang, L. L., et al. "Perinatal hypoxia and cognitive functioning in relation to behavioral development of children." Paper given at Annual Meeting, International Neuropsychological Society. Lahti, Finland, July 1988.

7. Eichlseder, W. "Ten years' experience with 1,000 hyperactive children in a private practice." *The American Academy of Pediatrics* 76, 1985, pp. 176–84.

8. "Debate grows on classroom's 'Magic Pill.'" *Education Week*, October 21, 1987.

9. McGuinness, D. *When Children Don't Learn*. New York: Basic Books, 1985.

10. Obler, L. K., and D. Fein, eds. *The Exceptional Brain*. New York: Guilford Press, 1988, p. 7.

11. Pennington, B. "Genotype and phenotype analysis of familial dyslexia." Address presented at the Annual Meeting of the Orton Dyslexia Society. Tampa, FL, November 1988.

12. Vail, P. *Smart Kids with School Problems*. New York: Dutton, 1987.

13. Duffy, F., and N. Geshwind. *Dyslexia*. Boston: Little Brown, 1985.

14. Obler, L. K., and D. Fein, eds. Op. cit.

15. Geshwind, N. "The brain of a learning disabled individual." *Annals of Dyslexia* 34, 1984.

16. Geshwind, N., and P. Behan. "Left-handedness: Association with immune disease, migraine, and developmental learning disorder." Proceedings of the National Academy of Sciences, USA, 79, 1982, pp. 5097–5100.

17. Galaburda, A. Personal communication. November 1988.

18. Galaburda, A. "Ordinary and extraordinary brains: Nature, nurture, and dyslexia." Address presented at the Annual Meeting of the Orton Dyslexia Society. Tampa, FL, November 1988.

19. Duane, D. D. "Dyslexia: pure and plus: A model behavioral syndrome." Address presented at the Annual Meeting of the Orton Dyslexia Society. Tampa, FL, November 1988.

20. Rourke, B. "The syndrome of nonverbal learning disorders." *The Clinical Neuropsychologist* 2 (4), 1988, pp. 293–330.
21. Potchen, E. J. "Disorders of the language system including dyslexia and learning disabilities." Address presented at the Annual Meeting of the Orton Dyslexia Society. Tampa, FL, November 1988.

CHAPTER 8: WHY CAN'T THEY PAY ATTENTION?

1. Aubin, M. Personal communication. October 1988.
2. Picton, T., et al. "Attention and the brain." In S. Friedman et al., *The Brain, Cognition, and Education*. New York: Academic Press, 1986.
3. Posner, M. "Attention and the control of cognition." In S. Friedman et al., op. cit.
4. Johnston, W., and V. Dark. "Selective attention." *Annual Review of Psychology* 37, 1986, pp. 43–75.
5. Ceci, S., ed. *Handbook of Cognitive, Social, and Neuropsychological Aspects of Learning Disabilities*, Vol. II. Hillsdale, NJ: Lawrence Erlbaum Associates, 1987.
6. Whalen, C., and B. Henker. *Hyperactive Children*. New York: Academic Press, 1980.
7. Bigler, N., et al. "Educational perspectives on attention deficit disorder." Paper presented at the international ACLD Conference. Las Vegas, February 1988.
8. Whalen, C., and B. Henker. *Hyperactive Children*. New York: Academic Press, 1980.
9. Kirby, E., and L. Grimley. *Understanding and Treating Attention Deficit Disorder*. New York: Pergamon, 1986.
10. Pelham, W. "The combination of behavior therapy and methylphenidate in the treatment of attention deficit disorders: A therapy outcome study." In L. Bloomingdale, ed., *Attention Deficit Disorder*, Vol 3. Oxford: Pergamon, 1988.
11. Silver, L. "The confusion relating to Ritalin." *ACLD Newsbriefs*, September 1988.
12. McGuinness, D. *When Children Don't Learn*. New York: Basic Books, 1985, pp. 200–201.
13. Cohen, N. "Physiological concomitants of attention in hyperactive children." Unpublished Ph.D. dissertation, McGill University, 1970.
14. Barkley, R. "Attention-deficit hyperactivity disorder." Address presented at symposium: The Many Faces of Intelligence. Washington, D.C., Kingsbury Center, September 1988.
15. Barkley, R. "An overview of attention deficit and related disorders in childhood and adolescence." Address presented at course: Neurodevelopment and Its Implications for Attention, Emotion, and Cognition: California Neuropsychology Services. Long Beach, CA, November 1988.
16. Jacobvitz, D., and L. Sroufe. "The early caregiver-child relationship and attention deficit disorder with hyperactivity in kindergarten: A prospective study." *Child Development* 58, 1987, pp. 1496–1504.
17. Mattson, A., et al. "40 Hertz EEG activity in LD and normal children." Poster presentation, International Neuropsychological Society. Vancouver, BC, February 1989.

18. Best, C. T., ed. *Hemispheric Function and Collaboration in the Child*. New York: Academic Press, 1985.

19. Welsh, M., and B. Pennington. "Assessing frontal lobe functioning in children: Views from developmental psychology." *Developmental Neuropsychology* 4 (3), 1988, pp. 199–230.

20. Brody, J. "Widespread abuse of drugs by pregnant women is found." *New York Times*, August 30, 1988.

21. *Education Week*, June 1, 1988.

22. "Get the lead out of your water." *PTA Today*, February 1988.

23. *New York Times*, April 12, 1989, p. 1.

24. Hartman, D. *Neuropsychological Toxicology*. New York: Pergamon, 1988.

25. Flax, E. "Pesticides in schools: Focus shifting from indifference to concern." *Education Week*, April 20, 1988.

26. "In California district, chemicals are used as last resort." *Education Week*, April 20, 1988.

27. Levine, A., and D. Krahn. "Food and behavior." In Morley, J., et al., eds., *Nutritional Modulation of Neural Functioning*. New York: Academic Press, 1988.

28. Wurtman, R., and J. Wurtman. *Nutrition and the Brain*, vols. 4, 6, and 7. New York: Raven, 1979, 1983, 1986.

29. Winick, M. *Nutrition in Health and Disease*. New York: Wiley, 1980.

30. Winick, M. *Malnutrition and Brain Development*. New York: Oxford University Press, 1976.

31. Kane, P. *Food Makes the Difference*. New York: Simon and Schuster, 1985.

32. Chollar, S. "Food for thought." *Psychology Today*, April 1988, pp. 30–34.

33. Conners, K. *Feeding the Brain: How Foods Affect Children*. New York: Plenum Press, 1989.

34. Conners, K. "The phenomenology and neurophysiology of attention: Foods, drugs and attention in children." Address presented at course: Neurodevelopment and Its Implications for Attention, Emotion, and Cognition: California Neuropsychology Services. Long Beach, CA, November 1988.

35. Wurtman, R., and E. Ritter-Walker. *Dietary Phenylalanine and Brain Function*. Boston: Birkhauser, 1988.

36. *Nation's School Report* 14 (2), 1988.

37. "Army softens basic training." *Cleveland Plain Dealer*, April 17, 1989, p. 1.

38. Allen, G. "Why we need to improve youth fitness." *PTA Today*, February 1987.

39. *Nation's School Report* 14 (2), 1988.

40. Miller, N., and L. Melamed. "Neuropsychological correlates of academic achievement." Poster presentation, International Neuropsychological Society. Vancouver, BC, February 1989.

41. Phillips, S. "The toddler and the preschooler." Unit for Child Studies, Selected Papers no. 29, New South Wales University, 1984 (ED 250 097).

42. Ayres, A. J. *Sensory Integration and Learning Disorders*. Los Angeles Western Psychological Services, 1972.

43. Ayres, A. J. "Improving academic scores through integration." *Journal of Learning Disabilities* 11, 1978, pp. 242–45.

44. Weikart, P. *Round the Circle: Key Experiences in Movement*. Ypsilanti, MI: High Scope Press, 1986.

45. Weikart, P. Personal communication. November 1988.

46. Mills, J. "Noise and children." *Journal of the Acoustical Society of America* 58 (4), 1975, p. 776.

47. Deutsch, D., ed. *The Psychology of Music*. New York: Academic Press, 1982.

48. Breitling, D., et al. "Auditory perception of music measured by brain electrical activity mapping." *Neuropsychologia* 25 (5), 1987, pp. 765–74.

49. Pareles, J. "What'd they say? A wop-bop a loo-bop." *New York Times*, August 8, 1988.

50. Pareles, J. "New-age music booms softly." *New York Times*, November 29, 1988.

51. Zentall, S., and T. Zentall. "Optimal stimulation: A model of disordered activity and performance in normal and deviant children." *Psychological Bulletin* 94 (3), 1983, pp. 446–71.

52. Luddington-Hoe, S. "Infant development and care." Symposium sponsored by Symposia Medicus. Cleveland, November 1988.

53. Levy, J. Personal communication. November 1988.

54. Schreckenberg, G., and H. Bird. "Neural plasticity of MUS musculus in response to disharmonic sound." *Bulletin of the New Jersey Academy of Sciences* 32, 1987, pp. 77–86.

CHAPTER 9: THE STARVING EXECUTIVE

1. Posner, M., and F. Friedrich. "Attention and the control of cognition." In Klivington et al., eds., *The Brain, Cognition, and Education*. New York: Academic Press, 1986, p. 100.

2. Denckla, M. Personal communication. September 1988.

3. Snyder, V. "Use of self-monitoring of attention with LD students: Research and application." *Learning Disability Quarterly* 10 (2), 1987, pp. 139–51.

4. Palfrey et al. "The emergence of attention deficits in early childhood: A prospective study." *Developmental and Behavioral Pediatrics* 6 (6), 1986, pp. 339–348.

5. Lambert, N. "Adolescent outcomes for hyperactive children." *American Psychologist* 43 (10), 1988, pp. 786–99.

6. Pollard, S., et al. "The effects of parent training and Ritalin on the parent-child interactions of hyperactive boys." *Family and Behavior Therapy* 5 (4), 1983, pp. 51–69.

7. Barkley, R. "What is the role of parent group training in the treatment of ADD children?" *Journal of Children in Contemporary Society* 19 (1, 2), 1986, pp. 143–51.

8. Rapport, M. "Ritalin vs. response cost in the control of hyperactive children: A within-subject comparison." *Journal of Applied Behavior Analysis* 15 (2), 1982, pp. 205–16.

9. Wells, K. "What do we know about the use and effects of behavior therapies in the treatment of ADD?" *Journal of Children in Contemporary Society* 19 (1, 2), 1986, pp. 111–22.

10. Paternite, C., and J. Loney. "Childhood hyperkinesis and home environment." In C. Whalen and B. Henker, eds., *Hyperactive Children*. New York: Academic Press, 1980.

11. Campbell, W., et al. "Correlates and predictors of hyperactivity and aggression." *Journal of Abnormal Child Psychology* 14 (2), 1986, pp. 217–34.

12. Meichenbaum, D. *Cognitive-Behavior Modification: An Integrative Approach*. New York: Plenum, 1977.
13. Vocate, D. R. *The Theory of A. R. Luria*. Hillsdale, NJ: Lawrence Erlbaum Associates, 1987, p. 136.
14. Vygotsky, L. *Thought and Language*. A. Kozulin, ed. Cambridge: MIT Press, 1986.
15. Ibid., p. 228.
16. Waters, H., and V. Tinsley. "The development of verbal self-regulation." In Kuczai, S., ed., *Language Development*, Vol 2. Hillsdale, NJ: Lawrence Erlbaum Associates, 1982.
17. Ibid.
18. Duckworth, E. "Understanding children's understandings." Paper presented at the Ontario Institute for Studies in Education. Toronto, 1981, pp. 51–52.
19. Cazden, C. *Classroom Discourse*. Portsmouth, New Hampshire: Heineman, 1988, p. 102.
20. Bruner, J. *Actual Minds, Possible Worlds*. Cambridge: Harvard University Press, 1986.
21. Rakic, P., and P. Goldman-Rakic. Development and modifiability of the cerebral cortex." *Neurosciences Research Program Bulletin* 20 (4), 1982.
22. Noava, O., and A. Ardilla. "Linguistic abilities in patients with prefrontal damage." *Brain and Language* 30, 1987, pp. 206–25.
23. Goldman-Rakic, P. "Development of cortical circuitry and cognitive function." *Child Development* 58, pp. 601–22.
24. Becker, M., Isaac, W., and G. Hynd. "Neuropsychological development of nonverbal behaviors attributed to frontal lobe functioning." *Developmental Neuropsychology* 3 (3, 4), 1987, pp. 275–98.
25. Welsh, M., and B. Pennington. "Assessing frontal-lobe functioning in children." *Developmental Neuropsychology* 4 (3), 1988, pp. 199–230.
26. Friedman, S., K. Klivington, and R. Peterson. *The Brain, Cognition, and Education*. New York: Academic Press, 1986.
27. Klivington, K. Personal communication. August 1988.

CHAPTER 10: TV, VIDEO GAMES, AND THE GROWING BRAIN

1. e.g., Palmer, E. *Television and American Children: A Crisis of Neglect*. New York: Oxford University Press, 1988. Greenfield, P. *Mind and Media*. Cambridge: Harvard University Press, 1984.
2. Fox, N., and M. Fanyo. "Turn off the television and turn on reading." *Reading Today*, April/May 1988, p. 11.
3. Winick, M., and J. Wehrenberg. *Children and TV Two*. Washington: ACEI, 1982.
4. Walberg, H., and T. Shanahan. "High school effects on individual students." *Educational Researcher* 12 (7), 1983, pp. 4–9.
5. Winn, M. *Unplugging the Plug-In Drug*. New York: Penguin, 1987.
6. Liebert, R., and J. Sprafkin. *The Early Window*. New York: Pergamon, 1988.
7. Languis, M., and M. Wittrock. "Integrating neuropsychological and cognitive research: A perspective for bridging the brain-behavior relationship." In J. Obrzut and G. Hynd, eds., *Child Neuropsychology*, vol. 1. New York: Academic Press, 1986.

8. Anderson, D., and P. Collins. *The impact on children's education: Television's influence on cognitive development.* Office of Educational Research and Improvement, U.S. Department of Education, April 1988, p. 34.

9. Anderson, D. Personal communication. March 1989.

10. Singer, J. Personal communication. March 1989.

11. Beentjes, J., and T. Van der Voort. "Television's impact on children's reading skills: A review of research." *Reading Research Quarterly* 23 (4), 1988, pp. 389–413.

12. Goleman, D. "Infants under 2 seem to learn from TV." *New York Times,* November 22, 1988.

13. Liebert, R., and J. Sprafkin. *The Early Window.* New York: Pergamon, 1988.

14. Reeves, B., et al. "Attention to television: Intrastimulus effects of movement and scene changes on alpha variation over time." *International Journal of Neuroscience* 27, 1985, pp. 241–55.

15. Moody, K. *Growing Up on Television.* New York: Times Books, 1980.

16. Mander, J. *Four Arguments for the Elimination of Television.* New York: Morrow Quill, 1978.

17. Emery, F., and M. Emery. *A Choice of Futures: To Enlighten or Inform?* Canberra: Center for Continuing Education, Australian National University, 1975.

18. Anderson, D., and P. Collins. Op. cit., p. 52.

19. Reeves, B. Personal communication. March 1989.

20. Bryant, J. Personal communication. March 1989.

21. Anderson, D. "The influence of television on children's attentional abilities." Paper commissioned by Children's Television Workshop, University of Massachusetts, 1985.

22. Anderson, D., and P. Collins. Op. cit., p. 34.

23. Ibid., p. 65.

24. Krugman, H. "Brain wave measures of media involvement." *Journal of Advertising Research* 2 (1), 1971, pp. 3–9.

25. Emery, M., and F. Emery. "The vacuous vision: The TV medium." *Journal of University Film Association* 32 (1, 2), 1980, pp. 27–31.

26. Mulholand, T. "Objective EEG methods for studying covert shifts in visual attention." In F. J. McGuigan and R. Schoonover, eds., *The Psychophysiology of Thinking.* New York: Academic Press, 1973.

27. Featherman, G., et al. *Electroencephalographic and Electrooculographic Correlates of Television Viewing.* Final Technical Report: National Science Foundation Student-Oriented Studies. Amherst: Hampshire College, 1979.

28. Walker, J. "Changes in EEG rhythms during television viewing." *Perceptual and Motor Skills* 51, 1980, pp. 255–61.

29. Radlick, M. "The processing demands of television." Unpublished doctoral dissertation. Troy, NY: Rensselaer Polytechnic Institute, 1980.

30. Burns, J., and D. Anderson. "Cognition and watching television." In D. Tupper and K. Cicerone, eds., *Neuropsychology of Everyday Life.* Boston: Kluwer, in press.

31. Yosawitz, A. Personal communication. February 1989.

32. Turkle, S. *The Second Self: Computers and the Human Spirit.* New York: Simon and Schuster, 1984.

33. Bracy, O., et al. "Cognitive Retaining Through Computers: Fact or Fad?" *Cognitive Rehabilitation*, March 1985, pp. 10–23.

34. Siegel, L. Personal communication, February 1989.

35. Harter, R. Personal communication. March 1989.

36. Singer, J. "The power and limitations of television: A cognitive-affective analysis." In P. Tannenbaum, ed., *The Entertainment Functions of Television*. Hillsdale, NJ: Lawrence Erlbaum Associates, 1980, p. 61.

37. Winn, M. *The Plug-In Drug*. New York: Viking Press, 1977, pp. 42, 47.

38. Emery, M., and F. Emery. "The vacuous vision: The TV medium." *Journal of the University Film Association* 32 (1, 2), 1980, p. 30.

39. See, e.g., S. Weinstein et al., "Brain-activity responses to magazine and television advertising." *Journal of Advertising Research* 20 (3), 1980, pp. 57–63.

40. Springer, S., and G. Deutsch. *Left Brain, Right Brain*, revised edition. New York: W. H. Freeman, 1985.

41. Kirk, U. *Neuropsychology of Language, Reading, and Spelling*. New York: Academic Press, 1983.

42. Calvert et al. "The relation between selective attention to television forms and children's comprehension of content." *Child Development* 53, 1982, pp. 601–10.

43. de Kerckhove, D. "Critical brain processes." In D. de Kerckhove and C. Lumsden, eds., *The Alphabet and the Brain*. Berlin: Springer-Verlag, 1988, p. 417.

44. Ibid. General Introduction.

45. Maehara, K., et al. "Handedness in the Japanese." *Developmental Neuropsychology* 4 (2), 1988, pp. 117–27.

46. Springer, S., and G. Deutsch. *Left Brain, Right Brain*, revised edition. New York: W. H. Freeman, 1985.

47. Neville, H., et al. "ERP studies of cerebral specialization during reading." *Brain and Language* 16, 1982, pp. 316–37.

48. Bakker, D., and J. Vinke. "Effects of hemisphere-specific stimulation on brain activity and reading in dyslexics." *Journal of Clinical and Experimental Neuropsychology* 7 (5), 1985, pp. 505–25.

49. Bakker, D. "The brain as a dependent variable." *Journal of Clinical Neuropsychology* 6 (1), 1984, pp. 1–16.

50. Bakker, D., and S. Glaude. "Prediction and prevention of L- and P-type dyslexia." Poster Session, Annual Meeting: International Neuropsychological Society. Vancouver, BC, February 1989.

51. Heller, W. Personal communication. April 1989.

52. Best, C. *Hemispheric Function and Collaboration in the Child*. New York: Academic Press, 1985.

53. Witelson, S., and D. Kigar. "Anatomical development of the corpus callosum in humans." In D. Molfese and S. Segalowitz, eds., *Brain Lateralization in Children: Developmental Implications*. New York: Guilford Press, 1988.

54. Levy, J. "Single-mindedness in the asymmetric brain." In Best, op. cit., p. 27.

55. Levy, J. Personal communication. November 1989.

56. Segalowitz, S. Personal communication. February 1989.

57. Welsh, M., and K. Cuneo. "Perseveration in young children." Poster session, Annual Meeting: International Neuropsychological Society. Vancouver, BC, February 1989.

CHAPTER 11: *SESAME STREET* AND THE DEATH OF READING

1. Katz, L. *Engaging Children's Minds*. Norwood, NJ: Ablex, 1989.
2. Katz, L. "Engaging children's minds." Address presented at Annual Meeting, National Association of Independent Schools. Chicago, March 1989.
3. *Sesame Street*. Morning edition, National Public Radio, December 1988.
4. Kaufman, F., vice president for public affairs, Children's Television Workshop. Personal communication. March 1989.
5. *Education Week*, June 15, 1988, p. 5.
6. Mielke, K., vice president for research, Children's Television Workshop. Personal communication. March, 1989.
7. Benbow, M. "Development of handwriting." Lecture presented at Smith College Day School. Northampton, MA, October 1989.
8. Healy, J. *Your Child's Growing Mind*. New York: Doubleday, 1989.
9. Beck, I., and P. Carpenter. "Cognitive approaches to word reading." *American Psychologist* 41 (10), 1986, pp. 1098–1105.
10. Beck, I., and P. Carpenter. "Cognitive approaches to understanding reading." *American Psychologist* 41 (10), 1986, pp. 1098–1105.
11. Lundberg, I., and T. Hoien. "Case studies of reading development among normal and disabled readers in Scandinavia." Paper presented at 39th Annual Conference, Orton Dyslexia Society. Tampa, FL, November 1988.
12. Rice, M., and P. Haight. " 'Motherese' of Mr. Rogers: A description of the dialogue of educational television programs." *Journal of Speech and Hearing Disorders* 51, 1986, pp. 282–87.
13. Jensen, J., and D. Neff. "Differential maturation of auditory abilities in preschool children." Paper presented Annual Meeting: International Neuropsychological Society. Vancouver, BC, February 1989.
14. Jensen, J. Personal communication. February 1989.
15. Wood, K., and L. Richman. "Developmental trends within memory-deficient reading-disability subtypes." *Developmental Neuropsychology* 4 (4), 1988, pp. 261–74.
16. Rice, M., and L. Woodsmall. "Lessons from television." *Child Development* (in press).
17. Singer, J. "The power and limitations of television: A cognitive-affective analysis." In P. Tannenbaum, ed., *The Entertainment Functions of Television*. Hillsdale, NJ: Lawrence Erlbaum Associates, 1980.
18. Rice, M., et al. *Words from Sesame Street: Learning Vocabulary while Viewing*. Lawrence: University of Kansas Press, in press.
19. Cook, T., et al. *Sesame Street Revisited*. New York: Russell Sage, 1975.
20. Aulls, M. "Research into practice." *Reading Today,* February 3, 1988, p. 6.
21. Postman, N. *Amusing Ourselves to Death*. New York: Elizabeth Sifton/Viking, 1985.
22. *Statement of instructional goals for the twentieth experimental season of* Sesame Street (1988–89).
23. Meringoff, L. "Influence of the medium on children's story apprehension." *Journal of Educational Psychology* 72, 1980, pp. 240–49.
24. Tamis-LeMonda, C., and M. Bornstein. "Is there a 'sensitive period' in human mental development?" In M. Bornstein, ed., *Sensitive Periods in Development*. Hillsdale: NJ: Lawrence Erlbaum Associates, 1987.

25. Halpern, W. "Turned-on toddlers." *Journal of Communication*, Autumn 1975, pp. 66–70.
26. Singer, J., ibid., p. 55.
27. Singer, ibid., p. 54.
28. Ibid., p. 55.
29. Burns, J., and D. Anderson. "Cognition and watching television." In D. Tupper and K. Cicerone, eds., *Neuropsychology of Everyday Life*. Boston: Kluwer, in press.
30. Pressley, M., et al. "Short term memory, verbal competence, and age as predictors of imagery instructional effectiveness." *Journal of Experimental Child Psychology* 43, 1987, pp. 194–211.
31. Greenfield, P., et al. "Is the medium the message?" *Journal of Applied Developmental Psychology* 7, 1986, pp. 201–18.
32. *Sesame Street*. Morning edition, National Public Radio, December 1988.

Chapter 12: "Disadvantaged" Brains

1. Lerner, R., and K. Hood. "Plasticity in development: Concepts and issues for intervention." *Journal of Applied Developmental Psychology* 7, 1986, pp. 139–52.
2. *Education Week*, February 22, 1989, p. 15.
3. Winick, M., et al. "Malnutrition and environmental enrichment by early adoption." *Science* 190, 1975, pp. 1173–86.
4. Hechinger, F. "A better start." Address given at Annual Meeting, National Association of Independent Schools. New York, February 1988.
5. Brooks, A. "Children of fast-track parents." Address given at Annual Meeting, National Association of Independent Schools. New York, February 1988.
6. Brooks, A. *Children of Fast-Track Parents*, New York: Viking, 1989.
7. Brooks, A. Personal communication. March 1989.
8. *New York Times*, December 26, 1988.
9. Brislin, R. W. "Human diversity: Race, culture, class, and ethnicity." G. Stanley Hall Address presented at Annual Meeting, American Psychological Association. New York, August 1987.
10. Cazden, C. *Classroom Discourse*. Portsmouth, NH: Heinemann, 1988.
11. Havighurst, R. "The relative importance of social class and ethnicity in human development." *Human Development* 19, 1976, pp. 56–64.
12. Graham, S. "Can attribution theory tell us something about motivation in blacks?" *Educational Psychologist* 23 (1), 1988, pp. 3–21.
13. Largo, R., et al. "Language development of term and preterm children during the first five years of life." *Developmental Medicine and Child Neurology* 28, 1986, pp. 333–50.
14. Gunarsa, S., et al. "Cognitive development of children." Symposium: Preparation for Adulthood, Third Asian Workshop on Child and Adolescent Development. Malaysia, 1984.
15. Reeves, S. "Self-interest and the common weal: Focusing on the bottom half." *Education Week*, April 27, 1988.
16. Wells, G. *Language, Learning, and Education*. Philadelphia: NFER-NELSON, 1985.
17. Thanks to Dr. Elyse Fleming for her suggestion of this term.

18. Schorr, L., and D. Schorr. *Within Our Reach*. New York: Anchor/Doubleday, 1988.

19. Laboratory of Comparative Human Cognition. "Contributions of cross-cultural research to educational practice." *American Psychologist*, October 1986, p. 1053.

20. McCall, R. "Developmental function, individual differences, and the plasticity of intelligence." In J. Gallagher and C. Ramey, eds., *The Malleability of Children*. Baltimore: Paul H. Brookes, 1987, p. 33.

21. Pogrow, S. "Teaching thinking to at-risk elementary students." *Educational Leadership*, April 1988, p. 80.

22. Coles, R. *The Call of Stories: Teaching and the Moral Imagination*. Boston: Houghton Mifflin, 1989.

23. Whimbey, A., and J. Lockheed. *Problem Solving and Comprehension*. Philadelphia: The Franklin Institute, 1982.

24. Smith, J., and J. Caplan. "Cultural differences in cognitive style development." *Developmental Psychology* 24 (1), 1988, pp. 46–52.

25. Laboratory of Comparative Human Cognition, op. cit., p. 1053.

26. Alvarez, G. "Effects of material deprivation on neurological functioning." *Social Science and Medicine* 17 (16), 1983, pp. 1097–1105.

27. Blount, B., and M. Sanches. *Sociocultural Dimensions of Language Change*. New York: Academic Press, 1977.

28. Siegel, L. "Home environmental influences of cognitive development in preterm and full-term children during the first five years." In A. Gottfried, ed., *Home Environment and Early Cognitive Development*. Orlando, FL: Academic Press, 1984.

29. Norman-Jackson, E. "Family interactions, language development and primary reading achievement of black children in families of low income." *Child Development* 53, 1982, pp. 349–58.

30. Cazden, C., op. cit.

31. Hemphill, L. "Context and conversational style." Doctoral dissertation, Harvard University, UMI no. 86-20, 1986, p. 703.

32. Cazden, C., op. cit., p. 192.

33. Bruner, J. *Actual Minds, Possible Worlds*. Cambridge: Harvard University Press, 1986.

34. Heath, S. "What no bedtime story means: Narrative skills at home and school." *Language in Society* 11, 1982, pp. 49–76.

35. Whitehurst, G., et al. "The effects of parent questions on children's reading abilities." *Developmental Psychology* 24, 1988, pp. 552–59.

36. Alvarez, G., op. cit., pp. 1099, 1102.

37. Flashman, L., and I. Knopf. "The relationship between sustained attention and short-term memory in kindergarten children." Poster session, Annual Meeting, International Neuropsychological Society. Vancouver, BC, February 1989.

38. Geffner, D., and I. Hochberg. "Ear laterality performance of children from low and middle socioeconomic levels on a verbal dichotic listening task." *Cortex* 7, 1971, pp. 193–203.

39. Borowy, R., and R. Goebel. "Cerebral lateralization of speech: The effects of age, sex, race, and social class." *Neuropsychologia* 14, 1976, pp. 363–70.

40. Barwick, M., L. Siegel, and J. Van Duzer. "The nature of reading disability in an adult population." Poster session, Annual Meeting, International Neuropsychological Society. Vancouver, BC, February 1989.

41. Waber, D., et al. "SES-related aspects of neuropsychological performance." *Child Development* 55, 1984, pp. 1878–86.

42. Waber, D. "The biological boundaries of cognitive styles: A neuropsychological analysis." In T. Globerson and T. Zelniker, eds., *Cognitive Style and Cognitive Development*. New York: Ablex, in press.

43. Springer, S., and G. Deutsch. *Left Brain, Right Brain.* San Francisco: W. H. Freeman, 1981, p. 142.

44. Springer, S., and G. Deutsch. *Left Brain, Right Brain,* 2nd edition. San Francisco: W. H. Freeman, 1985, p. 242.

45. Scott, S., et al. "Cerebral speech lateralization in the Native American Navajo." *Neuropsychologia* 17, 1979, pp. 89–92.

46. Rogers, L., et al. "Hemispheric specialization of language: An EEG study of bilingual Hopi Indian children." *International Journal of Neuroscience* 8, 1977, pp. 1–6.

47. McKeever, L., et al. "Language dominance in Navajo children: Importance of the language context." Poster session, Annual Meeting, International Neuropsychological Society. Vancouver, BC, February 1989.

48. Becker, M., et al. "Neuropsychological development of nonverbal behaviors attributed to 'frontal lobe' functioning." *Developmental Neuropsychology* 3 (4), 1987, pp. 275–98.

49. Waber, D. Personal communication. March 1989.

50. Angoff, W. "The nature-nurture debate, aptitudes, and group differences." *American Psychologist* 43 (9), 1988, p. 713.

51. Scarr, S., and R. Weinberg. "IQ test performance of black children adopted by white families." *American Psychologist* 31, 1976, pp. 726–39.

52. Scarr, S., and J. Arnett. "Malleability: Lessons from intervention and family studies." In J. Gallagher and C. Ramey, eds., *The Malleability of Children.* Baltimore: Paul H. Brookes, 1987, pp. 78–9.

53. Duyme, M. "School and social class: An adoption study." *Developmental Psychology* 24 (2), 1988, pp. 203–9.

54. Scarr, S., and R. Weinberg. "The influence of "family background" on intellectual attainment." *American Sociological Review* 43, 1978, pp. 674–92.

55. Diamond, M. *Enriching Heredity.* New York: Free Press, 1988, p. 96.

56. Kiyono, S., et al. "Facilitative effects of maternal environmental enrichment on maze learning in rat offspring." *Physiology & Behavior* 34, 1985, pp. 431–35.

57. Scarr, S., and J. Arnett, op cit., p. 74.

58. Schorr, L., and D. Schorr, op. cit.

59. Scholnick, E. "Influences on plasticity: Problems of definition." *Journal of Applied Developmental Psychology* 7, 1986, pp. 131–38.

60. Manrique, B. Personal communication. June 1988.

61. Manrique, B. Personal communication. June 1988.

62. Caldwell, B. "Sustaining intervention effects." In Gallagher, J., and C. Ramey, eds., *The Malleability of Children.* Baltimore: Paul H. Brookes, 1987, p. 91.

63. Rothman, R. "A district ties goals to success." *Education Week,* March 22, 1989.

64. Bracey, G. "Advocates of basic skills 'know what ain't so.' " *Education Week,* April 5, 1989.

65. Zigler, E., and J. Freedman. "Early experience, malleability, and Head Start." In J. Gallagher and C. Ramey, eds., *The Malleability of Children.* Baltimore: Paul H. Brookes, 1987, p. 91.

CHAPTER 13: NEW BRAINS: NEW SCHOOLS?

1. Costa, A. "The school as home for the mind." Address delivered at Education Summit Conference. Fairfax, VA, June 1988.
2. Costa, A. Personal communication. June 1988.
3. White, Merry. *The Japanese Educational Challenge*. New York: The Free Press, 1987.
4. Kohn, A. *No Contest: The Case Against Competition*. Boston: Houghton Mifflin, 1986.
5. "Teachers complain of lack of parental support." *New York Times*, December 12, 1988.
6. Comer, J. *Issues '88*. Washington: National Education Association, 1988.
7. White, B. "Helping children actualize their potential." *Human Intelligence Newsletter* 9 (3), 1988, pp. 3–5.
8. Bartolome, Paz. "The changing family and early childhood education." In *Changing Family Lifestyles*. Washington: ACEI, 1982, p. 11.
9. Pratt, M., et al. "Mothers and fathers teaching 3-year-olds." *Developmental Psychology* 24 (6), 1988, pp. 832–39.
10. McGuinness, D. "Reading failure: Causes and cures." Paper presented at Annual Meeting, Orton Dyslexia Society. Tampa, FL, November 1988.
11. Lindamood, P. Personal communication. November 1988.
12. Blachman, B. Discussant, Symposium on Phonological Processes in Literacy. Annual Meeting, Orton Dyslexia Society. Tampa, FL, November 1988.
13. Winn, D. "Develop listening skills as a part of the curriculum." *The Reading Teacher*, November 1988, pp. 144–46.
14. Cazden, C. *Classroom Discourse*. Portsmouth, NH: Heinemann, 1988.
15. Hamilton, A. J. "Challenging verbal passivity." *NEATE Leaflet* 85 (1), 1986, p. 22.
16. Taxonomy of questions adapted from B. Bloom et al. *Taxonomy of Educational Objectives: Cognitive Domain*. New York: McKay, 1956.
17. Goodman, K. *What's Whole in Whole Language?* Exeter, NH: Heinemann, 1986.
18. Calkins, L. *The Art of Teaching Writing*. Exeter, NH: Heinemann, 1986.
19. Newman, J. *Whole Language: Theory in Use*. Exeter, NH: Heinemann, 1985.
20. Altwerger, B., et al. "Whole Language: What's New?" *The Reading Teacher*, November 1987.
21. Harman, S., and C. Edelsky. "The risks of whole language literacy: Alienation and connection." *Language Arts* 66 (4), 1989, pp. 392–406.
22. Heath, S. "Questioning at home and at school." In G. Spindler, ed., *Doing the Ethnography of Schooling*. New York: Holt, Rinehart, & Winston, 1982.
23. Tharp, R. "Psychocultural variables and constants." *American Psychologist* 44 (2), 1989, pp. 349–59.
24. "Peer mediation: When students agree not to disagree." *Education Week*, May 25, 1988.
25. "Schoolyard diplomacy." *Children*, June 1988.
26. Barbieri, E. "Talents unlimited." *Educational Leadership*, April 1988, p. 35.

Chapter 14: Teaching the New Generation to Think: Human and Computer Models at School and at Home

1. Wilson, M. "Critical thinking: Repackaging or revolution?" *Language Arts* 65 (6), 1988, pp. 543–51.
2. Perkins, D. "Mindware: The new science of learnable intelligence." Address delivered at Education Summit Conference. Fairfax, VA, June 1988.
3. Wiggins, G. "10 'radical' suggestions for school reform." *Education Week*, March 9, 1988, p. 28.
4. *Education Week*, October 19, 1988, p. 5.
5. Eisner, E. "The ecology of school improvement." *Educational Leadership*, February 1988, pp. 24–29.
6. Resnick, L. "On learning research." *Educational Leadership*, December 1988, p. 12.
7. Kiewra, B. "Verbal control processes and working memory." *Educational Psychologist*, Winter 1988, p. 42.
8. Feuerstein, R. "Mediated learning: An open system." Address delivered at Education Summit Conference. Fairfax, VA, June 1988.
9. Ibid.
10. Hirsch, E. D., Jr. *Cultural Literacy: What Every American Needs to Know.* Boston: Houghton Mifflin, 1987.
11. Kett, J. Personal communication. October 1988.
12. *New York Times*, "Education Life," April 9, 1989.
13. Palmer, E. *Television and America's Children: A Crisis of Neglect.* New York: Oxford University Press, 1988.
14. Ibid., p. xxii.
15. Greenfield, P. *Mind and Media.* Cambridge: Harvard University Press, 1984.
16. Posner, M. Personal communication. August 1988.
17. Herron, J. Personal communication. April 1989.
18. Schwartz, J. "Closing the gap between education and the schools." In M. A. White, ed., *What Curriculum for the Information Age?* Hillsdale, NJ: Lawrence Erlbaum Associates, 1987, p. 70.
19. Weizenbaum, J. *Computer Power and Human Reason.* San Francisco: W. H. Freeman, 1976.
20. Boden, M. *Artificial Intelligence and Natural Man.* New York: Basic Books, 1987.
21. Rutkowsa, J., and C. Crook. *Computers, Cognition, and Development.* New York: John Wiley, 1987.
22. *Forbes*, August 27, 1984, p. 156.
23. Katz, L. Personal communication. March 1989.
24. Frith, U. *Autism: Explaining the Enigma.* Oxford: Basil Blackwell, 1989.

Chapter 15: Expanding Minds

1. Ogbu, J. "Cultural influences on plasticity in human development." In J. Gallagher and C. Ramey, eds., *The Malleability of Children.* Baltimore: Paul H. Brookes, 1987, p. 159.
2. Gould, S. J. *The Mismeasure of Man.* New York: Norton, 1981, p. 325.
3. Ibid., p. 331.

4. Gould, S. J. *Ever Since Darwin*. New York: Norton, 1977, p. 45.

5. Potts, R. Quoted in *U.S. News and World Report*, January 27, 1989, p. 59.

6. Bruner, J. Personal communication. September 15, 1988.

7. *Education for a Democratic Future*. Committee on Correspondence on the Future of Public Education, New York, 1984.

8. *Technology and the American Tradition*. Washington, D.C.: Government Printing Office, 1988.

9. Vail, P. Personal communication. June 1988.

10. White, M. A. "The third learning revolution." *Electronic Learning*, January 1988, p. 6.

11. Schwartz, J. "Closing the gap between education and the schools." In M. A. White, ed., *What Curriculum for the Information Age?* Hillsdale, NJ: Lawrence Erlbaum Associates, 1987.

12. Zukav, G. *The Dancing Wu Li Masters*. New York: Bantam Books, 1979.

13. John-Steiner, V. *Notebooks of the Mind*. New York: Harper & Row, 1985.

14. Ferguson, E. "The mind's eye: Nonverbal thought in technology." *Science* 197 (4306), 1977, pp. 827–36.

15. Grubb, R. Personal communication. June 1988.

16. Weiskrantz, L. *Thought Without Language*. Oxford: Clarendon Press, 1988.

17. O'Neill, C. Personal communication. October 1988.

18. Logan, R. *The Alphabet Effect*. New York: St. Martin's Press, 1986.

19. de Kerckhove, D. "Critical brain processes involved in deciphering the Greek alphabet." In D. de Kerckhove and C. Lumsden, eds., *The Alphabet and the Brain*. New York: Springer-Verlag, 1987, pp. 416–17.

20. John-Steiner, V. Op. cit.

21. Hunt, M. *The Universe Within*. New York: Simon and Schuster, 1982, p. 315.

22. Ravitch, D. "Technology and the curriculum." In White, M. A., ed., *What Curriculum for the Information Age?* Hillsdale, NJ: Lawrence Erlbaum Associates, 1987.

Index

ENDANGERED MINDS

DISCUSSION QUESTIONS

1. The author suggests that the "habits of mind"–and even the brains–of today's students have been changed by contemporary media and fast-paced lifestyles. Do you think it is possible? If so, have you seen any evidence to support this assertion?

2. What might account for the fact that young children's IQ scores appear to be rising at the same time older students' academic achievement scores are a cause for widespread concern?

3. The concept of "critical" or "sensitive" periods implies that if appropriate stimulation is lacking at the time when the brain is most receptive to it, the resulting skill development may be impaired. Acquiring the accent of a non-native language is given as an example. Can you think of any other life skills for which there seem to be critical/sensitive periods?

4. Chapters 4 and 5 stress the importance of language development for a wide variety of academic and personal skills. Which of these skills might be especially important for today's youngsters' future success, and why is language development involved? Can you think of any others that are not mentioned here?

5. Have you noticed any specific problems with listening abilities or critical thinking in today's culture? How would you rate the quality of language available in various media? Comment on the potential effects–political, social, or economic–for a society in which young people grow up unaccustomed to "elaborated" language or unable to comprehend material requiring extended reading or listening. Would our culture be improved or diminished with less complex language usage?

6. Research suggests that children are learning language skills before they even begin to understand or say words. What do parents or other caregivers do that is important in this development? React to Dr. Scheibel's comment, ". . . I think it would be very important to tell parents that they are participating with the physical development of their youngsters' brains to the exact degree that they interact with them, communicate with them."

7. The author implies that some cases of "learning disabilities" are more a question of a misfit between child and school than of something "wrong" with the child. Comment on this viewpoint. Should we change our schools to fit today's kids? Is it possible that much of the "disability" called ADHD is actually normal behavior in a developmentally inappropriate school setting (e.g., too restrictive, too pressured, or too permissive)?

8. Discuss the issue of whether "biology is destiny" (i.e., if you inherited it, it can't be changed) as far as learning is concerned. How much importance would you place on heredity or environment in accounting for learning or behavioral differences among individuals? (Don't worry if you don't have a final answer—neither do the scientists!)

9. Can you speculate about why there is still so little objective research about how television or other video use affects children's brain development? If you were planning a research study, what specific questions or hypotheses would you like to explore?

10. Do you have experiences in your own life to support or discount the negative influences that the author attributes to excessive TV viewing?

11. Most children's programs spawn commercial products related to a show's characters. What do you think this trend says about our culture's attitude toward childhood? Would you defend such marketing efforts or not?

12. Why do you think research consistently finds differences in the way adults talk to children among different socioeconomic groups? What implications does this have for a kindergarten teacher?

13. Summarize some of the issues involved in testing students for academic "competency." Why is it harder than it looks? Debate what your school district's policy should be in testing children to determine whether they should pass a grade or graduate.

14. What do you remember best about your school experience? On this basis, what advice would give to someone who was trying to start a new school from scratch?

15. Comment on the discussion presented in Chapter 15 about whether or not the evolution of the human brain is being changed by electronic media. What examples of nonverbal reasoning are given here? Do you think that either verbal or nonverbal reasoning is better than the other? What is most commonly valued in most schools? Do you agree with this emphasis? Why?

16. Comment on the author's suggestion that curiosity may be the human brain's most important attribute in the long run. If you had to propose one intellectual quality as most important for "future minds," what would it be?